The Unity of Scripture

**Understanding
the Mysteries of God**

Daniel Brown

Cover Art from Photos.com Istockphoto/JamesSteidl/photos.com

Interior Art and diagrams by Daniel Brown (author)

ISBN (978-0-9834214-0-5)

Printed in USA by createspace (www.createspace.com)

Dedication

This book is dedicated to the Lord Jesus Christ. Without his love, obedience and sacrifice none of us could be saved. He paid the price we could not pay.

This book is also dedicated to my parents, Harold and Stella Brown. They have been the stabilizing force in my life. I cannot overstate my love or gratitude for all they have done for me throughout my life.

Table of Contents

Origins

Symbolism

Prophecy

Appendix

Preface

This book has been on my mind constantly since about 1995. My pastor originally asked me to give a brief presentation about future prophetic events at a prophecy seminar he was putting together. This gave me the motivation to study the Bible's prophetic passages with greater scrutiny than I had previously been used to. I focused on the Olivet discourse accounts in Matt, Mark and Luke. I discovered they paralleled the Seal and Trumpet judgments in the Book of Revelation. This simple insight inspired me to continue probing the scriptures to obtain more understanding. I deliberately made the choice to forget everything I had been taught about the Bible and read it as if it were all brand new. This is when the Bible was unlocked for me. It started making sense. It was not contrary to science or unreasonable. Christianity (believing the Bible and following Jesus) became the most reasonable of faiths. Even though the prophecy seminar was only intended for our local assembly and the attendance was small, that endeavor has ultimately resulted in this book.

This book has been a long time coming. I had a car accident around 1998. The county I was living in had a summer long drought. I was driving down a winding country road in my restored 1966 Mustang. It started to sprinkle and the road became as slick as glass. The antique suspension on the car didn't hold to the road very well in slick conditions and it began spinning out of control. For a moment, time slowed down and a question appeared in my mind. The question was phrased like this, "Do you want to live?" I actually had to consider it. Two things immediately came to mind. First, I didn't want to leave my parents alone in this world (I am an only child.) Secondly, I hadn't finished my book yet, so I said "yes, I want to live." The voice in my mind said, "Close your eyes." So I did. The last image I had was dirt and gravel flying toward my face. The car plowed into an embankment and flipped all the way over. It finally came to rest in the upright position. Eventually, someone drove up and called an ambulance. The paramedics told me to keep my eyes closed until I got to the hospital. When I got there, the doctor couldn't believe my eyes were O.K. My head was covered in glass splinters, but my eyes were fine. This was a huge blessing but my back did get injured. Even though it took me about a year to recover, I'm still thankful for the experience. I don't know if it was God or an angel but there was something outside of me that spoke to my mind during that time and this book was part of my justification for living. I hope God will judge it to be worthy for his service.

Introduction

It is my hope that this book will help the reader understand the Bible in a completely new way. The reader will see God's plan from the beginning and he will see how things fit together to accomplish God's ultimate goal.

This book is separated into three sections. These sections are Origins, Symbolism and Prophecy. These are the three dimensions of the Bible. They form framework of scripture to tell the story of Jesus and the redemption he has provided for his people. Origins, Symbolism and Prophecy are separate and yet they are interconnected. All three must be taken together before understanding can take form. Of course, there are other ways to classify the scriptures. The Jews separate the Old Testament scriptures, which they call the Tanakh, into three classifications. They classify the scriptures as being the Law (Torah), the Prophets (Nevi'im) and the Writings (Kevtuvim). The word "Tanakh" is formed from the first letter of each classification (TaNaKh). For the purposes of this book, we will use the classifications of Origins, Symbolism and Prophecy (I guess the abbreviation for this would be **OSaP**.)

The first portion of this book deals with origins. While many Christians are familiar with the books of Moses, It is my hope this book will give you a new level of understanding that will bring these foundational books alive to you. This book also has the potential to take you deeper into Biblical symbolism and prophecy than you have ever been.

The overall goal of this book is to show the reader how the Bible is interconnected on so many different levels. The books of the Bible were not arbitrarily assembled but rather they were purposely and divinely ordained to be God's word to us in written form. There are no extra books in the Bible and none were accidentally left out. Every thing fits together into one complete unit. This is why the title of this book is "The Unity of Scripture".

God speaks to those who have ears to hear.

> Rev 2:7He that hath an ear, let him hear what the Spirit saith unto the churches; To him that overcometh will I give to eat of the tree of life, which is in the midst of the paradise of God.

It is my prayer that you will have "ears to hear" and God will use this book to talk to you.

While salvation my utmost desire for everyone, this book is not focused on trying to inspire someone to "get saved". This book is more for the Christian who wants a deeper understanding of God's word. This book is about the "how's" and "why's" of scripture. God uses many ways to draw men unto him. If he uses this book to break down the barriers of unbelief in someone's life and it results in their salvation, then I will praise the Lord forever.

This book is the talent the Lord has entrusted to me. It is my prayer that it will be spiritually profitable and I will be able to show him an increase when he comes.

Some of the formatting in this book may seem strange. Many times in this book, we will be looking at lengthy scriptural passages, such as the entire Book of Revelation, and we will insert similar passages from other parts of the Bible at the appropriate spots. To distinguish the inserted passages from the main text I use extra indentations. Hopefully these indentations will make things less confusing.

Chapter One

Understanding the Bible:

Cause and Effect:

How can a man understand the mind of an infinite God?

Our attempts must seem laughable to him.

> Is 55:8For my thoughts *are* not your thoughts, neither *are* your ways my ways, saith the LORD.

> 9For *as* the heavens are higher than the earth, so are my ways higher than your ways, and my thoughts than your thoughts.

God has communicated to us through his Bible. Within its pages, paper and ink come together to form a tangible link to God. The link is established when we read the Bible. The goal is to understand what God is saying and to form a relationship with him. We can't begin to understand God in his completeness but we can endeavor to understand the Bible he has given us.

Understanding the Bible is not a quick process. It is a gradual process. It is built layer upon layer. The foundation of understanding must be initially laid. Reading and considering the scriptures with a desire for truthful understanding is the first step. As the Bible is read and reread the interconnectedness of the scriptures becomes apparent. Prophecy is an example of this. Specific events are prophesied in different ways by men who where separated by centuries. By studying the scriptures and comparing them to one another, a more complete image of the prophesied events will emerge. The Prophet Isaiah says it this way...

> Is 28:9Whom shall he teach knowledge? and whom shall he make to understand doctrine? *them that are* weaned from the milk, *and* drawn from the breasts.

10

[10]For precept *must be* upon precept, precept upon precept; line upon line, line upon line; here a little, *and* there a little:

The Word of God is the ultimate truth. The Bible, specifically the King James Version, does an excellent job of bringing the word of God to us. Unfortunately, there are barriers which interfere with our comprehension of Gods word. These include translational problems (subtleties of particular words can be lost). Cultural differences between the people of Biblical times and today can also cause confusion. Then there is the biggest barrier of all to the correct understanding of scripture... It is our preconceived notions and our man made doctrines.

Many times, as people are raised in the church, doctrines are taught and accepted as fact because of the respect the people have for their pastor and their faith in his understanding of scripture. While Pastors, teachers, and knowledgeable individuals are valuable resources, they cannot replace your own individual study. Nor can this book replace your individual study.

I desire to share what understanding I have of the scriptures with you. I hope this book will inspire you to study the scriptures for yourself. My greatest exhortation to you is to put aside your preconceived notions and read the Bible in context. Read it as if you were reading it for the first time. I have done this and my understanding of the scriptures has been completely changed. Consider what I have to say and compare it with scripture. A sincere desire for truthful understanding and willingness to labor in the scriptures will be rewarded.

The Underlying Theme of the Scriptures.

This book will attempt to shed light on the many mysteries of the Bible. Origins, Symbolism, and Prophecy will be studied in detail. Before we begin we will need to understand the underlying theme of scripture. This theme spans the eons. Various aspects of it were revealed to prophets and to godly men throughout the ages. Each of these godly men received pieces of the puzzle, but these pieces would not fit together until the last days. These men accepted their individual revelations by faith without completely understanding the full meaning of their visions.

The Underlying Theme of Scripture
is the Love and Justice of God.

God is love. It permeates everything he is but it is not his only attribute. God is Holy. He is Righteous and he is Just. His love does not negate his holiness, righteousness or his justice. God's love remains even when we are unrighteous and we sin. God's love is independent of our actions but how he responds to us is not independent of our actions. His holiness and righteousness requires justice to be satisfied. Satan's plan was to use God's nature against him. He would set up a situation where God's holiness, righteousness and justice would be pitted against his love. The thing Satan didn't understand was the extent to which God would go to restore his creation.

God is all powerful and all knowing. This being said, it is hard to imagine why God would allow Lucifer/Satan to rebel. Nothing forced God to create Lucifer/Satan. So why would he bring into existence a creature who was destined to fall? This is unanswerable to our finite minds. Nevertheless, God did bring Lucifer/Satan into existence and he was created perfect in his ways.

> Ez 28:14Thou *art* the anointed cherub that covereth; and I have set thee *so:* thou wast upon the holy mountain of God; thou hast walked up and down in the midst of the stones of fire.
>
> 15Thou *wast* perfect in thy ways from the day that thou wast created, till iniquity was found in thee.

Consider that God knows everything past, present, and future. God is the only one who does. Satan did not know the future. If he knew the ultimate consequence of his rebellion, it's unlikely he would have rebelled against God. And yet, God (knowing that Lucifer/Satan would fall) created him anyway. Why would God do this? The answer is the justice of God.

God, as well as the law of man, judges people based on what they have done, not on what they will do in the future. There has to be a cause and effect relationship between actions and consequences for justice to be understood.

Imagine if it were possible for you to go back in time and kill a baby who you knew would grow up to be a murderous monster. Would you be justified in killing the baby? The baby would be innocent because it hadn't yet done anything. And yet you know what the baby will do when it grows up. How could you convince the mother and everyone else that her baby should die? You couldn't. They would question your knowledge of the future. What if the baby's name were Adolph Hitler? Would that make a difference? Do the ends justify the means?

Along the same line, imagine the police show up at your door and arrest you because you were going to commit a crime tomorrow. You have no idea what they are talking about. They assure you their predictions are always accurate. Would you think that was just? Would you take their word for it? No! You would question their knowledge of the future.

God allows everyone to make their own decisions (even though he knows what decision they will eventually make). If God had destroyed Lucifer/Satan before he fell, there would have been confusion in Heaven. Why would God do such a thing? Lucifer/Satan hadn't done anything. Satan would have appeared innocent. The rest of the angels, not knowing the future, would never know if Lucifer/Satan would have done the evil things God accused him of. A preemptive strike by God against Lucifer would have caused fear and uncertainty in Heaven. If God could attack someone as prominent as Lucifer, who apparently hadn't done anything, would anyone be safe? Who would be taken next without warning? The fear and uncertainty caused by such a preemptive attack would have been unacceptable. God would prove his judgments are just by letting Lucifer and the other rebellious angels do their worst. The cause and effect relationship between Satan's actions and God's judgment will be unmistakable. When the time for judgment comes, the entire universe will know that God's judgment against Satan, his fallen angels and sinful men is totally just.

Opportunity to Sin

God understood the condition of Lucifer's heart so he set up a situation that would convince Lucifer/Satan to make his move and reveal his true nature. God created a man in his own image and Satan went down the rebellious path just as God had anticipated. Satan would try to drive a wedge between God and his creation. Maybe if Satan could cause men to rebel against God, then God would abandon his creation (Satan figured God's love would prevent him from destroying his creation). Satan would come in and take over. Satan wanted to put God in a situation where his love would prevent his justice and by doing so God would no longer be righteous or holy. Satan would become the god of this world. Unfortunately for Satan, God had no intention of giving up his creation. Satan would have to learn this the hard way.

God created man and placed a tree in the midst of the garden. It was the Tree of Knowledge of Good and Evil. He instructed Adam not to eat from it and Adam instructed Eve.

Satan saw the opportunity he needed to drive in the wedge. He entered into a serpent and convinced Eve to question what God had said. Eve gave in and ate the fruit. She also convinced Adam to eat it. Satan was successful in his efforts to make man fall.

Adam and Eve had sinned by their disobedience. The justice of God requires sin to be judged, but Satan had misled them. It was not completely Adam or Eve's fault they fell.

Satan wanted God to abandon his creation, but God chose redemption instead.

Redemption is what reconciles God's love with his justice. This is a profound truth for all generations.

Adam and Eve would eventually die but God would give them and their children an opportunity for redemption. As for Lucifer/Satan, he will not have the opportunity for redemption because he was not deceived. He knew what he was doing and he rebelled deliberately.

From this point on, Satan's only hope is to thwart Gods plan for redemption.

Opportunity for Redemption

From the time of Adam throughout the Old Testament period, blood sacrifices were required as payment for sins. Since the blood sacrifices were not adequate to completely pay the price for their sin they had to keep offering the sacrifices year after year. The Old Testament saints obeyed this without fully understanding the meaning of the sacrifices.

> Lev 14:13And he shall slay the lamb in the place where he shall kill the sin offering and the burnt offering, in the holy place: for as the sin offering *is* the priest's, *so is* the trespass offering: it *is* most holy:

> Num 6:14And he shall offer his offering unto the LORD, one he lamb of the first year without blemish for a burnt offering, and one ewe lamb of the first year without blemish for a sin offering, and one ram without blemish for peace offerings,

The Final Payment for Sin

It was not until God took human form (Jesus) that the plan of God for the redemption of mankind could be fully understood. Now we can look back at the Old Testament sacrifices, the Tabernacle and the Hebrew Holy Days and see how they symbolized the ultimate sacrifice Jesus would make for the sins of men.

> John 1:29The next day John seeth Jesus coming unto him, and saith, Behold the Lamb of God, which taketh away the sin of the world.

> 1 Peter 1:19But with the precious blood of Christ, as of a lamb without blemish and without spot: 20Who verily was foreordained before the foundation of the world, but was manifest in these last times for you, 21Who by him do believe in God, that raised him up from the dead, and gave him glory; that your faith and hope might be in God.

The life of a lamb is not an adequate price to pay for sin. It was never intended to be the payment for sin. It was rather Gods promise to pay for the sins of men at a later date. The Old Testament saints, through faith, obeyed God by performing the sacrifices he told them to perform. Symbolically they were identifying themselves with the perfect sacrifice that would come in the future (Jesus). To put it in financial terms, The Old Testament Saints were only paying the interest on the principal. It was not until Jesus paid the whole price for our sins that the principle was paid. He graciously gave us this gift even though we did not deserve it.

> Ep 2:8For by grace are ye saved through faith; and that not of yourselves: *it is* the gift of God: 9Not of works, lest any man should boast.

God's Justice required that death was the price for sin. This price was paid in full when Jesus died in our place. His life was worth more than all of humanity put together. God's justice has been satisfied and we can now come to him as sons if we desire or we can reject him and not accept his gift of salvation. God loved us so much he paid the ultimate price to satisfy his requirements of justice, holiness and righteousness. God's love didn't contradict his justice but rather fulfilled it.

> Gal 4:4But when the fullness of the time was come, God sent forth his Son, made of a woman, made under the law, 5To redeem them that were under the law, that we might receive the adoption of sons.

> Rom 6:23For the wages of sin *is* death; but the gift of God *is* eternal life through Jesus Christ our Lord.

The End of the Age

Just as God sent Jesus in the fullness of time to redeem man, he will also deal with Satan in the fullness of time. The time for God to judge Satan is quickly approaching and the prophecies of the Bible are coming into sharper focus. Their meanings are becoming clearer. God's justice will be served regarding Satan and his angels.

> Dan 12:4But thou, O Daniel, shut up the words, and seal the book, *even* to the time of the end: many shall run to and fro, and knowledge shall be increased.

I am convinced that judgment day will grieve God. Lucifer was also God's creation and I'm sure God still loves him, but his righteousness requires Satan to be judged. Redemption for

Satan is not possible. His rebellion originated in his own heart. He was not deceived. The same holds true for the other fallen angels.

> Prov 24:17Rejoice not when thine enemy falleth, and let not thine heart be glad when he stumbleth:

This book is going to look into the mysteries of God in an attempt to gain an understanding of God's ways and his purpose. The Bible must be considered in its entirety. The Old Testament is the key to our understanding of the New Testament. Together these two provide the unity of scripture that is known as the Word of God.

Let us begin our study by looking at the most foundational book of the Bible, the Book of Genesis.

Chapter Two

Understanding Genesis:

The Creation

The first three chapters of the book of Genesis are among the most controversial in the entire Bible. This is largely due to the modern "Darwinist" view of origins. (For an explanation of why the theory of Evolution is wrong, refer to Appendix A) Evolution has become almost universally accepted as fact. Evolution supposes natural processes, rather than divine intervention, are responsible for the existence of all living things. The belief in evolution inevitably affects a person's worldview. If you believe in evolution you must either discount the validity of the Biblical scriptures or dismiss the Biblical account of creation as some sort of allegory. I believe it would be a mistake to approach the Biblical account of creation in either of these ways. I also believe a person can believe the Biblical account without turning off his (or her) brain. Admittedly, there are barriers to our understanding of what the Bible says. Among these barriers is the vocabulary of the people to whom the scriptures where given. Imagine trying to reveal concepts and visions to primitive people who could not understand what they were seeing. How would an ancient prophet describe a nuclear explosion, radiation, or a mushroom cloud? These things where unknown until the twentieth century. How about missiles or even basic concepts of science like time, space, matter, and gravity? The prophet would have to explain these things with his own inadequate words. The Bible was never meant to be a scientific document but, when correctly understood, its accuracy is mind boggling.

Let's consider some of what the Biblical account of creation says:

Gen 1:1In the beginning God created the heaven and the earth.

2And the earth was without form, and void; and darkness *was* upon the face of the deep. And the Spirit of God moved upon the face of the waters.

3And God said, Let there be light: and there was light.

4And God saw the light, that *it was* good: and God divided the light from the darkness.

[5]And God called the light Day, and the darkness he called Night. And the evening and the morning were the first day.

[6]And God said, Let there be a firmament in the midst of the waters, and let it divide the waters from the waters.

[7]And God made the firmament, and divided the waters which *were* under the firmament from the waters which *were* above the firmament: and it was so.

[8]And God called the firmament Heaven. And the evening and the morning were the second day.

[9]And God said, Let the waters under the heaven be gathered together unto one place, and let the dry *land* appear: and it was so.

[10]And God called the dry *land* Earth; and the gathering together of the waters called he Seas: and God saw that *it was* good.

When I read the preceding verses I see God setting up the parameters of the physical universe.

Consider Genesis 1:1, In the beginning God created the heaven and the earth.

"In the beginning…"   This denotes the creation of Time.

"God created the heaven…"   This denotes the creation of Space.

"and the earth."   This denotes the creation of Matter.

This interpretation of Genesis 1:1 requires a more liberal interpretation of what heaven and earth are, but considering the vocabulary available to Moses at the time this scripture was given, this interpretation seems reasonable. Assuming my interpretation is correct, we see in one verse Time, Space, and Matter created. These are the most basic properties of the physical universe.

Continuing on we see a description of a formless, empty and dark "earth".

> Gen 1:2 And the earth was without form, and void; and darkness *was* upon the face of the deep. And the Spirit of God moved upon the face of the waters.

We could consider this "earth" to be an undefined mass floating around in empty space. Some people make a big deal of the darkness and say this darkness was the result of the fall of Satan. Darkness symbolizes evil therefore it must be from Satan. I believe this is incorrect in this instance. Darkness, by definition, is the absence of light. Darkness does not exist as a thing, but rather it is the absence of a thing.... Light! Why was there no light? Because it hadn't been created yet! This would come next.

> Gen 1:3 And God said, Let there be light: and there was light.

Light is radiant energy. Radio waves and other forms of radiant energy could also have been created at this time, but God used words that the people would understand. At this point God has described the creation of Time, Space, Matter, and Energy. What would be next?

> Gen 1:4 And God saw the light, that *it was* good: and God divided the light from the darkness.

God divided the light from the darkness. How could this occur? We have already pointed out that darkness is not a thing but rather the absence of a thing... light. So how could God separate the light from the darkness? The same way we experience day being separate from night. The mass God created in verse 1 is obviously coming together, taking form, and demonstrating another property of matter.... Gravity! Light is no longer able to pass through the mass as it comes together. The light shines on the side facing the light source while the other side of the mass is dark. In this way the light is separated from the darkness. This also demonstrates the light source, which existed before the Sun was created, shone from one particular direction rather than shining from all directions. At this point Genesis has described the creation of **Time, Space, Matter, Energy and Gravity!** We can now consider the high degree of scientific insight contained within this controversial book.

Consider Einstein's now famous equation...

$$E = MC^2$$

$$\downarrow$$

Energy = Mass * the Speed of light².

$$\downarrow \qquad \downarrow \qquad \downarrow$$

Energy = Mass * (Distance / Time)²

$$\downarrow \qquad \downarrow \qquad \downarrow$$

Energy = Matter * (Space / Time)²

Energy = Mass * the Speed of light². The speed of light is 186,000 miles per second. Miles per second is a way measuring speed. Speed is defined as distance divided by time. So, within Einstein's theory we see the factors for **Energy, Matter** (with its **Gravity**), **Space** (distance), and **Time**. Notice that these are exactly the same factors God defined on the first day!

> Gen 1:5 And God called the light Day, and the darkness he called Night. And the evening and the morning were the first day.

This is the end of the first day and verse 5 implies the mass of the Earth was rotating thereby setting up the day/night cycle. The question is... Was this the end of the first day because 24 hours had passed or was it because time could be measured now in days because of the rotation of the Earth? Could days be measured independently from the rotation of the Earth? The answer to me seems simple. Even we humans can keep track of time independently of the rotation of the Earth. Any cheap digital watch can demonstrate this. So, if we can do it, why should we question the ability of the creator of the universe to keep track of time? When God says a day has passed, there is no reason to expect anything other than a regular 24 hour day.

> Gen 1:6 And God said, Let there be a firmament in the midst of the waters, and let it divide the waters from the waters.

⁷And God made the firmament, and divided the waters which *were* under the firmament from the waters which *were* above the firmament: and it was so.

⁸And God called the firmament Heaven. And the evening and the morning were the second day.

God separated the waters that were under the firmament from the waters that were above the firmament. Firmament can mean space, atmosphere, or sky. This is obvious because later God placed the Sun and Moon in the firmament of the heaven. Also, the birds fly in the open firmament of heaven. As far as the word Heaven goes, there are three Heavens. There is the first Heaven where the birds fly. The second Heaven is space, where the Sun, Moon, and Stars are. The third Heaven is Gods spiritual Heaven (the third Heaven is mentioned in 2 Corinthians 12:2). The waters that are above the firmament will become important later when considering the extreme ages the first few generations enjoyed. The waters above the firmament may also explain why our Carbon 14 dating methods are totally inaccurate. (This is explained in Appendix A).

^{Gen 1:9}And God said, Let the waters under the heaven be gathered together unto one place, and let the dry *land* appear: and it was so.

¹⁰And God called the dry *land* Earth; and the gathering together of the waters called he Seas: and God saw that *it was* good.

Here is a further display of gravity. As the matter God created continues to come together. The water flows off the land and into the lower-lying basins. As the water collects, the land emerges.

^{Gen 1:11}And God said, Let the earth bring forth grass, the herb yielding seed, *and* the fruit tree yielding fruit after his kind, whose seed *is* in itself, upon the earth: and it was so.

¹²And the earth brought forth grass, *and* herb yielding seed after his kind, and the tree yielding fruit, whose seed *was* in itself, after his kind: and God saw that *it was* good.

¹³And the evening and the morning were the third day.

God creates the plant life on the third day. These plants will become the food source for all of the animals to come. Light exists but the Sun has not yet been created. When God creates the Sun, it will become the light source.

> ᴳᵉⁿ ¹:¹⁴And God said, Let there be lights in the firmament of the heaven to divide the day from the night; and let them be for signs, and for seasons, and for days, and years:
>
> ¹⁵And let them be for lights in the firmament of the heaven to give light upon the earth: and it was so.
>
> ¹⁶And God made two great lights; the greater light to rule the day, and the lesser light to rule the night: *he made* the stars also.
>
> ¹⁷And God set them in the firmament of the heaven to give light upon the earth,
>
> ¹⁸And to rule over the day and over the night, and to divide the light from the darkness: and God saw that *it was* good.
>
> ¹⁹And the evening and the morning were the fourth day.

Here is where God creates the lights of heaven. The Sun is where the majority of our light is created. The moon is the source of reflected light for the nighttime hours. The stars are also mentioned. The stars seem to be mentioned almost as an after thought, but it would follow that the stars could not be more ancient than the Earth because God had just set up the parameters of the universe. At this point, nothing in this universe could have existed more than 4 days.

The question always arises about the distance of the stars and the speed of light. The question usually goes something like this. "If the universe is only about 6000 years old, how can we see the light from stars that are more than 6000 light years away?" The answer is not as difficult as you might think. God created a mature universe just as he created a mature Adam. If we could have seen Adam the day after he was created, he would have probably appeared to be about 20 years old but, in fact, he would be only be 2 days old. The same holds true for the universe. The universe appears to be much older than it is because it was created mature. The Earth, Adam, animals and plants must have been created in a mature state otherwise the living creatures could not have survived. Imagine if Adam was created as an infant and he was placed in a garden that God had freshly planted with seeds. Would the infant be able to lie around and wait for the plants to grow before he could have something to eat? How long could Adam or any of the baby animals survive without food?

^{Gen 1:20}And God said, Let the waters bring forth abundantly the moving creature that hath life, and fowl *that* may fly above the earth in the open firmament of heaven.

²¹And God created great whales, and every living creature that moveth, which the waters brought forth abundantly, after their kind, and every winged fowl after his kind: and God saw that *it was* good.

²²And God blessed them, saying, Be fruitful, and multiply, and fill the waters in the seas, and let fowl multiply in the earth.

²³And the evening and the morning were the fifth day.

The fifth day sees the creation of the fish and the birds.

^{Gen 1:24}And God said, Let the earth bring forth the living creature after his kind, cattle, and creeping thing, and beast of the earth after his kind: and it was so.

²⁵And God made the beast of the earth after his kind, and cattle after their kind, and every thing that creepeth upon the earth after his kind: and God saw that *it was* good.

²⁶And God said, Let us make man in our image, after our likeness: and let them have dominion over the fish of the sea, and over the fowl of the air, and over the cattle, and over all the earth, and over every creeping thing that creepeth upon the earth.

²⁷So God created man in his *own* image, in the image of God created he him; male and female created he them.

[28]And God blessed them, and God said unto them, Be fruitful, and multiply, and replenish the earth, and subdue it: and have dominion over the fish of the sea, and over the fowl of the air, and over every living thing that moveth upon the earth.

[29]And God said, Behold, I have given you every herb bearing seed, which *is* upon the face of all the earth, and every tree, in the which *is* the fruit of a tree yielding seed; to you it shall be for meat.

[30]And to every beast of the earth, and to every fowl of the air, and to every thing that creepeth upon the earth, wherein *there is* life, *I have given* every green herb for meat: and it was so.

[31]And God saw every thing that he had made, and, behold, *it was* very good. And the evening and the morning were the sixth day.

The sixth day sees the completion of God's creation with the creation of the land animals and man. It took 6 days. Not billions of years! Everything we see is the result of Gods' deliberate design and established order.

The so called "scientists" would have us believe the universe came about as a result of a "big bang" of something (we don't know what). They blindly accept an unexplained explosion as the creator of the universe without any need to explain the source of the explosion and yet, they reject the idea of God creating the universe because we can't answer the question, "Where did God come from?"

There is another observation about the creation account that should be brought out. It is interesting that **time** was the first thing God defined in the universe. Einstein demonstrated that matter and energy are interchangeable and both are linked by the speed of light time constant. (For a further discussion of Einstein and Genesis see Appendix B).

In the next chapter we will consider Adam.

Chapter Three

Understanding Genesis:

About Adam

Genesis Chapter 2 picks up at the end of day 6.

^{Gen 2:1}Thus the heavens and the earth were finished, and all the host of them.

²And on the seventh day God ended his work which he had made; and he rested on the seventh day from all his work which he had made.

³And God blessed the seventh day, and sanctified it: because that in it he had rested from all his work which God created and made.

These three verses should have been the last 3 verses of Chapter 1 and verse 4 should have been the start of Chapter 2. It is important to note that the chapter divisions of the Bible were not part of the Biblical text but were included later to aid in locating and cross referencing scriptures. Chapter divisions were not divinely inspired and at times they were not placed in the best possible locations.

^{Gen 2:4}These *are* the generations of the heavens and of the earth when they were created, in the day that the LORD God made the earth and the heavens,

⁵And every plant of the field before it was in the earth and every herb of the field before it grew: for the LORD God had not caused it to rain upon the earth, and *there was* not a man to till the ground.

⁶But there went up a mist from the earth, and watered the whole face of the ground.

The first mention of it ever raining was during the flood of Noah in Gen 7:4. There is a good reason to believe it didn't rain before the flood of Noah and the mist in Gen 2:6 was the mechanism for watering the plants before the flood. (More on this later.)

> Gen 2:7 And the LORD God formed man *of* the dust of the ground, and breathed into his nostrils the breath of life; and man became a living soul.

God spoke the rest of creation into existence, but he took special interest in creating man. He formed man from the dust of the Earth and breathed life into him thereby making him a living soul. In this way man was distinct from the rest of God's creation.

> Gen 2:8 And the LORD God planted a garden eastward in Eden; and there he put the man whom he had formed.

> 9 And out of the ground made the LORD God to grow every tree that is pleasant to the sight, and good for food; the tree of life also in the midst of the garden, and the tree of knowledge of good and evil.

God makes a habitat especially for Adam.

> Gen 2:15 And the LORD God took the man, and put him into the garden of Eden to dress it and to keep it.

> 16 And the LORD God commanded the man, saying, Of every tree of the garden thou mayest freely eat:

> 17 But of the tree of the knowledge of good and evil, thou shalt not eat of it: for in the day that thou eatest thereof thou shalt surely die.

God places Adam in the garden and prohibits him from eating from the Tree of Knowledge of Good and Evil.

> Gen 2:18 And the LORD God said, *It is* not good that the man should be alone; I will make him an help meet for him.

¹⁹And out of the ground the LORD God formed every beast of the field, and every fowl of the air; and brought *them* unto Adam to see what he would call them: and whatsoever Adam called every living creature, that *was* the name thereof.

²⁰And Adam gave names to all cattle, and to the fowl of the air, and to every beast of the field; but for Adam there was not found an help meet for him.

²¹And the LORD God caused a deep sleep to fall upon Adam and he slept: and he took one of his ribs, and closed up the flesh instead thereof;

²²And the rib, which the LORD God had taken from man, made he a woman, and brought her unto the man.

²³And Adam said, This *is* now bone of my bones, and flesh of my flesh: she shall be called Woman, because she was taken out of Man.

²⁴Therefore shall a man leave his father and his mother, and shall cleave unto his wife: and they shall be one flesh.

²⁵And they were both naked, the man and his wife, and were not ashamed.

God created the living creatures on days 5 and 6. Later God brought them to Adam to be named and to see if any of them would be a suitable help meet for Adam (verses 19-20). This seems odd. God should have known that none of the animals were physically (sexually) compatible with Adam, but maybe this was not what God meant by trying to find Adam a "help meet". We have assumed it meant "mate" but God obviously knew Adam was not capable of mating with any of the animals. I think "help meet" probably meant something like "suitable companion".

The Bible says Angels do not marry, which implies they are not joined in sexual relationships. Angels are thought to have been created directly by God, just as Adam was. Maybe Adam was initially created as a complete being in a way that was similar to the angels. It is unclear how Adam would have procreated without Eve, but when Adam did not find a suitable companion among the animals, God decided to custom make the perfect companion for him. God took a part of Adam (his rib) and with it he made the woman. She would be separate and independent from Adam but neither could be complete without the other. Adam became a sexual creature who would have to cleave to his wife to become one flesh.

When the woman was brought to Adam, he seemed fully aware of where she came from and what her purpose was. As verse 24 suggests, God must have explained the concepts of father, mother and children to Adam before the operation. It can therefore be concluded that Adam and Eve were intended to reproduce by sexual means even if they had never fallen into sin. Sex would not have been associated with lust or sin. Their nakedness was not even thought about before the fall.

> Gen 3:1 Now the serpent was more subtil than any beast of the field which the LORD God had made. And he said unto the woman, Yea, hath God said, Ye shall not eat of every tree of the garden?

The serpent was said to be more subtle than any beast of the field which the Lord had made. What does this mean? It is unclear. The first thing that seems odd is the fact that the serpent spoke. Did all animals speak before the fall or was this part of the subtlety of the serpent. Was the serpent more intelligent than the other animals?

It is unlikely the animals could speak as humans do because of the physical differences in their mouths, tongues and vocal chords, but it would be reasonable to speculate Adam and Eve could understand the animals and the animals could understand them. I expect, after the fall, the ability to understand each other was taken away. The ability to understanding the languages of the animals was probably blocked in a way similar to what happened at the tower of Babel.

> Gen 3:2 And the woman said unto the serpent, We may eat of the fruit of the trees of the garden:
>
> 3 But of the fruit of the tree which *is* in the midst of the garden, God hath said, Ye shall not eat of it, neither shall ye touch it, lest ye die.
>
> 4 And the serpent said unto the woman, Ye shall not surely die:
>
> 5 For God doth know that in the day ye eat thereof, then your eyes shall be opened, and ye shall be as gods, knowing good and evil.

It is unclear what Adam was doing during this conversation. The serpent was contradicting what God said and implying God had selfish reasons for telling them not to eat of the fruit of the Tree of Knowledge of Good and Evil. It should also be noted that the serpent didn't exactly lie. Instead, he misled Eve.

> ^{Gen 3:6}And when the woman saw that the tree *was* good for food, and that it *was* pleasant to the eyes, and a tree to be desired to make *one* wise, she took of the fruit thereof, and did eat, and gave also unto her husband with her; and he did eat.

> ⁷And the eyes of them both were opened, and they knew that they *were* naked; and they sewed fig leaves together, and made themselves aprons.

Eve believed the serpent and ate the fruit. Adam also ate the fruit but we are not sure why he chose to follow Eve's lead. At this point, it is easy to condemn Adam and Eve for their disobedience, but it's not that simple. Adam and Eve had never heard a lie or been misled before. They were naïve like children and were easy prey for someone who had evil intentions.

When they ate the fruit their innocence left them. They were suddenly given the knowledge of good and evil. Their nakedness was the first thing that became obvious. They tried to cover themselves with fig leaves.

> ^{Gen 3:8}And they heard the voice of the LORD God walking in the garden in the cool of the day: and Adam and his wife hid themselves from the presence of the LORD God amongst the trees of the garden.

> ⁹And the LORD God called unto Adam, and said unto him, Where *art* thou?

> ¹⁰And he said, I heard thy voice in the garden, and I was afraid, because I *was* naked; and I hid myself.

Their disobedience had changed everything. They were scared to face God.

> ^{Gen 3:11}And he said, Who told thee that thou *wast* naked? Hast thou eaten of the tree, whereof I commanded thee that thou shouldest not eat?

[12]And the man said, The woman whom thou gavest *to be* with me, she gave me of the tree, and I did eat.

[13]And the L ORD God said unto the woman, What *is* this *that* thou hast done? And the woman said, The serpent beguiled me, and I did eat.

Just like children, Adam tried to shift the blame to Eve, and Eve tried to shift the blame to the serpent. God dealt with each one separately.

Gen 3:14 And the L ORD God said unto the serpent, Because thou hast done this, thou *art* cursed above all cattle, and above every beast of the field; upon thy belly shalt thou go, and dust shalt thou eat all the days of thy life:

It is thought that Satan was operating through the serpent when he misled Eve and convinced her to eat the forbidden fruit. Genesis does not explicitly say the serpent was possessed by Satan, but other verses in the Bible link Satan to the serpent.

Rev 12: 9 And the great dragon was cast out, that old serpent, called the Devil, and Satan, which deceiveth the whole world: he was cast out into the earth, and his angels were cast out with him.

Rev 20:2 And he laid hold on the dragon, that old serpent, which is the Devil, and Satan, and bound him a thousand years,

The serpent was obviously more than a mere puppet of Satan because God cursed him physically. If the serpent was an innocent puppet of Satan who had no ability to resist, then it would have been wrong for God to punish him.

On some level, the serpent must have willingly cooperated with Satan to cause the downfall of Adam and Eve.

This is a foreshadowing of the conflict between Jesus and Satan.

> Gen 3:15And I will put enmity between thee and the woman, and between thy seed and her seed; it shall bruise thy head, and thou shalt bruise his heel.

> Rom 16:20And the God of peace shall bruise Satan under your feet shortly. The grace of our Lord Jesus Christ *be* with you. Amen.

> Gen 3:16Unto the woman he said, I will greatly multiply thy sorrow and thy conception; in sorrow thou shalt bring forth children; and thy desire *shall be* to thy husband, and he shall rule over thee.

God said he would multiply Eve's sorrow and her conception. He seems to be saying her punishment will be painful childbirths and she will end up having more children than she otherwise would have. Also, Adam will have the authority over her,

> Gen 3:17And unto Adam he said, Because thou hast hearkened unto the voice of thy wife, and hast eaten of the tree, of which I commanded thee, saying, Thou shalt not eat of it: cursed *is* the ground for thy sake; in sorrow shalt thou eat *of* it all the days of thy life;

> 18Thorns also and thistles shall it bring forth to thee; and thou shalt eat the herb of the field;

> 19In the sweat of thy face shalt thou eat bread, till thou return unto the ground; for out of it wast thou taken: for dust thou *art,* and unto dust shalt thou return.

Adam's punishment would be a life filled with hard work.

> Gen 3:20And Adam called his wife's name Eve; because she was the mother of all living.

> 21Unto Adam also and to his wife did the LORD God make coats of skins, and clothed them.

God made coats of skins to cover Adam and Eve. Blood had to be shed in order to provide a covering for Adam and Eve. This was the beginning of the sacrifices that would be offered for sin. These sacrifices were necessary because the penalty for sin is death and without the shedding of blood there is no remission of sin. Jesus would eventually die in Adam and Eves (and everyone's) place but until then, the blood sacrifices offered for them would serve as God's promise to pay the ultimate price for their sins in the future.

As for God's statement… they would surely die in the day they ate of the Tree of Knowledge of Good and Evil… God did not lie.

Before they ate, there was no reason they would ever die. After they ate of it, their deaths were inevitable. The day they ate the forbidden fruit, they knew they would surely die.

> Gen 3:22 And the LORD God said, Behold, the man is become as one of us, to know good and evil: and now, lest he put forth his hand, and take also of the tree of life, and eat, and live for ever:

"the man is become as one of us, to know good and evil"

Who is God talking to?

He could have been talking to the other members of the Godhead. God the father, God the Son and God the Holy Ghost or he could have been talking to the angels. I would expect the angels to understand the difference between good and evil especially after the fall of Lucifer.

Gen 3:22 also mentions another tree… the Tree of Life. What is this all about?

> Prov 3:13 Happy *is* the man *that* findeth **wisdom**, and the man *that* getteth **understanding**.

> Prov 3:18 She *is* a **tree of life** to them that lay hold upon her: and happy *is every one* that retaineth her.

Proverbs identifies wisdom and understanding as a tree of life.

It's curious the two trees specifically mentioned in the book of Genesis are associated with concepts like Knowledge, Understanding and Wisdom.

Knowledge, Understanding and Wisdom are the three levels of learning.

Knowledge answers the questions ……… Who, What, When, and Where?

Understanding answers the question ….. How?

Wisdom answers the question of ……….. Why?

Just having the knowledge of good and evil does not bring salvation. You must also understand God's plan and his purpose.

God did not initially prohibit Adam and Eve from eating of the Tree of Life. What would have happened if they had eaten from the Tree of Life first?

Both the Tree of Knowledge of Good and Evil and the Tree of Life are mentioned as being prominently located in the "midst of the garden". Is it reasonable to believe Adam and Eve would have ignored the fruit growing on the Tree of Life which was in the midst of their garden? Wouldn't they have tried the fruit of all the trees? Did they not get around to trying it or was their another reason they didn't eat of its fruit?

It may not have been possible to eat from the Tree of Life because its fruit was not in season. One must have knowledge before they can obtain understanding or wisdom.

Why would God prevent Adam from eating of a tree that would give him the knowledge of good and evil?

It is possible that Adam and Eve were not ready. There are certain things parents command their children not to do. They may say, "You are not allowed to use matches." They do this for the child's own good. They understand the child is not ready to use matches. As the child grows and matures, there will come a time when he will be mature enough to use something as potentially dangerous as matches.

In the same way, it is a crime for a 12 year old child to drive a car, but when a person reaches driving age, it is good for him to learn to drive.

I expect same thing applies to the Tree of Knowledge of Good and Evil. I expect God would have allowed them to eat of it eventually but they disobeyed and ate of it before they were ready.

> Gen 3:23Therefore the LORD God sent him forth from the garden of Eden, to till the ground from whence he was taken.

> 24So he drove out the man; and he placed at the east of the garden of Eden Cherubim, and a flaming sword which turned every way, to keep the way of the tree of life.

The disobedience of Adam and Eve had disastrous unforeseen consequences. They were driven from the Garden of Eden. Since they were not ready for the knowledge of good and evil, they definitely weren't ready for the Tree of Life.

If they had waited until God gave them permission to eat of the tree of the knowledge of good and evil then the results of their actions may have been very different. God said in the day they ate of it they would surely die. Would that statement have remained true forever? If they were obedient and waited until God allowed them to eat from that tree, would they still have died or was the tree meant to remain in the midst of the garden forever as a never ending test of men's obedience? It is impossible to say but it seems reasonable to assume that since God, the angels and Jesus have the knowledge of good and evil then it must not be a bad thing in and of itself. God was not angry because of their having this knowledge. He was angry because of their disobedience. Even though God had set up a situation were it was possible for them to sin, he did not make them sin. He told them what the consequences were and they used their own free will to disobey him. This set into action God's plan for redemption and put Satan's true nature on display for the entire universe to see. There is no turning back for Satan. He and his fallen angels will be judged and everyone will know God's judgment against them is just.

As for God's proclamation that Adam would die when he ate of the Tree of the Knowledge of Good and Evil, let's consider what death is. Death is a separation. We understand death as being when the body stops functioning. The soul separates from the body. This is the literal definition of physical death, but the death God was referring to was most likely spiritual death. Adam was spiritually separated from God by his disobedience. This happened immediately when he ate the fruit of the Tree of Knowledge. His separation from God was his spiritual death. He would continue to function physically for a while and he would father children (spiritually dead children). From this point on, spiritual life would only be provided on an individual basis.

Jesus alluded to this when he talked to Nicodemus…

John 3:3 Jesus answered and said unto him, Verily, verily, I say unto thee, Except a man be born again, he cannot see the kingdom of God.

4 Nicodemus saith unto him, How can a man be born when he is old? can he enter the second time into his mother's womb, and be born?

5 Jesus answered, Verily, verily, I say unto thee, Except a man be born of water and *of* the Spirit, he cannot enter into the kingdom of God.

6 That which is born of the flesh is flesh; and that which is born of the Spirit is spirit.

7 Marvel not that I said unto thee, Ye must be born again.

8 The wind bloweth where it listeth, and thou hearest the sound thereof, but canst not tell whence it cometh, and whither it goeth: so is every one that is born of the Spirit.

If Adam and Eve would have waited until they were allowed to eat of the Tree of the Knowledge of Good and Evil then I suspect their bodies would have "died" or "transformed" but their spirits would have lived (similar to the way a caterpillar transforms into a butterfly). They would have become truly spiritual beings. As it happened, they ate the fruit in disobedience, their spirits died and they became truly physical beings. The only hope we have now is through Jesus. He can breathe spiritual life into us individually so that we can be reborn as spiritual beings.

I believe the Tree of Knowledge of Good and Evil and the Tree of Life were literal, physical trees in the Garden of Eden. Their fruit had significance beyond that of mere food. The fruit was logically meant to be eaten, but it should have been eaten at the proper time and in the proper way.

The nearest thing I can compare it to would be the communion. The juice (wine) and the bread are given significance beyond their value as food. They are to be eaten with the understanding of what they mean and they are to be taken in a respectful way that is worthy of their meaning.

1 Cor 11:24And when he had given thanks, he brake *it,* and said, Take, eat: this is my body, which is broken for you: this do in remembrance of me.

25After the same manner also *he took* the cup, when he had supped, saying, This cup is the new testament in my blood: this do ye, as oft as ye drink *it,* in remembrance of me.

26For as often as ye eat this bread, and drink *this* cup, ye do shew the Lord's death till he come.

27Wherefore whosoever shall eat this bread, and drink this cup of the Lord, unworthily, shall be guilty of the body and blood of the Lord.

28But let a man examine himself, and so let him eat of *that* bread, and drink of *that* cup.

29For he that eateth and drinketh unworthily, eateth and drinketh damnation to himself, not discerning the Lord's body.

The communion Jesus had with his disciples was to be a symbolic reminder of his death on the cross as atonement for the sins of all mankind. Jesus took upon himself all of the sins of mankind and died upon a tree (the cross) so we could have salvation and eternal life.

Gal1:13 Christ hath redeemed us from the curse of the law, being made a curse for us: for it is written, Cursed *is* every one that hangeth on a tree:

In a sense, the Cross became the spiritual Tree of Life for humanity and Jesus became the fruit of the Tree of Life.

> Rom 1:18 Therefore as by the offence of one *judgment came* upon all men to condemnation; even so by the righteousness of one *the free gift came* upon all men unto justification of life.

By partaking in the communion in a worthy manner, we are associating ourselves with the atonement Jesus provided. He traded places with us. He took upon himself our sins so we could take upon ourselves his righteousness.

We now symbolically eat of it through Jesus, but in the future Jesus will give us the literal fruit to eat.

> Rev 2:7He that hath an ear, let him hear what the Spirit saith unto the churches; To him that overcometh will I give to eat of the tree of life, which is in the midst of the paradise of God.

The Tree of Life will be located in the New Jerusalem that will come down from Heaven when God creates a New Heaven and a New Earth.

> Rev 22:1And he shewed me a pure river of water of life, clear as crystal, proceeding out of the throne of God and of the Lamb.
>
> 2In the midst of the street of it, and on either side of the river, *was there* the tree of life, which bare twelve *manner* of fruits, *and* yielded her fruit every month: and the leaves of the tree *were* for the healing of the nations.
>
> Rev 22:14Blessed *are* they that do his commandments, that they may have right to the tree of life, and may enter in through the gates into the city.

Humanity will finally be restored to its proper place with God. It has been a long and painful process, but thanks to the faithfulness of Jesus, we will have been restored.

Rev 21:1 And I saw a new heaven and a new earth: for the first heaven and the first earth were passed away; and there was no more sea.

2 And I John saw the holy city, new Jerusalem, coming down from God out of heaven, prepared as a bride adorned for her husband.

3 And I heard a great voice out of heaven saying, Behold, the tabernacle of God *is* with men, and he will dwell with them, and they shall be his people, and God himself shall be with them, *and be* their God.

4 And God shall wipe away all tears from their eyes; and there shall be no more death, neither sorrow, nor crying, neither shall there be any more pain: for the former things are passed away.

Chapter Four

Understanding Genesis:

Cain and Family

Genesis 4 begins with Adam and Eve having two sons, Cain and Abel.

Cain was a tiller of the ground and Abel was a keeper of sheep. At one point, both sons made offerings to the Lord. Cain offered the fruit of the ground which he had grown. Abel brought the best of his flock, as an offering. God was pleased with the offering Abel made but God did not respect Cain's offering

The question is… **Why would God favor Abel's offering and not Cain's?**

The obvious answer would be because Abel's offering was a blood sacrifice which typified the blood sacrifice Jesus would offer for us in the future. This answer is reasonable but I think there is more to it. God mentions the quality of the offering Abel made.

> Gen 4:4And Abel, he also brought of the firstlings of his flock and of the fat thereof. And the LORD had respect unto Abel and to his offering:

Abel brought the best he had to God. There is no mention of the quality of Cain's offering. I suspect if Cain's heart were in the right place, God would have been pleased with Cain. Grain, in the form of meal and cakes, was used in the worship of God during the times of the Tabernacle and Temples. Bloodless offerings do have their place. The problem probably had more to do with Cain's attitude than with his offering.

We are told Cain talked with Abel and when they were in the field, Cain rose up and killed Abel. We are not told what they were talking about, but it angered Cain enough to attack his brother.

Did Cain intend to kill his brother? Did Cain even understand what death was? Did he understand the consequences?

We must give Cain the benefit of the doubt. He was not like us. He did not grow up in a culture where death was commonplace. In his day no one had died from wars, murders, illnesses, accidents or old age. As far as we know, the only experience he had with death was observing Abel offer his sheep to God. Cain may not have realized his attack would cause his brother to die. This could be why God didn't punish Cain as badly as we might have expected.

God judged Cain for the murder of Abel and sentenced him to exile.

> Gen 4:16And Cain went out from the presence of the LORD, and dwelt in the land of Nod, on the east of Eden.

> 17And Cain knew his wife; and she conceived, and bare Enoch: and he builded a city, and called the name of the city, after the name of his son, Enoch.

Who was Cain's wife and where did she come from?

Many people look at Cain's wife as a mystery or as evidence there were other humans around who were not part of the line of Adam. There is NO Biblical support for this. The Bible calls Eve the mother of ALL living.

> Gen 3:20And Adam called his wife's name Eve; because she was the mother of all living.

The only option Cain had was to marry one of his sisters. The Bible doesn't name any of the daughters of Adam and Eve but we are told they had sons and daughters. Chances are they had many children during their 900+ year life spans.

> Gen 5:4And the days of Adam after he had begotten Seth were eight hundred years: and he begat sons and daughters:

Doesn't the Bible say brothers and sisters should not marry each other?

The Law of Moses does prohibit marriage between close relatives, but this mandate was not given until the time of Moses. The law forbidding the marriages of close relatives makes sense. Close relatives are more likely to have many of the same genetic flaws. If two closely related people have children, it is more likely the genetic errors will compound and cause birth defects.

Genetic errors initially wouldn't have been a problem because Adam and Eve were created perfectly by God and had no genetic errors to pass on. It would take many generations for genetic errors to occur and to become significant enough to make it necessary to prohibit marriages between close relatives.

Abraham, Isaac and Jacob are the examples proving it was not wrong to marry close relatives before the time of Moses. Abraham married his half sister. Isaac and Jacob married their cousins

Marrying close relatives was not an issue during the time of Cain.

Jewish tradition states Adam and Eve had 33 sons and 23 daughters.
(Flavius Josephus, *Antiquities*, bk 1, ch 2, vs 3, footnote).

Josephus also says Cain took his wife with him to the land of Nod. This is consistent with what Genesis says.

> Gen 4:16 And Cain went out from the presence of the LORD, and dwelt in the land of Nod, on the east of Eden.
>
> 17And Cain knew his wife; and she conceived, and bare Enoch: and he builded a city, and called the name of the city, after the name of his son, Enoch.

Genesis says Cain went to the land of Nod where he knew his wife (had sexual relations with her.) It does not say he met her in Nod. There is no reason to continue to question who Cain's wife was. She was simply his sister.

The rest of Genesis 4 gives a brief description of the descendants of Cain. For the most part, the rest of this chapter is unremarkable, but there are two interesting things that should be pointed out.

Firstly, it says Tubalcain was an artificer in brass and iron.

> ^{Gen 4:22}And Zillah, she also bare Tubal-cain, an instructer of every artificer in brass and iron: and the sister of Tubal-cain *was* Naamah.

This is amazing considering Tubalcain was only seven generations from Adam. How did he come by his knowledge of metallurgy? Did God teach men how to refine and use metal?

The Book of Enoch suggests the fallen angels taught men how to use metals. Of course, the Book of Enoch cannot be assumed to be accurate, but it does provide an interesting answer to how Tubalcain learned to use metals.

> Enoch 8:1
>
> And Azazel taught men to make swords, and knives, and shields, and breastplates, and made known to them the metals (of the earth) and the art of working them, and bracelets, and ornaments, and the use of antimony, and the beautifying of the eyelids, and all kinds of costly stones, and all 2 colouring tinctures.

(The Book of Enoch is a pseudepigraphal apocryphal work attributed to Enoch, the great-grandfather of Noah.)

The second interesting thing remaining in this chapter is in verse 26.

> ^{Gen 4:26}And to Seth, to him also there was born a son; and he called his name Enos: then began men to call upon the name of the LORD.

Men began calling upon the name of the Lord after Enos was born. Enos was only two generations from Adam. Enos was born 235 years after the creation of Adam. Why did it take more than 235 years for men to begin calling upon the name of the Lord?

I think this passage means God was directly accessible to Adam and his children until then. At some point God stepped back and became a less direct influence in their lives. Men would have to call on him.

Would men continue to seek him or would they become evil?

Genesis 5 is called The Book of the Generations of Adam. It describes the lineage from Adam to Noah. To see this in the form of a family tree see Appendix E.

44

Chapter Five

Understanding Genesis:

Giants

Genesis 6

^{Gen 6:1}And it came to pass, when men began to multiply on the face of the earth, and daughters were born unto them,

²That the sons of God saw the daughters of men that they *were* fair; and they took them wives of all which they chose.

³And the LORD said, My spirit shall not always strive with man, for that he also *is* flesh: yet his days shall be an hundred and twenty years.

⁴There were giants in the earth in those days; and also after that, when the sons of God came in unto the daughters of men, and they bare *children* to them, the same *became* mighty men which *were* of old, men of renown.

These verses refer to two groups that came together during the time before the flood. One group was referred to as the "sons of God". The other group was called "the daughters of men."

It has been suggested the sons of God were the descendants of Seth while the daughters of men were the descendants of Cain. This makes no sense. Both Seth and Cain were sons of Adam. Both were normal human beings. Everyone currently alive is a descendant of Seth. Does that also make us Sons of God? The book of John says no.

^{John 1:12}But as many as received him, to them gave he power to become the sons of God, *even* to them that believe on his name:

Only those who receive Jesus can BECOME the sons of God.

There is no reason to think marriages between the children of Seth and the children of Cain would result in giants.

Who were the "sons of God"?

To understand who the fathers of the giants were (the mysterious sons of God), it is necessary to see how this term is used throughout the rest of the Bible.

Adam was identified as the son of God.

> Luke 3:38Which was *the son* of Enos, which was *the son* of Seth, which was *the son* of Adam, which was *the son* of God.

Jesus was also identified as the son of God.

> Mat 8:29And, behold, they cried out, saying, What have we to do with thee, Jesus, thou Son of God? art thou come hither to torment us before the time?

> Mark 1:1The beginning of the gospel of Jesus Christ, the Son of God;

Adam was created directly by God and was therefore God's son.

Jesus was the only begotten son of God.

> John 3:16For God so loved the world, that he gave his only begotten Son, that whosoever believeth in him should not perish, but have everlasting life.

Jesus was the only "begotten" son of God. He was physically born from a woman. God was the Father. Mary was the mother.

The sons of God in Genesis were obviously not just sons of Adam and they were not fathered by God as Jesus was. These sons of God were created by God in a way similar to Adam but they were not born like Jesus. These sons apparently were angels which were created directly by God. These angels decided to take to themselves human wives and they fathered children. These angel/human hybrid children grew to be giants. Angels were not meant to be sexual beings (see Mark 12:20-25). They were obviously acting in disobedience. From this, we can conclude the sons of God were fallen angels.

The verses referring to the sons of God imply several interesting things. Angels can obviously take on a physical form and father children. This means angels are physiologically similar enough to mate with humans. The resulting children are somewhat different from either parent. Similar to the way a mule results from the mating of a horse and a donkey.

> Gen 6:5 And GOD saw that the wickedness of man *was* great in the earth, and *that* every imagination of the thoughts of his heart *was* only evil continually.
>
> 6 And it repented the LORD that he had made man on the earth, and it grieved him at his heart.
>
> 7 And the LORD said, I will destroy man whom I have created from the face of the earth; both man, and beast, and the creeping thing, and the fowls of the air; for it repenteth me that I have made them.
>
> 8 But Noah found grace in the eyes of the LORD.
>
> 9 These *are* the generations of Noah: Noah was a just man *and* perfect in his generations, *and* Noah walked with God.
>
> 10 And Noah begat three sons, Shem, Ham, and Japheth.
>
> 11 The earth also was corrupt before God, and the earth was filled with violence.
>
> 12 And God looked upon the earth, and, behold, it was corrupt; for all flesh had corrupted his way upon the earth.

¹³And God said unto Noah, The end of all flesh is come before me; for the earth is filled with violence through them; and, behold, I will destroy them with the earth.

Wickedness was associated with the era of the giants. The sinfulness of mankind was great and God was sorry he had created men. Sinful angelic (demonic) beings had corrupted the human bloodlines. God decided to destroy the Earth but Noah found grace in the eyes of the Lord. God calls Noah "perfect in his generations". This probably meant his genes were free of the demonic contamination. God would cleanse the world of the demonic bloodlines and would start fresh with Noah and his family. There was more to Noah than just a perfect bloodline. Ezekiel implies Noah was one of the most righteous men who ever lived.

> Ezek 14:14Though these three men, Noah, Daniel, and Job, were in it, they should deliver *but* their own souls by their righteousness, saith the Lord GOD.

> Ezek 14:18Though these three men *were* in it, *as* I live, saith the Lord GOD, they shall deliver neither sons nor daughters, but they only shall be delivered themselves.

> Ezek 14:20Though Noah, Daniel, and Job, *were* in it, *as* I live, saith the Lord GOD, they shall deliver neither son nor daughter; they shall *but* deliver their own souls by their righteousness.

Gen 6:17And, behold, I, even I, do bring a flood of waters upon the earth, to destroy all flesh, wherein *is* the breath of life, from under heaven; *and* every thing that *is* in the earth shall die.

¹⁸But with thee will I establish my covenant; and thou shalt come into the ark, thou, and thy sons, and thy wife, and thy sons' wives with thee.

¹⁹And of every living thing of all flesh, two of every *sort* shalt thou bring into the ark, to keep *them* alive with thee; they shall be male and female.

²⁰Of fowls after their kind, and of cattle after their kind, of every creeping thing of the earth after his kind, two of every *sort* shall come unto thee, to keep *them* alive.

²¹And take thou unto thee of all food that is eaten, and thou shalt gather *it* to thee; and it shall be for food for thee, and for them.

²²Thus did Noah; according to all that God commanded him, so did he.

God intended to start over. Noah and his immediate family would be the only humans who were allowed to survive the flood. The giants as well as everyone else would die.

The question then becomes… What would prevent the "Sons of God" from fathering children (giants) and tainting the bloodlines after the flood?

The Bible indicates the "Sons of God" may have fathered children even after the flood.

> ᴳᵉⁿ ⁶:⁴There were giants in the earth in those days; and also after that, when the sons of God came in unto the daughters of men, and they bare *children* to them, the same *became* mighty men which *were* of old, men of renown.

The Bible mentions giants several times after the flood.

> ᴺᵘᵐ ¹³:³²And they brought up an evil report of the land which they had searched unto the children of Israel, saying, The land, through which we have gone to search it, is a land that eateth up the inhabitants thereof; and all the people that we saw in it *are* men of a great stature.

> ³³And there we saw the giants, the sons of Anak, *which come* of the giants: and we were in our own sight as grasshoppers, and so we were in their sight.

Who was Anak? Was he one of the fallen "Sons of God" who fathered giant children?

There were other giants who were either identified with Anak or they were compared to the sons of Anak. Among these were the Emims and the Zamzummims. Og, the king of Bashan, was said to be the last of the remnant of the giants.

> ^{Deut 3:11}For only Og king of Bashan remained of the remnant of giants; behold, his bedstead *was* a bedstead of iron; is it not in Rabbath of the children of Ammon? nine cubits was the length thereof, and four cubits the breadth of it, after the cubit of a man.

> ^{Josh 13:12}All the kingdom of Og in Bashan, which reigned in Ashtaroth and in Edrei, who remained of the remnant of the giants: for these did Moses smite, and cast them out.

The giants were finished off during the time of Moses. This would indicate the "Sons of God" had, at some point, been prevented from fathering any more children. We don't know exactly why they stopped.

Rev 9:14 shows at least 4 angels have been bound in the river Euphrates. Could these be the troublesome "Sons of God" who kept fathering children with the daughters of men? It is impossible to say. It's obvious the angels are not still fathering giants; therefore it's reasonable to conclude the angels have been restrained or otherwise prevented from mating with human women.

> ^{Rev 9:14}Saying to the sixth angel which had the trumpet, Loose the four angels which are bound in the great river Euphrates.

There were times when God instructed the Israelites to destroy the men, women and children in cities they took. Could this have been to remove whatever demonic genetic material had found its way back into the human gene pool? God specifically instructed Moses to kill everyone in the cities of Og the giant, king of Bashan.

> ^{Deut 3:3}So the LORD our God delivered into our hands Og also, the king of Bashan, and all his people: and we smote him until none was left to him remaining.

^{Deut 3:6}And we utterly destroyed them, as we did unto Sihon king of Heshbon, utterly destroying the men, women, and children, of every city.

We have discussed the interesting implications of the fallen angels who fathered giant offspring. Angels were never meant to mate with humans but they did it anyway. The Earth became so desperately wicked God decided to start over with the only righteous man who was perfect in his generations… Noah. As we shall see in the next chapter, God destroys every living thing upon the Earth with a great flood except for those who were with Noah.

52

Chapter Six

Understanding Genesis:

The Great Flood

Genesis 7

^{Gen 7:1}And the LORD said unto Noah, Come thou and all thy house into the ark; for thee have I seen righteous before me in this generation.

²Of every clean beast thou shalt take to thee by sevens, the male and his female: and of beasts that *are* not clean by two, the male and his female.

³Of fowls also of the air by sevens, the male and the female; to keep seed alive upon the face of all the earth.

⁴For yet seven days, and I will cause it to rain upon the earth forty days and forty nights; and every living substance that I have made will I destroy from off the face of the earth.

God instructs Noah to take into his Ark two of every kind of animal and seven of the clean animals and birds. Notice the animals are taken by their "kinds" not by their varieties. This would reduce the amount of animals necessary to be taken. Noah would only need to take two dogs. Not two of every type of dog. He would take two cats. Not two of every type of cat. He would take two monkeys, two bears etc.

The great variety of animals we now see on the Earth have arisen from the ancestors Noah placed on the Ark. Their genetic diversity was sufficient to allow the animals to specialize into thousands of varying forms.

^{Gen 7:5}And Noah did according unto all that the LORD commanded him.

[6]And Noah *was* six hundred years old when the flood of waters was upon the earth.

The flood waters came when Noah was 600 yrs old. Let's see what we can determine from the ages given concerning Noah and his ancestors.

Contemporaries Before the Flood.

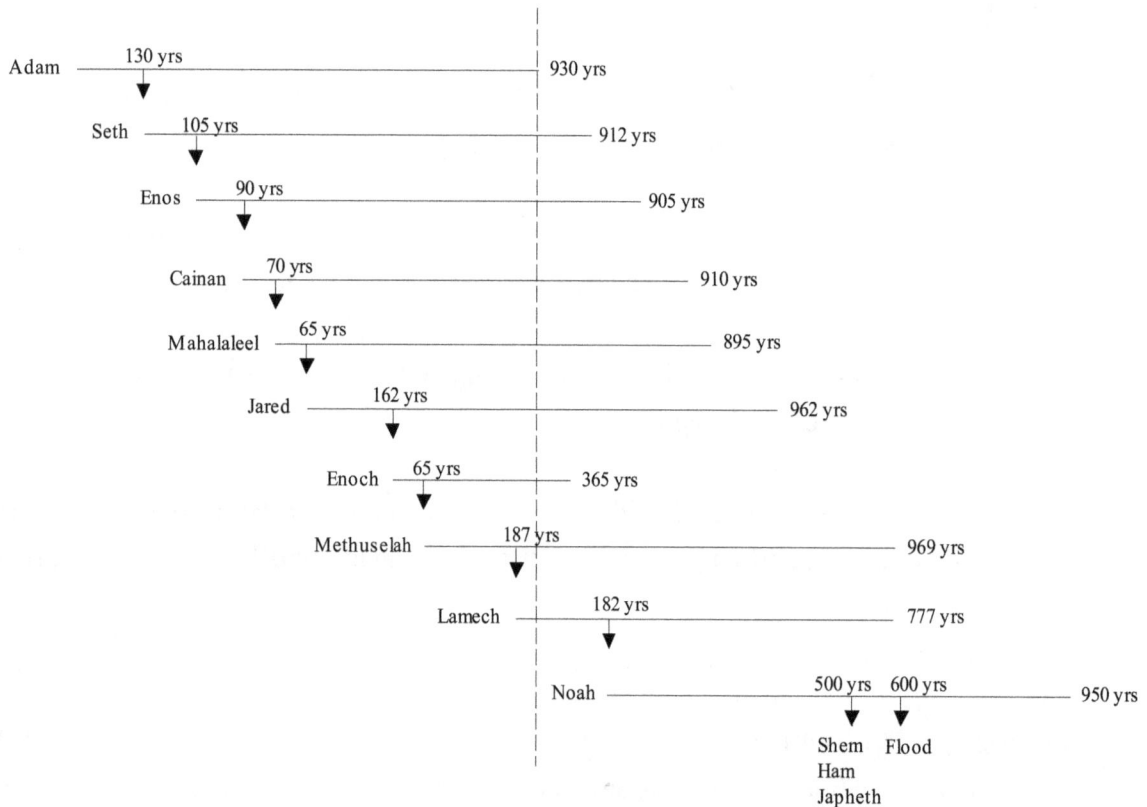

From the above graphic, Noah was the first in his line that was not alive during the lifetime of Adam. Noah's father Lamech as well as all of Noah's grandparents would have probably known Adam directly and would have been able to speak with him face to face. It would have been fascinating to hear the Adam's story directly from him. Noah would have to be satisfied listening to the creation story second hand from his parents and his grandparents.

We can also see Methuselah and Lamech were alive during the period Noah was building the ark. Lamech died approximately 5 years before the flood. Methuselah lived right up until the time of the flood. Methuselah's death coincides exactly with the beginning of the great flood. It was as if God was waiting for Methuselah to die before sending his judgement.

The great flood finally came in the 600th year of Noah's life.

> ^{Gen 7:11}In the six hundredth year of Noah's life, in the second month, the seventeenth day of the month, the same day were all the fountains of the great deep broken up, and the windows of heaven were opened.
>
> ¹²And the rain was upon the earth forty days and forty nights.
>
> ¹³In the selfsame day entered Noah, and Shem, and Ham, and Japheth, the sons of Noah, and Noah's wife, and the three wives of his sons with them, into the ark;
>
> ¹⁴They, and every beast after his kind, and all the cattle after their kind, and every creeping thing that creepeth upon the earth after his kind, and every fowl after his kind, every bird of every sort.
>
> ¹⁵And they went in unto Noah into the ark, two and two of all flesh, wherein *is* the breath of life.

Understanding what the Bible says about the fountains of the great deep being broken up, and the windows of heaven being opened explains a lot. It explains how the fossil beds around the world were formed. It explains where our fossil fuels came from and how all of that organic material became buried.

Breaking up all the fountains of the great deep would require an incredible amount of energy. God could have caused this cataclysm to occur with just a word or he could have used a natural catastrophe, like a massive meteor impact, to break apart the Earth's crust and release the fountains of the deep. Considering the fault lines which correspond with the volcanic "ring of fire" an extreme meteor impact seems like a reasonable explanation.

The impact of a meteor large enough to cause the crust of the Earth to crack would have a devastating effect on the whole planet. It is theorized that before the flood the oceans were smaller because a great deal of the Earth's water was contained in subterranean chambers (the fountains of the great deep). This water could have had the effect of moderating the temperatures planet wide. When the meteor hit it caused faults in the crust of the Earth which propagated around the planet. The water contained in the underground chambers escaped through the faults in the crust. The water would have been highly pressurized because of the weight of the earth bearing down on it. This highly pressurized water would have caused an incredible amount of erosion as it shot out of the faults. The eroded earth would have been carried along with the water and would eventually settle out as the turbulence lessened. The sedimentary deposits caused by the erosion would have encased many animals and plants thereby setting up the necessary conditions for the fossilization process to begin.

There is an entire field of study which looks at the broken crust of the Earth called Plate Tectonics. Scientists in this field attribute the creation of mountain ranges, volcanoes and earthquakes to the friction caused by the movement of these plates. It seems to make sense because the mountain ranges around the world tend to run parallel to the edges of the plates. It is as if the upper crust of the Earth is sliding in one direction and when it encounters enough resistance, the upper crust starts to buckle and thrust up forming the mountain ranges. Volcanoes also tend to occur along the Earth's fault lines. There is a lot of evidence to support Plate Tectonic theories, and I think the sudden breaking apart of the Earth's crust with the sudden expulsion of massive quantities of water and sediment explains all of the available evidence.

A different twist on Plate Tectonics

Let's imagine the Earth was very different before the Great Flood. The crust of the Earth was intact much like the shell of an egg. The crust being intact would make the Earth very stable. No shifting plates to cause earthquakes or volcanoes or huge mountain ranges. There was an ocean but it was smaller because much of the water was contained in subterranean chambers.

Now let's imagine a huge meteorite slams into the planet and cracks the crust of the Earth. The crack quickly propagates around the entire planet. The water in the subterranean vaults rushes to the surface which causes almost instantaneous flooding of the relatively flat landscape. The cracked crust of the Earth begins to move. The water under the cracked plates acts as lubrication as they slide. As the plates move, some plates move toward each other while others move away. The plates moving toward each other are forced to either slide over or under the other plate.

As the remaining water under the plates escapes, the resistance between the plates becomes greater. The plates begin to crack and buckle. The plates thrust upward as they buckle forming the great mountain ranges.

Where the plates were moving apart, great basins are formed. These basins become our modern day oceans. As the water on the land drains into these basins the land begins to appear once again.

The impact of the meteorite would have caused a huge amount of dust and dirt to be thrown into the upper atmosphere. This dust would provide condensation sites for the water vapor in the canopy above the Earth. The canopy would collapse in the form of a worldwide torrential rain.

The Ark rested 150 days after the flood started but it was 3 more months before the tops of the other mountains were seen.

> Gen 7:18 And the waters prevailed, and were increased greatly upon the earth; and the ark went upon the face of the waters. 19And the waters prevailed exceedingly upon the earth; and all the high hills, that *were* under the whole heaven, were covered. 20Fifteen cubits upward did the waters prevail; and the mountains were covered.

> Gen 7:24 And the waters prevailed upon the earth an hundred and fifty days.

> Gen 8:1 And God remembered Noah, and every living thing, and all the cattle that *was* with him in the ark: and God made a wind to pass over the earth, and the waters asswaged; 2The fountains also of the deep and the windows of heaven were stopped, and the rain from heaven was restrained; 3And the waters returned from off the earth continually: and after the end of the hundred and fifty days the waters were abated. 4And the ark rested in the seventh month, on the seventeenth day of the month, upon the mountains of Ararat. 5And the waters decreased continually until the tenth month: in the tenth *month,* on the first *day* of the month, were the tops of the mountains seen.

It took a little over 1 year from the start of the flood to the time when the Earth was dry enough to release the animals. This was a second beginning for mankind and God gave them the same instructions, to be fruitful and multiply upon the Earth.

> Gen 8:13And it came to pass in the six hundredth and first year, in the first *month,* the first *day* of the month, the waters were dried up from off the earth: and Noah removed the covering of the ark, and looked, and, behold, the face of the ground was dry.

> 14And in the second month, on the seven and twentieth day of the month, was the earth dried.

> 15And God spake unto Noah, saying,

> 16Go forth of the ark, thou, and thy wife, and thy sons, and thy sons' wives with thee.

> 17Bring forth with thee every living thing that *is* with thee, of all flesh, *both* of fowl, and of cattle, and of every creeping thing that creepeth upon the earth; that they may breed abundantly in the earth, and be fruitful, and multiply upon the earth.

Noah's first order of business after leaving the Ark was to build an altar and offer God a sacrifice. Noah made offerings of all of the clean beasts. He was able to do this because he took 7 of each clean animal. He could sacrifice one of each to God and three pair of each type of clean animals would remain.

> Gen 8:20And Noah builded an altar unto the LORD; and took of every clean beast, and of every clean fowl, and offered burnt offerings on the altar.

> 21And the LORD smelled a sweet savour; and the LORD said in his heart, I will not again curse the ground any more for man's sake; for the imagination of man's heart *is* evil from his youth; neither will I again smite any more every thing living, as I have done.

²²While the earth remaineth, seedtime and harvest, and cold and heat, and summer and winter, and day and night shall not cease.

God establishes a new covenant with Noah and with every creature upon the Earth. He will never again destroy the world with a flood.

Gen 9:9 And I, behold, I establish my covenant with you, and with your seed after you;

¹⁰And with every living creature that *is* with you, of the fowl, of the cattle, and of every beast of the earth with you; from all that go out of the ark, to every beast of the earth.

¹¹And I will establish my covenant with you; neither shall all flesh be cut off any more by the waters of a flood; neither shall there any more be a flood to destroy the earth.

¹²And God said, This *is* the token of the covenant which I make between me and you and every living creature that *is* with you, for perpetual generations:

¹³I do set my bow in the cloud, and it shall be for a token of a covenant between me and the earth.

The "sign" of a bow in the clouds implies there was no rain before the flood. A rainbow is an optical effect resulting from light refracting through water droplets. The rainbow was something new which Noah had never seen before (supporting the idea of no rain before the flood). God decided to link this new optical phenomenon with his promise not to destroy the world with a flood again. It would be a reminder of God's promise to Noah and all of his descendants.

Gen 9:14 And it shall come to pass, when I bring a cloud over the earth, that the bow shall be seen in the cloud:

[15]And I will remember my covenant, which *is* between me and you and every living creature of all flesh; and the waters shall no more become a flood to destroy all flesh.

[16]And the bow shall be in the cloud; and I will look upon it, that I may remember the everlasting covenant between God and every living creature of all flesh that *is* upon the earth.

[17]And God said unto Noah, This *is* the token of the covenant, which I have established between me and all flesh that *is* upon the earth.

Understanding the significance of the Great Flood and its consequences is fundamental to understanding geology and the fossil record. For a further discussion on these topics refer to Appendix A.

Chapter Seven

Understanding Genesis:

After the Flood

The flood is over. Noah and his family have been given the task of being fruitful and multiplying to replenish the Earth. There is no record of Noah having any children after the flood but his three sons had several children. See the family tree in Appendix E.

It's curious to note how the life spans changed after the flood.

Gen 9: 28 And Noah lived after the flood three hundred and fifty years.

29 And all the days of Noah were nine hundred and fifty years: and he died.

Noah lived 350 years after the flood which made him 950 yrs old when he died.

Shem (Noah's first born) lived about 500 yrs after the flood which made him about 600 yrs old when he died

Shem's son Arphaxad only lived to be 438 yrs old.

Within 10 generations the life spans had dropped to less than 200 yrs.

Today, anyone who remains alive for 90 yrs is considered to be very old.

The next chart we have will graphically show how the life spans dropped off in a non-linear fashion after the flood. The chart gives the false impression that Enoch died at a relatively young age, in reality he didn't die at all. He was taken up to Heaven by God in his 365th yr.

Before the flood, Lamech had the shortest life span of 777 yrs. Even this was substantially longer than the life span of anyone after the flood (except Noah). Noah probably reached such an old age because the majority of his years were lived before the flood. It is also important to note that the life spans after the flood decreased over time. They did not instantly drop. Arphaxad was among the first generation that was born after the flood and he still achieved an age of 438 years before he died. Ten generations after Arphaxad, the life spans had decreased to 147 years. Of course we make the assumption that all of these recorded life spans were typical for their generation. The general slope of the curve would tend to support this hypothesis.

A nonlinear decrease rather than an instantaneous (stair-step) decrease in life spans would suggest that either some beneficial remnant of the pre-flood environment was still available after the flood (but was being depleted over time) or the post-flood environment was detrimental to life spans. If the latter is the case, then the detrimental effects would seem to compound from one generation to the next. It may even be a combination of both of these factors. We will consider these possibilities shortly.

Life Spans Before and After
The Great Flood

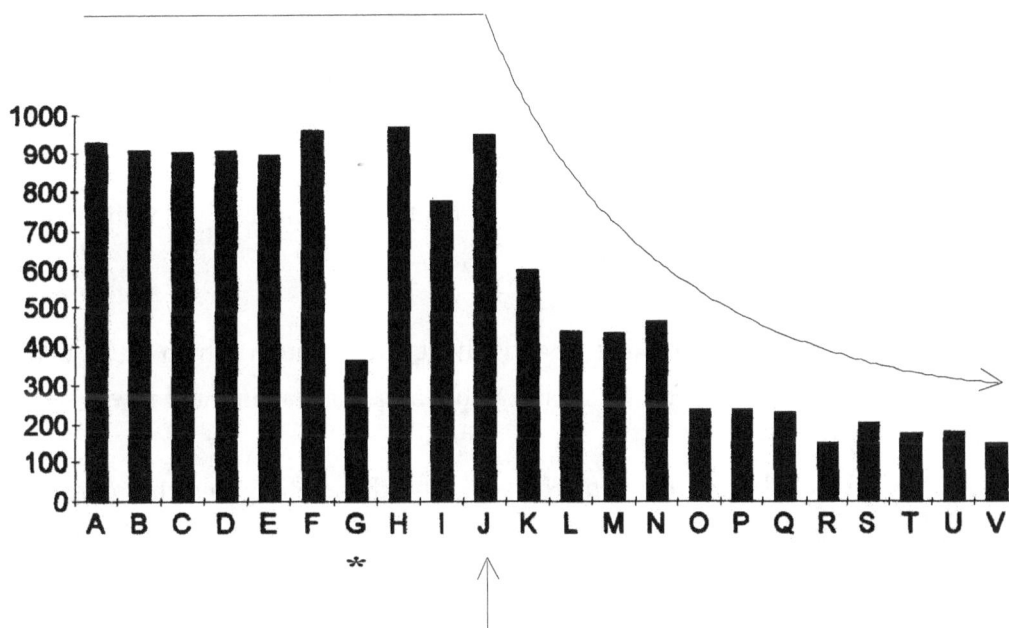

The great flood occurs here.

A	Adam	930	L	Arphaxad	438
B	Seth	912	M	Salah	433
C	Enos	905	N	Eber	464
D	Cainan	910	O	Peleg	239
E	Mahalaleel	895	P	Reu	239
F	Jared	962	Q	Serug	230
G	Enoch (*)	365	R	Nahor	148
H	Methuselah	969	S	Terah	205
I	Lamech	777	T	Abraham	175
J	Noah	950	U	Isaac	180
K	Shem	600	V	Jacob	147

* Enoch's lifespan was artificially low
because he did not die a natural death.

Why would the life spans drop after the flood?

Something dramatic had obviously happened to cause life spans to plummet after the flood but what could it have been? I believe the primary cause was the lower atmospheric pressure after the flood.

The Bible says the firmament separated the waters that were above the firmament from the waters below the firmament.

> Gen 1:6 And God said, Let there be a firmament in the midst of the waters, and let it divide the waters from the waters.
>
> 7 And God made the firmament, and divided the waters which *were* under the firmament from the waters which *were* above the firmament: and it was so.
>
> 8 And God called the firmament Heaven. And the evening and the morning were the second day.

Firmament can mean space, sky, or atmosphere. God placed the Sun and Moon in the firmament of the heaven (space). He also said the birds fly in the open firmament of the heaven (the sky or atmosphere). From the context, it is easy to see it was the atmosphere that separated the waters from the waters.

The above verses suggest there was a substantial amount of water in the upper atmosphere. I suspect it was a dense, transparent water vapor canopy.

Atmospheric pressure is a measure of the weight of the atmosphere directly above you. The atmosphere stretches upwards for miles. The weight of the air above you today is typically about 14.7 pounds per square inch. If additional mass (as from a water vapor canopy) were added to this, the atmospheric pressure would be correspondingly higher.

It's has been shown that lower atmospheric pressures have detrimental effects on oxygen breathing animals. Conversely, it would seem reasonable that higher pressures might provide beneficial effects to oxygen breathers.

Consider why mountain climbers require additional oxygen when they climb above a certain elevation. Is it because the ratio of Oxygen to Nitrogen is too low up there? NO! The ratio is the same, the difference is the pressure. The pressure is so low the density of Oxygen is inadequate to supply their bodily needs.

By increasing the pressure, you increase the density of the oxygen in a given volume of air. This is why high compression internal combustion engines produce more horsepower than low compression engines of the same size. The compression increases the density of oxygen which allows the fuel to burn quicker and causes a more explosive combustion.

The additional mass from the water vapor canopy would effectively cause the entire Earth to be one big hyperbaric (pressurized) chamber.

The medical profession has discovered the beneficial effects of hyperbaric chambers. These pressurized oxygen enriched chambers have been found to be useful in the treatment of diabetic wounds, non healing bone infections, carbon monoxide poisoning, and severe burns.

The higher atmospheric pressure before the flood was probably the primary beneficial effect on life spans but it was not the only factor. If it were the only reason for the long life spans then the life spans after the flood should have dropped instantaneously rather than decreasing incrementally from generation to generation.

If the sudden substantial decrease in atmospheric pressure was the only factor in the reduction of life spans then we would have expected to see a sudden (stair-step) decrease in life spans. This is not what we see. The decrease is non-linear but still takes generations. The atmospheric pressure would not have taken generations to stabilize. It would have reached equilibrium soon after the vapor canopy collapsed.

Other likely factors for increased life spans may have been indirectly due to the higher atmospheric pressures before the flood. We have demonstrated why an increased atmospheric pressure is beneficial to oxygen breathing life forms but would it also have beneficial effects on plant life?

Just as a higher atmospheric pressure increases the oxygen density available to animals, it also increases the carbon dioxide and nitrogen density available to the plants.

Plants use carbon dioxide to perform photosynthesis and nitrogen is one of the main ingredients in fertilizer. Some plants, such as legumes, can absorb nitrogen directly from the atmosphere and "fix" the nitrogen into the soil. I suspect the increased atmospheric pressure allowed plants to absorb the nitrogen they needed much more efficiently than they do today. When these plants died their richness would fertilize the earth. I suspect the plants before the flood were super nutritious because of their ideal growing conditions. Even after the flood, the earth may have still been "super" fertile and the nutritional value of the foods would still be good but, over time, the fertility of the ground would become less and less. The food would be less and less nutritious and the life spans would continue to drop.

The final factor in the decreasing life spans may have been due to the missing water vapor canopy. It no longer provided the same level of shielding from the Sun's cosmic rays. Cellular damage and genetic mutations would occur which could cause health problems over time. Such genetic damage would slowly build up over time and could easily be responsible for the continual decrease in life spans after the flood.

The Genesis account of the flood (when properly understood) is the most scientifically reasonable way to explain everything to do with origins. Unfortunately, it is not given the credibility it deserves. The "scientists" are covering their eyes and plugging their ears. They are clinging to their big-bang, Darwinist theories in spite of the overwhelming evidence supporting the Genesis account.

When the "scientists" of old said the Earth was flat, the Bible said it was round and hung upon nothing.

> [Isa 40:22]*It is* he that sitteth upon the circle of the earth…

> [Job 26:7]He stretcheth out the north over the empty place, *and* hangeth the earth upon nothing

Eventually, the Bible was proven to be correct. As always, the Bible believers get the last laugh.

Chapter Eight

Understanding Genesis:

The Tower of Babel and the Dispersion:

Genesis 11

Gen 11:1-4And the whole earth was of one language, and of one speech. ²And it came to pass, as they journeyed from the east, that they found a plain in the land of Shinar; and they dwelt there. ³And they said one to another, Go to, let us make brick, and burn them throughly. And they had brick for stone, and slime had they for morter. ⁴And they said, Go to, let us build us a city and a tower, whose top *may reach* unto heaven; and let us make us a name, lest we be scattered abroad upon the face of the whole earth

The descendants of Noah began to increase upon the face of the Earth. The people where all part of the same family and had a common language. If a charismatic leader could convince such a unified people to do his will, they could accomplish anything they put their minds to (for good or evil).

Gen 11:5-6And the LORD came down to see the city and the tower, which the children of men builded. ⁶And the LORD said, Behold, the people *is* one, and they have all one language; and this they begin to do: and now nothing will be restrained from them, which they have imagined to do

The Bible distinguishes one of Noah's descendants as being a great one in the Earth.

Gen 10:8-10And Cush begat Nimrod: he began to be a mighty one in the earth. ⁹He was a mighty hunter before the LORD: wherefore it is said, Even as Nimrod the mighty hunter before the LORD. [10]And the beginning of his kingdom was Babel, and Erech, and Accad, and Calneh, in the land of Shinar.

Nimrod was the founder of the City of Babel and was most likely the charismatic leader who convinced the people to build the great tower, but what would God think of this tower?

Gen 11:7-9Go to, let us go down, and there confound their language, that they may not understand one another's speech. [8]So the LORD scattered them abroad from thence upon the face of all the earth: and they left off to build the city. [9]Therefore is the name of it called Babel; because the LORD did there confound the language of all the earth: and from thence did the LORD scatter them abroad upon the face of all the earth.

From the above passage, God obviously disapproved of the tower and took steps to prevent its construction. But why? Was God afraid that Nimrod would be able to build a tower so high he could walk right into heaven? Obviously not.

Making a tower unto heaven probably meant the tower was being built to worship or use divination by observing the heavens. Similar to what we call Astrology.

It had only been 2 generations since the flood and the people were already being led astray. God decided to block their efforts by confounding their language. The question then becomes… How could the descendants of Noah fall into paganism so soon after the flood and where was Noah when all of this was going on?

Noah was the only one who God noted as being righteous in his generation.

Gen 7:1And the LORD said unto Noah, Come thou and all thy house into the ark; for thee have I seen righteous before me in this generation.

While Noah's wife, his sons, and their wives were with Noah in the Ark, God did not say they were righteous. It is reasonable to speculate Noah's family may have brought some of their pre-flood sinful ideas with them. The belief in Astrology could have been one of these ideas. As for Noah, Genesis says he planted a vineyard and became a husbandman.

> Gen 9:20 And Noah began *to be* an husbandman, and he planted a vineyard:

This implies Noah had settled in one area and he most likely remained there. The Bible doesn't tell us anything else about Noah's post-flood movements but we can be assured he didn't have anything to do with the construction of the tower of Babel.

At one point, Noah became drunk from the wine of his vineyard. Ham came into his tent and saw his father was naked. Rather than covering the nakedness of his father he chose to go out and tell his brothers about their father's nakedness. The brothers then did what Ham should have done. They covered their father's nakedness and took deliberate efforts not to look at him in that condition.

> Gen 9:21 And he drank of the wine, and was drunken; and he was uncovered within his tent. 22And Ham, the father of Canaan, saw the nakedness of his father, and told his two brethren without. 23And Shem and Japheth took a garment, and laid *it* upon both their shoulders, and went backward, and covered the nakedness of their father; and their faces *were* backward, and they saw not their father's nakedness.

When Noah awoke, he knew what had happened and he was angry at Ham. Noah then cursed Ham's son Canaan but he blessed Shem and Japheth.

> Gen 9:24 And Noah awoke from his wine, and knew what his younger son had done unto him. 25And he said, Cursed *be* Canaan; a servant of servants shall he be unto his brethren.

> Gen 9:26 And he said, Blessed *be* the LORD God of Shem; and Canaan shall be his servant. 27God shall enlarge Japheth, and he shall dwell in the tents of Shem; and Canaan shall be his servant.

It is unclear what part Canaan played in regard to Noah's drunken nakedness, but it was bad enough for Noah to curse his descendants.

Ham was the black sheep of the family because of his treatment of Noah. He was not blessed by Noah like his other brothers were. His son Canaan was cursed. Ham's grandson was Nimrod, the founder of Babel. The Hamites were most likely responsible for building the Tower of Babel.

When God confounded the language of the people, they separated and were forced to seek out those who shared their language. These groups then scattered throughout the world.

This separation of the people by language is most likely what was ultimately responsible for the creation of the races. Even though the life spans after the flood were extremely long by our standards, the population of the Earth at this point would still have been relatively small.

Separating such a small population into groups would reduce the available amount of genetic diversity to whatever was available within their own group. With such small breeding populations, it is reasonable to think that certain physical characteristics would become the norm for that group. These characteristics over time would become more and more exaggerated. Characteristics like skin color, hair color and eye color could be affected. These characteristics are not the result of evolution because the characteristics for all of these things were already in the genetic code of Noah and his children. Certain characteristics became dominant within these small groups due to the lack of genetic variation. (See Appendix A)

It is curious to note that Noah had 3 sons and there are 3 races of men on the Earth. Until recently, the races were very distinct. Caucasoid (white), Negroid (black), and Mongoloid (yellow). This is not to say that any race is better, worse, or more "evolved" than any other race. We are all just variations of a theme just as Black Labradors, Chocolate Labs and Yellow Labs are variations of the Labrador theme.

Recently, with our modern ability to travel quickly around the world, the races are intermarrying and giving birth to children of mixed race. The lines between the races are beginning to blur. This is not necessarily a bad thing. Genetically, it means the genetic diversity of these mixed race children is being increased. This is a beneficial thing physically for our population as a whole. Survival of the fittest directly depends on the amount of genetic diversity within a population. As far as health goes, the more genetic diversity the better. It should also be pointed out; the Bible does not prohibit mixed race marriages.

The rest of the Book of Genesis tells the story of Abraham, Isaac and Jacob. It continues until the death of Joseph. From this point on, Genesis focuses directly on God's relationship with Abraham and his descendants.

In eleven chapters, the Book of Genesis describes the creation of the Heaven and the Earth. It describes how men came to be under the curse of sin. Genesis gives us the ability to explain how the billions of fossils were quickly buried in sediment. It also helps us to explain where the different languages and the different races came from. Genesis does all this in a manner that is scientifically reasonable and consistent with the physical evidence.

It is beyond reason to believe an ancient author could have written such a profound, insightful and scientifically accurate document without divine revelation.

Chapter Nine

Understanding Genesis:

God's Promise to Abraham:

The Promise:

^{Gen 12:1}Now the LORD had said unto Abram, Get thee out of thy country, and from thy kindred, and from thy father's house, unto a land that I will shew thee: ²And I will make of thee a great nation, and I will bless thee, and make thy name great; and thou shalt be a blessing: ³And I will bless them that bless thee, and curse him that curseth thee: and in thee shall all families of the earth be blessed.

Abram (Abraham) found favor in the sight of Lord. Because of this the Lord made a seven part promise to him.

The Lord promised to make of him a great nation.

I will bless thee.

I will make thy name great.

Thou shalt be a blessing.

I will bless them that bless thee

I will curse him that curseth thee.

In thee shall all families of the Earth be blessed.

What a blessing for God to bestow on a human. Why was Abraham so greatly favored by God? The Bible doesn't really say. The best we can do is remember what God told the prophet Samuel… "for man looketh on the outward appearance, but the LORD looketh on the heart.."

Abraham must have been an exceptional individual

God had long term plans for Abraham and his descendants. God promised to make him a great nation. For this to happen, Abraham would have to father children. Unfortunately, Sarai (Sarah) was barren. This bothered Sarai so much that she offered Hagar (her handmaid) to Abraham as a surrogate to bare him a child. Abraham thought this may have been the way God's promise would come to fruition. Abraham was trying to make it happen rather than waiting on God. This turned out to be such a huge mistake the children of Israel are still suffering from it,

> Gen 16:2 And Sarai said unto Abram, Behold now, the LORD hath restrained me from bearing: I pray thee, go in unto my maid; it may be that I may obtain children by her. And Abram hearkened to the voice of Sarai.

> Gen 16:15 And Hagar bare Abram a son: and Abram called his son's name, which Hagar bare, Ishmael.

There was a lingering hostility between Sarah and Hagar because of Hagar's attitude after she bore Ishmael to Abraham. Abraham didn't want anything to do with the awkward situation between the two women.

> Gen 16:4 And he went in unto Hagar, and she conceived: and when she saw that she had conceived, her mistress was despised in her eyes.

> 5And Sarai said unto Abram, My wrong *be* upon thee: I have given my maid into thy bosom; and when she saw that she had conceived, I was despised in her eyes: the LORD judge between me and thee.

> 6But Abram said unto Sarai, Behold, thy maid *is* in thy hand; do to her as it pleaseth thee. And when Sarai dealt hardly with her, she fled from her face.

The Lord later made it known that Ishmael wasn't the child God had promised. Abraham's barren wife Sarai would bare him the son God had promised.

> Gen 16:15 And God said unto Abraham, As for Sarai thy wife, thou shalt not call her name Sarai, but Sarah *shall* her name *be.*

> 16 And I will bless her, and give thee a son also of her: yea, I will bless her, and she shall be *a mother* of nations; kings of people shall be of her.

Abraham questioned God about Ishmael.

> Gen 17:18 And Abraham said unto God, O that Ishmael might live before thee!

> Gen 17:20 And as for Ishmael, I have heard thee: Behold, I have blessed him, and will make him fruitful, and will multiply him exceedingly; twelve princes shall he beget, and I will make him a great nation.

God promised he would bless and multiply Ishmael, but he also told Hagar Ishmael would be a wild man. Everyone would be his enemy.

> Gen 16:12 And he will be a wild man; his hand will be against every man, and every man's hand against him; and he shall dwell in the presence of all his brethren.

Sarah eventually brought forth the son that God had promised Abraham.

> Gen 21:2: For Sarah conceived, and bare Abraham a son in his old age, at the set time of which God had spoken to him. 3 And Abraham called the name of his son that was born unto him, whom Sarah bare to him, Isaac. 4 And Abraham circumcised his son Isaac being eight days old, as God had commanded him.

Isaac grew and, at one point, Sarah saw Ishmael mocking. This infuriated Sarah and she insisted Abraham cast out Hagar and Ishmael.

> Gen 21:8 And the child grew, and was weaned: and Abraham made a great feast the *same* day that Isaac was weaned. 9And Sarah saw the son of Hagar the Egyptian, which she had born unto Abraham, mocking. 10Wherefore she said unto Abraham, Cast out this bondwoman and her son: for the son of this bondwoman shall not be heir with my son, *even* with Isaac.

Two great lineages can be traced back to Abraham. Ishmael was the first born but he was not the child God had promised. The child Sarah would have in her old age would be the miracle child by which all the nations of the Earth would be blessed. The lineage of Isaac would eventually bring forth Jesus.

Ishmael was the child that Abraham wanted but Isaac was the child God wanted for Abraham. One son can be seen as the work of the flesh while the other was the work of the spirit.

Both sons would be blessed and multiplied. But the son of the flesh (Ishmael) and his descendants would be a constant source of grief and trouble. There is no peace with Ishmael.

Isaac married Rebekah who was also barren but the Lord eventually answered Isaac's prayer and gave them two sons.

> Gen 25: 21 And Isaac intreated the LORD for his wife, because she *was* barren: and the LORD was intreated of him, and Rebekah his wife conceived.

> 22And the children struggled together within her; and she said, If *it be* so, why *am* I thus? And she went to enquire of the LORD.

> 23And the LORD said unto her, Two nations *are* in thy womb, and two manner of people shall be separated from thy bowels; and *the one* people shall be stronger than *the other* people; and the elder shall serve the younger.

> 24And when her days to be delivered were fulfilled, behold, *there were* twins in her womb.

> 25And the first came out red, all over like an hairy garment; and they called his name Esau.

26And after that came his brother out, and his hand took hold on Esau's heel; and his name was called Jacob: and Isaac *was* threescore years old when she bare them.

The two boys were very different.

Gen 25: 27And the boys grew: and Esau was a cunning hunter, a man of the field; and Jacob *was* a plain man, dwelling in tents.

28And Isaac loved Esau, because he did eat of *his* venison: but Rebekah loved Jacob.

Esau was the oldest and was entitled to the birthright but he didn't value it as highly as he should have. Jacob wanted the birthright and was willing to do whatever it took to obtain it.

Gen 25: 29And Jacob sod pottage: and Esau came from the field, and he *was* faint:

30And Esau said to Jacob, Feed me, I pray thee, with that same red *pottage;* for I *am* faint: therefore was his name called Edom.

31And Jacob said, Sell me this day thy birthright.

32And Esau said, Behold, I *am* at the point to die: and what profit shall this birthright do to me?

33And Jacob said, Swear to me this day; and he sware unto him: and he sold his birthright unto Jacob.

34Then Jacob gave Esau bread and pottage of lentiles; and he did eat and drink, and rose up, and went his way: thus Esau despised *his* birthright.

Jacob purchased the birthright from Esau and Jacob's mother convinced him to deceive Isaac into giving him the blessing that was intended for Esau.

Gen 25: [14]And he went, and fetched, and brought *them* to his mother: and his mother made savoury meat, such as his father loved.

[15]And Rebekah took goodly raiment of her eldest son Esau, which *were* with her in the house, and put them upon Jacob her younger son:

[16]And she put the skins of the kids of the goats upon his hands, and upon the smooth of his neck:

[17]And she gave the savoury meat and the bread, which she had prepared, into the hand of her son Jacob.

[18]And he came unto his father, and said, My father: and he said, Here *am* I; who *art* thou, my son?

[19]And Jacob said unto his father, I *am* Esau thy firstborn; I have done according as thou badest me: arise, I pray thee, sit and eat of my venison, that thy soul may bless me.

[20]And Isaac said unto his son, How *is it* that thou hast found *it* so quickly, my son? And he said, Because the LORD thy God brought *it* to me.

[21]And Isaac said unto Jacob, Come near, I pray thee, that I may feel thee, my son, whether thou *be* my very son Esau or not.

[22]And Jacob went near unto Isaac his father; and he felt him, and said, The voice *is* Jacob's voice, but the hands *are* the hands of Esau.

[23]And he discerned him not, because his hands were hairy, as his brother Esau's hands: so he blessed him.

Jacob acquired the birthright and the blessings through opportunism and deception but God honored the transfer from Esau to Jacob.

79

The fact Esau was so willing to sell his birthright for a quick bowl of soup proved his unworthiness. His choice of wives also demonstrated his poor judgment.

> Gen 25: 34And Esau was forty years old when he took to wife Judith the daughter of Beeri the Hittite, and Bashemath the daughter of Elon the Hittite:
>
> 35Which were a grief of mind unto Isaac and to Rebekah.
>
> Gen 36: 2Esau took his wives of the daughters of Canaan; Adah the daughter of Elon the Hittite, and Aholibamah the daughter of Anah the daughter of Zibeon the Hivite;
>
> 3And Bashemath Ishmael's daughter, sister of Nebajoth.

Jacob's treacherous behavior was in no way justifiable but he proved he valued God's blessings more than his brother Esau. God seemed to respect his determination and his willingness to pursue a blessing. Maybe this is why God accepted him as Esau's replacement. Jacob was given a new name (Israel) after wrestling with what he described as a man all night long. The man was more likely an angel or a manifestation of God himself. In any event, the "man" renamed Jacob. It was as if Jacob was starting over with God and he would now be called Israel.

> Gen 32: 24And Jacob was left alone; and there wrestled a man with him until the breaking of the day.
>
> 25And when he saw that he prevailed not against him, he touched the hollow of his thigh; and the hollow of Jacob's thigh was out of joint, as he wrestled with him.
>
> 26And he said, Let me go, for the day breaketh. And he said, I will not let thee go, except thou bless me.
>
> 27And he said unto him, What *is* thy name? And he said, Jacob.
>
> 28And he said, Thy name shall be called no more Jacob, but Israel: for as a prince hast thou power with God and with men, and hast prevailed.

Jacob (Israel) married two sisters and he later took their two handmaidens as wives. Rachael was the younger of the two sisters and was Jacob's favorite. Unfortunately, she was barren. The older of the two sisters was Leah. She gave Jacob a total of six sons and one daughter. Rachael, feeling empty because of her inability to have children, gave Jacob her handmaiden Bilhah so she might have children as a surrogate for Rachael. Not to be outdone, Leah gave Jacob her handmaiden Zilpah to have children in her place. Both handmaidens ended up having two sons each. Finally, Rachael conceived and bore Jacob two sons. She died in childbirth while having Benjamin (the second of her sons).

There was a special place in Jacob's heart for the sons of Rachael, especially Joseph. The other sons of Jacob perceived this and were frustrated at the preferential treatment their father showed toward Joseph. At one point Joseph told his family about a dream he had where his whole family was bowing to him. The brothers were indignant and their hatred for Joseph grew. One day Joseph came to them while they were tending the sheep. Joseph's brothers grabbed him and threw him into a pit. They then sold him into slavery and told their father he had been killed by a beast.

Joseph was taken to Egypt and eventually became the second most powerful man in Egypt. The brothers eventually had to go to Egypt to buy food to get them through a famine. They didn't recognize Joseph but Joseph knew who they were. Joseph put together a scheme to make them bring their youngest brother the next time they came. Joseph set a trap to make it appear the youngest brother had stolen a silver cup. The youngest brother, Benjamin, would be forced to stay and be Joseph's servant. The other brothers begged and pleaded Joseph to let the boy return to his father. They said their father would die if they returned without Benjamin.

Joseph broke down and revealed himself to his brothers and he forgave them. Joseph told them to bring the whole family to Egypt where they could be taken care of. The brothers returned to their father and told him what had happened. Jacob and the entire family went to Egypt to live with Joseph. This is how the children of Israel came to be in Egypt.

When Jacob (Israel) was approaching death he called his sons to him and he told them what would befall them in the Last days.

A blessing was given to Judah. Kings would come from him but the birthright would go to Joseph.

> ^{Gen 49:} ⁸Judah, thou *art he* whom thy brethren shall praise: thy hand *shall be* in the neck of thine enemies; thy father's children shall bow down before thee. ⁹Judah *is* a lion's whelp: from the prey, my son, thou art gone up: he stooped down, he couched as a lion, and as an old lion; who shall rouse him up? ¹⁰The sceptre shall not depart from Judah, nor a lawgiver from between his feet, until Shiloh come; and unto him *shall* the gathering of the people *be*. ¹¹Binding his foal unto the vine, and his ass's colt unto the choice vine; he washed his garments in wine, and his clothes in the blood of grapes: ¹²His eyes *shall be* red with wine, and his teeth white with milk.

The Birthright was given to Joseph

> ^{Gen 49:} ²²Joseph *is* a fruitful bough, *even* a fruitful bough by a well; *whose* branches run over the wall: ²³The archers have sorely grieved him, and shot *at him,* and hated him: ²⁴But his bow abode in strength, and the arms of his hands were made strong by the hands of the mighty *God* of Jacob; (from thence *is* the shepherd, the stone of Israel:) ²⁵*Even* by the God of thy father, who shall help thee; and by the Almighty, who shall bless thee with blessings of heaven above, blessings of the deep that lieth under, blessings of the breasts, and of the womb: ²⁶The blessings of thy father have prevailed above the blessings of my progenitors unto the utmost bound of the everlasting hills: they shall be on the head of Joseph, and on the crown of the head of him that was separate from his brethren.

We know the tribe of Judah was the kingly tribe and the messiah (Jesus) would come through this tribe, but the question is… Why? Judah was not the firstborn nor was he the most upright of the sons of Jacob.

Reuben was the firstborn son. Judah was son number four.

Reuben lost his birthright when he had an elicit affair with his father's concubine Bilhah.

> Gen 35: 22And it came to pass, when Israel dwelt in that land, that Reuben went and lay with Bilhah his father's concubine: and Israel heard *it*.

> Gen 49: 3Reuben, thou *art* my firstborn, my might, and the beginning of my strength, the excellency of dignity, and the excellency of power: 4Unstable as water, thou shalt not excel; because thou wentest up to thy father's bed; then defiledst thou *it:* he went up to my couch.

Simeon and Levi were the second and third sons of Jacob. They lost their birthright when they violently killed a man.

> Gen 34: 26And they slew Hamor and Shechem his son with the edge of the sword, and took Dinah out of Shechem's house, and went out.

> Gen 49: 5Simeon and Levi *are* brethren; instruments of cruelty *are in* their habitations. 6O my soul, come not thou into their secret; unto their assembly, mine honour, be not thou united: for in their anger they slew a man, and in their selfwill they digged down a wall. 7Cursed *be* their anger, for *it was* fierce; and their wrath, for it was cruel: I will divide them in Jacob, and scatter them in Israel.

Judah was next in line to receive the birth right but he was not worthy of it either.

The only son of Jacob who was truly exceptional was Joseph. Therefore, God wanted the birthright to go to him. It was customary for the firstborn son to get a double portion of the father's inheritance. During the time of Moses, The descendants of Joseph's two sons would be counted as separate tribes. They would be known as the tribes of Ephraim and Manasseh. They would separately receive an inheritance equal to the descendants of the rest of the tribes. In this way Joseph's descendants would end up with the double portion that would normally go to the firstborn son.

The book of First Chronicles says it this way…

> 1 Chron 5:1Now the sons of Reuben the firstborn of Israel, (for he *was* the firstborn; but, forasmuch as he defiled his father's bed, his birthright was given unto the sons of Joseph the son of Israel: and the genealogy is not to be reckoned after the birthright. 2For Judah prevailed above his brethren, and of him *came* the chief ruler; but the birthright *was* Joseph's:)

There are a couple of things that are worthy of mention concerning Abraham, Isaac, and Jacob.

Firstly, the favored wives of these men were all initially barren.

* Sarah was about 90 years old when she bore Isaac.
* Rebekah tried to have children for twenty years before she was successful.
* Rachel was barren for an unspecified amount of time but she was the last of Jacob's wives to have children.

God did not immediately fulfill his promises to make Abraham the father of many nations. God required faith and patience from Abraham, Isaac, and Jacob. Sarah and Rachael tried to take things into their own hands by using their handmaidens as surrogate mothers. This is not what God wanted. God would miraculously provide the promised children when he was ready. The births of Isaac, Jacob, and Joseph to previously barren mothers highlighted the fact that they were special and showed God could provide even when things seemed impossible.

The second thing worthy of noting is the first born sons of Abraham, Isaac, and Jacob did not receive the covenant or the birthright. Abraham would have been happy to have God bless Ishmael with the birthright, but God would bless Isaac.

> Gen 17: 18And Abraham said unto God, O that Ishmael might live before thee!

> 19And God said, Sarah thy wife shall bear thee a son indeed; and thou shalt call his name Isaac: and I will establish my covenant with him for an everlasting covenant, *and* with his seed after him.

Isaac preferred his firstborn son Esau but Esau didn't value the birthright.

> Gen 17: 28And Isaac loved Esau, because he did eat of *his* venison: but Rebekah loved Jacob.

Jacob gave the birthright to his eleventh son Joseph because he was the only one who was worthy.

The rejection of firstborn shows that God can bless whoever he wishes. He is sovereign. No one is entitled to the birthright. If Reuben had behaved honorably, then chances are his tribe would have been the Kingly tribe and would have brought forth the Messiah.

John the Baptist tried to make the point that being a descendant of Abraham is not an entitlement. God honors faith, obedience and holiness.

> Mat 3: 9And think not to say within yourselves, We have Abraham to *our* father: for I say unto you, that God is able of these stones to raise up children unto Abraham.

The book of Genesis ends with the death of Joseph and his instructions to his children to carry his bones with them when they leave Egypt. He knew it was not God's will for the children of Israel to remain in Egypt forever because he remembered the promise God made to Abraham.

> Gen 50: 24And Joseph said unto his brethren, I die: and God will surely visit you, and bring you out of this land unto the land which he sware to Abraham, to Isaac, and to Jacob.

> 25And Joseph took an oath of the children of Israel, saying, God will surely visit you, and ye shall carry up my bones from hence.

> 26So Joseph died, *being* an hundred and ten years old: and they embalmed him, and he was put in a coffin in Egypt.

The Bible continues with Exodus which tells the story of Moses and how God delivered the children of Israel from Egypt. The law is then given, followed by the history of Israel, its

Kings and its Prophets. The Old Testament points to the New Testament with its two focal points. The first focal point is when the deliverer (Messiah) pays the final price (sacrifice) for our sins. The second focal point when the Messiah returns to put down evil and to take possession of the world. The Old and New Testaments use Symbolism and Prophecy to continually point to these two focal points.

The rest of this book will be devoted to the understanding of the Symbolism and the Prophecies of the Bible. In many instances the Symbolism and Prophecy will be intertwined.

Chapter Ten

Symbolism:

Revealing Greater Truths:

The use of symbolism is a way of using one thing to represent something else. It is something we humans do very well. It is a vital part of our intellect. It sets us apart from the animals. Symbolism gives us the ability to communicate complex ideas with one another. It also gives us the ability to see beyond the obvious.

Starting at birth, a baby struggles to understand the world around it. The baby starts with only two concepts… comfort and discomfort. Comfort is good. Discomfort is bad. When the baby experiences discomfort, it cries. When it's wet, it cries. When it's hungry it cries. When it cries the mother feeds it or changes its diaper. From this instinctual reaction the baby learns "When I cry things happen, Mama comes and the discomfort goes away." This is the only way the baby can communicate.

As the baby grows, it hears the sounds the people around it are making. It watches everything and learns. Over time the baby begins to associate words with objects and concepts. "Mama", "Daddy", "No" and "Mine" all come to have meaning. The baby's use of specific sounds to get what it wants is a form of symbolism. This word means this. That word means that.

As the baby grows into childhood it learns to rely on sound, in the form of words, to communicate with other people. When the child is taught to read and write, the child learns that sounds can be symbolized by letters and letters can be arranged to symbolize words. Before long, the child will be able to read and write. Reading becomes a different way to communicate. In effect, reading becomes a way of hearing with your eyes and writing becomes a way of speaking with your hands. Everything depends on the human ability to associate or symbolize.

Numbering systems are also symbolic. They symbolize quantity. The number 5 has a different meaning to us than the number 1000. We have a general idea of how big a foot is or how long a mile is. The binary system of 1's and 0's can be used to symbolize what happens inside a computer. Variables such as "X" and "Y" are used in mathematics to symbolize unknown quantities.

Symbolism requires the ability to recognize patterns and similarities. God has placed this ability in all of us. In many instances, we find patterns to be pleasant such as with the hearing of music. If there is a melody or a beat we will recognize it, anticipate it and our bodies will even react to it. We may tap our feet, clap our hands or dance. Music is powerful. It affects our brains consciously as well as unconsciously. We quickly learn songs because of their pattern and rhyme. Is there any wonder why David wrote so many Psalms (songs)? His psalms were written in Hebrew and they would have had a verbal symmetry (rhyme) that wouldn't have translated well into any other language. Add music to the Psalm and the total effect would have been awe inspiring. He would use verbal imagery (symbolism) to convey ideas and the melody would capture the ear of the hearer.

The problem with any symbolism is its lack of precision. When I say "dog", you may visualize a four legged, hairy animal with a wet nose and a tendency to bark. The word "dog" symbolizes these types of characteristics, but what type of dog is it? There's not enough information in the word "dog" by itself. Adding more descriptive words to the word "dog" will be required to make the image more precise.

With language we can communicate ideas. We describe what we see as best we can, but in the end, words can only give an approximation of what we are describing. The saying, "A picture is worth a thousand words." is true. Words are only approximations of what we are describing.

It is curious that God created the entire universe using words.

Gen 1: 3**And God said**, Let there be light: and there was light.

Gen 1: 6**And God said**, Let there be a firmament in the midst of the waters, and let it divide the waters from the waters.

Gen 1: 9**And God said**, Let the waters under the heaven be gathered together unto one place, and let the dry *land* appear: and it was so.

^{Gen 1: 11}**And God said**, Let the earth bring forth grass, the herb yielding seed, *and* the fruit tree yielding fruit after his kind, whose seed *is* in itself, upon the earth: and it was so.

^{Gen 1: 14}**And God said**, Let there be lights in the firmament of the heaven to divide the day from the night; and let them be for signs, and for seasons, and for days, and years:

^{Gen 1: 20}**And God said**, Let the waters bring forth abundantly the moving creature that hath life, and fowl *that* may fly above the earth in the open firmament of heaven.

^{Gen 1: 24}**And God said**, Let the earth bring forth the living creature after his kind, cattle, and creeping thing, and beast of the earth after his kind: and it was so.

^{Gen 1: 26}**And God said**, Let us make man in our image, after our likeness: and let them have dominion over the fish of the sea, and over the fowl of the air, and over the cattle, and over all the earth, and over every creeping thing that creepeth upon the earth.

Could it be the language of God is so complete that his words do not approximate reality, they actually take form as reality? There is a unique relationship between God and his word. They are intertwined in a way that is not fully comprehensible to us.

^{John 1:1}**In the beginning was the Word**, and **the Word was with God**, and **the Word was God**. ²The same was in the beginning with God. ³All things were made by him; and without him was not any thing made that was made. ⁴In him was life; and the life was the light of men. ⁵And the light shineth in darkness; and the darkness comprehended it not.

^{John 1:14}And **the Word was made flesh**, and dwelt among us, (and we beheld his glory, the glory as of the only begotten of the Father,) full of grace and truth.

^{Heb 11:3}Through faith we understand that **the worlds were framed by the word of God, so that things which are seen were not made of things which do appear.**

We cannot begin to understand the infinite mind of God with his perfect language. Fortunately, he is able to communicate with us through finite, simple words. He has revealed himself to us through the Bible and he uses symbolism extensively. I believe there are two reasons for this. Firstly, symbolism is used to make concepts more easily understandable and secondly, it can cloak or hide greater truths in plain sight. Sometimes this cloaked symbolism can only be understood in retrospect. The parables of Jesus are prime examples of cloaked symbolism.

Mat 13:10And the disciples came, and said unto him, Why speakest thou unto them in parables? 11He answered and said unto them, Because it is given unto you to know the mysteries of the kingdom of heaven, but to them it is not given. 12For whosoever hath, to him shall be given, and he shall have more abundance: but whosoever hath not, from him shall be taken away even that he hath. 13Therefore speak I to them in parables: because they seeing see not; and hearing they hear not, neither do they understand. 14And in them is fulfilled the prophecy of Esaias, which saith, By hearing ye shall hear, and shall not understand; and seeing ye shall see, and shall not perceive: 15For this people's heart is waxed gross, and *their* ears are dull of hearing, and their eyes they have closed; lest at any time they should see with *their* eyes, and hear with *their* ears, and should understand with *their* heart, and should be converted, and I should heal them. 16But blessed *are* your eyes, for they see: and your ears, for they hear. 17For verily I say unto you, That many prophets and righteous *men* have desired to see *those things* which ye see, and have not seen *them;* and to hear *those things* which ye hear, and have not heard *them.*

We have already seen symbolism demonstrated in the book of Genesis starting with the Tree of Knowledge and the Tree of Life. Animal sacrifices were symbolic of the sacrifice Jesus would make for our sins. Abraham offering up Isaac was symbolic of God offering up Jesus. God used symbolism to tell the story of salvation over and over again so that when the ultimate sacrifice was made (the crucifixion of Jesus) we would be able to understand it.

Understanding symbolism is vital to a correct understanding of scripture. We need to look beyond the obvious to be able to see how deep the scriptures really go. Seeing the interconnectedness and the consistency within the 66 books of the Bible supports their authenticity and should increase our faith. By exploring the symbolism of the Bible we will be able to probe its depths and obtain greater understanding.

Symbolism has the power to reveal hidden truths and can provide many epiphanies regarding the nature of God, ourselves and the universe.

One of the primary keys to understanding Biblical symbolism is to pay attention whenever the Bible gives details. Details provide information that may be significant later. Pay particular attention when God himself gives specific instructions or details. When God gives details, they are always significant (Such as his instructions concerning the construction of the Tabernacle.)

Our journey will continue in the next chapter with a study of the Tabernacle.

Chapter Eleven

Symbolism

The Tabernacle

To study the symbolism of the Tabernacle we need to become familiar with what it was and how it was laid out. Its contents and dimensions were very significant. The first part of this chapter will be a matter of fact description of the Tabernacle. The second part of this chapter will explain the symbolism and its prophetic meaning. The diagrams of the holy objects are based on the Biblical descriptions but we don't know exactly how they looked. The diagrams will however, be adequate for purposes of demonstration.

> Ex 25:1 And the LORD spake unto Moses, saying, 2Speak unto the children of Israel, that they bring me an offering: of every man that giveth it willingly with his heart ye shall take my offering. 3And this *is* the offering which ye shall take of them; gold, and silver, and brass, 4And blue, and purple, and scarlet, and fine linen, and goats' *hair,* 5And rams' skins dyed red, and badgers' skins, and shittim wood, 6Oil for the light, spices for anointing oil, and for sweet incense, 7Onyx stones, and stones to be set in the ephod, and in the breastplate. 8And let them make me a sanctuary; that I may dwell among them. 9According to all that I shew thee, ***after the pattern of the tabernacle, and the pattern of all the instruments thereof, even so shall ye make*** *it.*

The Tabernacle was a mobile temple where God would meet with the priests on behalf of the people. God had a specific design for the Tabernacle. The Tabernacle was to be made according to a pattern that was shown to Moses. The pattern needed to be followed precisely. This precision was necessary because the Tabernacle was to have significance beyond its value as a tent. Its dimensions, construction and contents would all have symbolic meaning. Some of the symbolism is obvious while some is more subtle. Not all of the symbolism is understood. Some symbolism still remains waiting to be discovered, waiting for someone to dig deeper and uncover its hidden meaning.

94

Ex 26:15And thou shalt make boards for the tabernacle *of* shittim wood standing up. **16Ten cubits *shall be* the length of a board, and a cubit and a half *shall be* the breadth of one board.** 17Two tenons *shall there be* in one board, set in order one against another: thus shalt thou make for all the boards of the tabernacle. 18And thou shalt make the boards for the tabernacle, **twenty boards on the south side southward**. 19And thou shalt make forty sockets of silver under the twenty boards; two sockets under one board for his two tenons, and two sockets under another board for his two tenons. 20And for the second side of the tabernacle **on the north side *there shall be* twenty boards**: 21And their forty sockets *of* silver; two sockets under one board, and two sockets under another board. **22And for the sides of the tabernacle westward thou shalt make six boards.** 23And **two boards shalt thou make for the corners of the tabernacle in the two sides.** 24And they shall be coupled together beneath, and they shall be coupled together above the head of it unto one ring: thus shall it be for them both; they shall be for the two corners. **25And they shall be eight boards,** and their sockets *of* silver, sixteen sockets; two sockets under one board, and two sockets under another board.

There shall be 20 boards on the South side.
           20 boards on the North side
           6 boards on the West Side
           2 boards on the Corners of the West side

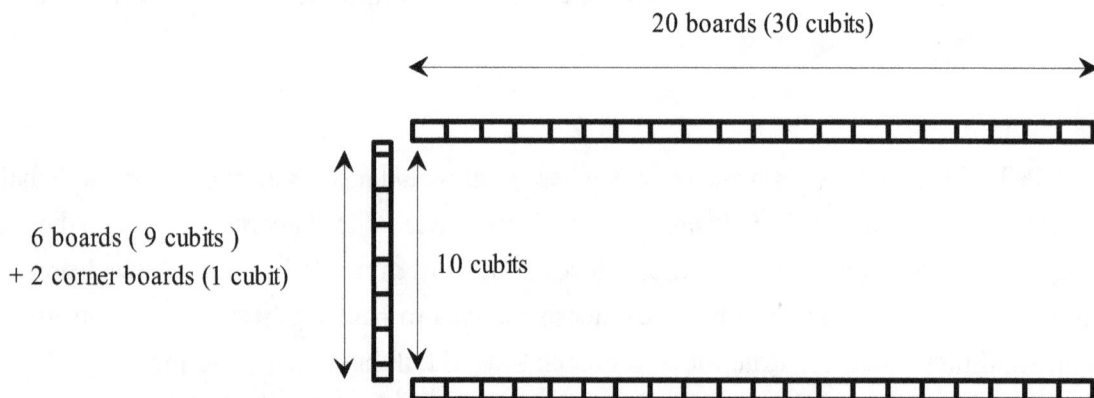

20 boards (30 cubits)

6 boards (9 cubits)
+ 2 corner boards (1 cubit)

10 cubits

The Bible doesn't specify the thickness of these boards. The boards are said to be one and a half cubits wide. We are told there are boards on the North, South and West sides. There are none on the East side. The boards on the West side are separated into two groups. There are 6 regular boards and there are 2 corner boards. The corner boards are obviously different from the boards on the sides. These corner boards would be used to tie together the three sides of the Tabernacle.

Were these corner boards also one and a half cubits wide? The Bible doesn't say specifically they had different dimensions, but the fact they are mentioned separately suggests they were different in someway.

To find out more information on the construction of the Tabernacle we must go to an extra-Biblical historical source. The most reputable of these would be the first century historian Josephus. While he was not alive during the construction or use of the Tabernacle, he was a Pharisee and it is reasonable to assume the information he had concerning the Tabernacle's dimensions would have been accurate.

With regard to the two corner boards, Josephus says they were made by cutting in half a single board which was 1 cubit wide. This would make each corner board a half a cubit wide.

When added to the other six boards making up the western wall of the Tabernacle the wall would become exactly ten cubits wide and ten cubits tall.

There were to be four pillars within the Tabernacle which would hold up a veil separating the Holy Place from the Most Holy Place.

> Ex 26:31 And thou shalt make a vail *of* blue, and purple, and scarlet, and fine twined linen of cunning work: with cherubims shall it be made:
>
> 32 And thou shalt hang it upon four pillars of shittim *wood* overlaid with gold: their hooks *shall be of* gold, upon the four sockets of silver.
>
> 33 And thou shalt hang up the vail under the taches, that thou mayest bring in thither within the vail the ark of the testimony: and the vail shall divide unto you between the holy *place* and the most holy.

30 cubits

10 cubits

10 cubits

N

W ← → E

S

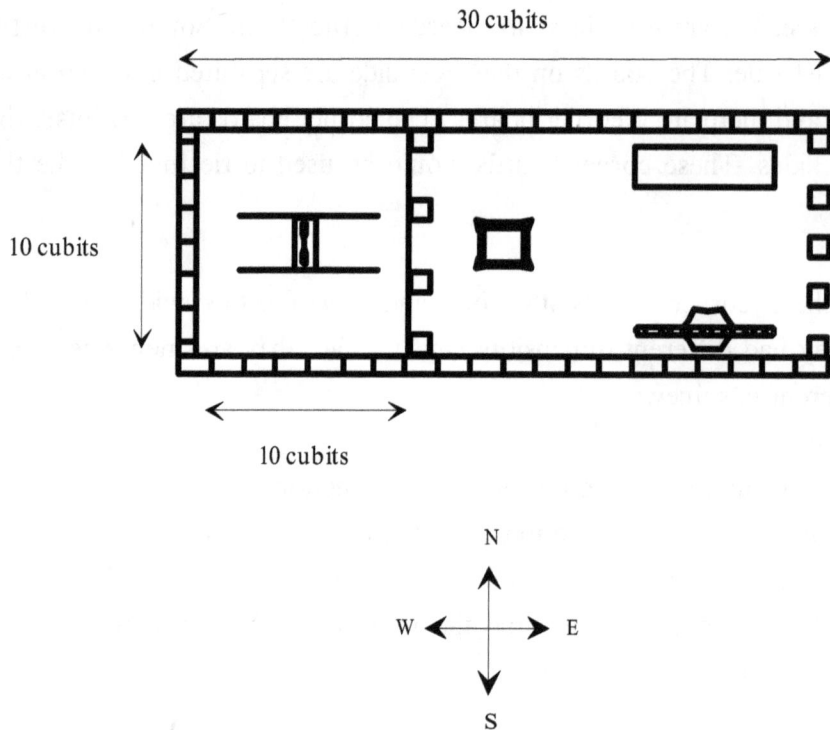

Once again, we refer to Josephus to give us more information about the veil and the four pillars supporting it. Josephus tells us the veil was ten cubits square and the pillars supporting the veil were placed 10 cubits from the western wall.

This would make the Most Holy Place a cube that measured ten cubits in each direction (Very symmetrical). Into this space the Ark of the Covenant would be placed.

The remaining two thirds of the interior space of the Tabernacle would be known as the Holy Place. This space would consist of the Table of Showbread, the Golden Lamp Stand, and the Altar of Incense. There were five pillars at the entrance to the Holy Place on the East Side.

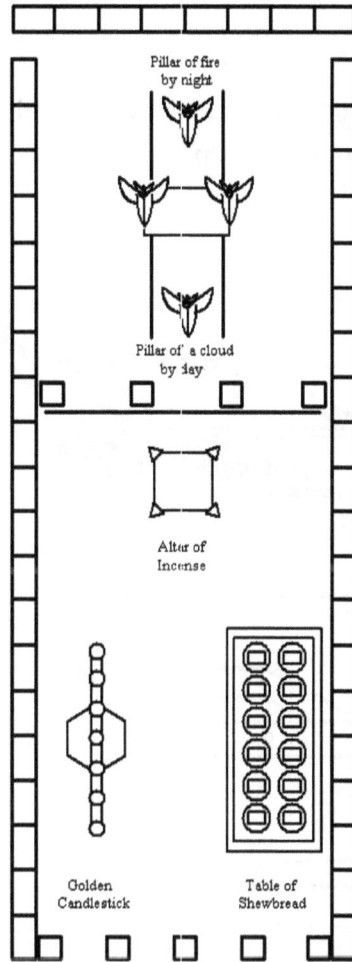

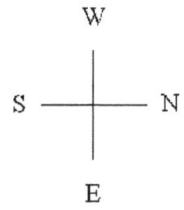

W

S ——┼—— N

E

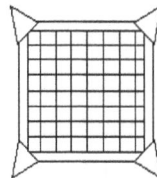

Brazen
Altar

Outside of the Tabernacle were the Brazen Altar and the Brazen Laver.

The Brazen Altar

The Brazen Altar was located east of the Tabernacle. It was near the entrance of the Tabernacle complex. This holy object was physically closest to the people. The offerings for sin would be burned here.

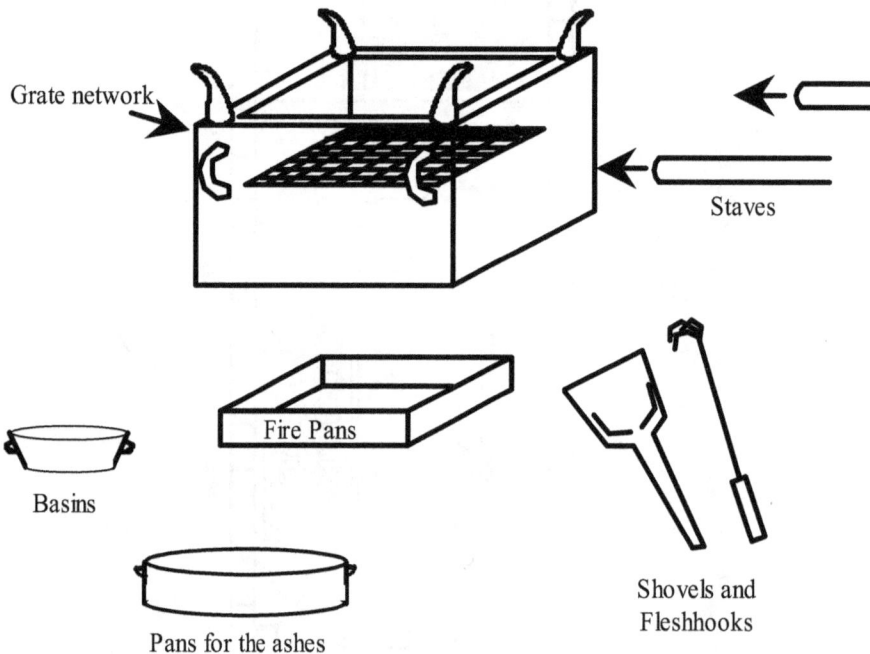

Grate network

Staves

Basins

Fire Pans

Pans for the ashes

Shovels and Fleshhooks

Ex 27:1 And thou shalt make an altar *of* shittim wood, five cubits long, and five cubits broad; the altar shall be foursquare: and the height thereof *shall be* three cubits. ²And thou shalt make the horns of it upon the four corners thereof: his horns shall be of the same: and thou shalt overlay it with brass. ³And thou shalt make his pans to receive his ashes, and his shovels, and his basons, and his fleshhooks, and his firepans: all the vessels thereof thou shalt make *of* brass. ⁴And thou shalt make for it a grate of network *of* brass; and upon the net shalt thou make four brasen rings in the four corners thereof. ⁵And thou shalt put it under the compass of the altar beneath, that the net may be even to the midst of the altar. ⁶And thou shalt make staves for the altar, staves *of* shittim wood, and overlay them with brass. ⁷And the staves shall be put into the rings, and the staves shall be upon the two sides of the altar, to bear it. ⁸Hollow with boards shalt thou make it: as it was shewed thee in the mount, so shall they make *it*.

Entering the Tabernacle

The priests were the only ones who were allowed to go into the Tabernacle. They were required to wear specific holy garments and to ritually cleanse themselves prior to entry. They would cleanse themselves by washing their hands and feet in the Brass Laver which was located just in front of the entrance of the Tabernacle on the East side.

Laver of Brass

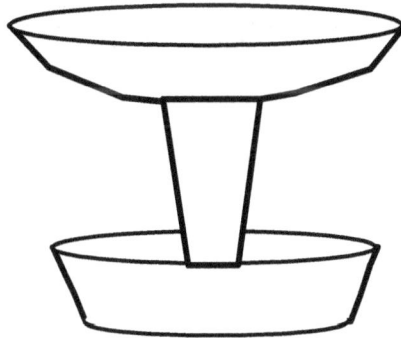

Ex 30: 17And the LORD spake unto Moses, saying, 18Thou shalt also make a laver *of* brass, and his foot *also of* brass, to wash *withal:* and thou shalt put it between the tabernacle of the congregation and the altar, and thou shalt put water therein. 19For Aaron and his sons shall wash their hands and their feet thereat: 20When they go into the tabernacle of the congregation, they shall wash with water, that they die not; or when they come near to the altar to minister, to burn offering made by fire unto the LORD: 21So they shall wash their hands and their feet, that they die not: and it shall be a statute for ever to them, *even* to him and to his seed throughout their generations.

When the priest was ready to enter the Tabernacle, he would pass through the five pillars at the entrance. He would then see the Table of Showbread on his right side.

The Table of Showbread

God instructed Moses to create a Table of Showbread and put it in the Holy Place along the northern wall. Every Sabbath the table would be furnished with twelve cakes of bread. These cakes would be made from the offerings that came from the children of Israel. Only the sons of Aaron would be allowed to eat these cakes.

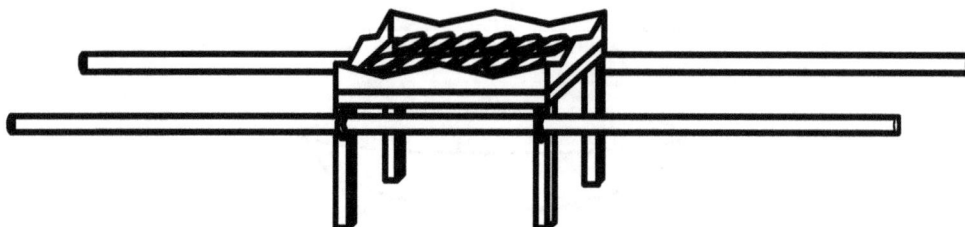

Ex 25: 23Thou shalt also make a table *of* shittim wood: two cubits *shall be* the length thereof, and a cubit the breadth thereof, and a cubit and a half the height thereof. 24And thou shalt overlay it with pure gold, and make thereto a crown of gold round about. 25And thou shalt make unto it a border of an hand breadth round about, and thou shalt make a golden crown to the border thereof round about. 26And thou shalt make for it four rings of gold, and put the rings in the four corners that *are* on the four feet thereof. 27Over against the border shall the rings be for places of the staves to bear the table. 28And thou shalt make the staves *of* shittim wood, and overlay them with gold, that the table may be borne with them. 29And thou shalt make the dishes thereof, and spoons thereof, and covers thereof, and bowls thereof, to cover withal: *of* pure gold shalt thou make them. 30And thou shalt set upon the table shewbread before me alway.

Lev 24: 5And thou shalt take fine flour, and bake twelve cakes thereof: two tenth deals shall be in one cake. 6And thou shalt set them in two rows, six on a row, upon the pure table before the LORD. 7And thou shalt put pure frankincense upon *each* row, that it may be on the bread for a memorial, *even* an offering made by fire unto the LORD. 8Every sabbath he shall set it in order before the LORD continually, *being taken* from the children of Israel by an everlasting covenant. 9And it shall be Aaron's and his sons'; and they shall eat it in the holy place: for it *is* most holy unto him of the offerings of the LORD made by fire by a perpetual statute.

Ex 40: 22And he put the table in the tent of the congregation, upon the side of the tabernacle northward, without the vail. 23And he set the bread in order upon it before the LORD; as the LORD had commanded Moses.

On the wall opposite the Table of Showbread was the Golden Candlestick.

The Golden Candlestick

Moses was also instructed to construct a Golden Candlestick. In the Hebrew language it is known as the Menorah. It was to be located in the Holy Place along the south wall directly across from the Table of Showbread. We aren't told how large the Candlestick was, but we are told it took a talent of pure gold to construct it.

Ex 25: [31]And thou shalt make a candlestick *of* pure gold: *of* beaten work shall the candlestick be made: his shaft, and his branches, his bowls, his knops, and his flowers, shall be of the same. [32]And six branches shall come out of the sides of it; three branches of the candlestick out of the one side, and three branches of the candlestick out of the other side: [33]Three bowls made like unto almonds, *with* a knop and a flower in one branch; and three bowls made like almonds in the other branch, *with* a knop and a flower: so in the six branches that come out of the candlestick. [34]And in the candlestick *shall be* four bowls made like unto almonds, *with* their knops and their flowers. [35]And *there shall be* a knop under two branches of the same, and a knop under two branches of the same, and a knop under two branches of the same, according to the six branches that proceed out of the candlestick. [36]Their knops and their branches shall be of the same: all it *shall be* one beaten work *of* pure gold. [37]And thou shalt make the seven lamps thereof: and they shall light the lamps thereof, that they may give light over against it. [38]And the tongs thereof, and the snuffdishes thereof, *shall be of* pure gold. [39]*Of* a talent of pure gold shall he make it, with all these vessels. [40]And look that thou make *them* after their pattern, which was shewed thee in the mount.

In front of the Golden Candlestick and the Table of Showbread was the Altar of Inscence.

The Altar of Incense

The Altar of Incense was located in the Holy Place just in front of the veil that separated the Holy Place from the Most Holy Place. The Altar of Incense was the second most holy object in the Tabernacle.

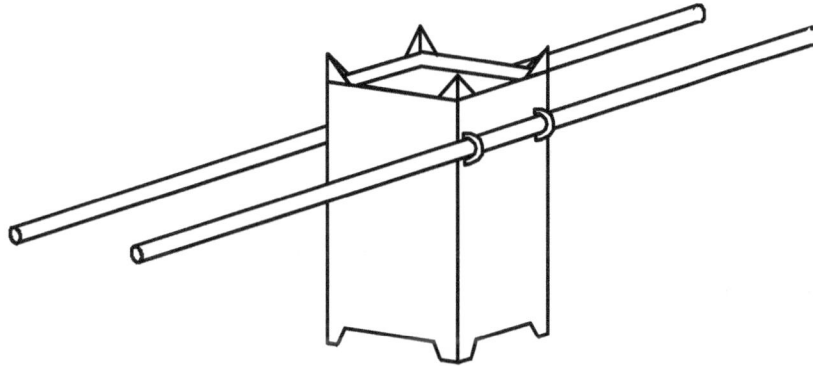

Ex 30:1And thou shalt make an altar to burn incense upon: *of* shittim wood shalt thou make it. 2A cubit *shall be* the length thereof, and a cubit the breadth thereof; foursquare shall it be: and two cubits *shall be* the height thereof: the horns thereof *shall be* of the same. 3And thou shalt overlay it with pure gold, the top thereof, and the sides thereof round about, and the horns thereof; and thou shalt make unto it a crown of gold round about. 4And two golden rings shalt thou make to it under the crown of it, by the two corners thereof, upon the two sides of it shalt thou make *it;* and they shall be for places for the staves to bear it withal. 5And thou shalt make the staves *of* shittim wood, and overlay them with gold. 6And thou shalt put it before the vail that *is* by the ark of the testimony, before the mercy seat that *is* over the testimony, where I will meet with thee. 7And Aaron shall burn thereon sweet incense every morning: when he dresseth the lamps, he shall burn incense upon it. 8And when Aaron lighteth the lamps at even, he shall burn incense upon it, a perpetual incense before the LORD throughout your generations. 9Ye shall offer no strange incense thereon, nor burnt sacrifice, nor meat offering; neither shall ye pour drink offering thereon. 10And Aaron shall make an atonement upon the horns of it once in a year with the blood of the sin offering of atonements: once in the year shall he make atonement upon it throughout your generations: it *is* most holy unto the LORD.

The Veil separated the Altar of Incense from the Ark of the Covenant.

The Ark of the Covenant

The Ark of the Covenant was the central focus of the Tabernacle. It was located in the Most Holy Place and was the most holy object in the Tabernacle.

Ex 25: [10]And they shall make an ark *of* shittim wood: two cubits and a half *shall be* the length thereof, and a cubit and a half the breadth thereof, and a cubit and a half the height thereof. [11]And thou shalt overlay it with pure gold, within and without shalt thou overlay it, and shalt make upon it a crown of gold round about. [12]And thou shalt cast four rings of gold for it, and put *them* in the four corners thereof; and two rings *shall be* in the one side of it, and two rings in the other side of it. [13]And thou shalt make staves *of* shittim wood, and overlay them with gold. [14]And thou shalt put the staves into the rings by the sides of the ark, that the ark may be borne with them. [15]The staves shall be in the rings of the ark: they shall not be taken from it.

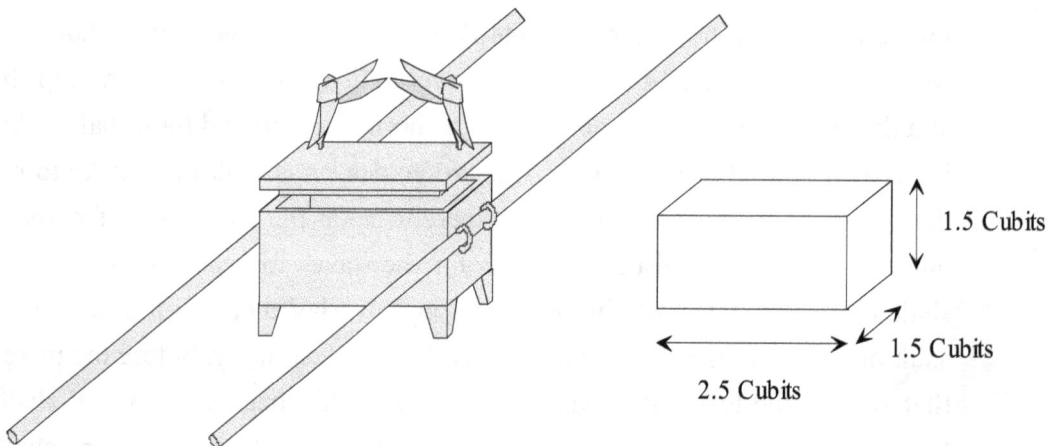

1.5 Cubits

1.5 Cubits

2.5 Cubits

The Ark was supposed to contain the "testimony" which God gave Moses. It would later contain the tables of the Ten Commandments, Aarons Rod, and a pot of Manna. Instructions were also given concerning the lid for the Ark. The lid would be called the Mercy Seat. It would be made of pure gold and would have Cherubs on top with their wings outstretched.

Ex 25: [16]And thou shalt put into the ark the testimony which I shall give thee. [17]And thou shalt make a mercy seat *of* pure gold: two cubits and a half *shall be* the length thereof, and a cubit and a half the breadth thereof. [18]And thou shalt make two cherubims *of* gold, *of* beaten work shalt thou make them, in the two ends of the mercy seat. [19]And make one cherub on the one end, and the other cherub on the other end: *even* of the mercy seat shall ye make the cherubims on the two ends thereof. [20]And the cherubim shall stretch forth *their* wings on high, covering the mercy seat with their wings, and their faces *shall look* one to another; toward the mercy seat shall the faces of the cherubims be. [21]And thou shalt put the mercy seat above upon the ark; and in the ark

The mercy seat is where the high priest would meet with God on behalf of the people. It would be the seat of God. We are told it was two and a half cubits long and one and a half cubits wide. The Bible doesn't tell us how thick it was.

Without knowing the thickness of the mercy seat, it would be difficult to determine how much it weighed, but if it were made of pure gold then it must have been very heavy.

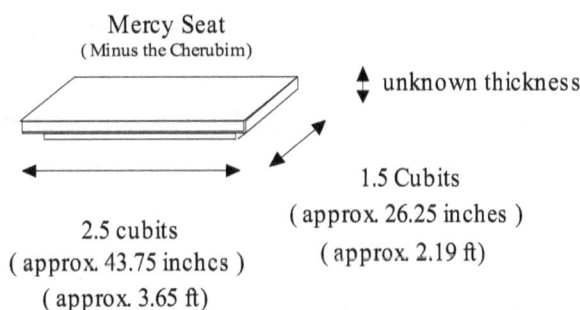

Mercy Seat
(Minus the Cherubim)

unknown thickness

2.5 cubits
(approx. 43.75 inches)
(approx. 3.65 ft)

1.5 Cubits
(approx. 26.25 inches)
(approx. 2.19 ft)

A cubit can measure anywhere from 17.5 to 25 inches long. The Royal Egyptian cubit is thought to have been about 20.6 inches long. Moses was educated in the house of Pharaoh so he would have most likely used the Royal Egyptian cubit.

If we make a few assumptions we can get an idea of how heavy this Mercy Seat was. Let's be conservative and use the smaller measure of the cubit (17.5 inches). This would make the Mercy Seat over three and a half feet long and two feet wide. If we assume the Mercy Seat was only half an inch thick, then the Mercy Seat would weigh over 400 pounds. As big as the Mercy Seat was it is unlikely it would have been any thinner than a half an inch because it would become too flimsy to support its own weight as well as the weight of the Golden Cherubim on top of it. The weight of the Golden Cherubim would have been substantial but we aren't given enough information about them to estimate their weight.

To do the math…

Gold weighs 1204 pounds per cubic foot.

The mercy seat is 3.65 feet x 2.19 feet x .0417 feet (½ inch) = .333 cubic feet

1204 pounds per cubic foot x .333 cubic feet = 401 Pounds

If we do the calculation using the larger Royal Egyptian Cubit then the weight of the Mercy Seat would be more than 522 pounds.

This raises the question. "How many Levites were required to carry the Ark?"

It was thought to have been carried by four Levites, but considering the excessive weight of the Mercy Seat alone, it is unlikely four men could have carried it for any appreciable distance. The weight of the Ark would include the Mercy Seat with the Golden Cherubs and the contents of the Ark. Of course, God could have miraculously made it possible for four men to carry it, but there is another option.

This is where symbolism will start increasing our understanding.

There is an account in the Bible where Ezekiel had a vision of God.

> Ezek 1: 1 Now it came to pass in the thirtieth year, in the fourth *month,* in the fifth *day* of the month, as I *was* among the captives by the river of Chebar, *that* the heavens were opened, and **I saw visions of God**.

> Ezek 1: 5 Also out of the midst thereof *came* the likeness of four living creatures. And this *was* their appearance; they had the likeness of a man. **6And every one had four faces, and every one had four wings.**

> Ezek 1: 9 Their wings *were* joined one to another; **they turned not when they went; they went every one straight forward.**

Ezek 1: [10]As for the likeness of their faces, they four had the face of a man, and the face of a lion, on the right side: and they four had the face of an ox on the left side; they four also had the face of an eagle.

Ezek 1: **[26]And above the firmament that** *was* **over their heads** *was* **the likeness of a throne**, as the appearance of a sapphire stone: and upon the likeness of the throne *was* the likeness as the appearance of a man above upon it. [27]And I saw as the colour of amber, as the appearance of fire round about within it, from the appearance of his loins even upward, and from the appearance of his loins even downward, I saw as it were the appearance of fire, and it had brightness round about. [28]As the appearance of the bow that is in the cloud in the day of rain, so *was* the appearance of the brightness round about. **This** *was* **the appearance of the likeness of the glory of the Lord**. And when I saw *it,* I fell upon my face, and I heard a voice of one that spake

The vision of Ezekiel shows <u>four creatures each having four faces</u> bearing the throne of the Lord.

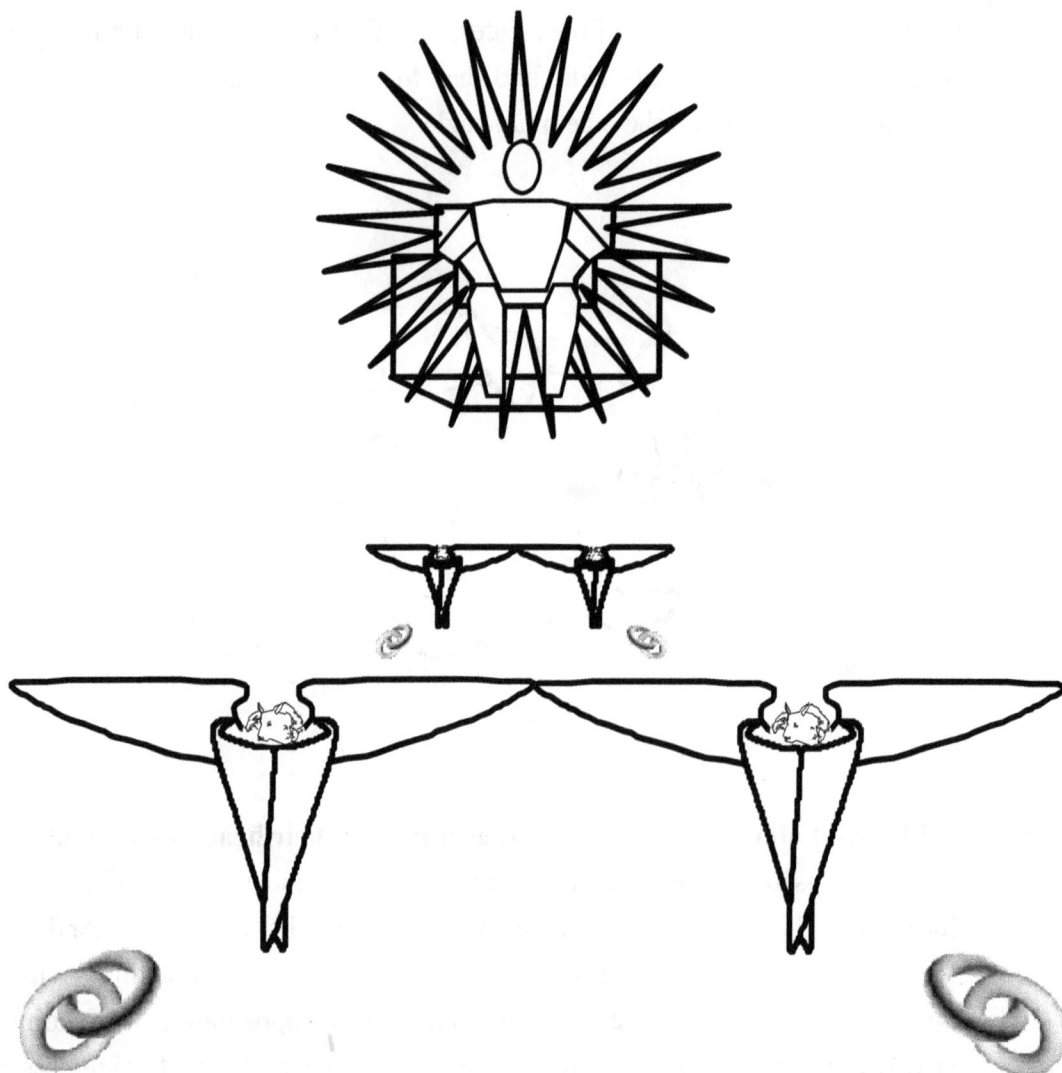

Could there have been more than four Levites carrying the Ark of the Covenant? Could there have been sixteen? If there were sixteen Levites then the weight of the Ark would be distributed among sixteen men rather than just four. This would also more closely match Ezekiel's vision. There would be four Levites on each corner of the Ark which would correspond to the four faces of the creatures bearing the throne of God. The fact the creatures were linked together and turned not when they went is similar to the way the Levites would have been linked as they each held the staves of the Ark. They would have to move in unison and always in the same direction.

Neither the Bible nor Josephus tells us how many Levites were required to carry the Ark, so my suggestion of sixteen Levites is plausible.

There will be more on the symbolism of Ezekiel's vision later.

For an additional discussion about the Ark of the Covenant and its potential functioning as a capacitor, see Appendix D.

The previous pages were a general description. Now we will consider the profound significance of the Tabernacle and its contents.

The structure of the Tabernacle is made up of 48 boards and 9 columns.

There are 5 columns at the entrance and 4 columns inside which separate the Holy Place from the Most Holy Place.

It is easy to see the 5 columns at the entrance of the Tabernacle correspond to the first five books of Moses known as the Pentateuch. These books are foundational to the whole Bible. They give the history of God's dealings with man and they also spell out God's law to his people.

The 4 columns inside the Tabernacle represent the 4 Gospels. These four books chronicle the life of Jesus the savior and explain how he was used to satisfy the Law of God for us.

110

The interpretation of these columns seems obvious, but can this symbolism be carried further?

Let's examine the 48 boards making up the North, South and Western walls of the Tabernacle. There are 66 books in our common Bible. Should there have been more? Do all of them belong there?

We should do the math...

    66   Books in the Bible
    - 5   Books of Moses
    - 4   Gospels
    ----
    57   Books remaining

There were 48 boards and 57 books remaining. So the question becomes, is there a correspondence between the number of books in the Bible and the number of boards in the Tabernacle or maybe 9 of the books in our Bible shouldn't be there?

Here is where we need to look beyond the obvious to see the truth. There is another option. There are several books in the Bible with multiple parts (Such as first and second Samuel and first and second Kings). If we combine these multi-part books together we end up with exactly 48 books remaining!

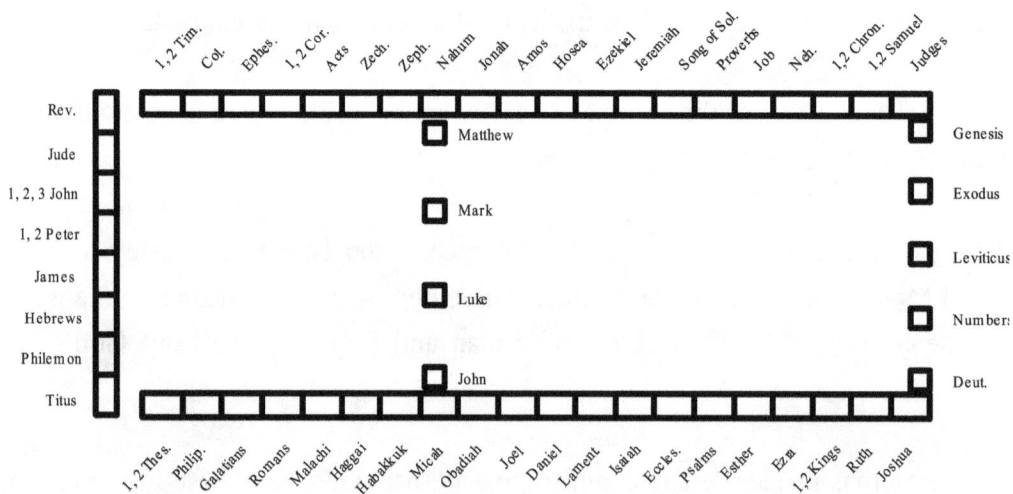

Is the exact correlation between the number of books in the Bible and the structure of the Tabernacle purely coincidental or did God play a divine part in the assemblage of our Bible? Does this symbolism bear witness to the authority of the Bible as a whole? I think it does.

The symbolism of the Tabernacle does not end with its structure. The contents of the Tabernacle also have profound meaning but we will need the Book of Revelation to help us understand.

John, in the Book of Revelation, is called up into Heaven to be shown what will happen in the future.

> Rev 1: 1 The Revelation of Jesus Christ, which God gave unto him, to shew unto his servants things which must shortly come to pass; and he sent and signified *it* by his angel unto his servant John:

The things John sees in Heaven correspond very closely to what was present in the Tabernacle.

The diagram on the following page puts the images John sees into the same configuration as the Tabernacle. As you can see, John's vision is totally consistent with the pattern of the Tabernacle. The Tabernacle of Moses was apparently meant to be an earthly representation of God's Heavenly Tabernacle.

The Heavenly Tabernacle

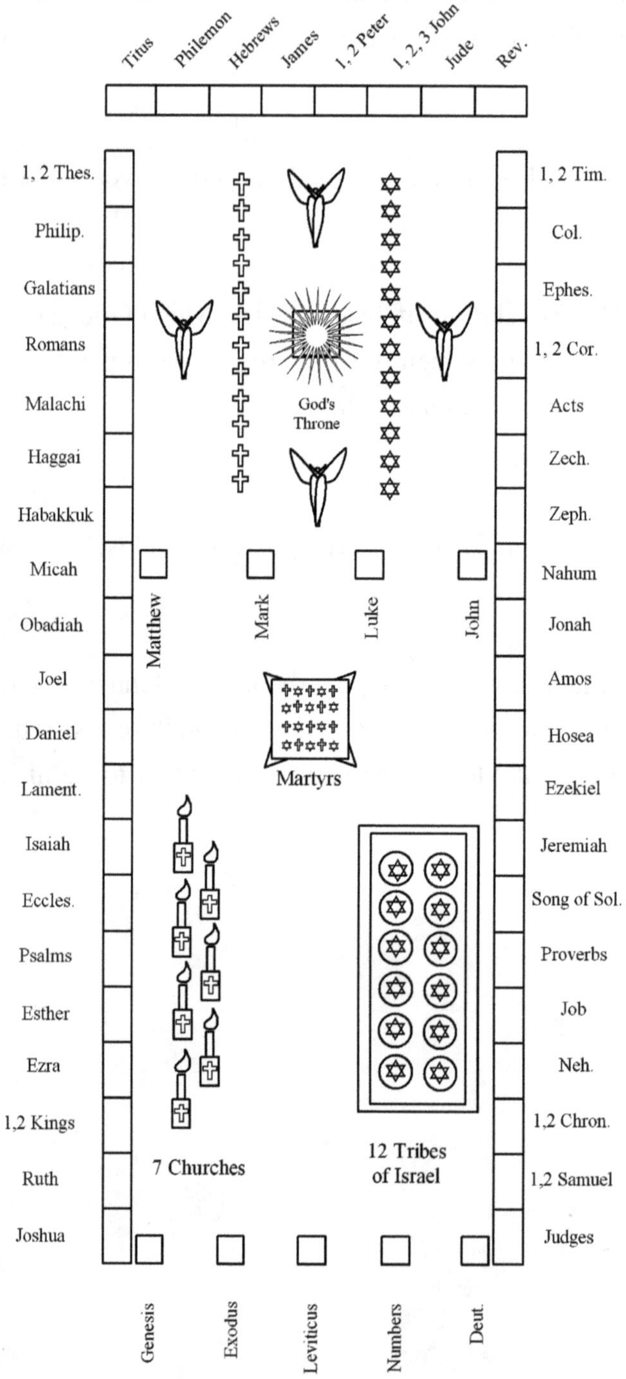
Titus
Philemon
Hebrews
James
1, 2 Peter
1, 2, 3 John
Jude
Rev.
1, 2 Thes.
Philip.
Galatians
Romans
Malachi
Haggai
Habakkuk
Micah
Obadiah
Joel
Daniel
Lament.
Isaiah
Eccles.
Psalms
Esther
Ezra
1,2 Kings
Ruth
Joshua
1, 2 Tim.
Col.
Ephes.
1, 2 Cor.
Acts
Zech.
Zeph.
Nahum
Jonah
Amos
Hosea
Ezekiel
Jeremiah
Song of Sol.
Proverbs
Job
Neh.
1,2 Chron.
1,2 Samuel
Judges
God's Throne
Matthew
Mark
Luke
John
Martyrs
7 Churches
12 Tribes of Israel
Genesis
Exodus
Leviticus
Numbers
Deut.

The Golden Candlestick

Rev 1: 10 I was in the Spirit on the Lord's day, and heard behind me a great voice, as of a trumpet,

11Saying, I am Alpha and Omega, the first and the last: and, What thou seest, write in a book, and send *it* unto the seven churches which are in Asia; unto Ephesus, and unto Smyrna, and unto Pergamos, and unto Thyatira, and unto Sardis, and unto Philadelphia, and unto Laodicea.

12And I turned to see the voice that spake with me. And being turned, I saw seven golden candlesticks;

Jesus was walking among the seven Golden Candlesticks. This is very similar to the Golden Candlestick in the Holy Place of the Tabernacle. The Golden Candlestick had seven branches just as there were seven Candlesticks in Heaven. Jesus then reveals the meaning of the seven Candlesticks.

Rev 1: 20 The mystery of the seven stars which thou sawest in my right hand, and the seven golden candlesticks. The seven stars are the angels of the seven churches: and the seven candlesticks which thou sawest are the seven churches.

The Golden Candlestick in the Tabernacle was used as a source of light.

Rev 5: 14 Ye are the light of the world. A city that is set on an hill cannot be hid.

15Neither do men light a candle, and put it under a bushel, but on a candlestick; and it giveth light unto all that are in the house.

16Let your light so shine before men, that they may see your good works, and glorify your Father which is in heaven.

The Candlesticks represent the Church.

The Table of Showbread

Even during the time of John's prophecy, God has his mind on Israel. This is shown by the Table of Showbread in the Tabernacle with its twelve Cakes. The Table of Showbread was not specifically mentioned in the Book of Revelation but the symbolism of the twelve cakes representing the twelve tribes is unmistakable. The Book of Revelation addresses the twelve tribes directly.

> Rev 7:2And I saw another angel ascending from the east, having the seal of the living God: and he cried with a loud voice to the four angels, to whom it was given to hurt the earth and the sea,
>
> 3Saying, Hurt not the earth, neither the sea, nor the trees, till we have sealed the servants of our God in their foreheads.
>
> 4And I heard the number of them which were sealed: *and there were* sealed an hundred *and* forty *and* four thousand of all the tribes of the children of Israel.

In the Tabernacle, the Table of Showbread stood beside the Golden Candlestick. This indicates there will be those of Israel during this timeframe who will be saved. They will stand beside the Church and the Church will stand beside them in the kingdom of God.

The Altar of Incense

The Altar of Incense was located just outside of the "Most Holy Place" in the Tabernacle. It was closer to the Most Holy Place than any of the other Holy Objects. The only thing that separated it from the Most Holy place was the Veil.

> Ex 30:1 And thou shalt make an altar to burn incense upon: *of* shittim wood shalt thou make it.
>
> 6And thou shalt put it before the vail that *is* by the ark of the testimony, before the mercy seat that *is* over the testimony, where I will meet with thee.

The Book of Revelation gives us an Idea of why the Altar of Incense was in the most prominent area closest to the Most Holy Place.

Rev 6: 9 And when he had opened the fifth seal, I saw **under the altar** the **souls** of them that were **slain for the word of God**, and for the testimony which they held:

[10]And they cried with a loud voice, saying, How long, O Lord, holy and true, dost thou not judge and avenge our blood on them that dwell on the earth?

[11]And white robes were given unto every one of them; and it was said unto them, that they should rest yet for a little season, until their fellowservants also and their brethren, that should be killed as they *were,* should be fulfilled.

Rev 8: 3And another angel came and stood at the altar, having a golden censer; and there was given unto him much incense, that he should offer *it* with the prayers of all saints upon the golden altar which was before the throne.

[4]And the smoke of the incense, *which came* with the prayers of the saints, ascended up before God out of the angel's hand.

The Altar of Incense in Heaven is actually a place reserved for the Martyrs. They were slain for the word of God and their testimony. It's no wonder they were so precious to God and were placed directly in front of his throne.

In the Tabernacle there was a veil separating the Holy Place from the Most Holy Place. This veil was not present when John had his vision. The reason is the veil had been torn in two when Jesus died. Jesus paid the price for our sins so we would no longer be separated from God.

Mar 15: 37And Jesus cried with a loud voice, and gave up the ghost.

[38]And the veil of the temple was rent in twain from the top to the bottom.

The veil is gone and we have direct access to God through Jesus our High Priest.

The Ark Of the Covenant

The Book of Revelation gives us a glimpse of the throne of God which was symbolized in the Tabernacle by the Ark of the Covenant.

> Rev 4: 2 And immediately I was in the spirit: and, behold, a throne was set in heaven, and *one* sat on the throne.
>
> ³And he that sat was to look upon like a jasper and a sardine stone: and *there was* a rainbow round about the throne, in sight like unto an emerald.
>
> ⁴And round about the throne *were* four and twenty seats: and upon the seats I saw four and twenty elders sitting, clothed in white raiment; and they had on their heads crowns of gold.
>
> ⁵And out of the throne proceeded lightnings and thunderings and voices: and *there were* seven lamps of fire burning before the throne, which are the seven Spirits of God.
>
> ⁶And before the throne *there was* a sea of glass like unto crystal: and in the midst of the throne, and round about the throne, *were* four beasts full of eyes before and behind.

There is a lot going on in the passage above but, with a little thought, we should be able to see how these things are reflected in the symbolism of the Tabernacle.

First we see God sitting upon his throne. This is shown in the Tabernacle by the Mercy Seat which was located on top of the Ark of the Covenant.

We see twenty four elders around the throne of God. Who are these twenty four elders? If we break down the number twenty four into two groups of twelve, then the numbers begin to take on more meaning. These were obviously exceptional men to be able to stand directly before God's throne. To stand before God's throne must be the highest honor and the greatest reward that can be bestowed on any man.

The first group of twelve is most likely the twelve disciples of Jesus. The second group of twelve is not as readily apparent. The obvious thought would be these are the patriarchs of the twelve tribes of Israel, but this solution is unlikely. This would mean the sons of Jacob would be honored more highly than Abraham, Isaac, or Jacob. The fact is, the patriarchs of the twelve tribes were not particularly holy or righteous men. Joseph was the only truly exceptional patriarch of the twelve.

Determining the identity of the second group of twelve elders requires speculation. If the first group of twelve is the disciples, which were New Testament saints, then the second group of twelve would likely consist of the Old Testament saints.

Who in the Old Testament would be worthy? As I said earlier, this requires speculation and may not be totally correct. The following candidates are my best guesses.

Daniel, Noah, Job (These three were examples of righteousness.
    See Ezekiel 14:14)
Abraham, Isaac, Jacob,
Moses, Joshua, David,
Enoch, Elijah, and John the Baptist

I believe these two groups of twelve elders are symbolized in the Tabernacle by the staves that were used to carry the Ark. These staves were inserted into the rings of the Ark and were never to be removed. These men were responsible for carrying the Law and the Gospel to the whole world.

Ex 25: 13 And thou shalt make staves *of* shittim wood, and overlay them with gold.

14And thou shalt put the staves into the rings by the sides of the ark, that the ark may be borne with them. 15The staves shall be in the rings of the ark: they shall not be taken from it.

Another prominent feature of the Ark of the Covenant was the cherubim on top of the mercy seat. There were two of them.

> Ex 25: 17 And thou shalt make a mercy seat *of* pure gold: two cubits and a half *shall be* the length thereof, and a cubit and a half the breadth thereof.

> 18And thou shalt make two cherubims *of* gold, *of* beaten work shalt thou make them, in the two ends of the mercy seat.

> 19And make one cherub on the one end, and the other cherub on the other end: *even* of the mercy seat shall ye make the cherubims on the two ends thereof.

> 20And the cherubim shall stretch forth *their* wings on high, covering the mercy seat with their wings, and their faces *shall look* one to another; toward the mercy seat shall the faces of the cherubims be.

These cherubs were similar to strange angelic beasts the Book of Revelation describes as being around the throne of God. These beasts constantly glorify and give thanks to God.

> Rev 4: 6 And before the throne *there was* a sea of glass like unto crystal: and in the midst of the throne, and round about the throne, *were* four beasts full of eyes before and behind.

> 7And the first beast *was* like a lion, and the second beast like a calf, and the third beast had a face as a man, and the fourth beast *was* like a flying eagle.

> 8And the four beasts had each of them six wings about *him;* and *they were* full of eyes within: and they rest not day and night, saying, Holy, holy, holy, Lord God Almighty, which was, and is, and is to come.

The descriptions of the Cherubs differ from the description of the four angelic beasts in a few ways. The Book of Revelation describes four angelic beast beasts around the throne of God, while the Book of Genesis only mentions two Cherubim being placed on the mercy seat.

Is this a contradiction? I don't think so. The Cherubim on the top of the mercy seat were not the only two angelic beings associated with the Tabernacle. There were two others. One angel appeared in a pillar of fire by night and the other appeared as a pillar of a cloud by day.

> Ex 13: 21 And the LORD went before them by day in a pillar of a cloud, to lead them the way; and by night in a pillar of fire, to give them light; to go by day and night:

> 22He took not away the pillar of the cloud by day, nor the pillar of fire by night, *from* before the people.

The previous verses say that the Lord went before the camp in a pillar of a cloud or in a pillar of fire but Exodus 14:19 shows that the Lord went before them in the form of an angel.

> Ex 14: 19 And the angel of God, which went before the camp of Israel, removed and went behind them; and the pillar of the cloud went from before their face, and stood behind them:

If the pillar of a cloud by day was an angel of God, wouldn't it seem reasonable the pillar of fire by night would also be an angel?

If we add the Daytime angel and the Nighttime angel to the two Cherubs on the mercy seat, then we see the symbolism of the Tabernacle matches the description of God's throne very accurately.

Solomon, when he was instructed how to built the first Temple, built two additional Cherubs to place within the Most Holy Place. The Temple was no longer mobile like the Tabernacle was so the symbolism of the Temple had to be adjusted to continue to accurately reflect God's throne.

The Daytime and the Nighttime angels were no longer needed to lead the people through the wilderness, so they would resume their place before the throne of God.

> 2 Chr 3:3 Now these *are the things wherein* Solomon was instructed for the building of the house of God…

120

2 Chr 3:10 And in the most holy house he made two cherubims of image work, and overlaid them with gold.

¹¹And the wings of the cherubims *were* twenty cubits long: one wing *of the one cherub was* five cubits, reaching to the wall of the house: and the other wing *was likewise* five cubits, reaching to the wing of the other cherub.

With both Tabernacles compared side by side it is easy to see their similarities.

The Symbolism of the Tabernacle

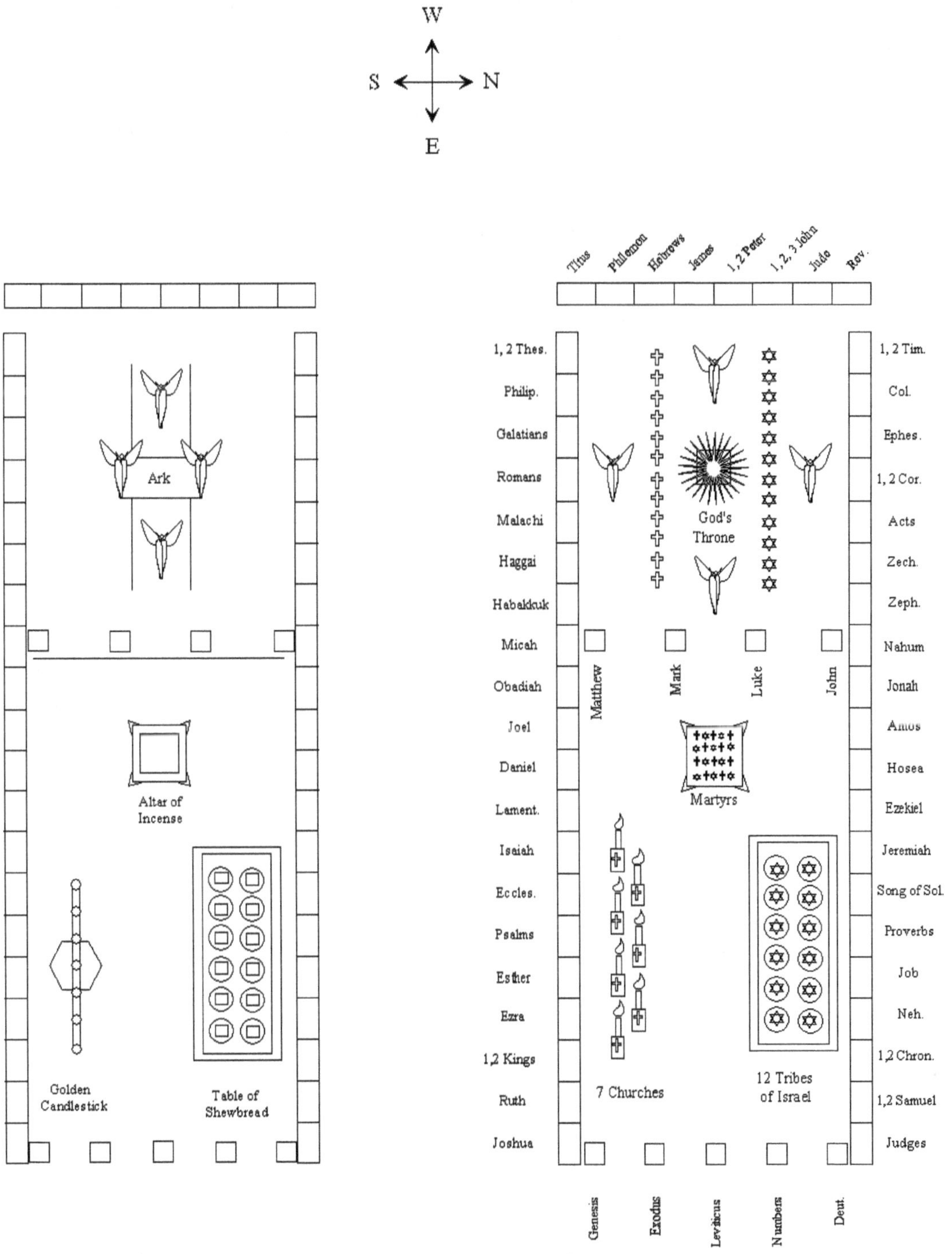

W
S ← → N
E

Left diagram:

Ark

Altar of
Incense

Golden
Candlestick

Table of
Shewbread

Right diagram:

Titus | Philemon | Hebrews | James | 1, 2 Peter | 1, 2, 3 John | Jude | Rev.

1, 2 Thes.		1, 2 Tim.
Philip.		Col.
Galatians		Ephes.
Romans		1, 2 Cor.
Malachi		Acts
Haggai		Zech.
Habakkuk		Zeph.
Micah		Nahum
Obadiah		Jonah
Joel		Amos
Daniel		Hosea
Lament.		Ezekiel
Isaiah		Jeremiah
Eccles.		Song of Sol.
Psalms		Proverbs
Esther		Job
Ezra		Neh.
1, 2 Kings		1, 2 Chron.
Ruth		1, 2 Samuel
Joshua		Judges

God's
Throne

Martyrs

Matthew | Mark | Luke | John

7 Churches

12 Tribes
of Israel

Genesis | Exodus | Leviticus | Numbers | Deut.

The Tabernacle was full of symbolic meaning. An entire book could be written on the symbolism of the Tabernacle, but that is not the purpose of this book. This book desires to show how the 66 books of the Bible fit together to demonstrate the unity of scripture. These books work in concert in such a consistent way as to be beyond coincidence. The symbolism helps us understand the purposes of God. When we understand the symbolism, even the strange visions of the prophets start to make more sense.

In the next chapter we will examine the Holy Days God established and their symbolism.

Chapter Twelve

Symbolism

The Holy Days

In this chapter we will talk about the Holy Days which were dictated to Moses by God. These days were meant to memorialize the Exodus from Egypt but they also had a prophetic component. These Holy Days anticipated key future events. There was a symbolism behind these Holy Days that was not readily apparent during the time of Moses. The true meaning behind the Holy Days would only be understood in retrospect. These Holy Days (holidays) would ultimately show us that God has always been in control. He has a plan and a purpose for his dealings with mankind. He knew exactly how and when he would redeem the world. He also knows how and when he will judge the world. Before we can fully understand the Holy Days, we must see them in their proper format. They are to be observed on specific calendar dates, but which calendar should be used?

Genesis Chapter 7 suggests a year was originally 360 days long.

> Gen 7:11 In the six hundredth year of Noah's life, in the **second month, the seventeenth day of the month**, the same day were all the fountains of the great deep broken up, and the windows of heaven were opened.

> Gen 8:3 And the waters returned from off the earth continually: and after the end of the **hundred and fifty days** the waters were abated.

> Gen 8:4 And the ark rested in the **seventh month, on the seventeenth day of the month,** upon the mountains of Ararat.

One Hundred and Fifty days elapsed before the waters of the great flood abated enough for the ark to come to rest..

It was exactly 5 months before the ark came to rest.

Therefore each month was exactly 30 days long. (150 days divided by 5 months)

Projecting this 30 day month over an entire year would result in a 360 day year.

The length of a year has obviously changed since the flood of Noah but the Bible seems to have continued marking time using the original calendar.

The timing of the Biblical Holy Days as well as many specific prophecies (such as those in the book of Daniel) seem to fit more easily into a 360 day per year time frame than into a 365 ¼ or into a 353 to 385 day per year (Jewish lunar year) timeframe. For this reason we will consider everything within a 360 day per year timeframe. For a more detailed discussion on the justification for using a 360 day calendar refer to Appendix C.

On the next page there is a 360 degree diagram which has the key Biblical Holy Days indicated. With the Holy Days drawn in this manner, it is easy to see the symmetry between the Holidays of the first month and the Holidays of the seventh month. There are some key Holidays that do not have counterparts six months later. The reasons for this will also be discussed.

The Holy Days

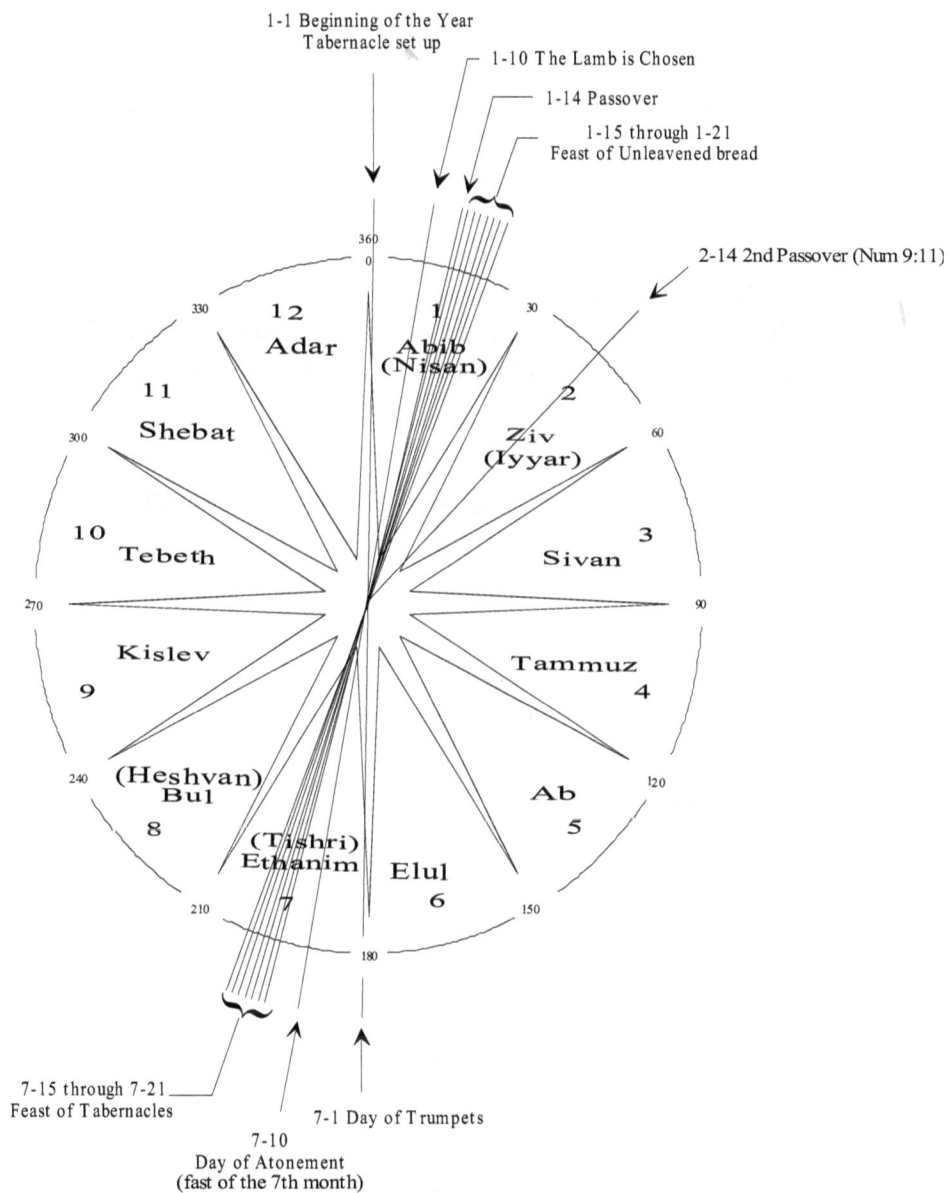

With the assumption that God based the timing of his Holy Days on the 360 day Calendar, let's see how these holidays fall. (Refer to the figure on the previous page.)

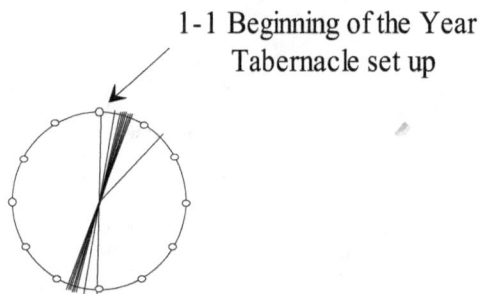

1-1 Beginning of the Year
Tabernacle set up

1-1   **(Abib 1)** The beginning of the year was not specifically called a Holy Day by Moses but it was significant as a new beginning. Also on this day Noah left the Ark along with the animals (on the first day of the first month).

> Gen 8:13 And it came to pass in the six hundredth and first year, in the first *month,* the first *day* of the month, the waters were dried up from off the earth: and Noah removed the covering of the ark, and looked, and, behold, the face of the ground was dry.

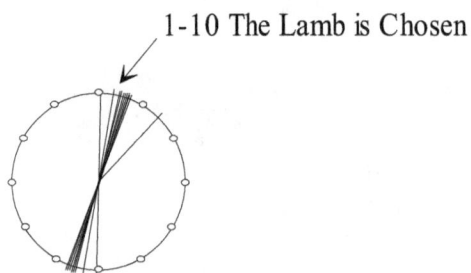

1-10 The Lamb is Chosen

1-10   **(Abib 10)** The Lamb is chosen for sacrifice.

> Ex 12: 3 Speak ye unto all the congregation of Israel, saying, In the tenth *day* of this month they shall take to them every man a lamb, according to the house of *their* fathers, a lamb for an house:

> Ex 12: 5 Your lamb shall be without blemish, a male of the first year: ye shall take *it* out from the sheep, or from the goats:

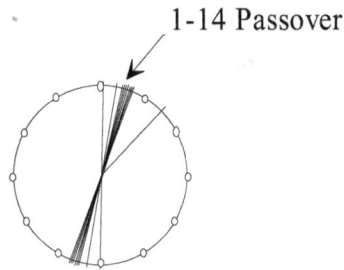

1-14 Passover

1-14   **(Abib 14)** The Lamb is sacrificed.

> Ex 12: 6And ye shall keep it up until the fourteenth day of the same month: and the whole assembly of the congregation of Israel shall kill it in the evening.
>
> 7And they shall take of the blood, and strike *it* on the two side posts and on the upper door post of the houses, wherein they shall eat it.
>
> 8And they shall eat the flesh in that night, roast with fire, and unleavened bread; *and* with bitter *herbs* they shall eat it.

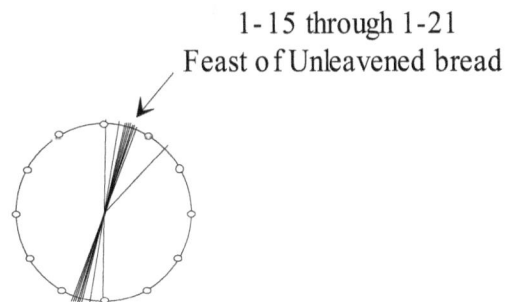

1-15 through 1-21
Feast of Unleavened bread

1-15 thru 1-21**(Abib 15-21)** The Feast of Unleavened Bread

> Lev 23:6 And on the fifteenth day of the same month *is* the feast of unleavened bread unto the LORD: seven days ye must eat unleavened bread.
>
> 7In the first day ye shall have an holy convocation: ye shall do no servile work therein.

[8]But ye shall offer an offering made by fire unto the LORD seven days: in the seventh day *is* an holy convocation: ye shall do no servile work *therein*

2-14
Second Passover (Num 9:11)

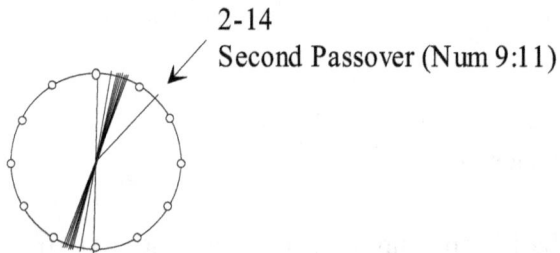

2-14   (**Ziv 14**) The Second Passover

Num 9: 10 Speak unto the children of Israel, saying, If any man of you or of your posterity shall be unclean by reason of a dead body, or *be* in a journey afar off, yet he shall keep the passover unto the LORD.

[11]The fourteenth day of the second month at even they shall keep it, *and* eat it with unleavened bread and bitter *herbs*.

[12]They shall leave none of it unto the morning, nor break any bone of it: according to all the ordinances of the passover they shall keep it.

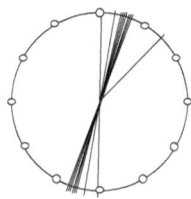

7-1 Day of Trumpets

7-1   (**Tishri 1**) Feast of Trumpets

> ^{Lev 23: 24} Speak unto the children of Israel, saying, In the seventh month, in the first *day* of the month, shall ye have a sabbath, a memorial of blowing of trumpets, an holy convocation.

> ²⁵Ye shall do no servile work *therein:* but ye shall offer an offering made by fire unto the LORD.

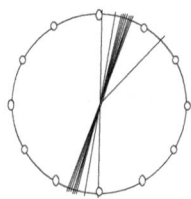

7-10
Day of Atonement
(fast of the 7th month)

7-10   (**Tishri 10**) Day of Atonement

> ^{Lev 23: 27} Also on the tenth *day* of this seventh month *there shall be* a day of atonement: it shall be an holy convocation unto you; and ye shall afflict your souls, and offer an offering made by fire unto the LORD.

> ²⁸And ye shall do no work in that same day: for it *is* a day of atonement, to make an atonement for you before the LORD your God.

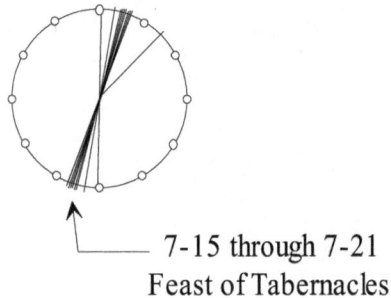

7-15 through 7-21
Feast of Tabernacles

7-15 thru 7-21 (**Tishri 15-21**) The Feast of Tabernacles

> Lev 23: 34 Speak unto the children of Israel, saying, The fifteenth day of this seventh month *shall be* the feast of tabernacles *for* seven days unto the LORD.
>
> 35On the first day *shall be* an holy convocation: ye shall do no servile work *therein.*
>
> 36Seven days ye shall offer an offering made by fire unto the LORD: on the eighth day shall be an holy convocation unto you; and ye shall offer an offering made by fire unto the LORD: it *is* a solemn assembly; *and* ye shall do no servile work *therein.*

When looking at the Holy Days superimposed on a 360 day calendar, it becomes apparent that most of the Holy Days are grouped in such a way as to be opposite one another. This is significant. There are two Holy Days which do not have corresponding Holy Days 6 months later. We will also consider the significance of this.

The Holy Days are arranged into two groups, the Holy Days of the first month and the Holy Days of the seventh month.

The Holy Days of the First Month
and
The Messianic Fulfillment

The group of Holy Days occurring in the first month commemorate events which happened during the exodus of the children of Israel from Egypt. Moses and the rest of Israel would have understood these holidays in this context but they also had profound prophetic significance.

The Holy Days of the first month, in addition to representing the exodus from Egypt, prophetically represented Jesus' sacrifice as the Lamb of God for the sins of the world.

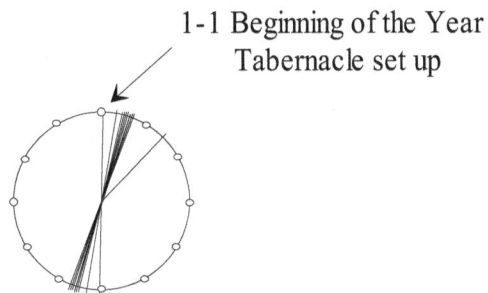

1-1 Beginning of the Year
Tabernacle set up

Abib 1 (the beginning of the year)

This commemorated the new beginning God established with Noah. God's covenant with Noah would be remembered on this day each year throughout all generations. God, by way of Jesus, would also establish a new beginning for the world.

Gen 8:13 And it came to pass in the six hundredth and first year, in the first *month,* the first *day* of the month, the waters were dried up from off the earth: and Noah removed the covering of the ark, and looked, and, behold, the face of the ground was dry.

132

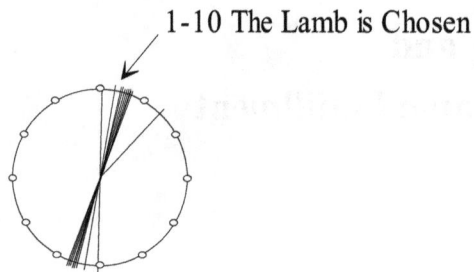

1-10 The Lamb is Chosen

Abib 10 (choosing the Lamb)

The fulfillment of Abib 10 occurred during what has come to be called Palm Sunday. On this day Jesus was proclaimed by the people to be the King of Israel. Four days later, the people would be yelling crucify him and free Barabbas.

> John 12:12On the next day much people that were come to the feast, when they heard that Jesus was coming to Jerusalem,

> 13Took branches of palm trees, and went forth to meet him, and cried, Hosanna: Blessed *is* the King of Israel that cometh in the name of the Lord.

1-14 Passover

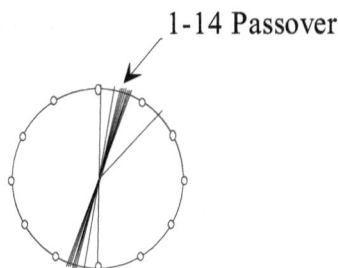

Abib 14 (the Passover)

The Passover was when the lamb was slain. The blood of the lamb caused the angel of death to pass over those who were obedient and did as God had instructed.

> Ex 12:13And the blood shall be to you for a token upon the houses where ye *are:* and when I see the blood, I will pass over you, and the plague shall not be upon you to destroy *you,* when I smite the land of Egypt.

Jesus was the ultimate Passover Sacrifice.

> John 1:29The next day John seeth Jesus coming unto him, and saith, Behold the Lamb of God, which taketh away the sin of the world.

> 1 Cor 5:7Purge out therefore the old leaven, that ye may be a new lump, as ye are unleavened. For even Christ our passover is sacrificed for us:

The Book of Exodus tells us the whole assembly of the congregation shall kill the lamb.

> Ex 12:6And ye shall keep it up until the fourteenth day of the same month: and the whole assembly of the congregation of Israel shall kill it in the evening.

Jesus was condemned by the congregation as a whole when the people shouted to Pilate "Let him be crucified!"

> ^{Mat 27:22}Pilate saith unto them, What shall I do then with Jesus which is called Christ? *They* all say unto him, Let him be crucified.

> ²³And the governor said, Why, what evil hath he done? But they cried out the more, saying, Let him be crucified.

There is no doubt. Jesus was the ultimate fulfillment of the Passover. Jesus was condemned by his own people but they were not the only ones responsible for the crucifixion of Jesus. We are equally responsible for sending Jesus to the cross. He sacrificed himself for every one of us because we are all guilty of sin.

> ^{Rom 5:8}But God commendeth his love toward us, in that, while we were yet sinners, Christ died for us.

Through the atoning sacrifice of Jesus we have been justified and reconciled to God. He is worthy of all our praise and honor and glory.

> ^{Rom 5:9}Much more then, being now justified by his blood, we shall be saved from wrath through him.

> ¹⁰For if, when we were enemies, we were reconciled to God by the death of his Son, much more, being reconciled, we shall be saved by his life.

> ¹¹And not only *so,* but we also joy in God through our Lord Jesus Christ, by whom we have now received the atonement.

It is curious Caiaphas the high priest, who was chiefly responsible for having Jesus executed, would make the following statement:

> ^{John 18:14}Now Caiaphas was he, which gave counsel to the Jews, that it was expedient that one man should die for the people.

By his very statement, Caiaphas was confirming Jesus should die for the people. He didn't understand how profoundly true his statement was.

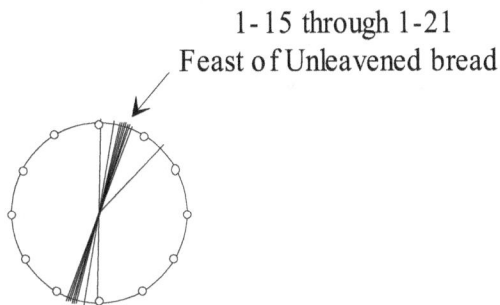

1-15 through 1-21
Feast of Unleavened bread

Abib 15-21 (The Feast of Unleavened Bread)

The Feast of Unleavened Bread directly follows the Passover. It is a seven day period that corresponds to the time of cleansing required for anyone who touches a dead body.

> Num 19: 11He that toucheth the dead body of any man shall be unclean seven days.
>
> 12He shall purify himself with it on the third day, and on the seventh day he shall be clean: but if he purify not himself the third day, then the seventh day he shall not be clean.

The feast of Unleavened Bread immediately follows the Passover. This holiday was a foreshadowing of the time when Jesus would be killed and buried for 3 days and 3 nights. After 3 days and 3 nights he would be raised and purified. Jesus foretold this event.

> Mat 12:40For as Jonas was three days and three nights in the whale's belly; so shall the Son of man be three days and three nights in the heart of the earth.

After 7 days Jesus fulfills all righteousness
and is considered ceremonially clean

| Abib 14 | Abib 15 | Abib 16 | Abib 17 | Abib 18 | Abib 19 | Abib 20 | Abib 21 |

| Abib 14 | Abib 15 | Abib 16 | Abib 17 | Abib 18 | Abib 19 | Abib 20 | Abib 21 |

Jesus Crucified

Jesus Resurrected
the third day and
is purified

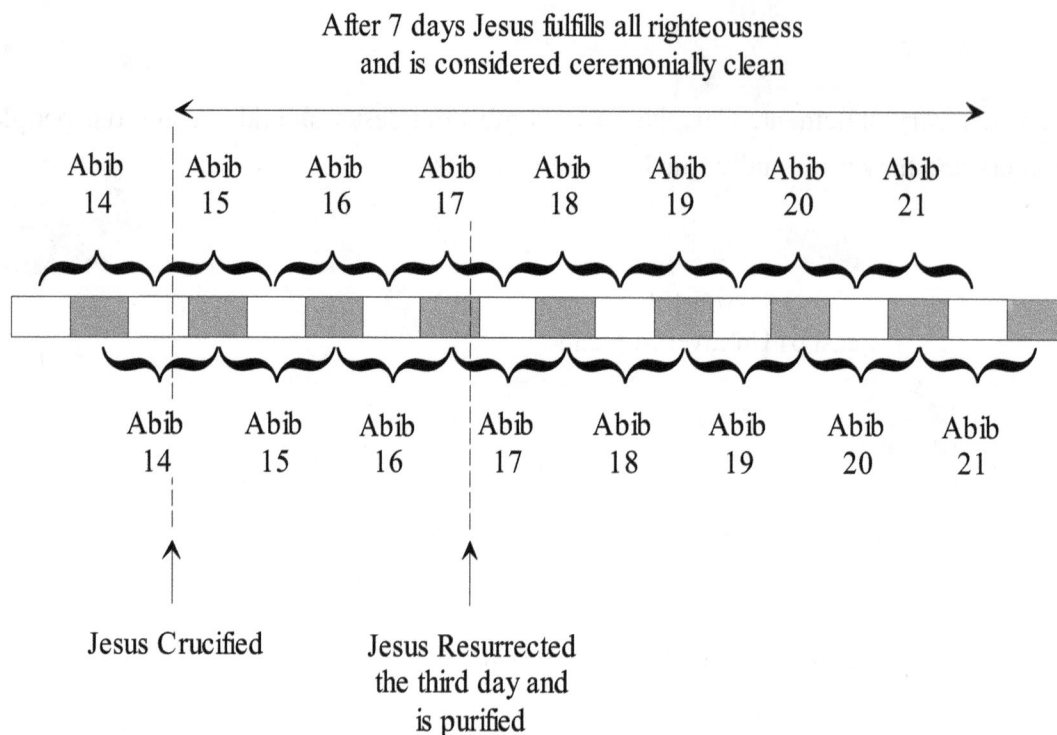

After Jesus' resurrection, he appeared to Mary but he would not allow her to touch him because he had not yet ascended to the father. He had to fulfill all righteousness.

> John 20:16 Jesus saith unto her, Mary. She turned herself, and saith unto him, Rabboni; which is to say, Master.
>
> 17 Jesus saith unto her, Touch me not; for I am not yet ascended to my Father: but go to my brethren, and say unto them, I ascend unto my Father, and your Father; and *to* my God, and your God.

The Feast of Unleavened Bread was a time of cleansing which predicted the death burial and resurrection of our Lord. The meaning of this Holy Day only becomes clear in retrospect.

> Acts 2: 22 Ye men of Israel, hear these words; Jesus of Nazareth, a man approved of God among you by miracles and wonders and signs, which God did by him in the midst of you, as ye yourselves also know: 23 Him, being delivered by the determinate counsel and foreknowledge of God, ye have taken, and by wicked hands have crucified and slain: 24 Whom God

hath raised up, having loosed the pains of death: because it was not possible that he should be holden of it. [25]For David speaketh concerning him, I foresaw the Lord always before my face, for he is on my right hand, that I should not be moved: [26]Therefore did my heart rejoice, and my tongue was glad; moreover also my flesh shall rest in hope: [27]Because thou wilt not leave my soul in hell, neither wilt thou suffer thine Holy One to see corruption

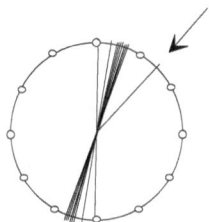

2-14 2nd Passover (Num 9:11)

(**Ziv 14**) The Second Passover

The second Passover occurred a month later than the first Passover. This second Passover was to allow those who were ceremonially unclean during the first Passover to participate later when they would be clean. There is no mention of a second Feast of Unleavened Bread because it was not necessary. Jesus would only need to be resurrected and cleansed once. Those who quickly prepared the body of Jesus for burial would have been ceremonially unclean. They would not be able to participate in the normal Passover. They would have to observe the second Passover a month later.

The First and Second Passovers did not have corresponding holidays six months later because the Passover symbolized the pivotal point in history. Jesus was the ultimate fulfillment of the Passover. This is when God paid the price to redeem us. He only had to pay the price once. There is no corresponding holiday six months later because there is nothing to compare to God's ultimate sacrifice.

The Holy Days of the Seventh Month
and
Their Future Fulfillment

The feasts of the seventh month commemorate events that have not happened yet. As with the feasts of the first month, these Holy Days are prophetic. The feasts of the first month dealt with the atoning sacrifice of Jesus. The feasts of the seventh month are concerned with events at the end of the age. The feasts of the first month could only be understood in retrospect. In the same way, it is doubtful we will be able to achieve a complete understanding of the feasts of the seventh month until they have been fulfilled. This being said, we can project ourselves into the future (to a degree) through the study of the prophetic texts. By doing this, we can look for key events that match the Holy Days. If these events are significant enough to be memorialized throughout the ages as holidays, then it would seem likely the prophetic text would at least mention them. The three remaining Holy Days describe the blowing of trumpets, atonement, and a seven day Feast.

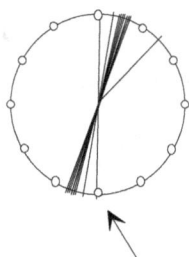

7-1 Day of Trumpets

(Tishri 1) The Feast of Trumpets

The Feast of Trumpets celebrates the resurrection of the dead and the transfiguration of the righteous. This has come to be known as the "Rapture". The rapture is undeniably associated with the blowing of a trumpet.

> 1 Cor 15:51 Behold, I shew you a mystery; We shall not all sleep, but we shall all be changed, 52 In a moment, in the twinkling of an eye, **at the last**

trump: for the trumpet shall sound, and the dead shall be raised incorruptible, and we shall be changed.

1Thes 4:16For the Lord himself shall descend from heaven with a shout, with the voice of the archangel, and **with the trump of God**: and the dead in Christ shall rise first: 17Then we which are alive *and* remain shall be caught up together with them in the clouds, to meet the Lord in the air: and so shall we ever be with the Lord.

Mat 24:30And then shall appear the sign of the Son of man in heaven: and then shall all the tribes of the earth mourn, and they shall see the Son of man coming in the clouds of heaven with power and great glory. 31And he shall send his angels with a great **sound of a trumpet**, and they shall gather together his elect from the four winds, from one end of heaven to the other.

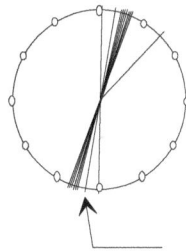

7-10
Day of Atonement
(fast of the 7th month)

(Tishri 10) Day of Atonement

The Day of Atonement is a day of judgment. It is when the ungodly are gathered for destruction. It will be a complete bloodbath.

Rev 14:19And the angel thrust in his sickle into the earth, and gathered the vine of the earth, and cast *it* into the great winepress of the wrath of God.

20And the winepress was trodden without the city, and blood came out of the winepress, even unto the horse bridles, by the space of a thousand *and* six hundred furlongs.

140

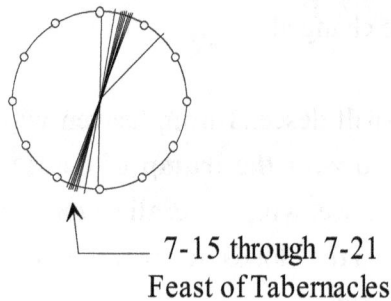

7-15 through 7-21
Feast of Tabernacles

(**Tishri 15-21**) The Feast of Tabernacles

The Feast of Tabernacles is also known as the Feast of Booths. This is a seven day feast where the people are supposed to live in temporary structures. They live in these structures in anticipation of finding a permanent home.

The events foretold by the feasts of the seventh month are easy to see when we look in the book of Revelation. The first thing we have to do is locate when the resurrection (rapture) occurs. This would be the event associated with the feast of Trumpets. The following passage happens at the last (seventh) trumpet.

> Rev 14:14And I looked, and behold a white cloud, and upon the cloud *one* sat like unto the Son of man, having on his head a golden crown, and in his hand a sharp sickle.

> 15And another angel came out of the temple, crying with a loud voice to him that sat on the cloud, Thrust in thy sickle, and reap: for the time is come for thee to reap; for the harvest of the earth is ripe.

> 16And he that sat on the cloud thrust in his sickle on the earth; and the earth was reaped.

After this we see a severe judgment against the ungodly which corresponds with the day of Atonement.

> Rev 14:17And another angel came out of the temple which is in heaven, he also having a sharp sickle.

¹⁸And another angel came out from the altar, which had power over fire; and cried with a loud cry to him that had the sharp sickle, saying, Thrust in thy sharp sickle, and gather the clusters of the vine of the earth; for her grapes are fully ripe.

¹⁹And the angel thrust in his sickle into the earth, and gathered the vine of the earth, and cast *it* into the great winepress of the wrath of God.

²⁰And the winepress was trodden without the city, and blood came out of the winepress, even unto the horse bridles, by the space of a thousand *and* six hundred furlongs.

The very next thing to be described is the seven angels who have the seven last plagues. Take note of the fact that the people couldn't enter the temple until the seven angels finished pouring out the seven vials full of Gods wrath. Waiting for the seven vials to be poured out corresponds perfectly to the seven days of temporary lodging required by the Feast of Tabernacles. For those on the Earth this will be a terrible time but it will be a time of eager anticipation for those in Heaven.

Rev 15:1And I saw another sign in heaven, great and marvellous, seven angels having the seven last plagues; for in them is filled up the wrath of God.

²And I saw as it were a **sea of glass mingled with fire**: and them that had gotten the victory over the beast, and over his image, and over his mark, *and* over the number of his name, **stand on the sea of glass, having the harps of God**.

Rev 15:5And after that I looked, and, behold, the temple of the tabernacle of the testimony in heaven was opened:

⁶And the seven angels came out of the temple, having the seven plagues, clothed in pure and white linen, and having their breasts girded with golden girdles.

^{Rev 15:8}And the temple was filled with smoke from the glory of God, and from his power; and **no man was able to enter into the temple, till the seven plagues of the seven angels were fulfilled**.

The Sea of glass corresponded to the Brazen Laver where the priest would perform a final purification of himself just prior to entering the Tabernacle.

^{Ex 30:18}Thou shalt also make a laver *of* brass, and his foot *also of* brass, to wash *withal:* and thou shalt put it between the tabernacle of the congregation and the altar, and thou shalt put water therein.

¹⁹For Aaron and his sons shall wash their hands and their feet thereat:

²⁰When they go into the tabernacle of the congregation, they shall wash with water, that they die not; or when they come near to the altar to minister, to burn offering made by fire unto the LORD:

²¹So they shall wash their hands and their feet, that they die not: and it shall be a statute for ever to them, *even* to him and to his seed throughout their generations.

The Holy Days are profound in their significance. They remind us of Gods sacrifice, his redemption, and his judgment. They are periodic reminders lest we forget. They are proof of Gods plan and his purpose. They tell us God is in control. Everything will be accomplished in his time.

Problems with the timing of the Passover and the Crucifixion of Jesus.

It would be easy to conclude this chapter without discussing the problems associated with the timeline of the Passover and the crucifixion of Jesus. These problems are substantial and should be addressed rather than avoided. To this end, I will try to offer possible solutions but in many instances there isn't enough information to form solid conclusions.

It is obvious the Holy Days of the first month were symbolic of key events in the life (and death) of Jesus but, when we look closely at the Gospel accounts, some apparent inconsistencies arise. These inconsistencies do not automatically mean the Gospel accounts are in error, but they do require additional consideration.

The main problem is with the timing of the Passover. The Gospels seem to describe the same Passover occurring on two different days.

The Bible clearly states the Passover is to be observed on the 14th day of the first month in the evening. Everyone in Israel would have known this. This is where timing becomes confusing. It appears as if Jesus observed the Passover with his disciples. He was arrested by the temple guards later that night and was crucified the following day **just prior** to the Passover.

Did Jesus observe the Passover a day early or was there another explanation? Let's look at the timeline.

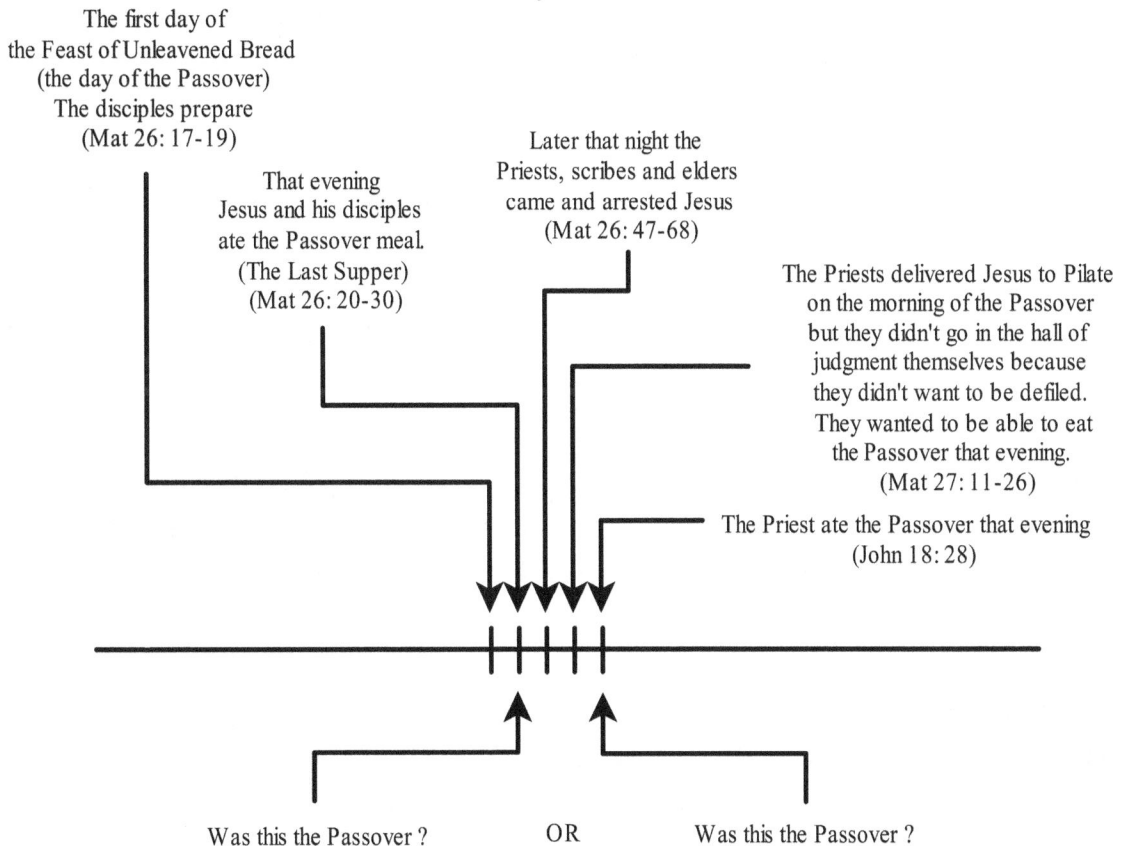

The first day of
the Feast of Unleavened Bread
(the day of the Passover)
The disciples prepare
(Mat 26: 17-19)

That evening
Jesus and his disciples
ate the Passover meal.
(The Last Supper)
(Mat 26: 20-30)

Later that night the
Priests, scribes and elders
came and arrested Jesus
(Mat 26: 47-68)

The Priests delivered Jesus to Pilate
on the morning of the Passover
but they didn't go in the hall of
judgment themselves because
they didn't want to be defiled.
They wanted to be able to eat
the Passover that evening.
(Mat 27: 11-26)

The Priest ate the Passover that evening
(John 18: 28)

Was this the Passover ?   OR   Was this the Passover ?

Jesus ate the Last Supper with his disciples on the evening of the Passover:

> Mat 26:17Now the first *day* of the *feast of* unleavened bread the disciples came to Jesus, saying unto him, Where wilt thou that we prepare for thee to eat the passover?

> Mat 26:19And the disciples did as Jesus had appointed them; and they made ready the passover.

> 20Now when the even was come, he sat down with the twelve.

Jesus was arrested later that night and taken to the house of the high priest Caiaphas for questioning.

> Mat 26:57And they that had laid hold on Jesus led *him* away to Caiaphas the high priest, where the scribes and the elders were assembled.

They decided to have Jesus put to death so they delivered him to Pontius Pilate in the morning but they didn't go into the hall of judgment because they didn't want to be defiled. They wanted to be able to eat the Passover that evening.

> Mat 27:1When the morning was come, all the chief priests and elders of the people took counsel against Jesus to put him to death:

> 2And when they had bound him, they led *him* away, and delivered him to Pontius Pilate the governor.

> John 18:28Then led they Jesus from Caiaphas unto the hall of judgment: and it was early; **and they themselves went not into the judgment hall, lest they should be defiled; but that they might eat the passover.**

Furthermore, the gospel of John tells us the custom for Pilate was to release one prisoner at the Passover, implying that the Passover celebration had not yet occurred.

If Jesus had eaten the Passover meal with his disciples the night before, why were the priests observing the Passover a day later?

Which Passover was the correct Passover? The Passover Jesus observed with his disciples or the Passover the priests were looking to observe a day later?

This appears to be a contradiction but is it? Most of the apparent contradictions in the Bible can be easily explained if we understand the way things were in Biblical times. Unfortunately, the explanation for this apparent contradiction is not simple or conclusive. The most likely solution to the "Two Passovers" problem involves speculation about how days were measured. There were several methods of counting days in the Bible. The most obvious was… the day starts in the morning.

> ^{Mat 28:} ¹In the end of the sabbath, as it began to dawn toward the first *day* of the week, came Mary Magdalene and the other Mary to see the sepulchre.

Notice how the Sabbath was ending at the dawn of the first day of the week. This suggests days were sometimes measured from dawn to dawn.

Days were also measured from evening to evening.

> ^{Lev 23:} ²⁷Also on the tenth *day* of this seventh month *there shall be* a day of atonement: it shall be an holy convocation unto you; and ye shall afflict your souls, and offer an offering made by fire unto the LORD. ²⁸And ye shall do no work in that same day: for it *is* a day of atonement, to make an atonement for you before the LORD your God. ²⁹For whatsoever soul *it be* that shall not be afflicted in that same day, he shall be cut off from among his people. ³⁰And whatsoever soul *it be* that doeth any work in that same day, the same soul will I destroy from among his people. ³¹Ye shall do no manner of work: *it shall be* a statute for ever throughout your generations in all your dwellings. ³²It *shall be* unto you a sabbath of rest, and ye shall afflict your souls: in the ninth *day* of the month at even, **from even unto even, shall ye celebrate your sabbath.**

146

To further compound the confusion, God said in the Book of Genesis "And the evening and the morning were the first day." What does this mean?

There are on average 12 hours between the evening and the morning. How could this describe a 24 hour day. The answer relies on our understanding of the terms Evening and Morning. If we define an evening as being from noon to midnight and a morning as being from midnight to noon then the entire 24 hour period is accounted for. This would mean a day would begin when the Sun is at its highest point in the sky and the next day would begin when the sun was once again at the highest point in the sky. The beginning of the day at noon could be easily measured by putting a stick into the ground. In the morning the stick would cast a long shadow. As the day passed the shadow cast by the stick would become shorter and shorter. When the shadow was at its shortest, it would be Noon. The shadow would then grow longer and longer as the evening progressed. This method would have been useful because of its precision but it would be awkward because the day changes during the most active part of the daylight hours. It would be much simpler to consider the day beginning in the morning when you woke up

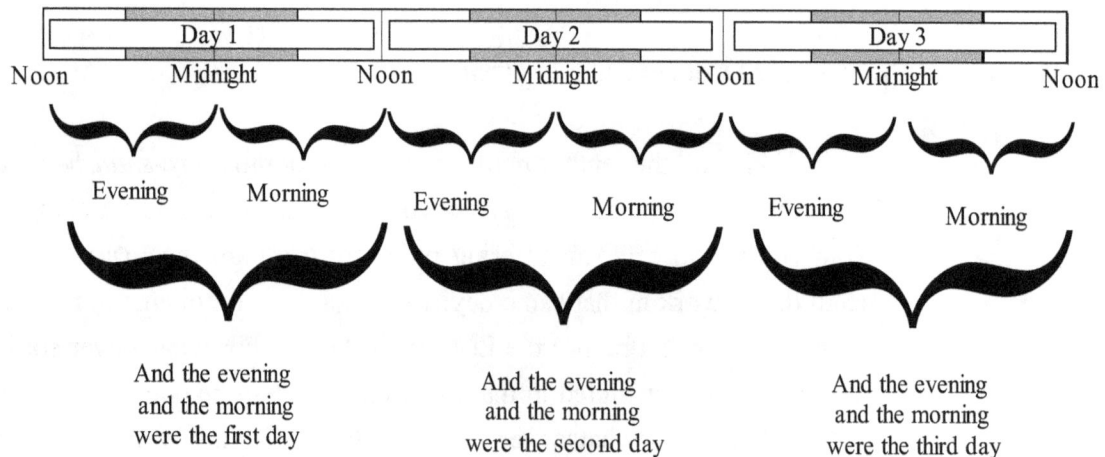

There was a third method of measuring days during the time of Jesus. It was the modern Roman method which measured a day starting at Midnight. The Roman day went from Midnight to Midnight so the transition from one day to the next would happen in the middle of the night.

Israel was under the control of the Romans but the Romans allowed Israel to continue with many of their religious practices. The Jews were allowed to continue observing the Passover and their other religious holidays. In some ways the Romans even encouraged these observances. They were mainly concerned with funding their empire. They didn't care how their subjects worshiped as long as they didn't threaten Rome. Keeping the peace so the tax revenue would continue was of primary importance. This is why Pontius Pilate made it a tradition to free one criminal during the Passover. It pleased the people and helped keep the peace.

It may have been the subtleties between the various timekeeping methods that allowed Jesus to eat the Passover meal 24 hours before the Sadducees would partake of it. It is possible the Sadducees adopted the Roman method of counting days as a matter of convenience. Rather than disrupting everything by changing days every day at Noon, it would be much simpler for everyone to do like the Romans and consider the new day to begin in the middle of the night. By doing this, the daylight periods wouldn't be split into separate days. Each morning when you woke up it would be a new day.

(The following is speculative but it does solve the Passover problem.)

If the traditional Jewish method were used, Jesus would have observed the Passover after sundown on Abib 14. Using the Roman method, Abib 14 would begin at Midnight but the Passover couldn't be observed until the next sundown. (See the diagram on page 149)

As unlikely as it seems for the Sadducees to follow the Roman calendar, they may not have had a choice. To keep down confusion, the Romans may have required the days to officially begin at midnight. Since the Jews could still observe their holidays in the evening the impact would be minimal. It was a minor change that few people would have objected to because of the convenience of it.

There may have been some (possibly the Pharisees) who would observe the Passover using the more traditional way of measuring days. For these people, Passover would come a day earlier than for those using the Roman system of timekeeping.

Having two separate days to perform the Passover rituals would be a big convenience for everyone. The sacrifices and the Passover ceremonies could be spread over two days rather than just one.

On the other hand, maybe Jesus and his disciples were the only people using the traditional method of timekeeping in their observance of the Passover. This would explain why eating lamb wasn't mentioned as part of the last supper. If they were observing the Passover a day earlier than everyone else, then the sacrificial lambs wouldn't have been sacrificed yet. In this instance Jesus was the Passover lamb and he symbolized the eating of his broken body through the breaking of the unleavened bread and his blood was symbolized by the wine they drank.

This change in timekeeping methods may have been part of God's plan for Jesus to fulfill all righteousness. It would allow him to observe the Passover with is disciples, explain its true significance to them and then offer himself as the spotless Passover lamb the next evening.

For this theory to have credibility it would mean the current Jewish interpretation of Biblical time keeping is incorrect. While this may sound outlandish, we must remember that it has been approximately 2000 years since the last temple sacrifices were offered. The Jewish people have been scattered to the four corners of the Earth and Israel didn't even exist as a nation until 1948. It is not unreasonable to conclude that some of their traditions may have become confused over all that time.

The question we must ask ourselves is… If reconciling the Biblical account with the current Jewish system of time measurement is not possible then is the Bible in error or are the current Jewish methods of time keeping different than they were in the days of Jesus?

In whom do you put your trust? The Bible or the current Jewish scholars?

Passover day begins

Passover meal is eaten by Jesus and his Disciples.

Passover day ends

Abib 14

Noon   Midnight   Noon

Evening   Morning

Jesus dies at about 3 pm on Abib 15 using the Evening to Evening Method.

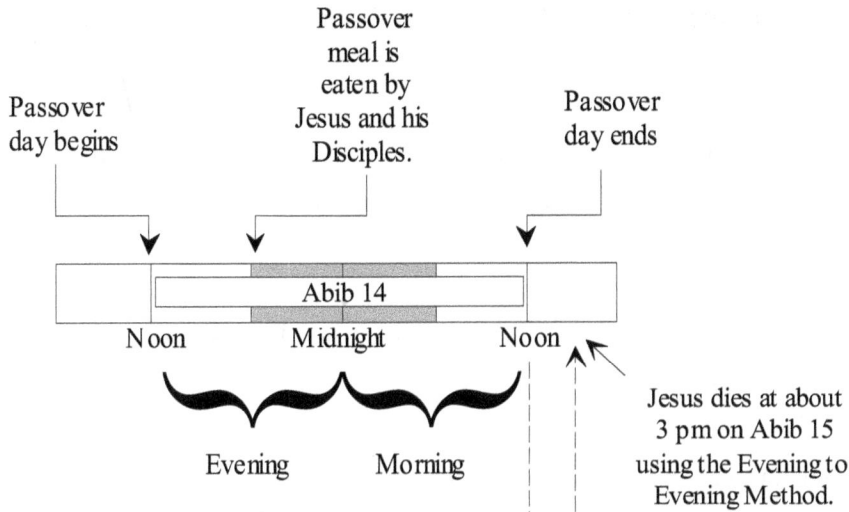

Evening to Evening method of counting days

Jesus and his disciples are thought to have used this method of counting days.

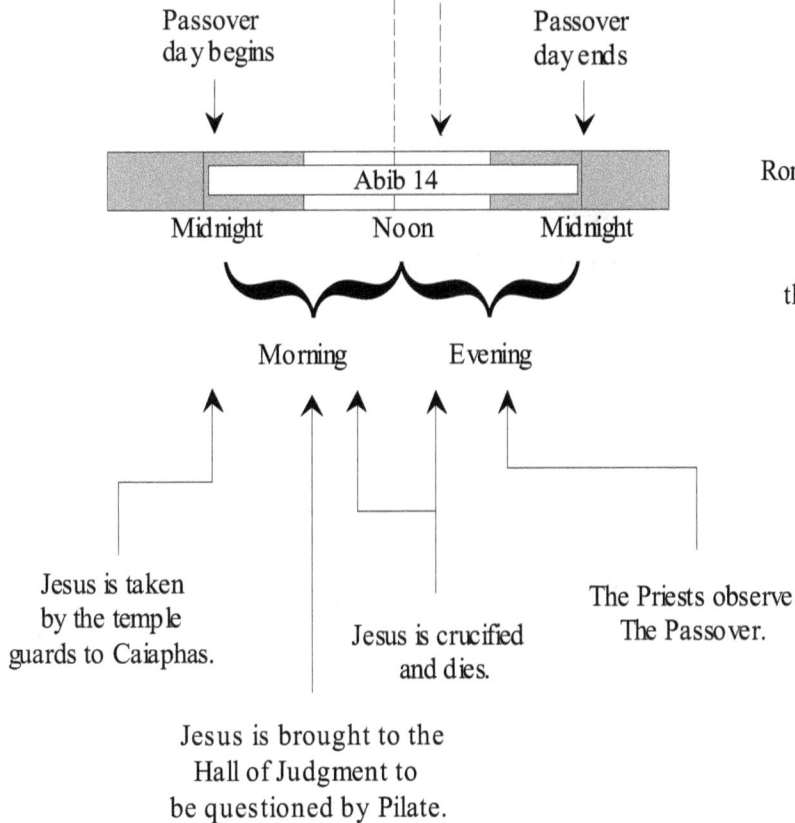

Passover day begins

Passover day ends

Abib 14

Midnight   Noon   Midnight

Morning   Evening

Roman method of counting days. Midnight to midnight.

The Priests are thought to have used this method of counting days.

Jesus is taken by the temple guards to Caiaphas.

Jesus is crucified and dies.

The Priests observe The Passover.

Jesus is brought to the Hall of Judgment to be questioned by Pilate.

To reiterate the timeline, Jesus ate the last supper with his disciples on the evening of the Passover:

> Mat 26:17Now the first *day* of the *feast of* unleavened bread the disciples came to Jesus, saying unto him, Where wilt thou that we prepare for thee to eat the passover?

> Mat 26:19And the disciples did as Jesus had appointed them; and they made ready the passover.

> 20Now when the even was come, he sat down with the twelve.

Jesus was arrested later that night and taken to the house of the high priest Caiaphas for questioning.

> Mat 26:57And they that had laid hold on Jesus led *him* away to Caiaphas the high priest, where the scribes and the elders were assembled.

They delivered Jesus to Pontius Pilate in the morning but they didn't go into the hall of judgment because they wanted to be able to eat the Passover that evening.

> Mat 27:1When the morning was come, all the chief priests and elders of the people took counsel against Jesus to put him to death:

> 2And when they had bound him, they led *him* away, and delivered him to Pontius Pilate the governor.

> John 18:28Then led they Jesus from Caiaphas unto the hall of judgment: and it was early; and they themselves went not into the judgment hall, lest they should be defiled; but that they might eat the passover.

The next thing to consider is what Jesus called "the sign of the prophet Jonas".

> Mat 12:39But he answered and said unto them, An evil and adulterous generation seeketh after a sign; and there shall no sign be given to it, but the sign of the prophet Jonas:

> 40For as Jonas was three days and three nights in the whale's belly; so shall the Son of man be three days and three nights in the heart of the earth.

Many people make the mistake of reading Mat 12:40 by itself without putting it within the context of everything else in the gospel accounts concerning the death, burial and resurrection of Jesus. By just looking at Mat 12:40 and ignoring the rest of the chronology, it is easy to come to the conclusion that 3 full days and 3 full nights had to pass to fulfill this prophecy. It should be pointed out Mat 12:40 doesn't specify full days or full nights. The next few pages will attempt to put the death, burial and resurrection of Jesus into the full and proper context.

The Sign of Jonah

(Matthew 12:40)

Jesus, using the Evening to Evening method
of counting days, observed the Passover here.

Jesus was arrested and brought before the High Priest.

Jesus was brought before Pilot. The priest didn't go in because they wanted to be
able to observe the passover meal later that evening.   John 18: 28

Jesus was crucified at about the 3rd hour of the day (9 am).   Mark 15:25

Darkness was across the land from the 6th to the 9th hour (Noon to 3pm)

Jesus died about the 9th hour of the day (3 pm).   Mat 27: 46

The preist using the Roman method of counting
days would observe the Passover here.

Jesus was resurrected early
on the first day of the week.
Mark 16: 9

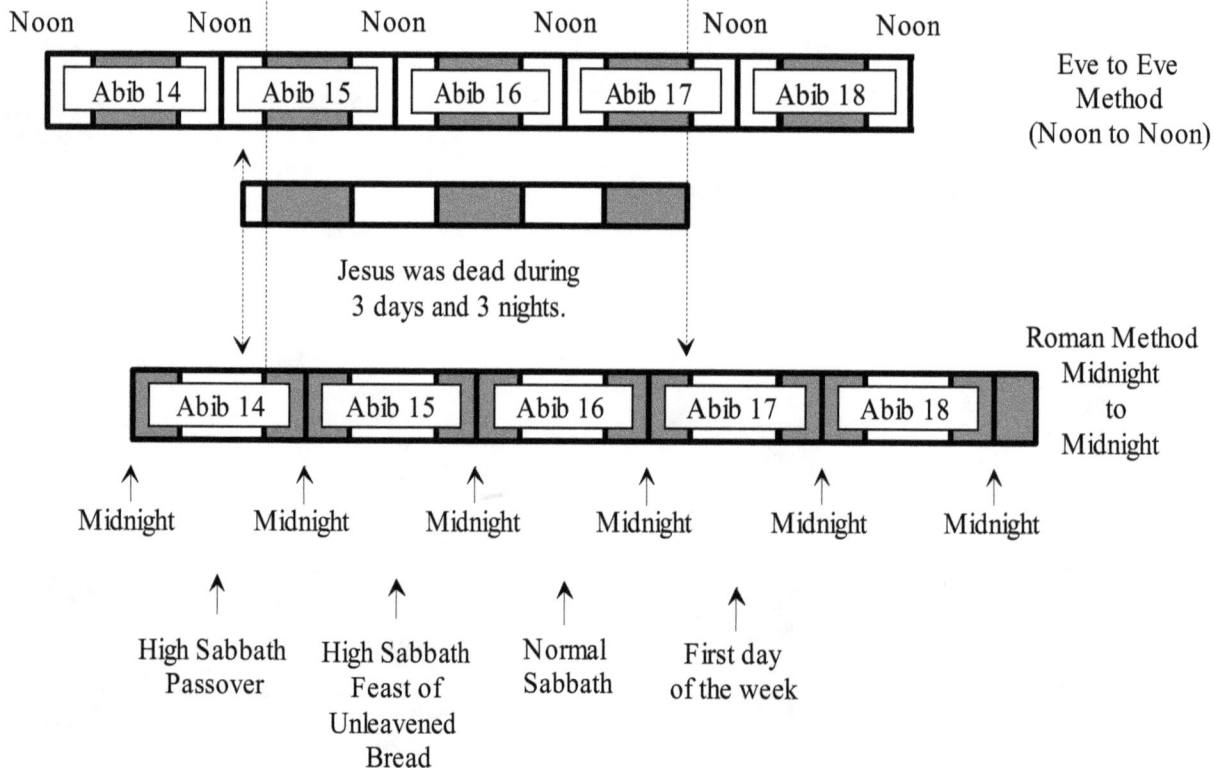

Noon	Noon	Noon	Noon	Noon	Noon

Abib 14	Abib 15	Abib 16	Abib 17	Abib 18

Eve to Eve
Method
(Noon to Noon)

Jesus was dead during
3 days and 3 nights.

Abib 14	Abib 15	Abib 16	Abib 17	Abib 18

Roman Method
Midnight
to
Midnight

Midnight	Midnight	Midnight	Midnight	Midnight	Midnight

High Sabbath Passover	High Sabbath Feast of Unleavened Bread	Normal Sabbath	First day of the week

If the Roman method of counting days were used, then the Passover meal
would occur 24 hours later than if the Evening to Evening method were used.

If you look at the "Sign of Jonah" diagram you will see Jesus was resurrected just before dawn on Abib 17.

> ^{Mat 28:1}In the end of the sabbath, as it began to dawn toward the first *day* of the week, came Mary Magdalene and the other Mary to see the sepulchre.

This was the end of the Sabbath just before dawn on the first day of the week. Mary Magdalene and the other Mary had to wait three days before going to attend to the body of Jesus because of the way the Sabbaths fell. It just so happened that the Passover (Abib 14) occurred on Thursday. The second day of the Feast of Unleavened Bread (Abib 15) was also a Sabbath which would have been on a Friday and the next day would be the normal Saturday Sabbath. Jesus' body would be allowed to lie undisturbed for three days and three nights before his resurrection thus fulfilling the sign of Jonah. Admittedly these were not 3 full days and three full nights, but the prophecy was correct nevertheless.

The Sign of Jonah diagram on the previous page shows Jesus being in the grave for 3 day periods and 3 night periods.

Jesus was dead during
3 days and 3 nights.

While this may not agree with our preconceived notions about what Jesus meant in Mat 12: 40, we have to ask ourselves if it is a reasonable solution.

For this to be considered a reasonable solution we must demonstrate the Bible counts any portion of a day as if it were a whole day. To do this we need to show other instances in the Bible where partial days were counted as whole days. Below are several instances of this.

> ^{Gen 42: 16}Send one of you, and let him fetch your brother, and ye shall be kept in prison, that your words may be proved, whether *there be any* truth in you: or else by the life of Pharaoh surely ye *are* spies. **¹⁷And he put them all together into ward three days. ¹⁸And Joseph said unto them the third day,** This do, and live; *for* I fear God:

1 Kings 20: 29And they **pitched one over against the other seven days**. And so it was, that **in the seventh day the battle was joined**: and the children of Israel slew of the Syrians an hundred thousand footmen in one day.

2 Chron 10:3And they sent and called him. So Jeroboam and all Israel came and spake to Rehoboam, saying, 4Thy father made our yoke grievous: now therefore ease thou somewhat the grievous servitude of thy father, and his heavy yoke that he put upon us, and we will serve thee. 5And he said unto them, **Come again unto me after three days**. And the people departed.

2 Chron 10:12So Jeroboam and all the people came to Rehoboam **on the third day**, as the king bade, saying, Come again to me on the third day.

In all of the previous examples a specific number of days are mentioned but the context shows these were not necessarily full days. In all of these instances the event occurred sometime on the last day but the last day was still counted as a day. The fact that the event occurred during the last day did not prevent the author from including the partial day in the day count. There was no suggestion that exactly 24 hours had to pass before a day could be counted. In the case of the death of Jesus, he died at about 3 pm but since the "day" wasn't over it still counted as a day. In this way Jesus was correct when he said he would be 3 days and 3 nights in the heart of the Earth (Mat 12:40).

The other issue many Christians may be reluctant to accept is the idea that more than one method of measuring days was used during the time of Jesus. The current Jewish/Seminary view of Biblical time keeping assumes that the days began in the evening at sunset. This idea has been so universally accepted that any suggestion otherwise is immediately ridiculed. Accepting the current Jewish or Bible seminary view in this regard can lead us to only one conclusion… The Biblical timeline is wrong.

This is another instance where we have to abandon our preconceived notions and consider exactly what the Bible says.

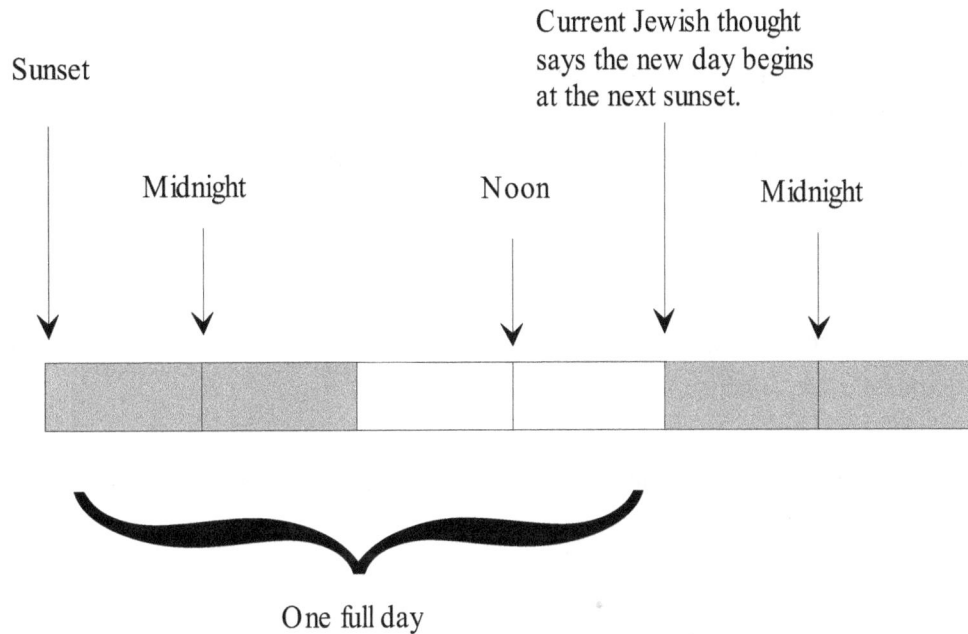

Sunset | Midnight | Noon | Current Jewish thought says the new day begins at the next sunset. | Midnight

One full day

There are biblical passages which support the idea that there were other methods of counting the days during the time of Jesus. The following passages show the evening was not always seen as the day's beginning.

> John 20:1**The first *day* of the week cometh Mary Magdalene early, when it was yet dark**, unto the sepulchre, and seeth the stone taken away from the sepulchre.

> John 20:18Mary Magdalene came and told the disciples that she had seen the Lord, and *that* he had spoken these things unto her.

> 19**Then the same day at evening, being the first *day* of the week**, when the doors were shut where the disciples were assembled for fear of the Jews, came Jesus and stood in the midst, and saith unto them, Peace *be* unto you.

If the evening is the beginning of a new day, then how could the evening in John 20:19 still be the same day as the day mentioned in John 20:1?

Consider the following verse regarding Mary.

> ^Mat 28:1^In the end of the sabbath, as it began to dawn toward the first *day* of the week, came Mary Magdalene and the other Mary to see the sepulchre.

If we hold to the generally accepted view of Jewish timekeeping where the day begins at sunset would Mat 28:1 make any sense?

Would the Sabbath end and first day of the week begin at dawn?

If we consider each of the above passages in the context of the Roman method of timekeeping, they both make perfect sense

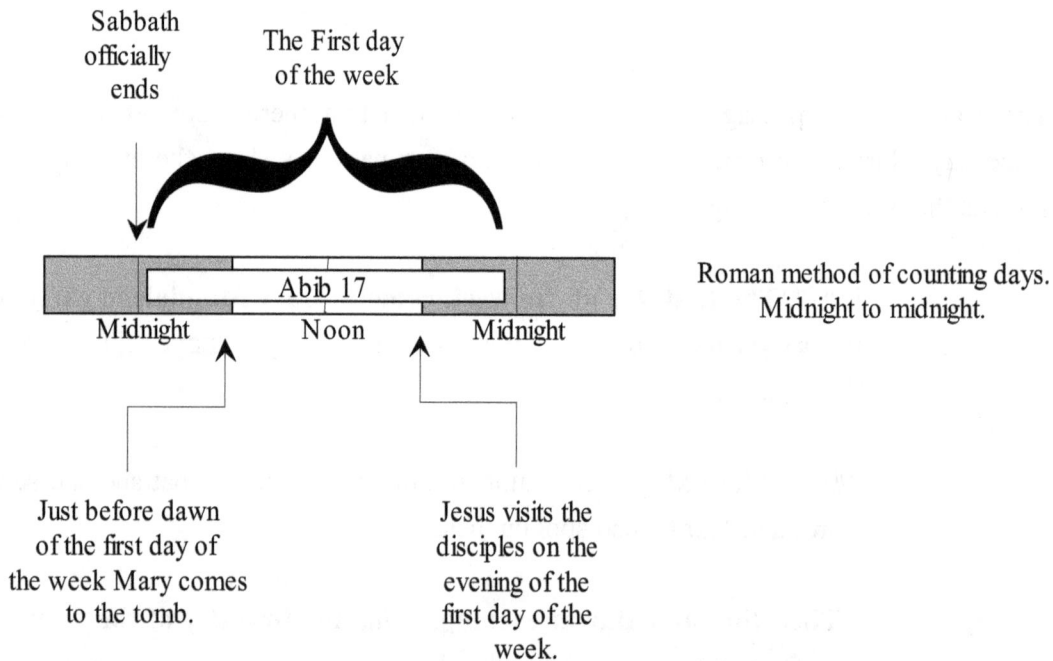

Roman method of counting days.
Midnight to midnight.

Using the Roman method of timekeeping, it is difficult to tell exactly when midnight occurs thereby ending the Sabbath. To be safe, Mary waited until just before dawn to go to the tomb to attend to Jesus. Later that same day, in the evening, Jesus appeared to his disciples.

The actual timing of the crucifixion is also confused because of the multiple methods of counting days. Let's compare the books of Mark and John.

Mark 15:24And when they had crucified him, they parted his garments, casting lots upon them, what every man should take.

25And it was **the third hour**, and **they crucified him**.

John 19:13When Pilate therefore heard that saying, he brought Jesus forth, and sat down in the judgment seat in a place that is called the Pavement, but in the Hebrew, Gabbatha.

14And it was the preparation of the passover, and **about the sixth hour**: and he saith unto the Jews, Behold your King!

15But they cried out, Away with *him,* away with *him,* **crucify him**. Pilate saith unto them, Shall I crucify your King? The chief priests answered, We have no king but Caesar.

16**Then delivered he him therefore unto them to be crucified**. And they took Jesus, and led *him* away.

As you can see, Mark 15 says Jesus was crucified in the third hour whereas John 19 clearly shows that Jesus wasn't crucified until after the sixth hour. How can this be? Here again it is because of the way people counted days.

The following diagram shows that Mark assumes the day begins at dawn. If we say the dawn occurs at approximately 6 am then the crucifixion of Jesus would have occurred at about 9 am.

158

Mark 15
Time measured
starting at dawn

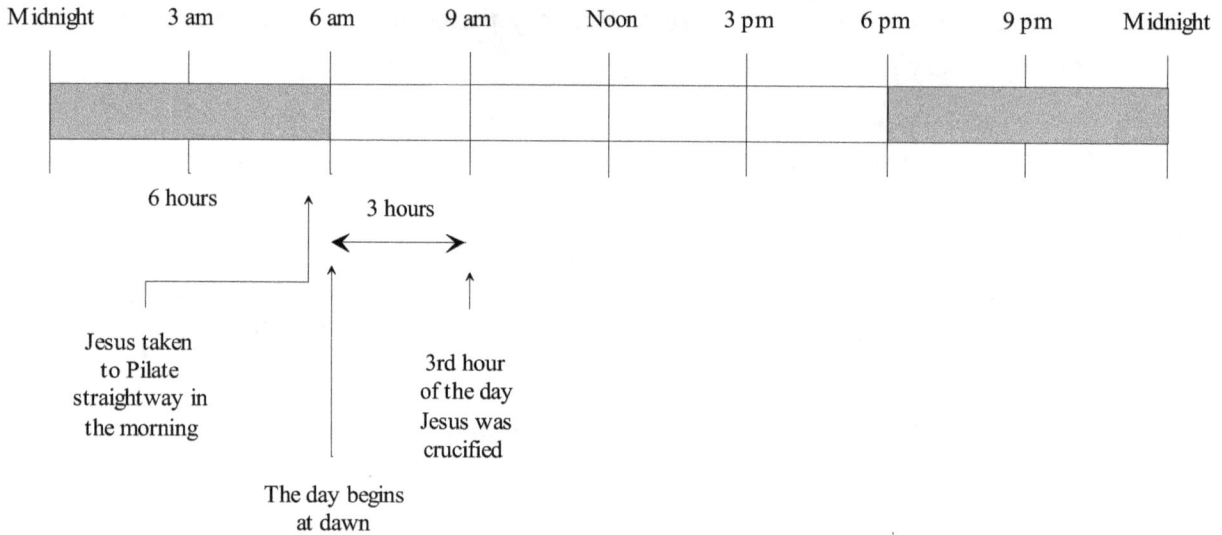

| Midnight | 3 am | 6 am | 9 am | Noon | 3 pm | 6 pm | 9 pm | Midnight |

6 hours   3 hours

Jesus taken
to Pilate
straightway in
the morning

3rd hour
of the day
Jesus was
crucified

The day begins
at dawn

The passage in John says the order to have Jesus crucified was given at about the sixth hour. This would mean the Roman method of time keeping must have been used. This method has the day begin at midnight. This would mean the order to have Jesus crucified would have been given at approximately 6 am.

John 18 & 19
Time measured
starting at Midnight

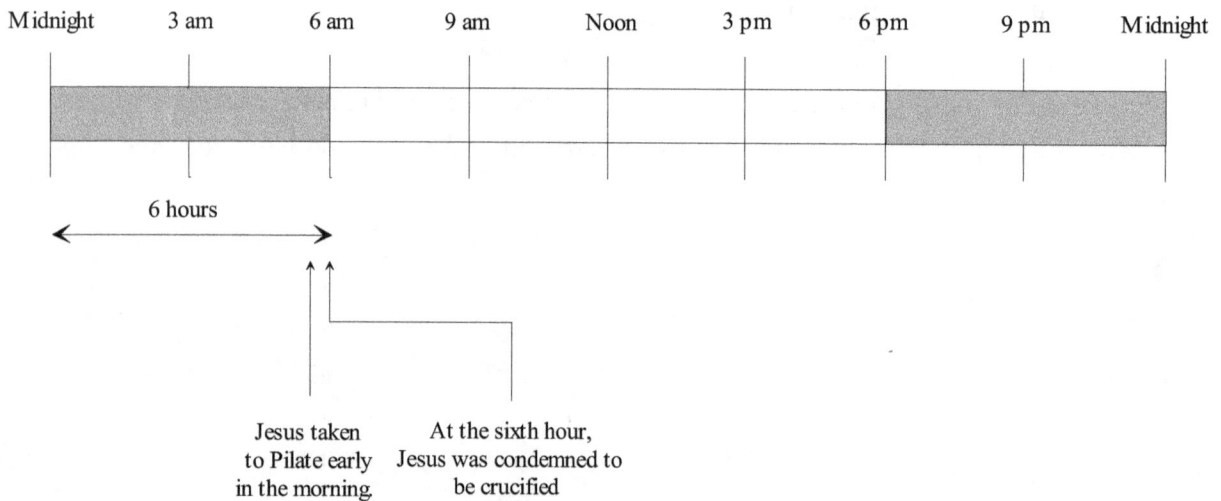

| Midnight | 3 am | 6 am | 9 am | Noon | 3 pm | 6 pm | 9 pm | Midnight |

6 hours

Jesus taken
to Pilate early
in the morning.

At the sixth hour,
Jesus was condemned to
be crucified

There are several other passages that say there was darkness over the land from the 6th to the 9th hour and that Jesus died in the ninth hour

[Mat 27:45]Now from the sixth hour there was darkness over all the land unto the ninth hour. [46]And about the ninth hour Jesus cried with a loud voice, saying, Eli, Eli, lama sabachthani? that is to say, My God, my God, why hast thou forsaken me?

[50]Jesus, when he had cried again with a loud voice, yielded up the ghost.

[Mark 15:33]And when the sixth hour was come, there was darkness over the whole land until the ninth hour. [34]And at the ninth hour Jesus cried with a loud voice, saying, Eloi, Eloi, lama sabachthani? which is, being interpreted, My God, my God, why hast thou forsaken me?

[37]And Jesus cried with a loud voice, and gave up the ghost.

[Luke 23:44]And it was about the sixth hour, and there was a darkness over all the earth until the ninth hour.

[46]And when Jesus had cried with a loud voice, he said, Father, into thy hands I commend my spirit: and having said thus, he gave up the ghost.

With our understanding of the different methods of counting days we can piece together a biblically consistent timeline for the crucifixion. (See the diagram on the next page)

The Timing of the Crucifixion

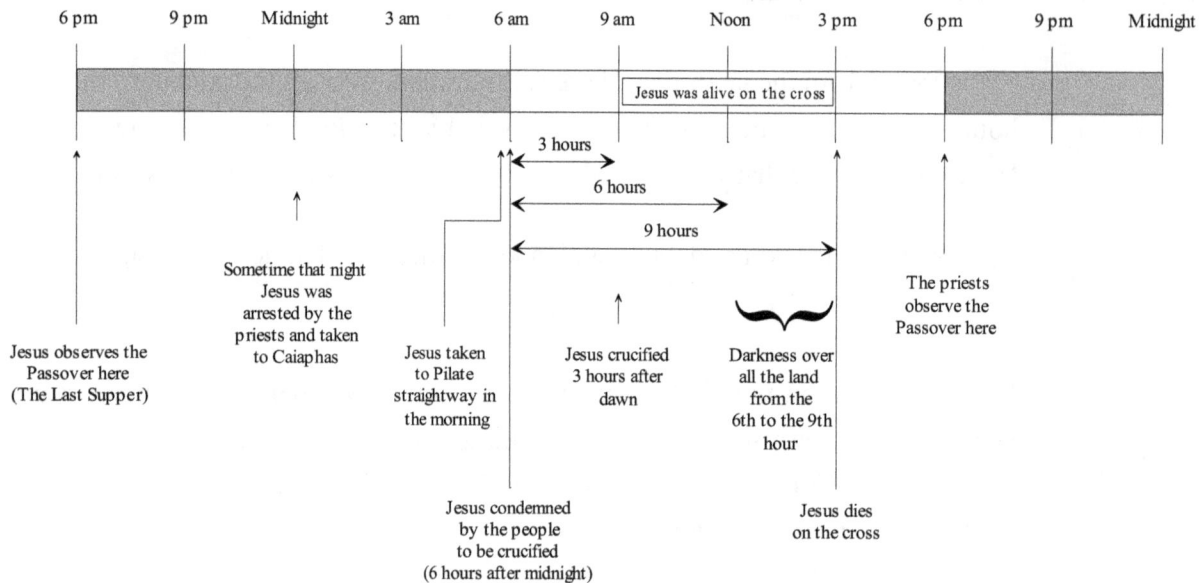

6 pm 9 pm Midnight 3 am 6 am 9 am Noon 3 pm 6 pm 9 pm Midnight

Jesus was alive on the cross

3 hours

6 hours

9 hours

Jesus observes the Passover here (The Last Supper)

Sometime that night Jesus was arrested by the priests and taken to Caiaphas

Jesus taken to Pilate straightway in the morning

Jesus crucified 3 hours after dawn

Darkness over all the land from the 6th to the 9th hour

The priests observe the Passover here

Jesus condemned by the people to be crucified (6 hours after midnight)

Jesus dies on the cross

The timing of the Passovers and the Crucifixion has been one of the favorite "contradictions" for those who would seek to discredit the Bible. Admittedly, these are difficult passages to resolve, but when we read the Bible in context and lay aside our preconceived notions we can see the accounts are consistent. The typical view that the biblical day begins at sundown is supported by modern Jewish customs but this does not necessarily mean the customs are always completely correct. We cannot allow the customs of men (even Jewish men) to be the ultimate authority in settling biblical questions. The better way to answer such questions is to go to the Bible directly. It is the closest thing to the ultimate authority (God) we have access to here on the Earth.

The precision and deliberacy of the timing of Jesus' crucifixion testifies to the fact God does not just react to events. He is in total control!

This chapter has shown us how symbolism can be directly linked with prophecy. We have seen how the complete significance of symbolism can only be understood in retrospect. In instances such as with the feasts of the first month, the symbolism had dual functions. It commemorated past events, like the death of the firstborn while, at the same time, it anticipated future, more significant events, like the crucifixion of Jesus (the ultimate Passover).

Understanding symbolism is the key to understanding prophecy. In the next chapter, we will consider the symbolism and the prophecies surrounding the life of Jesus.

Chapter Thirteen

Symbolism & Prophecy:

The Life of Jesus

Symbolism was a fundamental part of the ministry of Jesus. We can see this starting with the gifts the Magi brought to Jesus.

> Mat 2:11And when they were come into the house, they saw the young child with Mary his mother, and fell down, and worshipped him: and when they had opened their treasures, they presented unto him gifts; gold, and frankincense, and myrrh.

All three of these gifts had unique significance and were symbolic of the total Lordship of Jesus. Each one of these gifts appealed to a different part of our senses.

Gold is for the Eye.

> Ex 28:2And thou shalt make holy garments for Aaron thy brother for glory and **for beauty**.

> Ex 28:5And they shall take **gold**, and blue, and purple, and scarlet, and fine linen. 6And they shall make the ephod *of* **gold**, *of* blue, and *of* purple, *of* scarlet, and fine twined linen, with cunning work.

> Ex 28:8And the curious girdle of the ephod, which *is* upon it, shall be of the same, according to the work thereof; *even of* **gold**, *of* blue, and purple, and scarlet, and fine twined linen.

Behold Jesus

^{John 19:5}**Then came Jesus forth**, wearing the crown of thorns, and the purple robe. And *Pilate* saith unto them, **Behold the man**!

^{Zech 12:10}And I will pour upon the house of David, and upon the inhabitants of Jerusalem, the spirit of grace and of supplications: and **they shall look upon me whom they have pierced**, and they shall mourn for him, as one mourneth for *his* only *son,* and shall be in bitterness for him, as one that is in bitterness for *his* firstborn.

^{John 19:25}Now there stood by the cross of Jesus his mother, and his mother's sister, Mary the *wife* of Cleophas, and Mary Magdalene. ²⁶ When   **Jesus** therefore saw his mother, and the disciple standing by, whom he loved, he **saith** unto his mother, **Woman, behold thy son**!

^{John 1:29} The next day John seeth Jesus coming unto him, and saith, **Behold the Lamb of God, which taketh away the sin of the world**.

Just as the incorruptible beauty of gold is meant to be seen, the incorruptible beauty of Jesus was meant to be seen. Gold must be passed through the fire, beaten and formed to be made into beautiful objects. The eye is the only thing that can appreciate the beauty of gold. The eyes of the people would witness the works and the trials of Jesus. This would cause the redeemed to give glory unto God.

Frankincense is for the Smell.

^{Ex 30:34}And the LORD said unto Moses, Take unto thee sweet spices, stacte, and onycha, and galbanum; *these* sweet spices with pure **frankincense**: of each shall there be a like *weight:* ³⁵And thou shalt **make it a perfume**, a confection after the art of the apothecary, tempered together, pure *and* holy: ³⁶And thou shalt beat *some* of it very small, and put of it before the testimony in the tabernacle of the congregation, where I will meet with thee: it shall be unto you most holy.

Jesus is the sweet smelling savour.

> Ep 5:2 And walk in love, as Christ also hath loved us, and hath given himself for us an offering and a sacrifice to God for a sweet smelling savour.

Frankincense played two symbolic parts in connection with Jesus. It symbolized the pleasure God had for the total obedience of Jesus (it was like a sweet smelling aroma) while at the same time it symbolized the bitterness and pain Jesus would endure to secure our redemption.

Frankincense is also for the Taste.

> Lev 24:5 And thou shalt take fine flour, and bake twelve cakes thereof: two tenth deals shall be in one cake. ⁶And thou shalt set them in two rows, six on a row, upon the pure table before the LORD. ⁷And thou shalt **put pure frankincense** upon *each* row, that it may be **on the bread** for a memorial, *even* an offering made by fire unto the LORD.
> ⁸Every sabbath he shall set it in order before the LORD continually, *being taken* from the children of Israel by an everlasting covenant.
>
> ⁹And it shall be Aaron's and his sons'; and **they shall eat it in the holy place: for it *is* most holy unto him of the offerings** of the LORD made by fire by a perpetual statute.

Jesus tasted death in our place.

> Heb 2:9 But we see **Jesus**, who was made a little lower than the angels for the suffering of death, crowned with glory and honour; that he by the grace of God **should taste death for every man**.

Frankincense is a bitter tasting substance made from the resin of the Boswellia tree. These trees are renouned for their ability to survive even in the harshest of circumstances. They often grow directly out of the cracks in rocks. Their resin is extracted by slashing the bark of the trees and allowing the resin to secrete and harden into clumps called tears. Everything about Frankincense reminds us of the painful death Jesus endured for us.

Myrrh is for the Touch.

Ex 30:23 Take thou also unto thee principal spices, of **pure myrrh** five hundred *shekels,* and of sweet cinnamon half so much, *even* two hundred and fifty *shekels,* and of sweet calamus two hundred and fifty *shekels,* 24And of cassia five hundred *shekels,* after the shekel of the sanctuary, and of oil olive an hin: 25And **thou shalt make it an oil of holy ointment**, an ointment compound after the art of the apothecary: it shall be an holy anointing oil. 26And thou shalt anoint the tabernacle of the congregation therewith, and the ark of the testimony,

Jesus bore our pain in his body.

Isaiah 53:5But **he** *was* **wounded** for our transgressions, *he was* **bruised** for our iniquities: the chastisement of our peace *was* upon him; and **with his stripes we are healed**.

Jesus has become our healing ointment. His sacrifice was necessary for the healing of our souls as well as our bodies. He will wash away the sins of those who follow him.

The gifts of the Magi symbolically ministered to the senses of Sight, Smell, Taste, and Touch but there was nothing to minister to the sense of Hearing. The reason for this is obvious. Jesus himself was the word of God made flesh. He was the gift that God gave. He was meant to be heard!

The Word is for the hearing.

^{John 1:14}And the **Word was made flesh**, and dwelt among us, (and we beheld his glory, the glory as of the only begotten of the Father,) full of grace and truth.

^{Mat 17:5}While he yet spake, behold, a bright cloud overshadowed them: and behold a voice out of the cloud, which said, **This is my beloved Son**, in whom I am well pleased; **hear ye him**.

^{Rom 10:17}So then **faith *cometh* by hearing, and hearing by the word of God.**

Once again, symbolism is shown to have meaning beyond the obvious. The gifts of the Magi were prophetically acknowledging what Jesus would accomplish. This gives us a sense of how deliberate God's plan was and how everything fits together perfectly.

Jesus was the focal point of history. He was with God in the beginning. He sacrificed himself to pay the penalty for our sins and he will eventually return to set up his eternal kingdom here on Earth. It is not surprising such a key figure in history would be anticipated by the prophets. The question then becomes... What were the prophecies concerning Jesus and why don't the Jews accept him as their savior?

The prophecies concerning Jesus were given to the prophets without adequate context. The prophets recorded what God gave them without necessarily understanding the meaning of their prophecies. Some scriptures were understood to be referring to a coming savior (Messiah) while other scriptures were overlooked because they seemed to contradict the idea of a powerful deliverer for the Jews. The prophets prophesied about a suffering servant as well as a mighty king. In one place they compare him to a lamb while in another place they called him a lion. Who would have thought these scriptures would be describing a single man? Jesus would challenge all the preconceived notions the Jews had about their deliverer. This would be too much for most of them to accept. Especially the priests who wanted to retain their power and position.

The Messiah was supposed to come from the house of David.

^{Jer 23:5}Behold, the days come, saith the LORD, that I will raise unto David a righteous Branch, and a King shall reign and prosper, and shall execute judgment and justice in the earth. ⁶In his days Judah shall be saved, and Israel shall dwell

safely: and this *is* his name whereby he shall be called, THE LORD OUR RIGHTEOUSNESS.

^{Is 9:6}For unto us a child is born, unto us a son is given: and the government shall be upon his shoulder: and his name shall be called Wonderful, Counsellor, The mighty God, The everlasting Father, The Prince of Peace.

⁷Of the increase of *his* government and peace *there shall be* no end, upon the throne of David, and upon his kingdom, to order it, and to establish it with judgment and with justice from henceforth even for ever. The zeal of the LORD of hosts will perform this.

He would specifically come from the town of Bethlehem.

^{Mic 5:2}But thou, Bethlehem Ephratah, *though* thou be little among the thousands of Judah, *yet* out of thee shall he come forth unto me *that is* to be ruler in Israel; whose goings forth *have been* from of old, from everlasting.

It should be noted that these prophecies portray the Messiah in a very powerful, dominant role. This is the type of conquering leader the people were expecting. The people could rally around this type of leader. This is also what Satan expected but God had different plans.

^{Zech 9:9}Rejoice greatly, O daughter of Zion; shout, O daughter of Jerusalem: behold, thy King cometh unto thee: he *is* just, and having salvation; lowly, and riding upon an ass, and upon a colt the foal of an ass.

^{Is 53:7}He was oppressed, and he was afflicted, yet he opened not his mouth: he is brought as a lamb to the slaughter, and as a sheep before her shearers is dumb, so he openeth not his mouth.

Imagine Satan's delight when he realized Jesus didn't come as a powerful conqueror. He came as the son of a poor carpenter and wasn't warlike at all. His "turn the other cheek" and "love thy neighbor" philosophies would be considered signs of weakness. Surely, Satan would be able to overtake him.

Jesus was to be born of a virgin.

> Is 7:14Therefore the Lord himself shall give you a sign; Behold, a virgin shall conceive, and bear a son, and shall call his name Immanuel.

Mary was the virgin.

> Luke 1:30And the angel said unto her, Fear not, Mary: for thou hast found favour with God. 31And, behold, thou shalt conceive in thy womb, and bring forth a son, and shalt call his name JESUS. 32He shall be great, and shall be called the Son of the Highest: and the Lord God shall give unto him the throne of his father David: 33And he shall reign over the house of Jacob for ever; and of his kingdom there shall be no end. 34Then said Mary unto the angel, How shall this be, seeing I know not a man? 35And the angel answered and said unto her, The Holy Ghost shall come upon thee, and the power of the Highest shall overshadow thee: therefore also that holy thing which shall be born of thee shall be called the Son of God.

Let's examine if Jesus was really the son of David.

There is one genealogy of Jesus given in the book of Matthew and another given in the book of Luke. These genealogies are different and both claim to be the line of Jesus through Joseph. But why is the line of Joseph given at all? Considering he wasn't the real father of Jesus. (See the diagram on the next page)

From Adam to the Present

Adam — 130+800=930
Seth
Seth — 105+807=912
Enos
Enos — 90+815=905
Cainan
Cainan — 70+840=910
Mahalaleel
Mahalaleel — 65+830=895
Jared
Jared — 162+800=962
Enoch
Enoch — 65+300=365
Methuselah
Methuselah — 187+782=969
Lamech
Lamech — 182+595=777
Noah
Noah — 500+100+350=950
|
Shem |
Shem — Flood 100+500=600
Arphaxad
Arphaxad — 35+403=438
Salah
Salah — 30+403=433
Eber
Eber — 34+430=464
Peleg
Peleg — 30+209=239
Reu
Reu — 32+207=239
Serug
Serug — 30+200=230
Nahor
Nahor — 29+119=148
Terah
Terah — 70+135=205
Abram
Abram/Abraham — 100+75=175
Isaac
Isaac — 60+120 = 180
Jacob
Jacob / Israel — (lived 147 yrs)
Judah
Pharez
Hezron
Ram
Amminadab
Nahshon
Salmon
Boaz
Obed
Jesse
David

Number of years from Adams creation until Jacobs death. (2253 - 2274 years)

Solomon	Nathan
Roboam	Mattatha
Abia	Menan
Asa	Melea
Josaphat	Eliakim
Joram	Jonan
Ozias / *Ahaziah	Joseph
* Joash	Juda
* Amaziah	Simeon
* Azariah	Levi
Joatham	Matthat
Achaz	Jorim
Ezekias	Eliezer
Manasses	Jose
Amon	Er
Josias	Elmodam
*Jehoiakim	Cosam
Jechonias	Addi
Salathiel	Melchi
Zorobabel	Neri
Abiud	Salathiel
Eliakim	Zorobabel
Azor	Rhesa
Sadoc	Joanna
Achim	Juda
Eliud	Joseph
Eleazar	Semei
Matthan	Mattahias
Jacob	Maath
Joseph	Nagge
	Esli
	Naum
	Amos
	Mattathias
	Joseph
	Janna
	Melchi
	Levi
	Matthat
	Heli
	Joseph (via mary)

Lineage of Joseph (Mat 1:1-17)

The Presumed lineage of Jesus on his mothers side. (Luke 3:23-38)

Unknown Span of Time.

Jesus

* = Not found in the Mat text
Found in 1 Chr 3:10-17

} Approx. 2000 years from Jesus to the present

Present

figure 1.1

Lineages are always given in reference to the fathers. Since Jesus had no earthly father, his lineage was reckoned from the lineage of his adoptive father Joseph. The genealogy in Matthew was most likely the genealogy of Joseph and the genealogy in Luke was probably Mary's. The reason I say this is because in Matthew it says **Jacob begat Joseph**.

> Mat 1:16And Jacob begat Joseph the husband of Mary, of whom was born Jesus, who is called Christ.

In Luke Joseph was called the son of Heli

> Luke 3:23And Jesus himself began to be about thirty years of age, being (as was supposed) the son of Joseph, which was *the son* of Heli,

The term "begat" indicates Joseph was the son of Jacob by birth, while Joseph is merely called the son of Heli in Luke. The son of Heli most likely means the son-in-law of Heli. Since son-in-laws are still considered sons, the theory is reasonable. Nowhere does Luke say Heli begat Joseph.

With the assumption these two lineages belong to Joseph and Mary it becomes easy to see why Jesus could correctly be called the son of David. The lineage of Joseph goes through the line of Solomon. The lineage of Mary goes through Nathan. Both lineages intersect at King David.

> Mat 1:1The book of the generation of Jesus Christ, the son of David, the son of Abraham.

The lineage of Jesus confirms he was from the kingly line of David and his bloodlines were impeccable. He was qualified to be king in every way.

Physically he was the son of David through his birth by Mary.

According to the Law he was the son of David through his adoption by Joseph.

Spiritually he was the only begotten son of God.

You may have noticed there are stars beside several of the names in the line of Joseph. These men were not mentioned as being in the line of Joseph from the book of Matthew but they were included in the 1 Chronicles text. The diagram on the next page will compare the names from the two texts

Lineage From Matthew Chapter 1	Lineage From 1 Chronicles Chapter 3
David	David
Solomon	Solomon
Roboam	Rehoboam
Abia	Abia
Asa	Asa
Josaphat	Jehoshaphat
Joram	Joram
Ozias	Ahaziah
	* Joash
	* Amaziah
	* Azariah
Joatham	Jotham
Achaz	Ahaz
Ezekias	Hezekiah
Manasses	Manasseh
Amon	Amon
Josias	Josiah
	* Jehoiakim
Jechonias	Jeconiah
Salathiel	Salathiel
Zorobabel	
Abiud	
Eliakim	
Azor	
Sadoc	
Achim	
Eliud	
Eleazar	
Matthan	
Jacob	
Joseph	
Jesus	

With the exception of the obvious spelling differences the two lineages mirror each other very closely. The book of 1 Chronicles covered the time span up until the time of Salathiel. After the time of Salathiel we are forced to rely on the Matthew text for further information concerning the lineage of Jesus.

The Matthew lineage was not all inclusive. Several names were left out by Matthew. What was the reason for this?

The omission of names from a lineage would not normally bother me because a great grandson can still be referred to as a son. The troubling part is the observation Matthew makes concerning the number of generations between key events.

> ^{Matt 1:17}So all the generations from Abraham to David *are* fourteen generations; and from David until the carrying away into Babylon *are* fourteen generations; and from the carrying away into Babylon unto Christ *are* fourteen generations.

If we add the 4 omitted names to the Matthew lineage there are no longer 14 generations between David and the carrying away to Babylon. This would either mean this portion of Matthew is in error or there is a reason why these names were deliberately removed. Were these men judged to be unworthy to be counted as ancestors of Jesus?

Against Joash:

> ^{2 Chrn 24:22}Thus **Joash** the king remembered not the kindness which Jehoiada his father had done to him, but slew his son. And when he died, he said, The LORD look upon *it,* and require *it.*

> ^{2 Chrn 24:24}For the army of the Syrians came with a small company of men, and the LORD delivered a very great host into their hand, because they had forsaken the LORD God of their fathers. So they executed judgment against **Joash**.

Against Amaziah:

2Chron 25:14Now it came to pass, after that **Amaziah** was come from the slaughter of the Edomites, that he brought the gods of the children of Seir, and set them up *to be* his gods, and bowed down himself before them, and burned incense unto them.

Against Azariah:

2 Kings 14:21And all the people of Judah took **Azariah**, which *was* sixteen years old, and made him king instead of his father Amaziah.

2 Kings 14:24And he did *that which was* evil in the sight of the LORD: he departed not from all the sins of Jeroboam the son of Nebat, who made Israel to sin.

Against Jehoiakim:

2 Chron 36:5**Jehoiakim** *was* twenty and five years old when he began to reign, and he reigned eleven years in Jerusalem: and he did *that which was* evil in the sight of the LORD his God.

These men did evil in the sight of the Lord and they did not repent. They were not worthy to be considered to be in the line of Jesus. David also did evil in the eyes of the Lord with regard to Urias but he repented and was forgiven.

Timothy warns against getting too bogged down in endless genealogies.

1 Tim 1:4Neither give heed to fables and endless genealogies, which minister questions, rather than godly edifying which is in faith: *so do.*

Suffice it to say Jesus fulfilled the prophecy that he would be known as the son of David. He was born in Bethlehem and his mother was a virgin.

There are scores of prophecies which were undeniably fulfilled by Jesus during his earthly ministry. Among these are…

174

He would be betrayed for 30 pieces of silver and it would be used to purchase a potters field.

Zech 11:12And I said unto them, If ye think good, give *me* my price; and if not, forbear. So they weighed for my price thirty *pieces* of silver. 13And the LORD said unto me, Cast it unto the potter: a goodly price that I was prised at of them. And I took the thirty *pieces* of silver, and cast them to the potter in the house of the LORD.

Mat 26:15And said *unto them,* What will ye give me, and I will deliver him unto you? And they covenanted with him for thirty pieces of silver.

Mat 27:5And he cast down the pieces of silver in the temple, and departed, and went and hanged himself. 6And the chief priests took the silver pieces, and said, It is not lawful for to put them into the treasury, because it is the price of blood. 7And they took counsel, and bought with them the potter's field, to bury strangers in.

They would cast lots for his cloths.

Ps 22:18They part my garments among them, and cast lots upon my vesture

Mat 27:35And they crucified him, and parted his garments, casting lots: that it might be fulfilled which was spoken by the prophet, They parted my garments among them, and upon my vesture did they cast lots.

They pierced his hands, feet and side.

Ps 22:16For dogs have compassed me: the assembly of the wicked have inclosed me: they pierced my hands and my feet.

Zech 12:10And I will pour upon the house of David, and upon the inhabitants of Jerusalem, the spirit of grace and of supplications: and they shall look upon me whom they have pierced, and they shall mourn for him, as one mourneth for *his* only *son,* and shall be in bitterness for him, as one that is in bitterness for *his* firstborn.

Zech 13:6And *one* shall say unto him, What *are* these wounds in thine hands? Then he shall answer, *Those* with which I was wounded *in* the house of my friends.

Mat 27:35And they crucified him, and parted his garments, casting lots: that it might be fulfilled which was spoken by the prophet, They parted my garments among them, and upon my vesture did they cast lots.

John 19:34But one of the soldiers with a spear pierced his side, and forthwith came there out blood and water.

None of his bones would be broken.

Ps 34:20He keepeth all his bones: not one of them is broken.

John 19: 33But when they came to Jesus, and saw that he was dead already, they brake not his legs:

He would be killed as a criminal.

Is 53:12Therefore will I divide him *a portion* with the great, and he shall divide the spoil with the strong; because he hath poured out his soul unto death: and he was numbered with the transgressors; and he bare the sin of many, and made intercession for the transgressors.

Mark 15:27And with him they crucify two thieves; the one on his right hand, and the other on his left. 28And the scripture was fulfilled, which saith, And he was numbered with the transgressors.

Any objective person who examines the life of Jesus and compares it to the Old Testament scriptures will have to admit Jesus fulfilled too many scriptures to be explained away as coincidence.

So why wasn't he accepted as the Jewish Messiah?

We have already touched on part of the reason. Jesus, during his life, fulfilled some of the scriptures pertaining to the coming Messiah but he didn't fulfill them all. Jesus took them by surprise. No one expected the Messiah to come twice. They didn't expect the prophecies concerning the Messiah to be fulfilled in two separate stages which would be separated by two thousand years.

The Jews expected the Messiah to deliver them from the Romans and immediately set up his kingdom. The priests expected to be greatly exalted by the Messiah but Jesus came against them in no uncertain terms.

> Mat 23:13But woe unto you, scribes and Pharisees, hypocrites! for ye shut up the kingdom of heaven against men: for ye neither go in *yourselves,* neither suffer ye them that are entering to go in.
>
> 14Woe unto you, scribes and Pharisees, hypocrites! for ye devour widows' houses, and for a pretence make long prayer: therefore ye shall receive the greater damnation.
>
> 15Woe unto you, scribes and Pharisees, hypocrites! for ye compass sea and land to make one proselyte, and when he is made, ye make him twofold more the child of hell than yourselves.

Jesus made enemies of the scribes and Pharisees. His doctrine was about obeying the heart of the law. He talked directly to the people and taught as one with authority. The priests perceived him to be a threat to their way of life. It is no wonder the priests refused to accept Jesus as their Messiah. They would have done anything to discredit him.

Christians and Jews acknowledge the Old Testament as being the word of God. We both have these scriptures in common. Even the first century Jewish historian Josephus admits Jesus was a real historical figure. (See Josephus, Jewish Antiquities 18.3.3)

Some of the Old Testament prophecies are so specific and so obviously referring to Jesus it would be impossible to deny he was the fulfillment. Being curious as to how the Jews dealt with these scriptures I purchased a Jewish Tanach which is virtually the same thing as the Old Testament we Christians are used to. When I read the Tanach two things stood out. The first thing was how similar the translation of the Tanach was to the King James Version of the Old Testament. This gives credit to the skill of the translators who translated the King James Version of the Bible. The second thing that stood out was, just as I suspected, the scriptures which obviously referred to Jesus were different in the Tanach. I will not quote the Tanach verbatim in order to avoid any copyright issues. Instead I will quote from the King James Version of the Old Testament and then I will point out how the Tanach is different. (The King James Version of the Bible is copyright free therefore it can be quoted from directly.) I encourage you to look these verses up for yourself in the Tanach.

One example was regarding the virgin birth.

King James Version

Is 7:14Therefore the Lord himself shall give you a sign; Behold, a virgin shall conceive, and bear a son, and shall call his name Immanuel.

In the Tanach, the verse is virtually identical with the exception that the word virgin has been replaced with young woman.

Why would a young woman conceiving and bearing a son be considered a "sign"? Young women have children every day. There is nothing miraculous or even noteworthy about it. On the other hand, if a virgin conceived and had a son it would be an extraordinary thing. This would be a unique event that could be used as a sign.

The word virgin makes more sense in this instance. Is there some bias in the Tanach against the idea of a virgin birth because of its association with Jesus? Are the Jews willing to change any scriptures that support the claim of Jesus being the Messiah? Let's look at some other examples.

King James Version

Ps 22:16For dogs have compassed me: the assembly of the wicked have inclosed me: they pierced my hands and my feet.

Once again, the King James Version is a 100 % match with the life of Jesus but the Tanach version is different. Piercing of the hands and feet is an obvious reference to the crucifixion. The Tanach says, evil-doers enclosed me like a lion; they are at my hands and feet. The reference to the evil-doers inclosing someone like a lion being at their hands and feet doesn't really make sense. Lions typically go for the throat, not for the hands and feet.

Jesus was betrayed for 30 pieces of silver.

King James Version

Zech 11:12 And I said unto them, If ye think good, give *me* my price; and if not, forbear. So they weighed for my price thirty *pieces* of silver. [13]And the LORD said unto me, Cast it unto the potter: a goodly price that I was prised at of them. And I took the thirty *pieces* of silver, and cast them to the potter in the house of the LORD.

Notice the King James Version mentions the 30 pieces of silver being cast to the potter. The Tanach leaves out this important detail. It merely says the 30 pieces of silver were cast into the treasury of the house of the Lord. Did the translators of the Tanach deliberately leave this out? Did they leave it out because it was another bull's-eye for the Christian account?

Mat 27:3 Then Judas, which had betrayeth him, when he saw that he was condemned, repented himself, and brought again the thirty pieces of silver to the chief priests and elders, [4]Saying, I have sinned in that I have betrayed the innocent blood. And they said, What *is that* to us? see thou *to that.* [5]And he cast down the pieces of silver in the temple, and departed, and went and hanged himself. **[6]And the chief priests took the silver pieces**, and said, It is not lawful for to put them into the treasury, because it is the price of blood. [7]And they took counsel, **and bought with them the potter's field, to bury strangers in**.

These differences between the King James Version of the Old Testament and the Tanach seem to be deliberate but the King James Version seems to make more contextual sense.

The Jews will eventually recognize Jesus as there Messiah and they will mourn for all of the pain Jesus had to endure. It will be a wonderful day when the Jews are reconciled to God.

> ^{Zech 12:10}And I will pour upon the house of David, and upon the inhabitants of Jerusalem, the spirit of grace and of supplications: and they shall look upon me whom they have pierced, and they shall mourn for him, as one mourneth for *his* only *son,* and shall be in bitterness for him, as one that is in bitterness for *his* firstborn.

> ^{Zech 13:6}And *one* shall say unto him, What *are* these wounds in thine hands? Then he shall answer, *Those* with which I was wounded *in* the house of my friends.

Symbolism is the key to understanding the Bible. We have seen how it can be used to demonstrate profound truths which are not immediately obvious. Jesus also does this with his use of parables. They allow the believers to believe and understand while at the same time it allows the unbelievers to continue to disbelieve. Understanding Symbolism will be very important in our study of prophecy.

In the next chapter we will begin focusing on the prophecies concerning the end of the age. We will begin with the Book of Daniel.

Chapter Fourteen

Prophecy:

The Book of Daniel

Understanding the Book of Daniel is essential to gaining an accurate view of prophecy. This book is valuable because of its historical as well as its prophetic content. Most of the prophetic symbolism in the Book of Daniel is explained for the reader. This gives us a foundation to build upon in our understanding of prophecy.

Daniel's prophecies begin with the reign of King Nebuchadnezzar and extend beyond the tribulation period. The Book of Daniel can only be compared to the Book of Revelation in its prophetic significance. I cannot overstate its importance.

The one thing not immediately obvious when reading the Book of Daniel is its chapters are not arranged in chronological order.

Biblical Order		Chronological Order		
Chapter	1-4	Chapter	1-4	Nebuchadnezzar rules
Chapter	5	Chapter	7	Belshazzar rules
Chapter	6	Chapter	8	Belshazzar rules
Chapter	7	Chapter	5	Belshazzar rules
Chapter	8	Chapter	6	Darius rules
Chapter	9	Chapter	9	Darius rules
Chapter	10	Chapter	11	Darius rules
Chapter	11	Chapter	12	Darius rules
Chapter	12	Chapter	10	Cyrus rules

This raises the question: Why would the Book of Daniel be compiled out of sequence? The answer lies in the prophecies of the book. If you look at the way the Bible lays out the prophecies of Daniel you should notice the prophecies start out very broad. The first is the prophecy of Nebuchadnezzar's dream. It symbolically foretells the rise and fall of the kingdoms of this world. It symbolizes the kingdoms of this world as a statue of a man made with different materials. Nebuchadnezzar's kingdom is the first mentioned in the prophecy, being symbolized as the golden head of the image. The vision ends with the rock (Jesus) falling on the feet of the image and destroying it completely. The rock then fills all the Earth. This prophecy is the broadest and most basic prophecy in the Book of Daniel. All the other prophecies in the Book of Daniel are variations on this theme. Each new prophecy gives additional insight into the nature of these kingdoms and by chapter 9 the symbolism is dropped and literal descriptions of the future are given.

Nebuchadnezzar's Dream – The Foundation of Prophecy

In the second year of King Nebuchadnezzar's reign, the king had a dream that troubled him greatly. He couldn't remember the details of the dream but he was so disturbed by it that he called his magicians, astrologers, sorcerers, and Chaldeans to tell him what the dream was and what it meant. When they couldn't, the king was angry and would have killed them all but Daniel, one of the captured men of Judah, made the request that he and his friends be allowed to pray and seek an answer from his God concerning this dream. The king agreed and God revealed the meaning of the dream to Daniel. Daniel, in turn, revealed the dream to King Nebuchadnezzar.

> Dan 2:25Then Arioch brought in Daniel before the king in haste and said thus unto him, I have found a man of the captives of Judah, that will make known unto the king the interpretation. 26The king answered and said to Daniel, whose name *was* Belteshazzar, Art thou able to make known unto me the dream which I have seen, and the interpretation thereof? 27Daniel answered in the presence of the king, and said, The secret which the king hath demanded cannot the wise *men,* the astrologers, the magicians, the soothsayers, shew unto the king; 28But there is a God in heaven that revealeth secrets, and maketh known to the king Nebuchadnezzar what shall be in the latter days. Thy dream, and the visions of thy head upon thy bed, are these; 29As for thee, O king, thy thoughts came *into thy mind* upon thy bed, what should come to pass hereafter: and he that revealeth secrets maketh known to thee what shall come to pass. 30But as for me, this secret

is not revealed to me for *any* wisdom that I have more than any living, but for *their* sakes that shall make known the interpretation to the king, and that thou mightest know the thoughts of thy heart.

There are a few points in the above passage which need to be emphasized. Firstly, Notice Daniel's humility and how he gave all the credit for the revelation of Nebuchadnezzar's dream to the God in Heaven. By revealing the dream and its interpretation Daniel demonstrated God's superiority over all the false gods of Babylon. Secondly, Daniel stated the king was shown what would be in the "latter days". There is no doubt in my mind that we are living in the "latter days" and this prophecy is relevant to our time period.

Nebuchadnezzar's Dream

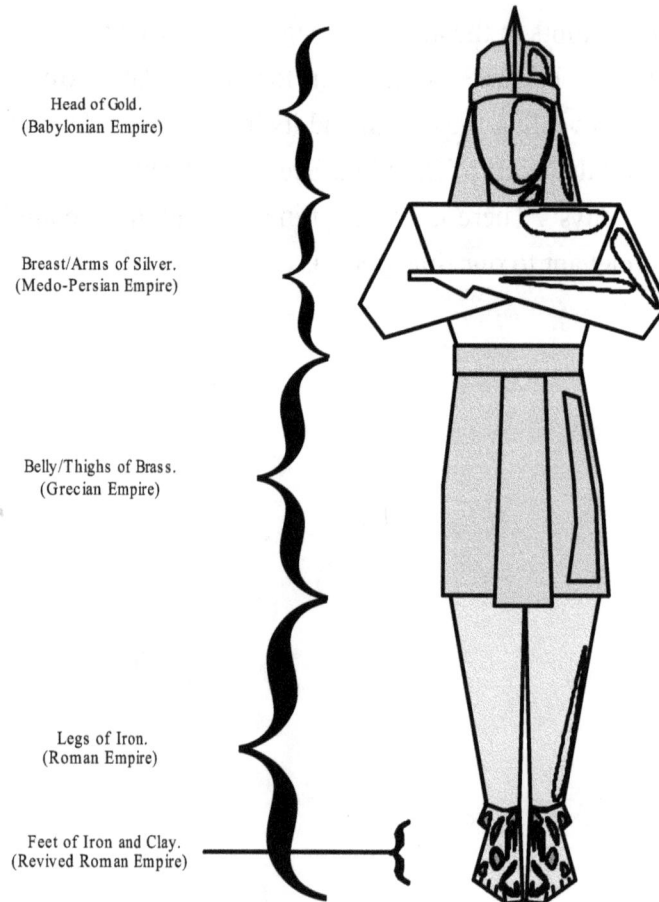

Head of Gold.
(Babylonian Empire)

Breast/Arms of Silver.
(Medo-Persian Empire)

Belly/Thighs of Brass.
(Grecian Empire)

Legs of Iron.
(Roman Empire)

Feet of Iron and Clay.
(Revived Roman Empire)

Figure 1

The dream...

Dan 2:31Thou, O king, sawest, and behold a great image. This great image, whose brightness was excellent, stood before thee; and the form thereof *was* terrible. 32This image's head *was* of fine gold, his breast and his arms of silver, his belly and his thighs of brass, 33His legs of iron, his feet part of iron and part of clay. 34Thou sawest till that a stone was cut out without hands, which smote the image upon his feet *that were* of iron and clay, and brake them to pieces. 35Then was the iron, the clay, the brass, the silver, and the gold, broken to pieces together, and became like the chaff of the summer threshingfloors; and the wind carried them away, that no place was found for them: and the stone that smote the image became a great mountain, and filled the whole earth.

The interpretation...

Dan 2:36This *is* the dream; and we will tell the interpretation thereof before the king. 37Thou, O king, *art* a king of kings: for the God of heaven hath given thee a kingdom, power, and strength, and glory. 38And wheresoever the children of men dwell, the beasts of the field and the fowls of the heaven hath he given into thine hand, and hath made thee ruler over them all. Thou *art* this head of gold. 39And after thee shall arise another kingdom inferior to thee, and another third kingdom of brass, which shall bear rule over all the earth. 40And the fourth kingdom shall be strong as iron: forasmuch as iron breaketh in pieces and subdueth all *things:* and as iron that breaketh all these, shall it break in pieces and bruise. 41And whereas thou sawest the feet and toes, part of potters' clay, and part of iron, the kingdom shall be divided; but there shall be in it of the strength of the iron, forasmuch as thou sawest the iron mixed with miry clay. 42And *as* the toes of the feet *were* part of iron, and part of clay, so the kingdom shall be partly strong, and partly broken. 43And whereas thou sawest iron mixed with miry clay, they shall mingle themselves with the seed of men: but they shall not cleave one to another, even as iron is not mixed with clay. 44And in the days of these kings shall the God of heaven set up a kingdom, which shall never be destroyed: and the kingdom shall not be left to other people, *but* it shall break in pieces and consume all these kingdoms, and it shall stand for ever. 45Forasmuch as thou sawest that the stone was cut out of the mountain without hands, and that it brake in pieces the iron, the brass, the clay, the silver, and the gold; the great God hath made known to the king what shall come to pass hereafter: and the dream is certain, and the interpretation thereof sure.

This prophetic dream tells us the great power of Babylon would be replaced by a second great power, which would be replaced by a third, and then a fourth. This fourth power would be destroyed and replaced by the rock. Nebuchadnezzar's dream covers the time period from his reign until the destruction of the kingdoms of this world. Then the rock (Jesus) becomes a mountain and fills the whole Earth.

Dan 2:46Then the king Nebuchadnezzar fell upon his face, and worshipped Daniel, and commanded that they should offer an oblation and sweet odours unto him. 47The king answered unto Daniel, and said, Of a truth *it is,* that your God is a God of gods, and a Lord of kings, and a revealer of secrets, seeing thou couldst reveal this secret. 48Then the king made Daniel a great man, and gave him many great gifts, and made him ruler over the whole province of Babylon, and chief of the governors over all the wise *men* of Babylon. 49Then Daniel requested of the king, and he set Shadrach, Meshach, and Abed-nego, over the affairs of the province of Babylon: but Daniel *sat* in the gate of the king.

Daniel was humble and gave God the credit nevertheless, in the end, Daniel was exalted. Daniel's humility perfectly demonstrated Mat 23:12.

Mat 2312And whosoever shall exalt himself shall be abased; and he that shall humble himself shall be exalted.

The image Nebuchadnezzar saw was divided into four parts symbolized by different types of metals (see figure 1). Daniel identified the head of gold to be representing Nebuchadnezzar's kingdom of Babylon. The second and third divisions are the two kingdoms that would follow. These will be identified later in the Book of Daniel as the Medo/Persian Empire and the Grecian Empire. The last division consists of the legs and feet of the statue. Both made of iron but the feet are mingled with clay. The legs and feet are not identified by name but they are easily identified historically. The legs are representative of the Roman Empire and the feet are a corrupted continuation of the Roman Empire. This last empire will continue until the Lord comes and destroys it. Then the Lord will set up his own kingdom.

Since the kingdoms represented here occur in a sequential fashion, it makes sense the rock (Jesus) falls on the last kingdom (the feet) and destroys the whole statue.

While the four kingdoms described by Nebuchadnezzar's dream were probably the greatest and most powerful kingdoms of their day, they did not rule the entire world. They did not control the oriental world or the great civilizations on the American continent. The thing these four kingdoms had in common was their control of Israel (or more accurately Judah.) These kingdoms were used to judge and chastise God's disobedient people. This prophecy predicts the succession of control from the time of Nebuchadnezzar until the Lord returns to set up his kingdom. Daniel's next prophecy will parallel Nebuchadnezzar's dream and will provide more detail.

In Chapter 7, Daniel tells us about a dream he had which troubled him greatly. God showed him the same kingdoms Nebuchadnezzar saw but this time the kingdoms were portrayed as four great beasts.

The Four Beasts

Dan 7:1In the first year of Belshazzar king of Babylon Daniel had a dream and visions of his head upon his bed: then he wrote the dream, *and* told the sum of the matters. 2Daniel spake and said, I saw in my vision by night, and, behold, the four winds of the heaven strove upon the great sea. 3And four great beasts came up from the sea, diverse one from another. 4The first *was* like a lion, and had eagle's wings: I beheld till the wings thereof were plucked, and it was lifted up from the earth, and made stand upon the

The Empires of Prophecy

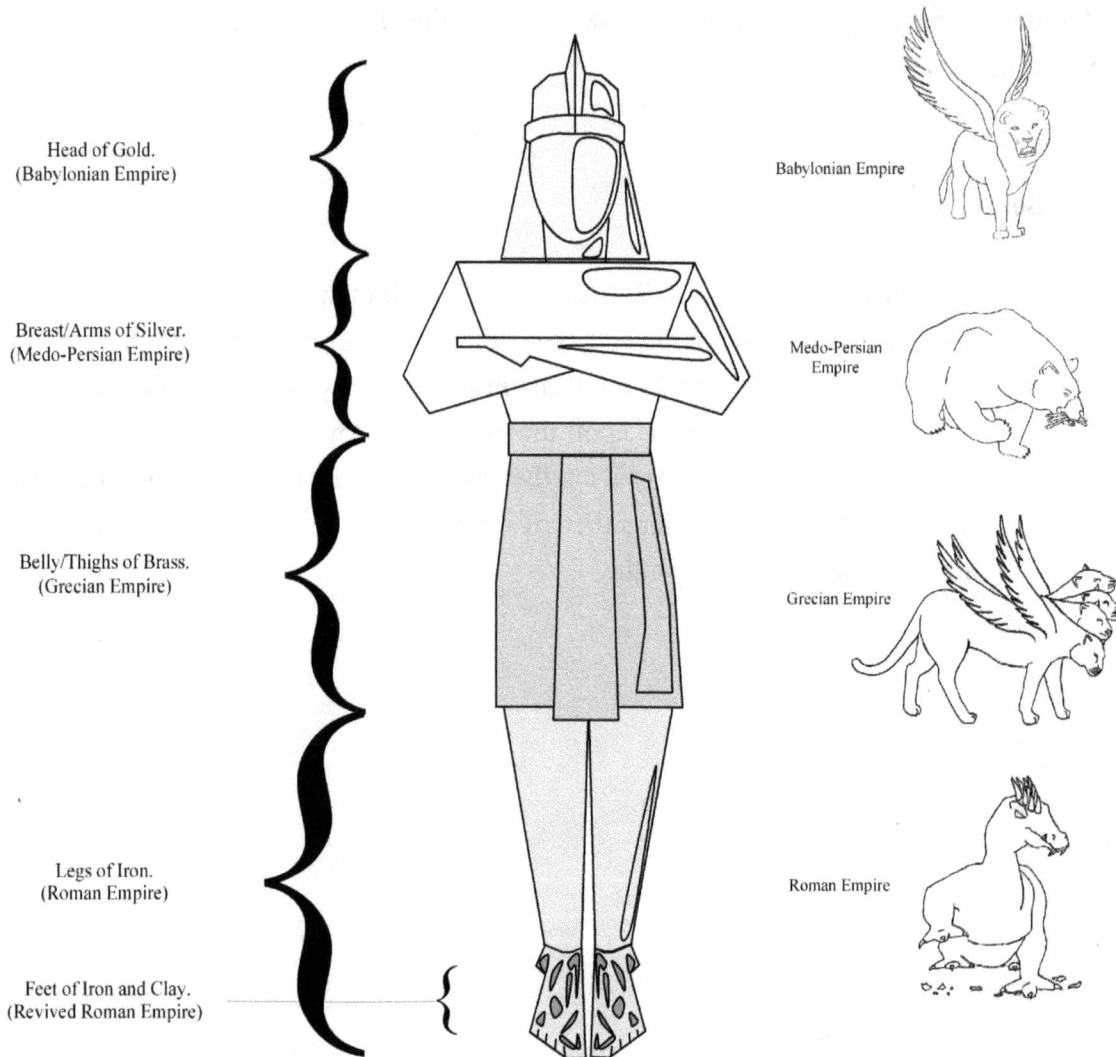

Head of Gold.
(Babylonian Empire)

Breast/Arms of Silver.
(Medo-Persian Empire)

Belly/Thighs of Brass.
(Grecian Empire)

Legs of Iron.
(Roman Empire)

Feet of Iron and Clay.
(Revived Roman Empire)

Babylonian Empire

Medo-Persian Empire

Grecian Empire

Roman Empire

feet as a man, and a man's heart was given to it. [5]And behold another beast, a second, like to a bear, and it raised up itself on one side, and *it had* three ribs in the mouth of it between the teeth of it: and they said thus unto it, Arise, devour much flesh. [6]After this I beheld, and lo another, like a leopard, which had upon the back of it four wings of a fowl; the beast had also four heads; and dominion was given to it. [7]After this I saw in the night visions, and behold a fourth beast, dreadful and terrible, and strong exceedingly; and it had great iron teeth: it devoured and brake in pieces, and stamped the residue with the feet of it: and it *was* diverse from all the beasts that *were* before it; and it had ten horns. [8]I considered the horns, and, behold, there came up among them another little horn, before whom there were three of the first horns plucked up by the roots: and, behold, in this horn *were* eyes like the eyes of man, and a mouth speaking great things.

Dan 7:9 I beheld till the thrones were cast down, and the Ancient of days did sit, whose garment *was* white as snow, and the hair of his head like the pure wool: his throne *was like* the fiery flame, *and* his wheels *as* burning fire. [10]A fiery stream issued and came forth from before him: thousand thousands ministered unto him, and ten thousand times ten thousand stood before him: the judgment was set, and the books were opened. [11]I beheld then because of the voice of the great words which the horn spake: I beheld *even* till the beast was slain, and his body destroyed, and given to the burning flame. [12]As concerning the rest of the beasts, they had their dominion taken away: yet their lives were prolonged for a season and time. [13]I saw in the night visions, and, behold, *one* like the Son of man came with the clouds of heaven, and came to the Ancient of days, and they brought him near before him. [14]And there was given him dominion, and glory, and a kingdom, that all people, nations, and languages, should serve him: his dominion *is* an everlasting dominion, which shall not pass away, and his kingdom *that* which shall not be destroyed.

The interpretation…

Dan 7:15 I Daniel was grieved in my spirit in the midst of *my* body, and the visions of my head troubled me. [16]I came near unto one of them that stood by, and asked him the truth of all this. So he told me, and made me know the interpretation of the things. [17]These great beasts, which are four, *are* four kings, *which* shall arise out of the earth. [18]But the saints of the most High shall take the kingdom, and possess the kingdom for ever, even for ever and ever. [19]Then I would know the truth of the fourth beast, which was diverse from all the others, exceeding dreadful, whose teeth *were of* iron, and his nails *of* brass; *which* devoured, brake in pieces, and stamped the residue with his feet; [20]And of the ten horns that *were* in his head, and *of* the other which came up, and before whom three fell; even *of* that horn that had eyes, and a mouth that spake very great things, whose look *was* more stout than his fellows. [21]I beheld, and the same horn made war with the

190

saints, and prevailed against them; ²²Until the Ancient of days came, and judgment was given to the saints of the most High; and the time came that the saints possessed the kingdom. ²³Thus he said, The fourth beast shall be the fourth kingdom upon earth, which shall be diverse from all kingdoms, and shall devour the whole earth, and shall tread it down, and break it in pieces. ²⁴And the ten horns out of this kingdom *are* ten kings *that* shall arise: and another shall rise after them; and he shall be diverse from the first, and he shall subdue three kings. ²⁵And he shall speak *great* words against the most High, and shall wear out the saints of the most High, and think to change times and laws: and they shall be given into his hand until a time and times and the dividing of time. ²⁶But the judgment shall sit, and they shall take away his dominion, to consume and to destroy *it* unto the end. ²⁷And the kingdom and dominion, and the greatness of the kingdom under the whole heaven, shall be given to the people of the saints of the most High, whose kingdom *is* an everlasting kingdom, and all dominions shall serve and obey him. ²⁸Hitherto *is* the end of the matter. As for me Daniel, my cogitations much troubled me, and my countenance changed in me: but I kept the matter in my heart.

There is obviously a direct correlation between the dream of Nebuchadnezzar (the statue) and the four beasts in Daniel's dream. Daniel lived to see the dominance of the first three empires but he was most curious about the fourth empire.

If we look at other prophetic texts for similar symbolism we start to see an underlying pattern. We see how the Book of Revelation and the Book of Daniel compliment each other demonstrating the perfect unity of scripture.

In the Book of Revelation we see a seven headed, ten horned beast rising out of the sea.

> Rev 13: ¹And I stood upon the sand of the sea, and saw a beast rise up out of the sea, having seven heads and ten horns, and upon his horns ten crowns, and upon his heads the name of blasphemy.
>
> ²And the beast which I saw was like unto a leopard, and his feet were as *the feet* of a bear, and his mouth as the mouth of a lion: and the dragon gave him his power, and his seat, and great authority.

The beast described in Revelation 13 has seven heads and ten horns. Let's compare this to what Daniel described in chapter 7.

> The first beast had 1 head (the head of a Lion).
> The second beast had 1 head (the head of a Bear).
> The third beast had 4 heads (four heads of a Leopard)
> The fourth beast had 1 head (the head of a diverse kind of beast)

There were a total of seven heads in Daniel's vision in chapter 7.

The fourth beast was the only beast that had horns. It had 10 horns. As we can see, the vision Daniel described in chapter 7 described seven heads and 10 horns similar to what we read about in Revelation chapter 13.

Furthermore, the characteristics of the beast described in Revelation chapter 13 are remarkably similar to the beasts in Daniel's vision.

> Rev 13: 2And the beast which I saw was like unto a leopard, and his feet were as *the feet* of a bear, and his mouth as the mouth of a lion: and the dragon gave him his power, and his seat, and great authority.

Babylonian Empire

Medo-Persian Empire

Grecian Empire

Roman Empire

The Scarlet Colored
Composite Beast of
Revelation

It is as if the beasts of Daniel's vision came together to form a single composite beast. I think this has profound prophetic significance. This merging seems to indicate these same empires will come together at the end of the age to form a combined super empire. It is unclear whether it will come in the form of the United Nations, the European Union or some other international organization but it will consist of the nations previously described in Daniel Chapter 7.

Daniel had one more vision which provides additional information regarding how history would unfold.

The vision of the Ram and the He goat:

In chapter 8 Daniel has a dream about a ram and a he goat.

^{Dan 8:1}In the third year of the reign of king Belshazzar a vision appeared unto me, *even unto* me Daniel, after that which appeared unto me at the first. ²And I saw in a vision; and it came to pass, when I saw, that I *was* at Shushan *in* the palace, which *is* in the province of Elam; and I saw in a vision, and I was by the river of Ulai. ³Then I lifted up mine eyes, and saw, and, behold, there stood before the river a ram which had *two* horns: and the *two* horns *were* high; but one *was* higher than the other, and the higher came up last. ⁴I saw the ram pushing westward, and northward, and southward; so that no beasts might stand before him, neither *was there any* that could deliver out of his hand; but he did according to his will, and became great. ⁵And as I was considering, behold, an he goat came from the west on the face of the whole earth, and touched not the ground: and the goat *had* a notable horn between his eyes. ⁶And he came to the ram that had *two* horns, which I had seen standing before the river, and ran unto him in the fury of his power. ⁷And I saw him come close unto the ram, and he was moved with choler against him, and smote the ram, and brake his two horns: and there was no power in the ram to stand before him, but he cast him down to the ground, and stamped upon him: and there was none that could deliver the ram out of his hand. ⁸Therefore the he goat waxed very great: and when he was strong, the great horn was broken; and for it came up four notable ones toward the four winds of heaven. ⁹And out of one of them came forth a little horn, which waxed exceeding great, toward the south, and toward the east, and toward the pleasant *land*. ¹⁰And it waxed great, *even* to the host of heaven; and it cast down *some* of the host and of the stars to the ground, and stamped upon them. ¹¹Yea, he magnified *himself* even to the prince of the host, and by him the daily *sacrifice* was taken away, and the place of his sanctuary was cast down. ¹²And an host was given *him* against the daily *sacrifice* by reason of transgression, and it cast down the truth to the ground; and it practised, and prospered.

194

The interpretation:

> ^{Dan 8:} ¹⁶And I heard a man's voice between *the banks of* Ulai, which called, and said, Gabriel, make this *man* to understand the vision. ¹⁷So he came near where I stood: and when he came, I was afraid, and fell upon my face: but he said unto me, Understand, O son of man: for at the time of the end *shall be* the vision. ¹⁸Now as he was speaking with me, I was in a deep sleep on my face toward the ground: but he touched me, and set me upright. ¹⁹And he said, Behold, I will make thee know what shall be in the last end of the indignation: for at the time appointed the end *shall be.* ²⁰The ram which thou sawest having *two* horns *are* the kings of Media and Persia. ²¹And the rough goat *is* the king of Grecia: and the great horn that *is* between his eyes *is* the first king. ²²Now that being broken, whereas four stood up for it, four kingdoms shall stand up out of the nation, but not in his power. ²³And in the latter time of their kingdom, when the transgressors are come to the full, a king of fierce countenance, and understanding dark sentences, shall stand up. ²⁴And his power shall be mighty, but not by his own power: and he shall destroy wonderfully, and shall prosper, and practise, and shall destroy the mighty and the holy people. ²⁵And through his policy also he shall cause craft to prosper in his hand; and he shall magnify *himself* in his heart, and by peace shall destroy many: he shall also stand up against the Prince of princes; but he shall be broken without hand. ²⁶And the vision of the evening and the morning which was told *is* true: wherefore shut thou up the vision; for it *shall be* for many days. ²⁷And I Daniel fainted, and was sick *certain* days; afterward I rose up, and did the king's business; and I was astonished at the vision, but none understood *it.*

The vision of the Ram and the He Goat is symbolic of the conflict between the Medo-Persian Empire and the Greco-Roman Empires. The Medes and the Persians are symbolized by the two horns on the Ram. The Greeks were symbolized by the Goat with a singular great horn. The great horn was the first king of the Greeks (Alexander the Great). When Alexander the Great was killed his kingdom was divided into four parts. The kings that took his place were Seleucus (King of Asia Minor), Ptolemy (King of Egypt), Lysimachus (King of Thrace) and Cassander (King of Macedonia). When considering the previous vision of Daniel, the four divisions of Alexander's empire remind us of the four headed leopard with the four wings of a foul.

The little horn would arise from one of these kings but he wouldn't arise until the time of the end. This indicates the goat spans the time period of both the Greeks and the Romans. It is unclear why this king is called the "little" horn. It could be because his kingdom is small or maybe he will be a notably short individual.

Daniel's Seventy Weeks

In chapter 9 Daniel desired understanding from the Lord. It's interesting to consider how he approached God for understanding.

By prayer, supplications, fasting, sackcloth and ashes.

> Dan 9: 3And I set my face unto the Lord God, to seek by prayer and supplications, with fasting, and sackcloth, and ashes:

By confessing his sins and the sins of his people.

> Dan 9: 4And I prayed unto the LORD my God, and made my confession, and said, O Lord, the great and dreadful God, keeping the covenant and mercy to them that love him, and to them that keep his commandments;
>
> 5We have sinned, and have committed iniquity, and have done wickedly, and have rebelled, even by departing from thy precepts and from thy judgments:
>
> 6Neither have we hearkened unto thy servants the prophets, which spake in thy name to our kings, our princes, and our fathers, and to all the people of the land.

By giving Praise.

> Dan 9: 9To the Lord our God *belong* mercies and forgivenesses, though we have rebelled against him;

By remembering the works God performed in the past.

> Dan 9: [15]And now, O Lord our God, that hast brought thy people forth out of the land of Egypt with a mighty hand, and hast gotten thee renown, as at this day; we have sinned, we have done wickedly.

The type of worship Daniel gave was not superficial, quick or easy. When he sought God he did so with determination and patience. He honored God for his works and for his merciful nature. He exalted God and did not try to exalt himself. He confessed his sins and the sins of his people. Daniel's sincere humility before God caused God to love him greatly and to answer his prayers for understanding.

> Dan 9: [21]Yea, whiles I *was* speaking in prayer, even the man Gabriel, whom I had seen in the vision at the beginning, being caused to fly swiftly, touched me about the time of the evening oblation.
>
> [22]And he informed *me,* and talked with me, and said, O Daniel, I am now come forth to give thee skill and understanding.
>
> [23]At the beginning of thy supplications the commandment came forth, and I am come to shew *thee;* for thou *art* greatly beloved: therefore understand the matter, and consider the vision.

We can learn a lot from the way Daniel prayed but it is not a "secret formula" for getting your prayers answered. It worked for Daniel because he was genuine. He desired to understand the visions God gave him. His prayers were not selfish attempts to manipulate God as many of our prayers are. His prayers had the right motivations.

Too often we try to convince God to do our will when we should be seeking to do his will. This is a key spiritual concept.

The angel Gabriel came to give Daniel understanding regarding his visions. From this point on, no further symbolism will be used. Gabriel will tell Daniel exactly what will happen in the future.

> Dan 9: 24Seventy weeks are determined upon thy people and upon thy holy city, to finish the transgression, and to make an end of sins, and to make reconciliation for iniquity, and to bring in everlasting righteousness, and to seal up the vision and prophecy, and to anoint the most Holy.

Seventy weeks are seventy periods of seven. 70 times 7 = 490 years.

> Dan 9: 25Know therefore and understand, *that* from the going forth of the commandment to restore and to build Jerusalem unto the Messiah the Prince *shall be* seven weeks, and threescore and two weeks: the street shall be built again, and the wall, even in troublous times.

The seventy weeks are not necessarily consecutive because they are divided into groups of 7 weeks and 62 weeks with 1 week remaining. (A week is thought to be a period of seven years.)

Another truth is revealed when comparing the Book of Daniel and Revelation. The truth Daniel revealed was there were spiritual forces at work behind these great empires.

> Dan 10: 5Then I lifted up mine eyes, and looked, and behold a certain man clothed in linen, whose loins *were* girded with fine gold of Uphaz:

> Dan 10: 12Then said he unto me, Fear not, Daniel: for from the first day that thou didst set thine heart to understand, and to chasten thyself before thy God, thy words were heard, and I am come for thy words.

> 13But the prince of the kingdom of Persia withstood me one and twenty days: but, lo, Michael, one of the chief princes, came to help me; and I remained there with the kings of Persia.

[14]Now I am come to make thee understand what shall befall thy people in the latter days: for yet the vision *is* for *many* days.

The "man" clothed in linen was most likely an angel. He told Daniel he had tried to come to him immediately when Daniel had set his heart to understand the vision, but the "Prince of Persia" withstood him. He was unable to get past the Prince of Persia until Michael came to help him. In Daniel chapter 12, Michael is called "the great prince which standeth for the children of thy people". Jude identifies Michael as an archangel and in Revelation chapter 12 he is shown to be a military leader of the angels.

The Prince of Persia was the demonic power which controlled the Persian Empire. He was a powerful spiritual being who could only be restrained by the strength of an Archangel. After the angel delivered his message to Daniel he said he would have to return and fight with the Prince of Persia and then the Prince of Grecia would come.

Dan 10: [20]Then said he, Knowest thou wherefore I come unto thee? and now will I return to fight with the prince of Persia: and when I am gone forth, lo, the prince of Grecia shall come.

[21]But I will shew thee that which is noted in the scripture of truth: and *there is* none that holdeth with me in these things, but Michael your prince.

The Prince of Grecia would be another spiritual power who would be the ultimate power behind the Grecian Empire.

Just as these empires were controlled by demonic spiritual forces, God's people have godly spiritual forces working in their behalf.

Another example of the spiritual forces behind the natural governments is seen in the Book of Revelation. We have already talked about the seven headed, ten horned beast in Revelation which corresponded to Daniel's vision of the four beasts. These four empires will unite at the end of the age and the spiritual forces controlling these empires will also unite. The Book of Revelation shows us a seven headed, ten horned dragon which is the spiritual power behind the combined empires at the end of the age.

7 Headed,

10 Horned Dragon.

(The spiritual principalities behind
the composite beast of Revelation.)

Rev 12: 3 And there appeared another wonder in heaven; and behold a great red dragon, having seven heads and ten horns, and seven crowns upon his heads.

Rev 12: 7 And there was war in heaven: Michael and his angels fought against the dragon; and the dragon fought and his angels,

Rev 12: 9 And the great dragon was cast out, that old serpent, called the Devil, and Satan, which deceiveth the whole world: he was cast out into the earth, and his angels were cast out with him.

Rev 13:1 And I stood upon the sand of the sea, and saw a beast rise up out of the sea, having seven heads and ten horns, and upon his horns ten crowns, and upon his heads the name of blasphemy.

2And the beast which I saw was like unto a leopard, and his feet were as *the feet* of a bear, and his mouth as the mouth of a lion: and the dragon gave him his power, and his seat, and great authority.

The dragon was clearly identified as Satan and his angels. Notice how the dragon is cast down to Earth. Then we see the seven headed, ten horned beast rising up out of the sea immediately after the dragon is cast down. The demonic spiritual forces will give rise to this final great government.

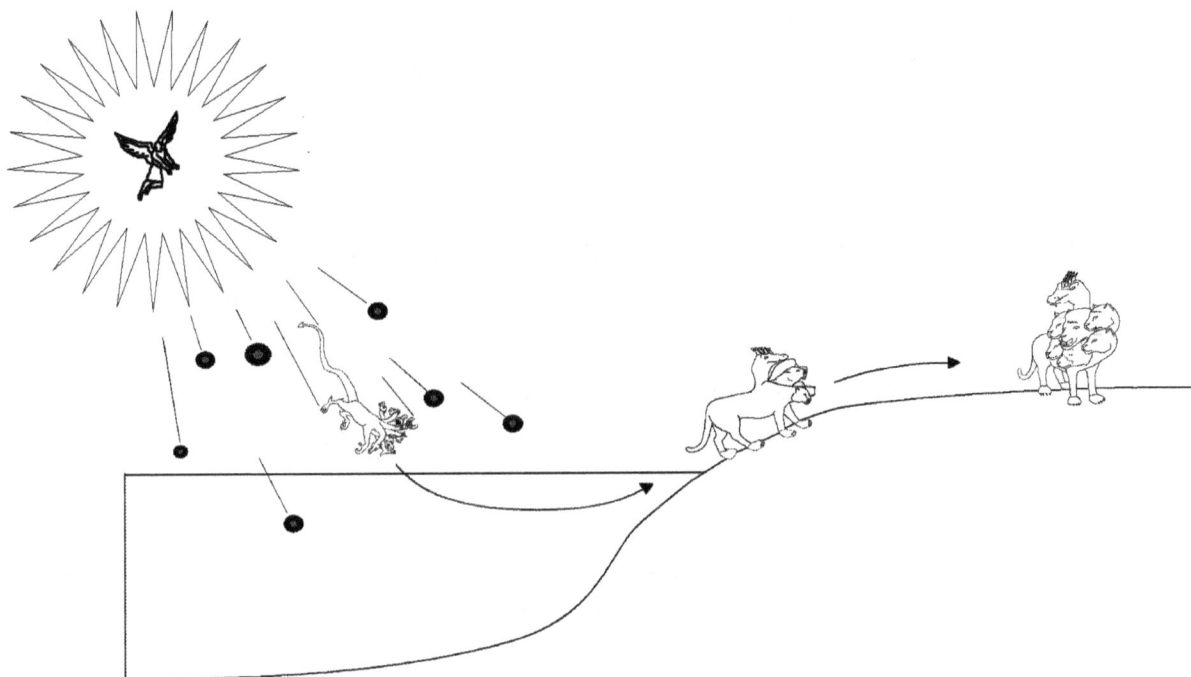

Rev 13:1 And I stood upon the sand of the sea, and saw a beast rise up out of the sea, having seven heads and ten horns, and upon his horns ten crowns, and upon his heads the name of blasphemy.

2 And the beast which I saw was like unto a leopard, and his feet were as *the feet* of a bear, and his mouth as the mouth of a lion: and the dragon gave him his power, and his seat, and great authority.

3 And I saw one of his heads as it were wounded to death; and his deadly wound was healed: and all the world wondered after the beast.

4And they worshipped the dragon which gave power unto the beast: and they worshipped the beast, saying, Who *is* like unto the beast? who is able to make war with him?

5And there was given unto him a mouth speaking great things and blasphemies; and power was given unto him to continue forty *and* two months.

6And he opened his mouth in blasphemy against God, to blaspheme his name, and his tabernacle, and them that dwell in heaven.

7And it was given unto him to make war with the saints, and to overcome them: and power was given him over all kindreds, and tongues, and nations.

8And all that dwell upon the earth shall worship him, whose names are not written in the book of life of the Lamb slain from the foundation of the world.

There is no doubt John the revelator and Daniel are talking about the same individual. The little horn will be empowered by the dragon, Satan.

Dan 7: 24And the ten horns out of this kingdom *are* ten kings *that* shall arise: and another shall rise after them; and he shall be diverse from the first, and he shall subdue three kings.

25And he shall speak *great* words against the most High, and shall wear out the saints of the most High, and think to change times and laws: and they shall be given into his hand until a time and times and the dividing of time.

Chapter 11, in the Book of Daniel, gives detailed descriptions of the kings described in the earlier visions. The last king described would be the one known as the little horn. He is said to be a vial person who obtains power through flatteries. He will take the place of a person who is described as a raiser of taxes.

> Dan 11: 20Then shall stand up in his estate a raiser of taxes *in* the glory of the kingdom: but within few days he shall be destroyed, neither in anger, nor in battle.

The ruler prior to the little horn was destroyed neither in anger, nor in battle. It is possible the rule of this "raiser of taxes" will be destroyed through an election.

> Dan 11: 21And in his estate shall stand up a vile person, to whom they shall not give the honour of the kingdom: but he shall come in peaceably, and obtain the kingdom by flatteries.

The little horn comes in peaceably and obtains the kingdom by flatteries. This little horn has all of the characteristics we have come to expect from a politician.

> Dan 11: 23And after the league *made* with him he shall work deceitfully: for he shall come up, and shall become strong with a small people.

> 24He shall enter peaceably even upon the fattest places of the province; and he shall do *that* which his fathers have not done, nor his fathers' fathers; he shall scatter among them the prey, and spoil, and riches: *yea,* and he shall forecast his devices against the strong holds, even for a time.

He will come against the king of the south but his plans will fail.

> Dan 11: 25And he shall stir up his power and his courage against the king of the south with a great army; and the king of the south shall be stirred up to battle with a very great and mighty army; but he shall not stand: for they shall forecast devices against him.

²⁶Yea, they that feed of the portion of his meat shall destroy him, and his army shall overflow: and many shall fall down slain.

A treaty will be agreed to by these two lying kings.

Dan 11: ²⁷And both these kings' hearts *shall be* to do mischief, and they shall speak lies at one table; but it shall not prosper: for yet the end *shall be* at the time appointed.

The little horn will be against the holy covenant.

Dan 11: ²⁸Then shall he return into his land with great riches; and his heart *shall be* against the holy covenant; and he shall do *exploits,* and return to his own land.

Dan 11: ³⁰For the ships of Chittim shall come against him: therefore he shall be grieved, and return, and have indignation against the holy covenant: so shall he do; he shall even return, and have intelligence with them that forsake the holy covenant.

What holy covenant was the little horn against? What holy covenant would he forsake? Could the covenant have been made when the two kings were speaking lies to one another in verse 27? If so, then why would an agreement between two lying men be considered holy? Could it be this agreement would allow the Jews to rebuild their temple and resume offering sacrifices? The next verse supports this idea.

Dan 11: ³¹And arms shall stand on his part, and they shall pollute the sanctuary of strength, and shall take away the daily *sacrifice,* and they shall place the abomination that maketh desolate.

This verse puts the message Gabriel brought to Daniel earlier in context.

Dan 9: ²⁷And he shall confirm the covenant with many for one week: and in the midst of the week he shall cause the overspreading of abominations he shall make *it* desolate, even until the consummation, and that determined shall be poured upon the desolate.

He shall confirm the covenant for one week (7 years) but in the middle of the week he will take away the daily sacrifice and replace it with an abomination.

He will persecute the godly people

Dan 11: ³²And such as do wickedly against the covenant shall he corrupt by flatteries: but the people that do know their God shall be strong, and do *exploits.*

³³And they that understand among the people shall instruct many: yet they shall fall by the sword, and by flame, by captivity, and by spoil, *many* days.

³⁴Now when they shall fall, they shall be holpen with a little help: but many shall cleave to them with flatteries.

³⁵And *some* of them of understanding shall fall, to try them, and to purge, and to make *them* white, *even* to the time of the end: because *it is* yet for a time appointed.

The Book of Revelation has a very similar passage to Dan 11: 35.

Rev 6: ⁹And when he had opened the fifth seal, I saw under the altar the souls of them that were slain for the word of God, and for the testimony which they held:

¹⁰And they cried with a loud voice, saying, How long, O Lord, holy and true, dost thou not judge and avenge our blood on them that dwell on the earth?

¹¹And white robes were given unto every one of them; and it was said unto them, that they should rest yet for a little season, until their fellowservants also and their brethren, that should be killed as they *were,* should be fulfilled.

The little horn will exalt himself above all other things and he will speak against the one true God.

> Dan 11: 36And the king shall do according to his will; and he shall exalt himself, and magnify himself above every god, and shall speak marvellous things against the God of gods, and shall prosper till the indignation be accomplished: for that that is determined shall be done.

He will not regard the God of his fathers but he will gain power by honoring another god.

> Dan 11: 37Neither shall he regard the God of his fathers, nor the desire of women, nor regard any god: for he shall magnify himself above all.
>
> 38But in his estate shall he honour the God of forces: and a god whom his fathers knew not shall he honour with gold, and silver, and with precious stones, and pleasant things.
>
> 39Thus shall he do in the most strong holds with a strange god, whom he shall acknowledge *and* increase with glory: and he shall cause them to rule over many, and shall divide the land for gain.

He was able to make a holy covenant that allowed the Jews resume sacrifices but since he turns his back on the "God of his fathers", it is reasonable to assume he will have a Jewish or Christian heritage.

He will honor the god of forces which his fathers knew not. He will acknowledge and increase the glory of a strange god.

I suspect the strange god he will give glory to will be Allah. This evil little horn will need to make alliances with the Moslem nations around Israel in order to be allowed to rebuild the temple on Mount Moriah. His glorification of this strange god along with his great political power will probably cause the Moslems to accept him as their Mahdi (Messiah). When he betrays Israel the land will be divided for gain. It is curious to note that Europe and America have become more Moslem in recent years due to massive Islamic immigration.

War will follow the little horn even until the end.

> Dan 11: 40And at the time of the end shall the king of the south push at him: and the king of the north shall come against him like a whirlwind, with chariots, and with horsemen, and with many ships; and he shall enter into the countries, and shall overflow and pass over.
>
> 41He shall enter also into the glorious land, and many *countries* shall be overthrown: but these shall escape out of his hand, *even* Edom, and Moab, and the chief of the children of Ammon.
>
> 42He shall stretch forth his hand also upon the countries: and the land of Egypt shall not escape.
>
> 43But he shall have power over the treasures of gold and of silver, and over all the precious things of Egypt: and the Libyans and the Ethiopians *shall be* at his steps.
>
> 44But tidings out of the east and out of the north shall trouble him: therefore he shall go forth with great fury to destroy, and utterly to make away many.
>
> 45And he shall plant the tabernacles of his palace between the seas in the glorious holy mountain; yet he shall come to his end, and none shall help him.

Verses 42 and 43 mention the little horn's conquest of Egypt. Isaiah 19 goes into great detail about this final conquest of Egypt.

> Is 19: 4 And the Egyptians will I give over into the hand of a cruel lord; and a fierce king shall rule over them, saith the Lord, the LORD of hosts.

We will discuss more about this later.

Chapter 12 is a continuation of chapter 11. This is where the people of God are delivered.

> ^{Dan 12: 1} And at that time shall Michael stand up, the great prince which standeth for the children of thy people: and there shall be a time of trouble, such as never was since there was a nation *even* to that same time: and at that time thy people shall be delivered, every one that shall be found written in the book.

The phrase "time of trouble, such as never was" is reminiscent of the term "great tribulation" used in the New Testament.

> ^{Mat 24: 21} For then shall be great tribulation, such as was not since the beginning of the world to this time, no, nor ever shall be.

The next verse sounds suspiciously like the Resurrection of the dead (rapture) but is it?

> ^{Dan 12: 2} And many of them that sleep in the dust of the earth shall awake, some to everlasting life, and some to shame *and* everlasting contempt.

> ³And they that be wise shall shine as the brightness of the firmament; and they that turn many to righteousness as the stars for ever and ever.

> ^{Rev 20: 4} And I saw thrones, and they sat upon them, and judgment was given unto them: and *I saw* the souls of them that were beheaded for the witness of Jesus, and for the word of God, and which had not worshipped the beast, neither his image, neither had received *his* mark upon their foreheads, or in their hands; and they lived and reigned with Christ a thousand years.

> ⁵But the rest of the dead lived not again until the thousand years were finished. This *is* the first resurrection.

> ^{Rev 20: 7}And when the thousand years are expired, Satan shall be loosed out of his prison,

Rev 20: 13And the sea gave up the dead which were in it; and death and hell delivered up the dead which were in them: and they were judged every man according to their works.

14And death and hell were cast into the lake of fire. This is the second death.

Daniel 12:2 appears to cover both resurrections, the first which is the rapture and the second which is the Great White Throne judgment described in the book of Revelation.

Daniel was told this prophecy was for the time of the end.

Dan 12: 4 But thou, O Daniel, shut up the words, and seal the book, *even* to the time of the end: many shall run to and fro, and knowledge shall be increased.

Then Daniel heard two men talking about the timeframe for these events.

Dan 12: 5Then I Daniel looked, and, behold, there stood other two, the one on this side of the bank of the river, and the other on that side of the bank of the river.

6And *one* said to the man clothed in linen, which *was* upon the waters of the river, How long *shall it be to* the end of these wonders?

7And I heard the man clothed in linen, which *was* upon the waters of the river, when he held up his right hand and his left hand unto heaven, and sware by him that liveth for ever that *it shall be* for a time, times, and an half; and when he shall have accomplished to scatter the power of the holy people, all these *things* shall be finished.

The wonders will last three and a half years. The end of these wonders (Dan 12:6) will obviously be at the end of the second half of the 7 year agreement because the sacrifices were being offered daily for the first three and a half years.

> Dan 12: 11 And from the time *that* the daily *sacrifice* shall be taken away, and the abomination that maketh desolate set up, *there shall be* a thousand two hundred and ninety days.
>
> 12Blessed *is* he that waiteth, and cometh to the thousand three hundred and five and thirty days.
>
> 13But go thou thy way till the end *be:* for thou shalt rest, and stand in thy lot at the end of the days.

The wording in Dan 12:11 is strange. It appears as if the abomination of desolation is set up 1290 days after the daily sacrifices are taken away. This is not likely because it would put the abomination of desolation outside of the seven year window Daniel told us about. Therefore, Daniel 12:11 must mean the abomination will take place 1290 days after the daily sacrifices begin. This is consistent with Daniel 9:27

> Dan 9: 27And he shall confirm the covenant with many for one week: **and in the midst of the week he shall cause the sacrifice and the oblation to cease**, and for the overspreading of abominations he shall make *it* desolate, even until the consummation, and that determined shall be poured upon the desolate.

This gives us a starting point for the prophetic time clock. Daniel's 70th week (also known as the 7 year tribulation period) will begin when the seven year covenant is renewed and shortly after that, Israel will begin offering their daily sacrifices to God.

Dan 12:12 says, blessed is he who comes to the 1335th day but it doesn't say what will happen then. Could this be when the rapture occurs? Does this go against what Jesus said concerning the timing of the rapture?

> Mark 13:32 But of that day and *that* hour knoweth no man, no, not the angels which are in heaven, neither the Son, but the Father.
>
> 33Take ye heed, watch and pray: for ye know not when the time is.

There is still uncertainty about what will happen on the 1335th day. Even if this is telling us when the rapture will occur, we still can't put an exact time on it because we don't know when prophetic clock will start ticking for those last seven years in Daniel's prophecy. Notice that Jesus' statement in Mark 13:32 was in the present tense. It didn't say we will never know when the day or the hour would come. I guess if you want to be very technical about it, there are 24 time zones on this planet, so the day and hour of Jesus' return would depend on where you are located on the planet. Nevertheless, if the 1335th day rapture theory is correct, once the daily sacrifices resume on the temple mount, we should be able to narrow down the timing of Jesus' return to within a day or so. Ultimately, we won't know if the 1335th day rapture theory is correct until the rapture actually occurs so, in the end, Mark 13:32 will remain true until the rapture occurs.

In later chapters we will show conclusively that the rapture will not happen at the beginning of the seven year tribulation. This is contrary to what most of the popular Christian authors say. The 1335th day is a reasonable candidate for the rapture.

On the next page is a diagram where I try to fit all of the time frames Daniel gives into one consistent timeline. The timeline may or may not be correct. There is much speculation involved, but I have taken every effort to ensure it is not contrary to the scriptures. Ultimately, we will only be able to judge its correctness in retrospect. The same holds true for all of the timelines in this book.

Daniel's Timeline

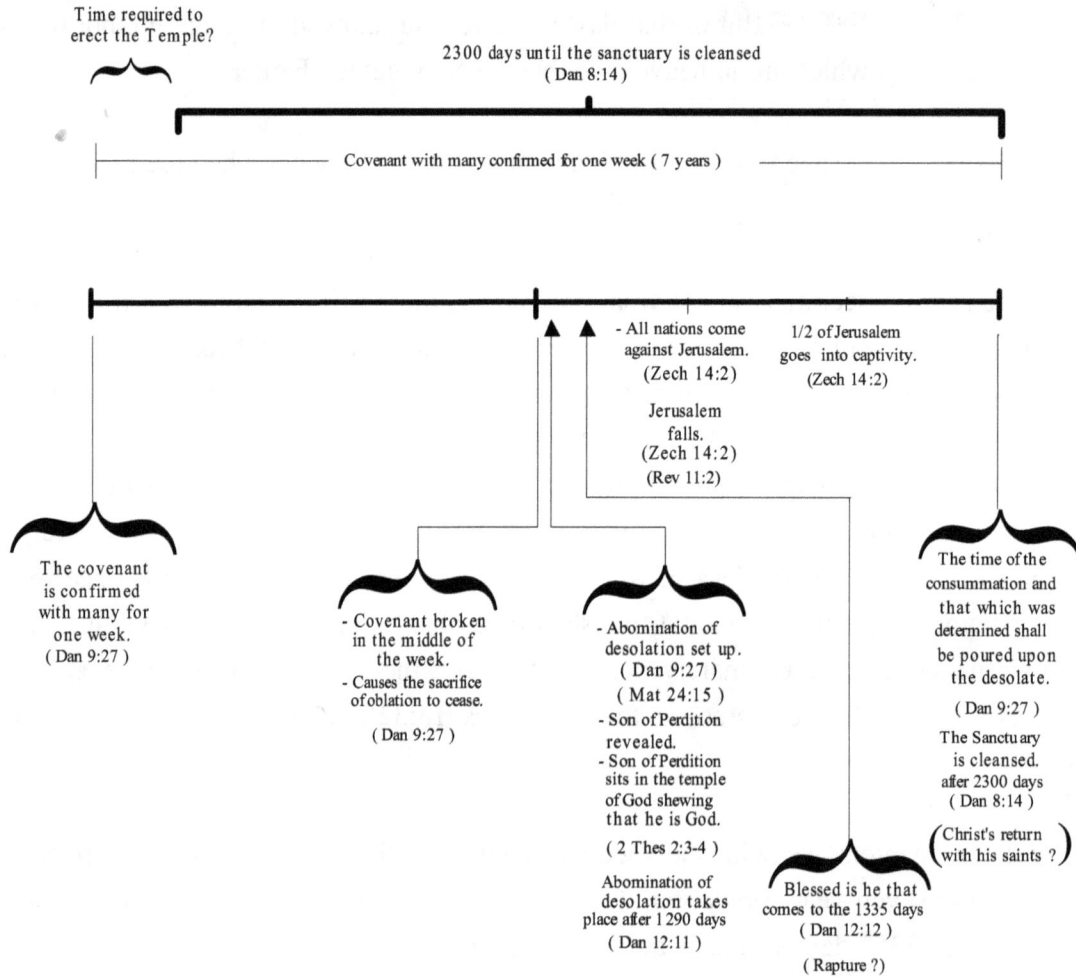

Time required to
erect the Temple?

2300 days until the sanctuary is cleansed
(Dan 8:14)

Covenant with many confirmed for one week (7 years)

- All nations come
against Jerusalem.
(Zech 14:2)

1/2 of Jerusalem
goes into captivity.
(Zech 14:2)

Jerusalem
falls.
(Zech 14:2)
(Rev 11:2)

The covenant
is confirmed
with many for
one week.
(Dan 9:27)

- Covenant broken
in the middle of
the week.
- Causes the sacrifice
of oblation to cease.

(Dan 9:27)

- Abomination of
desolation set up.
(Dan 9:27)
(Mat 24:15)
- Son of Perdition
revealed.
- Son of Perdition
sits in the temple
of God shewing
that he is God.

(2 Thes 2:3-4)

Abomination of
desolation takes
place after 1290 days
(Dan 12:11)

The time of the
consummation and
that which was
determined shall
be poured upon
the desolate.

(Dan 9:27)

The Sanctuary
is cleansed.
after 2300 days
(Dan 8:14)

Christ's return
with his saints ?

Blessed is he that
comes to the 1335 days
(Dan 12:12)

(Rapture ?)

The Book of Daniel gives the panorama of history and prophecy in a very organized and thorough manner. It is the foundation for our understanding of prophecy. The Book of Revelation has a narrower focus than the Book of Daniel but both books fit together like clockwork. We will see in later chapters how the Olivet discourse and the prophecies of various Old Testament prophets fit in to the overall picture. There is truly a unity to the scriptures. They are each part of a greater whole.

Chapter Fifteen

Prophecy:

The Book of Revelation

The Book of Daniel is a combination of history and prophecy. The Book of Revelation, on the other hand, is virtually all prophecy. Like Daniel, Revelation is highly organized. It focuses on the same timeframe as Daniel's 70th week. The Book of Revelation is, for the most part, sequential. Our previous study of Daniel will help us make sense of the symbolism and the imagery used in the Book of Revelation.

The first verse in Revelation tells us what the purpose of the book is.

> Rev 1: 1 The Revelation of Jesus Christ, which God gave unto him, to shew unto his servants things which must shortly come to pass; and he sent and signified *it* by his angel unto his servant John:.

The revelation was given to Jesus by God so Jesus could show his servants what would shortly come to pass. Jesus shared this revelation with John through the use of an angel.

> Rev 1: 3 Blessed *is* he that readeth, and they that hear the words of this prophecy, and keep those things which are written therein: for the time *is* at hand.

There are blessings for those who read, hear (understand), and keep the things written in this book.

> Rev 1: 4John to the seven churches which are in Asia: Grace *be* unto you, and peace, from him which is, and which was, and which is to come; and from the seven Spirits which are before his throne;

⁵And from Jesus Christ, *who is* the faithful witness, *and* the first begotten of the dead, and the prince of the kings of the earth. Unto him that loved us, and washed us from our sins in his own blood,

⁶And hath made us kings and priests unto God and his Father; to him *be* glory and dominion for ever and ever. Amen.

John reminds the seven churches in Asia of God's eternal nature and the importance of Jesus' sacrifice.

Rev 1: ⁷Behold, he cometh with clouds; and every eye shall see him, and they *also* which pierced him: and all kindreds of the earth shall wail because of him. Even so, Amen.

Jesus coming with clouds is a foreshadowing of the first resurrection (also known as the Rapture) which will occur later in the book. We will see that he does indeed come with clouds.

Rev 1: ⁸I am Alpha and Omega, the beginning and the ending, saith the Lord, which is, and which was, and which is to come, the Almighty.

Jesus is eternal just as God the father is eternal. His existence did not begin with his birth. He has always been.

John 1: ¹In the beginning was the Word, and the Word was with God, and the Word was God.

²The same was in the beginning with God.

³All things were made by him; and without him was not any thing made that was made.

Rev 1: 9I John, who also am your brother, and companion in tribulation, and in the kingdom and patience of Jesus Christ, was in the isle that is called Patmos, for the word of God, and for the testimony of Jesus Christ.

10I was in the Spirit on the Lord's day, and heard behind me **a great voice, as of a trumpet**,

11Saying, I am Alpha and Omega, the first and the last: and, What thou seest, write in a book, and send *it* unto the seven churches which are in Asia; unto Ephesus, and unto Smyrna, and unto Pergamos, and unto Thyatira, and unto Sardis, and unto Philadelphia, and unto Laodicea.

Rev 1:10 as well as Rev 4:1 has been used by many Christians to justify their belief Jesus will return for his people before the "tribulation period" begins. They equate the trumpet in these verses with the trumpet spoken of in 1Cor 15: 52.

Rev 1:10I was in the Spirit on the Lord's day, and heard behind me a great voice, **as of a trumpet**,

Rev 4:1After this I looked, and, behold, a door *was* opened in heaven: and the first voice which I heard *was* **as it were of a trumpet** talking with me; which said, Come up hither, and I will shew thee things which must be hereafter.

1Cor 15:52In a moment, in the twinkling of an eye, **at the last trump**: for the trumpet shall sound, and the dead shall be raised incorruptible, and we shall be changed.

The two verses in the book of Revelation are obviously not describing the same trumpet 1Cor 15:52 is describing. If you read the two verses in Revelation very carefully you will see there is no trumpet sounding but rather a trumpet-like voice is speaking. The trumpet-like voice John heard was speaking to him specifically. It told him to "come up hither" so he could be shown what would happen in the future. To say this "come up hither" is the resurrection of the saints at the end of the age goes far beyond what the verse actually says. Furthermore, the verse in Corinthians says the trumpet that sounds will be the "last trump". The phrase "at the last trump" implies there will be a series of trumpets preceding the last trump. The trumpet-like voice in Rev 4:1 was not associated with a series of trumpets and therefore could not have been the "last trumpet" described in 1Cor 15:52. We will see later in the Book of Revelation the series of trumpets which concludes with the dead rising **at the last trumpet** just as the book of Corinthians described.

We will deal extensively with the first resurrection (also known as the Rapture) later.

Rev 1:12And I turned to see the voice that spake with me. And being turned, I saw seven golden candlesticks;

13And in the midst of the seven candlesticks *one* like unto the Son of man, clothed with a garment down to the foot, and girt about the paps with a golden girdle.

14His head and *his* hairs *were* white like wool, as white as snow; and his eyes *were* as a flame of fire;

15And his feet like unto fine brass, as if they burned in a furnace; and his voice as the sound of many waters.

16And he had in his right hand seven stars: and out of his mouth went a sharp twoedged sword: and his countenance *was* as the sun shineth in his strength.

17And when I saw him, I fell at his feet as dead. And he laid his right hand upon me, saying unto me, Fear not; I am the first and the last:

18I *am* he that liveth, and was dead; and, behold, I am alive for evermore, Amen; and have the keys of hell and of death.

19Write the things which thou hast seen, and the things which are, and the things which shall be hereafter;

20The mystery of the seven stars which thou sawest in my right hand, and the seven golden candlesticks. The seven stars are the angels of the seven churches: and the seven candlesticks which thou sawest are the seven churches.

The seven golden candlesticks should remind us of the seven branched menorah in the Tabernacle of Moses. In fact, the Tabernacle of Moses was a physical representation of God's heavenly Tabernacle. The symbolism is unmistakable. (See Chapter 11 regarding the symbolism of the Tabernacle.)

Chapters 2 and 3 of the book of Revelation are messages to the seven churches in Asia. It has been thought these churches typify the character of the churches throughout history. This theory is intriguing and, if correct, it means the church in the final days will have characteristics similar to the Laodicean church.

> Rev 3:14And unto the angel of the church of the Laodiceans write; These things saith the Amen, the faithful and true witness, the beginning of the creation of God;
>
> 15I know thy works, that thou art neither cold nor hot: I would thou wert cold or hot.
>
> 16So then because thou art lukewarm, and neither cold nor hot, I will spue thee out of my mouth.
>
> 17Because thou sayest, I am rich, and increased with goods, and have need of nothing; and knowest not that thou art wretched, and miserable, and poor, and blind, and naked:
>
> 18I counsel thee to buy of me gold tried in the fire, that thou mayest be rich; and white raiment, that thou mayest be clothed, and *that* the shame of thy nakedness do not appear; and anoint thine eyes with eyesalve, that thou mayest see.

This description seems to pretty accurately describe the church today. At least it describes the church in America.

The church preceding the Laodicean church was the church of Philadelphia. It was highly spoken of by Jesus. A door was opened for them by God. They kept his word and did not deny his name. America was founded as a Christian nation and, for the most part, remained a Christian nation until recent years.

Rev 3:7 And to the angel of the church in Philadelphia write; These things saith he that is holy, he that is true, he that hath the key of David, he that openeth, and no man shutteth; and shutteth, and no man openeth;

8 I know thy works: behold, I have set before thee an open door, and no man can shut it: for thou hast a little strength, and hast kept my word, and hast not denied my name.

9 Behold, I will make them of the synagogue of Satan, which say they are Jews, and are not, but do lie; behold, I will make them to come and worship before thy feet, and to know that I have loved thee.

10 Because thou hast kept the word of my patience, I also will keep thee from the hour of temptation, which shall come upon all the world, to try them that dwell upon the earth.

11 Behold, I come quickly: hold that fast which thou hast, that no man take thy crown.

12 Him that overcometh will I make a pillar in the temple of my God, and he shall go no more out: and I will write upon him the name of my God, and the name of the city of my God, *which is* new Jerusalem, which cometh down out of heaven from my God: and *I will write upon him* my new name.

Jesus promised to keep the church of Philadelphia from the hour of temptation, which shall come upon the entire world, to try them that dwell upon the Earth. This sounds like Jesus is promising to remove them before the tribulation starts. Does this support the idea of a pre-tribulation rapture? Not necessarily.

If the seven churches symbolically represent seven church ages throughout history, it would make sense that the righteous Christians of the Philadelphia church age would die out before the hour of temptation falls on the rich, lukewarm Laodicean Christians. What does the hour of temptation mean? What temptation? The Laodicean church is fixated with money and wealth. What will they be willing to do to keep their money and their goods? How will they be able to buy gold tried in the fire, white raiment and eye salve from God? I suspect they will have to give up their earthly wealth and its security. They will have to avoid the temptation to save themselves and their wealth. They will have to refuse the mark of the beast and be willing to become martyrs for God. (The mark of the beast will be discussed later.)

By not taking the mark of the beast the Laodicean Christians will be forfeiting their wealth. They will lose control of all their possessions. In this way they will be able to purchase gold tried in the fire.

> Pr 13:7There is that maketh himself rich, yet *hath* nothing: *there is* that maketh himself poor, yet *hath* great riches. 8The ransom of a man's life *are* his riches: but the poor heareth not rebuke.

> Mat 19:29And every one that hath forsaken houses, or brethren, or sisters, or father, or mother, or wife, or children, or lands, for my name's sake, shall receive an hundredfold, and shall inherit everlasting life.

To buy white raiment the Laodicean Christians must be faithful even if it means dying as a martyr. Their white raiment will be the white robes of martyrdom.

> Rev 6:9And when he had opened the fifth seal, I saw under the altar the souls of them that were slain for the word of God, and for the testimony which they held:

> 10And they cried with a loud voice, saying, How long, O Lord, holy and true, dost thou not judge and avenge our blood on them that dwell on the earth?

> 11And white robes were given unto every one of them; and it was said unto them, that they should **rest yet for a little season, until their fellowservants also and their brethren, that should be killed as they** *were,* should be fulfilled.

Figure 15-1 is an outline of the Book of Revelation which will attempt to show the sequential nature of the book.

In this outline, the sequential nature of the Book of Revelation is shown by the use of blocks going from top to bottom. One block is followed by another and another. These blocks follow each other sequentially. The exception to this is shown by the use of indented blocks. The indented blocks are used when John deviates from the overall chronology to explain something in greater detail. These types of deviations are known as parenthetical passages. In the Book of Revelation, John tells us what will happen in sequential order but there are times in his narrative when he needs to explain something in greater detail. To do this he pauses the sequence, explains whatever needs explaining, and then returns to the sequence. The best example of this is the parenthetical passages which occur between the sixth trumpet judgment and the seventh trumpet judgment. The trumpet judgments are described in sequence 1 thru 6. There is a chapter and a half between trumpet judgment 6 and trumpet judgment 7. The chapter and a half in between trumpet 6 and 7 gives details about the seven thunders and the two witnesses. John then returns to the chronology right where he left off... at trumpet judgment 7.

When we separate the sequential passages from the parenthetical passages the Book of Revelation suddenly becomes more understandable.

The parenthetical passages tend to make the chronology harder to follow but if we concentrate on the sequential order of the judgments and study the parenthetical passages separately, the chronological nature of the book of Revelation becomes obvious.

Revelation Outline.

John's Greetings to the Churches.	John's Greetings to the Churches.
What John sees in Heaven (describes Jesus).	What John sees in Heaven (describes Jesus).
The Messages to the Seven Churches.	The Messages to the Seven Churches.
What John sees in Heaven (describes the Throne Room).	What John sees in Heaven (describes the Throne Room).
The Seal Judgments. (seals 1 thru 6)	The Seal Judgments. (seals 1 thru 6)
The Twelve Tribes Sealed.	The Twelve Tribes Sealed.
The Seal Judgments continued... (seal # 7)	The Seal Judgments continued... (seal # 7)
The Trumpet Judgments (trumps 1 thru 6)	The Trumpet Judgments (trumps 1 thru 6)

John's Greetings to the Churches.	John's Greetings to the Churches.	Rev 1:1-6
What John sees in Heaven (describes Jesus).	What John sees in Heaven (describes Jesus).	Rev 1:7-20
The Messages to the Seven Churches.	The Messages to the Seven Churches.	Rev 2:1-3:22
What John sees in Heaven (describes the Throne Room).	What John sees in Heaven (describes the Throne Room).	Rev 4:1-5:14
The Seal Judgments. (seals 1 thru 6)	The Seal Judgments. (seals 1 thru 6)	Rev 6:1-17
The Twelve Tribes Sealed.	The Twelve Tribes Sealed.	Rev 7:1-17
The Seal Judgments continued... (seal # 7)	The Seal Judgments continued... (seal # 7)	Rev 8:1-6
The Trumpet Judgments (trumps 1 thru 6)	The Trumpet Judgments (trumps 1 thru 6)	Rev 8:7-9:21
	(Parenthetical) Seven Thunders and Angel with little book.	Rev 10:1-11
	(Parenthetical) Two Witnesses.	Rev 11:1-13
The Trumpet Judgments continued... (trump # 7)	The Trumpet Judgments continued... (trump # 7)	Rev 11:14-19
	(Parenthetical) The Nature of the Struggle Between God, Israel and the Devil.	Rev 12:1-17
	(Parenthetical) The Nature of the Government in the Last Days and the Mark of the Beast.	Rev 13:1-18
	(Parenthetical) The Lords Presence is with his People.	Rev 14:1-5
	(Parenthetical) The Warning goes out against taking the Mark of the Beast.	Rev 14:6-13
Rapture! Gathering together of the Saints.	Rapture! Gathering together of the Saints.	Rev 14:14-16
Angel begins Gathering Ungodly for Destruction.	Angel begins Gathering Ungodly for Destruction.	Rev 14:17-20
	(Parenthetical) The Godly are in Heaven Now !	Rev 15:2-4
The Seven Vial Judgments.	The Seven Vial Judgments.	Rev 15:5-16:21
	(Parenthetical) Mystery Babylon (Symbolic historical representation of Babylon.)	Rev 17:1-18
	(Parenthetical) Babylon Judged.	Rev 18:1-24
There is Worshipping in Heaven and the Marriage Supper of the Lamb takes place.	There is Worshipping in Heaven and the Marriage Supper of the Lamb takes place.	Rev 19:1-10
Jesus Returns and Fights Against The Kings of the Earth, the Beast and the False Prophet.	Jesus Returns and Fights Against The Kings of the Earth, the Beast and the False Prophet.	Rev 19:11-21
Satan Bound 1000 yrs	Satan Bound 1000 yrs	Rev 20:1-3
Tribulation Saints Rule and Reign with Christ 1000 yrs.	Tribulation Saints Rule and Reign with Christ 1000 yrs.	Rev 20:4-6
Satan Loosed for a Short Season. He Deceives the Nations and Causes a Rebellion.	Satan Loosed for a Short Season. He Deceives the Nations and Causes a Rebellion.	Rev 20:7-10
The Great White Throne Judgment.	The Great White Throne Judgment.	Rev 20:11-15
A New Heaven and New Earth.	A New Heaven and New Earth.	Rev 21:1-5
God has Words for the Godly and the Ungodly.	God has Words for the Godly and the Ungodly.	Rev 21:6-8
New Jerusalem comes down from Heaven and is Described.	New Jerusalem comes down from Heaven and is Described.	Rev 21:9-22:5
God has some Closing Words for John.	God has some Closing Words for John.	Rev 22:6-21

Figure 15-1

The general chronology of the Book of Revelation is as follows:

There are seven Seal judgments.

When the seventh Seal is opened then seven Trumpets begin to sound.

When the LAST (7th) Trumpet is sounded the rapture immediately follows.

Then there are seven final Vial Judgments.

This pattern of judgments is not unique in the Bible. There was another instance where this exact pattern can be seen. It can be seen in the Book of Joshua at the fall of Jericho.

Josh 6:2And the LORD said unto Joshua, See, I have given into thine hand Jericho, and the king thereof, *and* the mighty men of valour. 3And ye shall compass the city, all *ye* men of war, *and* **go round about the city once. Thus shalt thou do six days.** 4And seven priests shall bear before the ark seven trumpets of rams' horns: and **the seventh day ye shall compass the city seven times, and the priests shall blow with the trumpets**. 5And it shall come to pass, that when they make a long *blast* with the ram's horn, *and* when ye hear **the sound of the trumpet**, all the people shall **shout with a great shout**; and the wall of the city shall fall down flat, and the people shall ascend up every man straight before him.

Josh 6:20So the people shouted when *the priests* blew with the trumpets: and it came to pass, when the people heard the sound of the trumpet, and the people shouted with a great shout, that the wall fell down flat, so that the people went up into the city, every man straight before him, and they took the city. 21**And they utterly destroyed all that *was* in the city, both man and woman, young and old, and ox, and sheep, and ass, with the edge of the sword.**

God's Pattern of Judgment

Beyond Coincidence

The Pattern from Joshua
When Jericho Fell

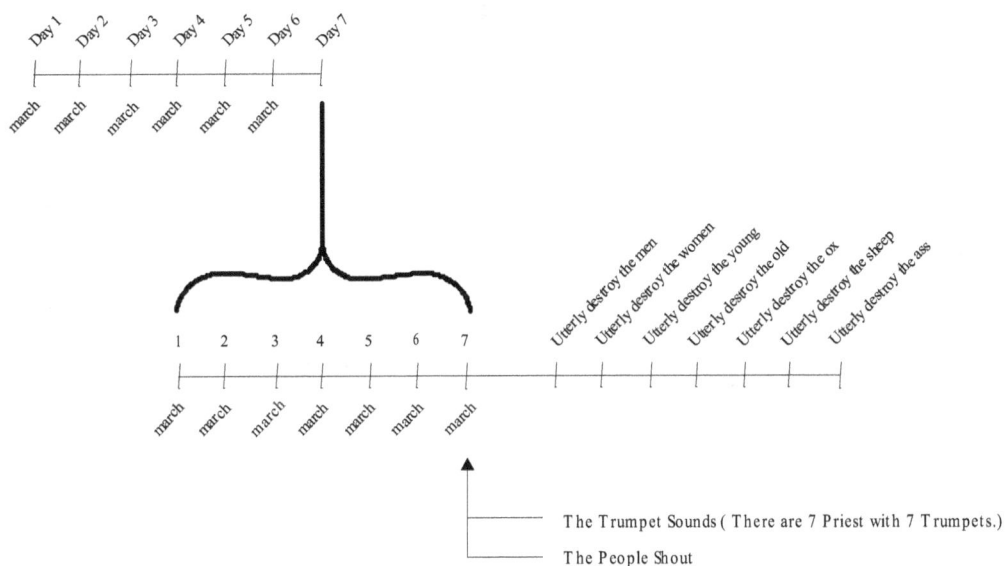

Day 1 Day 2 Day 3 Day 4 Day 5 Day 6 Day 7

march march march march march march

1 2 3 4 5 6 7

Utterly destroy the men
Utterly destroy the women
Utterly destroy the young
Utterly destroy the old
Utterly destroy the ox
Utterly destroy the sheep
Utterly destroy the ass

march march march march march march march

The Trumpet Sounds (There are 7 Priest with 7 Trumpets.)
The People Shout

The Pattern from Revelation

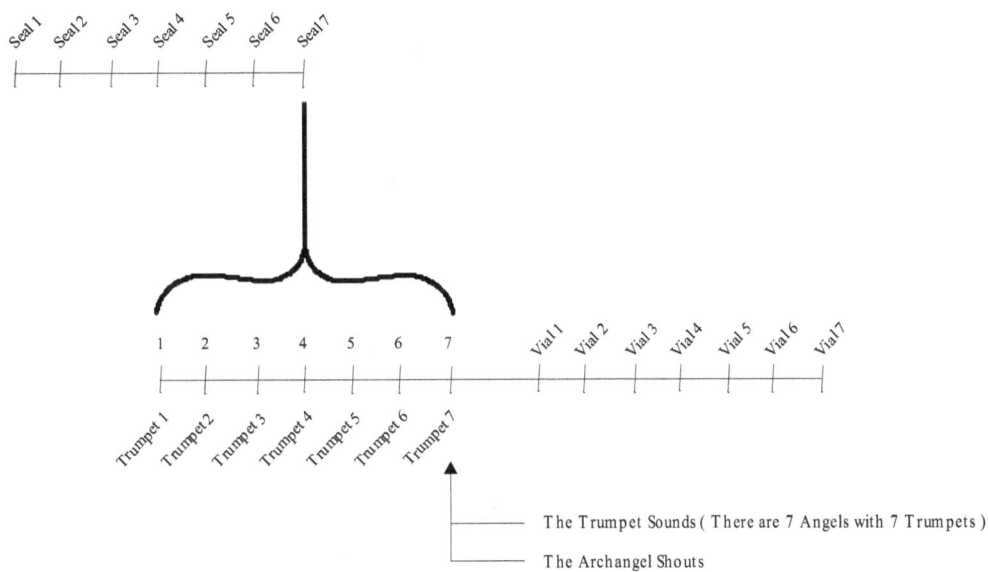

Seal 1 Seal 2 Seal 3 Seal 4 Seal 5 Seal 6 Seal 7

1 2 3 4 5 6 7

Vial 1 Vial 2 Vial 3 Vial 4 Vial 5 Vial 6 Vial 7

Trumpet 1 Trumpet 2 Trumpet 3 Trumpet 4 Trumpet 5 Trumpet 6 Trumpet 7

The Trumpet Sounds (There are 7 Angels with 7 Trumpets)
The Archangel Shouts

From the figure on the previous page, it is easy to see how the pattern from Joshua mimics the pattern of judgments laid out in the Book of Revelation. It seems unlikely such identical patterns would be purely coincidental.

If I were to put these judgments into mathematical form the equation would look something like this:

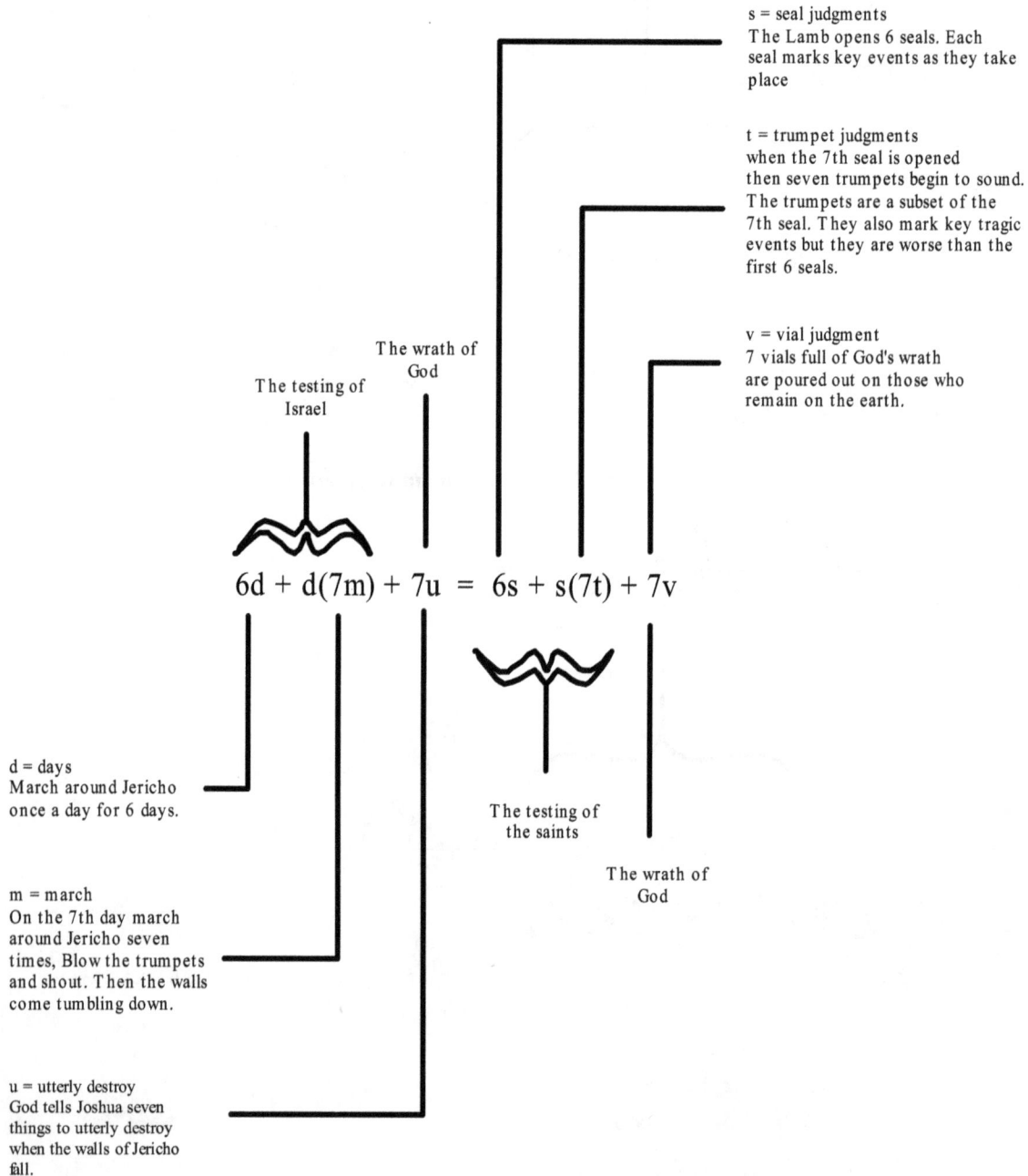

s = seal judgments
The Lamb opens 6 seals. Each seal marks key events as they take place

t = trumpet judgments
when the 7th seal is opened then seven trumpets begin to sound. The trumpets are a subset of the 7th seal. They also mark key tragic events but they are worse than the first 6 seals.

v = vial judgment
7 vials full of God's wrath are poured out on those who remain on the earth.

The wrath of God

The testing of Israel

$$6d + d(7m) + 7u \ = \ 6s + s(7t) + 7v$$

The testing of the saints

The wrath of God

d = days
March around Jericho once a day for 6 days.

m = march
On the 7th day march around Jericho seven times, Blow the trumpets and shout. Then the walls come tumbling down.

u = utterly destroy
God tells Joshua seven things to utterly destroy when the walls of Jericho fall.

God tested the children of Israel during their siege of Jericho. He tested their trust and their obedience. I'm sure it was no fun marching around an entire city in silence day after day and the people of Jericho must have thought the Israeli strategy was laughable. The seventh day was seven times worse than any of the first six days for the people of Israel (it was their great tribulation) but their obedience was rewarded with victory and God's judgment was poured out on the people of Jericho.

The people of God will also be tested during the tribulation to come. They will need to trust and obey God. It will not be pleasant and following God will seem laughable to unbelievers. We will need to march continually forward as the Seal and Trumpet judgments progress but if we endure to the end we will be saved. When the 7th trumpet sounds, we will be delivered and Satan's walls will fall. God will then pour out his wrath on those who remain.

Let's examine the Seal, Trumpet and Vial judgments in a little more detail to get an idea of what is coming.

The Seal, Trumpet and Vial judgments are shown on the next page. The diagram shows the seventh seal judgment initiates the seven trumpet judgments. These trumpet judgments can therefore be considered as a subset of the seventh seal. This will be important when we consider the events Jesus described in his Olivet discourse.

The Judgments of the book of Revelation.

7 Seals

7 Trumpets

7 Vials

Silence about a 1/2 an hour.

Woe 1

Woe 2

Woe 3

Woes 2 & 3 come in quick succession.

Church raptured.

A conquering leader comes on the scene.

War / civil unrest

Famine

Death by
- sword
- famine
- disease and
- wild beasts

Great martyrdom for Christ.

Great earthquake
- Sun & Moon darkened
- stars fall
- heaven departs as a scroll
- mountains & islands moved out of their places.
- Rich men hide in the rocks of the mountains.
- Winds halted
- 144,000 sealed of all the tribes of Israel.

Voices, thunderings, lightnings, and an earthquake.

7 trumpets begin to sound.

Hail and fire mingled with blood.
- 1/3 trees &
- All green grass burned up.

A mountain burning with fire cast into the sea and
- 1/3 sea life died.
- 1/3 ships destroyed.

A star called Wormwood falls upon 1/3 of the waters. Makes waters bitter and causes many to die.

1/3 Sun 1/3 Moon 1/3 stars smitten. Day & night shown not for 1/3 of them.

A star falls and the Bottomless pit opens. Smoke rises. Sun darkened by the smoke. Locusts come forth to torment those not sealed by God.

Torment lasts 5 months.

200,000,000 demon horsemen let loose to kill 1/3 of men.

Jesus returns sitting upon a cloud with a sickle and he gathers his saints. He also commands another angel to gather the clusters of grapes to be destroyed.

grievous sores come upon those with the mark of the beast.

Sea becomes blood and every living thing in it dies.

Rivers and fountains of waters become blood.

Sun scorches men with fire.

Beasts' kingdom is full of darkness. They gnaw their tongues because of the pain.

Euphrates dried up.

Kings gather to battle the Lord.

The last vial causes Voices, Thunderings, Lightnings, and the greatest of all Earthquakes

The islands and mountains cannot be found.

Great hail falls upon men.

By Daniel Brown

The Seven Seal Judgments

Seal Judgment 1

Rev 6:1 And I saw when the Lamb opened one of the seals, and I heard, as it were the noise of thunder, one of the four beasts saying, Come and see.

2 And I saw, and behold a white horse: and he that sat on him had a bow; and a crown was given unto him: and he went forth conquering, and to conquer.

Symbology:	A crown given to him.	He will be a head of state.
	He rides a white horse.	He appears to be one of the good guys.
	He has a Bow.	He has weapons that can kill from a distance

Seal Judgment 2

Rev 6:4 And there went out another horse *that was* red: and *power* was given to him that sat thereon to take peace from the earth, and that they should kill one another: and there was given unto him a great sword.

Symbology:	Red Horse takes peace from the Earth.	Widespread War
	He has a Sword	Weapon of close combat.
		Hand to hand combat.
		Civil unrest.

Seal Judgment 3

Rev 6:5 And when he had opened the third seal, I heard the third beast say, Come and see. And I beheld, and lo a black horse; and he that sat on him had a pair of balances in his hand.

6 And I heard a voice in the midst of the four beasts say, A measure of wheat for a penny, and three measures of barley for a penny; and *see* thou hurt not the oil and the wine.

Symbology:	Rode a Black Horse	Evil
	Rider carried balances	Instrument of commerce.
	Measuring food	Famine, inflation

Seal Judgment 4

Rev 6:7 And when he had opened the fourth seal, I heard the voice of the fourth beast say, Come and see.

8 And I looked, and behold a pale horse: and his name that sat on him was Death, and Hell followed with him. And power was given unto them over the fourth part of the earth, to kill with sword, and with hunger, and with death, and with the beasts of the earth.

Symbology:	Rode a Pale horse		Death, Pestilence, Disease.
	Kills with	Sword	War
		Hunger	Famine
		Death	Disease
		Beasts	Wild Animals

Seal Judgment 5

Rev 6:9 And when he had opened the fifth seal, I saw under the altar the souls of them that were slain for the word of God, and for the testimony which they held:

10 And they cried with a loud voice, saying, How long, O Lord, holy and true, dost thou not judge and avenge our blood on them that dwell on the earth?

11 And white robes were given unto every one of them; and it was said unto them, that they should rest yet for a little season, until their fellowservants also and their brethren, that should be killed as they *were,* should be fulfilled.

Symbology:	Altar of slain souls	Martyrs before God. Symbolized by the altar of incense in the Tabernacle of Moses.
	White robes given to them	Purity. Laodicean Church told to purchase white raiment from God. Martyrdom is the price of white robes.
	Told to be patient	Persecution of the saints continuing. Persecution lasts for a while.

Seal Judgment 6

^{Rev 6:12}And I beheld when he had opened the sixth seal, and, lo, there was a great earthquake; and the sun became black as sackcloth of hair, and the moon became as blood;

¹³And the stars of heaven fell unto the earth, even as a fig tree casteth her untimely figs, when she is shaken of a mighty wind.

¹⁴And the heaven departed as a scroll when it is rolled together; and every mountain and island were moved out of their places.

¹⁵And the kings of the earth, and the great men, and the rich men, and the chief captains, and the mighty men, and every bondman, and every free man, hid themselves in the dens and in the rocks of the mountains;

¹⁶And said to the mountains and rocks, Fall on us, and hide us from the face of him that sitteth on the throne, and from the wrath of the Lamb:

¹⁷For the great day of his wrath is come; and who shall be able to stand?

Symbology:	Sun is Black, Moon is as blood	Darkness, debris in atmosphere.
	Stars of heaven fall	Missiles? Meteors?
	Heaven departed as a scroll	Mushroom Cloud?
	Important men hide in the rocks	Fallout shelters?

Seal Judgment 7

^{Rev 8:1}And when he had opened the seventh seal, there was silence in heaven about the space of half an hour.

²And I saw the seven angels which stood before God; and to them were given seven trumpets.

³And another angel came and stood at the altar, having a golden censer; and there was given unto him much incense, that he should offer *it* with the prayers of all saints upon the golden altar which was before the throne.

⁴And the smoke of the incense, *which came* with the prayers of the saints, ascended up before God out of the angel's hand.

⁵And the angel took the censer, and filled it with fire of the altar, and cast *it* into the earth: and there were voices, and thunderings, and lightnings, and an earthquake.

⁶And the seven angels which had the seven trumpets prepared themselves to sound.

Symbology: Silence   Awe and anticipation of the
                                          coming 7 trumpet judgments.

The Seven Trumpet Judgments

Trumpet Judgment 1

Rev 8:7 The first angel sounded, and there followed hail and fire mingled with blood, and they were cast upon the earth: and the third part of trees was burnt up, and all green grass was burnt up.

Symbology: Hail, Fire, with Blood   Fallout? Meteors? Electrical storms? Solar flares? Contaminated rains?

Trees and grass burned.   Widespread fires.

Trumpet Judgment 2

Rev 8:8 And the second angel sounded, and as it were a great mountain burning with fire was cast into the sea: and the third part of the sea became blood;

9 And the third part of the creatures which were in the sea, and had life, died; and the third part of the ships were destroyed.

Symbology: Burning mountain cast into sea   Big Meteor? Volcano?

Trumpet Judgment 3

Rev 8:10 And the third angel sounded, and there fell a great star from heaven, burning as it were a lamp, and it fell upon the third part of the rivers, and upon the fountains of waters;

11 And the name of the star is called Wormwood: and the third part of the waters became wormwood; and many men died of the waters, because they were made bitter.

Symbology:	Burning Star falls	Missile? Meteor?
	Star named Wormwood	Bitter, Radioactive?. Ukrainian word for wormwood is Chernobyl. Chernobyl is synonymous with nuclear disaster.

Trumpet Judgment 4

^{Rev 8:12}And the fourth angel sounded, and the third part of the sun was smitten, and the third part of the moon, and the third part of the stars; so as the third part of them was darkened, and the day shone not for a third part of it, and the night likewise.

¹³And I beheld, and heard an angel flying through the midst of heaven, saying with a loud voice, **Woe, woe, woe,** to the inhabiters of the earth by reason of the other voices of the trumpet of the three angels, which are yet to sound!

Symbology:	The Sun, Moon, and Stars are smitten. They do not shine for a 1/3 part of the day or night.	Smoke or Dust in the atmosphere is blocking a substantial amount of incoming light?
	An angel proclaims the Severity of the next three trumpets	Woe, woe, woe An angel flies through the heavens warning of the severity of the events that will occur at the blowing of the next 3 trumpets

Trumpet Judgment 5

The First Woe.

^{Rev 9:1}And the fifth angel sounded, and I saw a star fall from heaven unto the earth: and to him was given the key of the bottomless pit.

²And he opened the bottomless pit; and there arose a smoke out of the pit, as the smoke of a great furnace; and the sun and the air were darkened by reason of the smoke of the pit.

³And there came out of the smoke locusts upon the earth: and unto them was given power, as the scorpions of the earth have power.

⁴And it was commanded them that they should not hurt the grass of the earth, neither any green thing, neither any tree; but only those men which have not the seal of God in their foreheads.

⁵And to them it was given that they should not kill them, but that they should be tormented five months: and their torment *was* as the torment of a scorpion, when he striketh a man.

⁶And in those days shall men seek death, and shall not find it; and shall desire to die, and death shall flee from them.

⁷And the shapes of the locusts *were* like unto horses prepared unto battle; and on their heads *were* as it were crowns like gold, and their faces *were* as the faces of men.

⁸And they had hair as the hair of women, and their teeth were as *the teeth* of lions.

⁹And they had breastplates, as it were breastplates of iron; and the sound of their wings *was* as the sound of chariots of many horses running to battle.

¹⁰And they had tails like unto scorpions, and there were stings in their tails: and their power *was* to hurt men five months.

¹¹And they had a king over them, *which is* the angel of the bottomless pit, whose name in the Hebrew tongue *is* Abaddon, but in the Greek tongue hath *his* name Apollyon.

¹²One woe is past; *and,* behold, there come two woes more hereafter.

The Fifth Trumpet is the beginning of the three Woes spoken of in Rev 8:13. The Fifth Trumpet is when the spiritual forces of Satan are unleashed. They will attack humans directly and they will be allowed to torment men for five months. Only those who have the seal of God in their forehead will avoid the demonic torture. The three woes will be the most horrific time the planet has ever known.

Symbology:	The bottomless pit is opened	A holding place for fallen angels?
	Locusts arise out of the smoke of the pit.	Demons are let loose upon the Earth.
	Their sole purpose is to torment men who do not have the seal of God in their foreheads for five months.	They cannot hurt God's people but they torment everyone else.

Rev 7:2And I saw another angel ascending from the east, having the seal of the living God: and he cried with a loud voice to the four angels, to whom it was given to hurt the earth and the sea, ³Saying, Hurt not the earth, neither the sea, nor the trees, till we have sealed the servants of our God in their foreheads. ⁴And I heard the number of them which were sealed: *and there were* sealed an hundred *and* forty *and* four thousand of all the tribes of the children of Israel.

Their shape is like horses prepared for battle; they have gold	The locust are described as having the characteristics of

236

Symbology: (continued)	crowns on their head, and their faces are like the faces of men. They have hair like women, Teeth like lions, breastplates of iron, wings and stinging tails like scorpions.	several types of creatures. Their composite descriptions are reminiscent of the descriptions of other known angelic beings like Seraphim and Cherubim.
	Men will seek death but will not Be able to find it. (Rev 9:6)	This inability to die is unprecedented in the Bible. Men will not be able to escape the torment of the demons by dying. The soul will not be able to separate itself from the body no matter how badly the body is injured.
	Their king's name is Abaddon or Apollyon.	Abaddon and Apollyon both mean Destroyer… Satan.

Trumpet Judgment 6

The Second Woe.

> ^{Rev 9:12} One woe is past; *and,* behold, there come two woes more hereafter.

> ¹³And the sixth angel sounded, and I heard a voice from the four horns of the golden altar which is before God,

The golden altar before God corresponds to the Altar of Incense in the Tabernacle. Rev 6:9 tells us this altar is the place where the martyrs reside.

> ¹⁴Saying to the sixth angel which had the trumpet, Loose the four angels which are bound in the great river Euphrates.

> ¹⁵And the four angels were loosed, which were prepared for an hour, and a day, and a month, and a year, for to slay the third part of men.

Using the 360 day calendar this calculates to 391 days and 1 hour or 9385 hours. This verse is very curious. Unfortunately, I do not understand the meaning of this time reference.

> ¹⁶And the number of the army of the horsemen *were* two hundred thousand thousand: and I heard the number of them.

> ¹⁷And thus I saw the horses in the vision, and them that sat on them, having breastplates of fire, and of jacinth, and brimstone: and the heads of the horses *were* as the heads of lions; and out of their mouths issued fire and smoke and brimstone.

> ¹⁸By these three was the third part of men killed, by the fire, and by the smoke, and by the brimstone, which issued out of their mouths.

> ¹⁹For their power is in their mouth, and in their tails: for their tails *were* like unto serpents, and had heads, and with them they do hurt.

[20]And the rest of the men which were not killed by these plagues yet repented not of the works of their hands, that they should not worship devils, and idols of gold, and silver, and brass, and stone, and of wood: which neither can see, nor hear, nor walk:

[21]Neither repented they of their murders, nor of their sorceries, nor of their fornication, nor of their thefts.

Trumpet Judgment 7

The Third Woe.

The Last Trumpet.

Several verses indicate the resurrection of the saints takes place at the Last (seventh) Trumpet. Unfortunately, the sequence of events in the book of Revelation is interrupted at this point by the inclusion of two parenthetical passages. While these parenthetical passages give us valuable insight into the warfare going on in the spiritual realm, they tend to distract us from the cause and effect relationship which exists between the sounding of the Seventh Trumpet and the resurrection of the saints.

For the sake of understanding, we will remove the parenthetical passages that are not part of the timeline. To show the chronological flow I have shaded out the parenthetical passages in my outline of the Book of Revelation (See Figure 15-1 on page 221). We will consider these parenthetical passages later.

> [Rev 11:15]And the seventh angel sounded; and there were great voices in heaven, saying, The kingdoms of this world are become *the kingdoms* of our Lord, and of his Christ; and he shall reign for ever and ever.
>
> [16]And the four and twenty elders, which sat before God on their seats, fell upon their faces, and worshipped God,
>
> [17]Saying, We give thee thanks, O Lord God Almighty, which art, and wast, and art to come; because thou hast taken to thee thy great power, and hast reigned.

[18]And the nations were angry, and thy wrath is come, and the time of the dead, that they should be judged, and that thou shouldest give reward unto thy servants the prophets, and to the saints, and them that fear thy name, small and great; and shouldest destroy them which destroy the earth.

[19]And the temple of God was opened in heaven, and there was seen in his temple the ark of his testament: and there were lightnings, and voices, and thunderings, and an earthquake, and great hail.

Rev 14:14-16 are the scriptures that describe the rapture taking place.

Rev 14:14 And I looked, and behold a white cloud, and upon the cloud *one* sat like unto the Son of man, having on his head a golden crown, and in his hand a sharp sickle.

Rev 1:7 Behold, he cometh with clouds; and every eye shall see him, and they *also* which pierced him: and all kindreds of the earth shall wail because of him. Even so, Amen.

Rev 14:15 And another angel came out of the temple, crying with a loud voice to him that sat on the cloud, Thrust in thy sickle, and reap: for the time is come for thee to reap; for the harvest of the earth is ripe.

[16]And he that sat on the cloud thrust in his sickle on the earth; and the earth was reaped.

1 Thes 4:17 Then we which are alive *and* remain shall be caught up together with them in the clouds, to meet the Lord in the air: and so shall we ever be with the Lord.

Rev 14:17-20 describe the gathering together of the ungodly for destruction.

> Rev 14:17And another angel came out of the temple which is in heaven, he also having a sharp sickle.

> 18And another angel came out from the altar, which had power over fire; and cried with a loud cry to him that had the sharp sickle, saying, Thrust in thy sharp sickle, and gather the clusters of the vine of the earth; for her grapes are fully ripe.

> 19And the angel thrust in his sickle into the earth, and gathered the vine of the earth, and cast *it* into the great winepress of the wrath of God.

> 20And the winepress was trodden without the city, and blood came out of the winepress, even unto the horse bridles, by the space of a thousand *and* six hundred furlongs.

The prophet Joel foresees the same gathering of the ungodly for destruction. Notice the similar wording with the reference to the harvest, the sickle and the winepress. The imagery is unmistakable.

> Joel 3:11Assemble yourselves, and come, all ye heathen, and gather yourselves together round about: thither cause thy mighty ones to come down, O LORD.

> 12Let the heathen be wakened, and come up to the valley of Jehoshaphat: for there will I sit to judge all the heathen round about.

> 13Put ye in the sickle, for the harvest is ripe: come, get you down; for the press is full, the fats overflow; for their wickedness *is* great.

> 14Multitudes, multitudes in the valley of decision: for the day of the LORD *is* near in the valley of decision.

To miss the resurrection and to experience the wrath of God is the ultimate Woe

The Last Trumpet has blown, the rapture has occurred and there are still 7 vial judgments to be poured out on those who remain.

The Seven Vial Judgments

Rev 15:1And I saw another sign in heaven, great and marvelous, seven angels having the seven last plagues; for in them is filled up the wrath of God.

Many pre-tribulation rapture believers justify their position by saying, "God has not appointed us to wrath" (quoting from 1Thes 5:9) therefore Christians will not take part in the tribulation period. This is only partially correct. The Christians were caught up into Heaven when the seventh trumpet sounded. They will not be here for the pouring out of the seven vials full of God's wrath.

The thing the pre-tribulation rapturist misunderstands is… The wrath the believers endure during the tribulation period is the wrath of Satan not the wrath of God.

Rev 12:12Therefore rejoice, *ye* heavens, and ye that dwell in them. Woe to the inhabiters of the earth and of the sea! for the devil is come down unto you, having great wrath, because he knoweth that he hath but a short time.

The Sea of Glass:

Rev 15:2And I saw as it were a sea of glass mingled with fire: and them that had gotten the victory over the beast, and over his image, and over his mark, *and* over the number of his name, stand on the sea of glass, having the harps of God.

This Sea of Glass may be what the Brazen Laver was symbolizing at the entrance of the Tabernacle of Moses. This was the final place of cleansing before the priest could enter the Holy Place. Also notice how the saints sing the "song of Moses" and how similar the vial judgments are to the plagues of Egypt.

Rev 15:3 And they sing the song of Moses the servant of God, and the song of the Lamb, saying, Great and marvellous *are* thy works, Lord God Almighty; just and true *are* thy ways, thou King of saints.

4 Who shall not fear thee, O Lord, and glorify thy name? for *thou* only *art* holy: for all nations shall come and worship before thee; for thy judgments are made manifest.

5 And after that I looked, and, behold, the temple of the tabernacle of the testimony in heaven was opened:

6 And the seven angels came out of the temple, having the seven plagues, clothed in pure and white linen, and having their breasts girded with golden girdles.

7 And one of the four beasts gave unto the seven angels seven golden vials full of the wrath of God, who liveth for ever and ever.

8 And the temple was filled with smoke from the glory of God, and from his power; and no man was able to enter into the temple, till the seven plagues of the seven angels were fulfilled.

Rev 16:1 And I heard a great voice out of the temple saying to the seven angels, Go your ways, and pour out the vials of the wrath of God upon the earth.

Vial Judgment 1

Rev 16:2And the first went, and poured out his vial upon the earth; and there fell a noisome and grievous sore upon the men which had the mark of the beast, and *upon* them which worshipped his image.

> Ex 9: 8And the LORD said unto Moses and unto Aaron, Take to you handfuls of ashes of the furnace, and let Moses sprinkle it toward the heaven in the sight of Pharaoh.

> 9And it shall become small dust in all the land of Egypt, and shall be a boil breaking forth *with* blains upon man, and upon beast, throughout all the land of Egypt.

> 11And the magicians could not stand before Moses because of the boils; for the boil was upon the magicians, and upon all the Egyptians.

Vial Judgment 2

Rev 16:3And the second angel poured out his vial upon the sea; and it became as the blood of a dead *man:* and every living soul died in the sea.

> Ex 7:19And the LORD spake unto Moses, Say unto Aaron, Take thy rod, and stretch out thine hand upon the waters of Egypt, upon their streams, upon their rivers, and upon their ponds, and upon all their pools of water, that they may become blood; and *that* there may be blood throughout all the land of Egypt, both in *vessels of* wood, and in *vessels of* stone.

> 20And Moses and Aaron did so, as the LORD commanded; and he lifted up the rod, and smote the waters that *were* in the river, in the sight of Pharaoh, and in the sight of his servants; and all the waters that *were* in the river were turned to blood.

Vial Judgment 3

Rev 16:4And the third angel poured out his vial upon the rivers and fountains of waters; and they became blood.

5And I heard the angel of the waters say, Thou art righteous, O Lord, which art, and wast, and shalt be, because thou hast judged thus.

6For they have shed the blood of saints and prophets, and thou hast given them blood to drink; for they are worthy.

7And I heard another out of the altar say, Even so, Lord God Almighty, true and righteous *are* thy judgments.

Vial Judgment 4

Rev 16:8And the fourth angel poured out his vial upon the sun; and power was given unto him to scorch men with fire.

9And men were scorched with great heat, and blasphemed the name of God, which hath power over these plagues: and they repented not to give him glory.

Vial Judgment 5

Rev 16:10And the fifth angel poured out his vial upon the seat of the beast; and his kingdom was full of darkness; and they gnawed their tongues for pain,

11And blasphemed the God of heaven because of their pains and their sores, and repented not of their deeds.

> Ex 10:21And the LORD said unto Moses, Stretch out thine hand toward heaven, that there may be darkness over the land of Egypt, even darkness *which* may be felt.

²²And Moses stretched forth his hand toward heaven; and there was a thick darkness in all the land of Egypt three days:

Vial Judgment 6

^{Rev 16:12}And the sixth angel poured out his vial upon the great river Euphrates; and the water thereof was dried up, that the way of the kings of the east might be prepared.

¹³And I saw three unclean spirits like frogs *come* out of the mouth of the dragon, and out of the mouth of the beast, and out of the mouth of the false prophet.

¹⁴For they are the spirits of devils, working miracles, *which* go forth unto the kings of the earth and of the whole world, to gather them to the battle of that great day of God Almighty.

¹⁵Behold, I come as a thief. Blessed *is* he that watcheth, and keepeth his garments, lest he walk naked, and they see his shame.

¹⁶And he gathered them together into a place called in the Hebrew tongue Armageddon.

> ^{Ex 8:5}And the LORD spake unto Moses, Say unto Aaron, Stretch forth thine hand with thy rod over the streams, over the rivers, and over the ponds, and cause frogs to come up upon the land of Egypt.

> ⁶And Aaron stretched out his hand over the waters of Egypt; and the frogs came up, and covered the land of Egypt.

Vial Judgment 7

Rev 16:17And the seventh angel poured out his vial into the air; and there came a great voice out of the temple of heaven, from the throne, saying, It is done.

18And there were voices, and thunders, and lightnings; and there was a great earthquake, such as was not since men were upon the earth, so mighty an earthquake, *and* so great.

19And the great city was divided into three parts, and the cities of the nations fell: and great Babylon came in remembrance before God, to give unto her the cup of the wine of the fierceness of his wrath.

20And every island fled away, and the mountains were not found.

21And there fell upon men a great hail out of heaven, *every stone* about the weight of a talent: and men blasphemed God because of the plague of the hail; for the plague thereof was exceeding great.

> Ex 9:22And the LORD said unto Moses, Stretch forth thine hand toward heaven, that there may be hail in all the land of Egypt, upon man, and upon beast, and upon every herb of the field, throughout the land of Egypt.
>
> 23And Moses stretched forth his rod toward heaven: and the LORD sent thunder and hail, and the fire ran along upon the ground; and the LORD rained hail upon the land of Egypt.
>
> 24So there was hail, and fire mingled with the hail, very grievous, such as there was none like it in all the land of Egypt since it became a nation.

The link between the vial judgments and the plagues of Moses is no coincidence. The pouring out of God's wrath on Egypt was a foreshadowing of the vial judgments. God's chosen people (the saints) are delivered from the bonds of Egypt (this world) and will enter in to the Promised Land (God's kingdom). Unfortunately, even after Gods deliverance, the people still murmured and complained. We will also see a degree of dissatisfaction during the millennial reign of Jesus. We will discuss this shortly.

Chapters 17 and 18 are also parenthetical and have been temporarily removed. The next thing to happen chronologically will be the return of Jesus.

Jesus returns to set up his millennial reign.

^{Rev 19:11}And I saw heaven opened, and behold a white horse; and he that sat upon him *was* called Faithful and True, and in righteousness he doth judge and make war.

¹²His eyes *were* as a flame of fire, and on his head *were* many crowns; and he had a name written, that no man knew, but he himself.

¹³And he *was* clothed with a vesture dipped in blood: and his name is called The Word of God.

¹⁴And the armies *which were* in heaven followed him upon white horses, clothed in fine linen, white and clean.

The armies following Jesus are most likely the raptured saints.

¹⁵And out of his mouth goeth a sharp sword, that with it he should smite the nations: and he shall rule them with a rod of iron: and he treadeth the winepress of the fierceness and wrath of Almighty God.

Verse 15 says Jesus will rule the nations with a "rod of iron". This implies two things. There will be un-raptured people who make it through the tribulation period. Secondly, the rebellious nature of man still lives on. Otherwise they would not need to be ruled with a rod of iron.

¹⁶And he hath on *his* vesture and on his thigh a name written, KING OF KINGS, AND LORD OF LORDS.

¹⁷And I saw an angel standing in the sun; and he cried with a loud voice, saying to all the fowls that fly in the midst of heaven, Come and gather yourselves together unto the supper of the great God;

¹⁸That ye may eat the flesh of kings, and the flesh of captains, and the flesh of mighty men, and the flesh of horses, and of them that sit on them, and the flesh of all *men, both* free and bond, both small and great.

¹⁹And I saw the beast, and the kings of the earth, and their armies, gathered together to make war against him that sat on the horse, and against his army.

²⁰And the beast was taken, and with him the false prophet that wrought miracles before him, with which he deceived them that had received the mark of the beast, and them that worshipped his image. These both were cast alive into a lake of fire burning with brimstone.

²¹And the remnant were slain with the sword of him that sat upon the horse, which *sword* proceeded out of his mouth: and all the fowls were filled with their flesh.

^{Rev 20:1}And I saw an angel come down from heaven, having the key of the bottomless pit and a great chain in his hand.

²And he laid hold on the dragon, that old serpent, which is the Devil, and Satan, and bound him a thousand years,

³And cast him into the bottomless pit, and shut him up, and set a seal upon him, that he should deceive the nations no more, till the thousand years should be fulfilled: and after that he must be loosed a little season.

The beast and the false prophet are thrown directly into the lake of fire in Rev 19:20 but Satan is thrown into the bottomless pit for 1000 years. After the 1000 years are finished, Satan will be loosed for a little season. Why would God allow this? Why not immediately throw him into the lake of fire with the beast and the false prophet? God undoubtedly has a purpose for doing this.

^{Rev 20:4}And I saw thrones, and they sat upon them, and judgment was given unto them: and *I saw* the souls of them that were beheaded for the witness of Jesus, and for the word of God, and which had not worshipped the beast, neither his image,

neither had received *his* mark upon their foreheads, or in their hands; and they lived and reigned with Christ a thousand years.

⁵But the rest of the dead lived not again until the thousand years were finished. This *is* the first resurrection.

⁶Blessed and holy *is* he that hath part in the first resurrection: on such the second death hath no power, but they shall be priests of God and of Christ, and shall reign with him a thousand years.

When Jesus returns at the end of the tribulation period, he will bring his armies with him. Verses 4-6 indicate there will be more than one resurrection. These verses indicate the first resurrection will consist of those who were martyred for Jesus and those Christians who died without receiving the mark of the beast. All of God's people throughout time do not seem to be included in this first resurrection. This is contrary to the commonly held idea of a general resurrection of all God's people at the time of the Rapture. Let's see what some other passages say about the "rapture".

> 1 Cor 15:51Behold, I shew you a mystery; We shall not all sleep, but **we shall all be changed,** ⁵²In a moment, in the twinkling of an eye, **at the last trump:** for the trumpet shall sound, and the dead shall be raised incorruptible, and we shall be changed. ⁵³For this corruptible must put on incorruption, and this mortal *must* put on immortality. ⁵⁴So when this corruptible shall have put on incorruption, and this mortal shall have put on immortality, then shall be brought to pass the saying that is written, Death is swallowed up in victory. ⁵⁵O death, where *is* thy sting? O grave, where *is* thy victory?

The previous passage tells us we (the believers) will ALL be changed… at the last trump.

> 1Thes 4:13But I would not have you to be ignorant, brethren, concerning them which are asleep, that ye sorrow not, even as others which have no hope. ¹⁴For if we believe that Jesus died and rose again, even so them also which sleep in Jesus will God bring with him. ¹⁵For this we say unto you

by the word of the Lord, that we which are alive *and* remain unto the coming of the Lord shall not prevent them which are asleep. [16]For the Lord himself shall descend from heaven with a shout, with the voice of the archangel, and with the trump of God: and the dead in Christ shall rise first: [17]Then we which are alive *and* remain shall be caught up together with them in the clouds, to meet the Lord in the air: and so shall we ever be with the Lord. [18]Wherefore comfort one another with these words.

There is an apparent inconsistency between Rev 20: 4-6 and the other passages referring to the resurrection. We know they are all describing the same event because they occur at the sounding of the last trump. The only explanation I can offer for this is that John was specifically focusing on those who died during the tribulation period. Notice how John's statement focused on the beast and his mark. These things would only apply to the tribulation saints.

> [Rev 20:4]And I saw thrones, and they sat upon them, and judgment was given unto them: and *I saw* the souls of them that were beheaded for the witness of Jesus, and for the word of God, and which had not worshipped the beast, neither his image, neither had received *his* mark upon their foreheads, or in their hands; and they lived and reigned with Christ a thousand years.

Many people will die during this time, but only those tribulation saints who were beheaded and died as martyrs or believers who died some other way without taking the mark, would be resurrected at the last trump.

> [Rev 20:5]But the rest of the dead lived not again until the thousand years were finished. This *is* the first resurrection.

Those who died after taking the mark and submitting to the beast would not be resurrected until the last resurrection (the second death) a thousand years later.

> [6]Blessed and holy *is* he that hath part in the first resurrection: on such the second death hath no power, but

they shall be priests of God and of Christ, and shall reign with him a thousand years.

While Rev 20:4-6 apparently focuses on the resurrection of those who died during the tribulation period, the other passages in the Bible referring to the "rapture" seem to be broader in scope and indicate that all believers throughout history will be resurrected at the same time as the martyrs in the Book of Revelation.

> Rev 20:7 And when the thousand years are expired, Satan shall be loosed out of his prison,
>
> 8 And shall go out to deceive the nations which are in the four quarters of the earth, Gog and Magog, to gather them together to battle: the number of whom *is* as the sand of the sea.
>
> 9 And they went up on the breadth of the earth, and compassed the camp of the saints about, and the beloved city: and fire came down from God out of heaven, and devoured them.
>
> 10 And the devil that deceived them was cast into the lake of fire and brimstone, where the beast and the false prophet *are,* and shall be tormented day and night for ever and ever.

In Rev 20:4 we are told those who take part in the first resurrection will rule and reign with Jesus for 1000 years. Who will they rule over? There will obviously be some regular people who will survive the tribulation period. At the end of the thousand years, when Satan is loosed from the bottomless pit, he will be able to convince these people to gather and make war against the camp of the saints.

After living with justice, peace and prosperity for 1000 yrs, how could Satan convince the people to rebel? Could it be our ideas about the millennium are incorrect? Maybe it will not be as heavenly as we have imagined. Maybe hard work will still be required for people to survive. Jesus will rule with a rod of iron and there will be consequences if the people rebel.

> Rev 19:15And out of his mouth goeth a sharp sword, that with it he should smite the nations: and **he shall rule them with a rod of iron**: and he treadeth the winepress of the fierceness and wrath of Almighty God. 16And he hath on *his* vesture and on his thigh a name written, KING OF KINGS, AND LORD OF LORDS.

> Zech 14:16And it shall come to pass, *that* every one that is left of all the nations which came against Jerusalem shall even go up from year to year to worship the King, the LORD of hosts, and to keep the feast of tabernacles. **17And it shall be, *that* whoso will not come up of *all* the families of the earth unto Jerusalem to worship the King, the LORD of hosts, even upon them shall be no rain. 18And if the family of Egypt go not up, and come not, that *have* no *rain;* there shall be the plague, wherewith the LORD will smite the heathen that come not up to keep the feast of tabernacles.**

Even with Satan bound the rebellious nature of man will still be intact during the millennial reign. Obedience to God will be easier during this time because Satan will not be around to distort or deceive. Any rebellion will come directly from the heart of the rebel. Ultimately, the people will have to do what is right or pay the consequences.

When the 1000 years are over, Satan will be loosed and he will stir up the people against the saints. This is where Satan fulfills his final purpose. He will be able to convince some of the people they can prevail against the camp of the saints. The people will have to choose who they will serve. The rebellious will gather together to make war and God destroys them. After this the great white throne judgment takes place.

> Rev 20:11And I saw a great white throne, and him that sat on it, from whose face the earth and the heaven fled away; and there was found no place for them.

[12]And I saw the dead, small and great, stand before God; and the books were opened: and another book was opened, which is *the book* of life: and the dead were judged out of those things which were written in the books, according to their works.

[13]And the sea gave up the dead which were in it; and death and hell delivered up the dead which were in them: and **they were judged every man according to their works**.

[14]And death and hell were cast into the lake of fire. This is the second death.

[15]And whosoever was not found written in the book of life was cast into the lake of fire.

Judgment day is the second resurrection. It is preferable to take part in the first resurrection. Those who took part in the first resurrection have already been judged to be worthy of salvation because of their faith in Jesus and his redemption. Everyone else will be judged by their works and everyone who is not found in the book of life will be cast into the lake of fire.

This may be the answer to the age old question, "How God can condemn someone who has never heard the Gospel?" The answer is… he doesn't. He will judge them by their works.

God will judge their works but salvation will come only through his grace.

God can write the name of whoever he wants into his Book of Life. He is God!

Those who have never heard the Gospel are like orphans who have not had the opportunity to know their father or receive anything good from him. Conversely, those who have heard and rejected the Gospel are like rebellious children who have not only rejected their father, they have also rejected the opportunity to live an abundant life with him and inherit everything he has for them. Which group will be more likely to receive mercy from God the father… the rebellious children or the orphans?

Both groups will be judged but those who have heard the Gospel will be held to a higher standard than those who have not.

> Luke 12:48But he that knew not, and did commit things worthy of stripes, shall be beaten with few *stripes*. For unto whomsoever much is given, of him shall be much required: and to whom men have committed much, of him they will ask the more.

God is the only one who can righteously judge the hearts of men. His judgments will be just and any salvation will be the direct result of his grace. Jesus paid the price for the sins of all men. I don't know what criteria God will use when he judges those who never had the opportunity to know him, but I know it will be totally just and all of the praise, honor and glory will go to Jesus. His atoning sacrifice is what made salvation possible.

After the final judgment God starts anew. He has overcome every enemy and redeemed his people. The sorrows of our previous lives will be past. Our future will be joyous and it will never end.

> Rev 21:1And I saw a new heaven and a new earth: for the first heaven and the first earth were passed away; and there was no more sea.
>
> 2And I John saw the holy city, new Jerusalem, coming down from God out of heaven, prepared as a bride adorned for her husband.
>
> 3And I heard a great voice out of heaven saying, Behold, the tabernacle of God *is* with men, and he will dwell with them, and they shall be his people, and God himself shall be with them, *and be* their God.

Just as the Tabernacle of Moses was a symbolic representation of the Heavenly Tabernacle, could it be the Heavenly Tabernacle is a symbolic representation of the "Ultimate Tabernacle" that will be created when the New Heaven and New Earth are created?

> Rev 21:4And God shall wipe away all tears from their eyes; and there shall be no more death, neither sorrow, nor crying, neither shall there be any more pain: for the former things are passed away.

⁵And he that sat upon the throne said, Behold, I make all things new. And he said unto me, Write: for these words are true and faithful.

⁶And he said unto me, It is done. I am Alpha and Omega, the beginning and the end. I will give unto him that is athirst of the fountain of the water of life freely.

⁷He that overcometh shall inherit all things; and I will be his God, and he shall be my son.

⁸But the fearful, and unbelieving, and the abominable, and murderers, and whoremongers, and sorcerers, and idolaters, and all liars, shall have their part in the lake which burneth with fire and brimstone: which is the second death.

⁹And there came unto me one of the seven angels which had the seven vials full of the seven last plagues, and talked with me, saying, Come hither, I will shew thee the bride, the Lamb's wife.

¹⁰And he carried me away in the spirit to a great and high mountain, and shewed me that great city, the holy Jerusalem, descending out of heaven from God,

¹¹Having the glory of God: and her light *was* like unto a stone most precious, even like a jasper stone, clear as crystal;

¹²And had a wall great and high, *and* had twelve gates, and at the gates twelve angels, and names written thereon, which are *the names* of the twelve tribes of the children of Israel:

¹³On the east three gates; on the north three gates; on the south three gates; and on the west three gates.

¹⁴And the wall of the city had twelve foundations, and in them the names of the twelve apostles of the Lamb.

¹⁵And he that talked with me had a golden reed to measure the city, and the gates thereof, and the wall thereof.

¹⁶And the city lieth foursquare, and the length is as large as the breadth: and he measured the city with the reed, twelve thousand furlongs. The length and the breadth and the height of it are equal.

¹⁷And he measured the wall thereof, an hundred *and* forty *and* four cubits, *according to* the measure of a man, that is, of the angel.

¹⁸And the building of the wall of it was *of* jasper: and the city *was* pure gold, like unto clear glass.

¹⁹And the foundations of the wall of the city *were* garnished with all manner of precious stones. The first foundation *was* jasper; the second, sapphire; the third, a chalcedony; the fourth, an emerald;

²⁰The fifth, sardonyx; the sixth, sardius; the seventh, chrysolite; the eighth, beryl; the ninth, a topaz; the tenth, a chrysoprasus; the eleventh, a jacinth; the twelfth, an amethyst.

²¹And the twelve gates *were* twelve pearls; every several gate was of one pearl: and the street of the city *was* pure gold, as it were transparent glass.

²²And I saw no temple therein: for the Lord God Almighty and the Lamb are the temple of it.

²³And the city had no need of the sun, neither of the moon, to shine in it: for the glory of God did lighten it, and the Lamb *is* the light thereof.

²⁴And the nations of them which are saved shall walk in the light of it: and the kings of the earth do bring their glory and honour into it.

²⁵And the gates of it shall not be shut at all by day: for there shall be no night there.

²⁶And they shall bring the glory and honour of the nations into it.

²⁷And there shall in no wise enter into it any thing that defileth, neither *whatsoever* worketh abomination, or *maketh* a lie: but they which are written in the Lamb's book of life.

^{Rev 22:1}And he shewed me a pure river of water of life, clear as crystal, proceeding out of the throne of God and of the Lamb.

²In the midst of the street of it, and on either side of the river, *was there* the tree of life, which bare twelve *manner* of fruits, *and* yielded her fruit every month: and the leaves of the tree *were* for the healing of the nations.

In the previous verse we see the Tree of Life. The Tree of Life brings our thoughts back to how it all began. The fall, the flood, the faith of Abraham, the Law of Moses, the reign of David, the carrying away into Babylon and the rebuilding of the Temple. God has done all he could to instruct his people and provide them a way of redemption.

The curse of sin came from Adam's disobedience in eating the fruit of the Tree of Knowledge of Good and Evil. Jesus took that curse upon himself when he was innocently hung upon the tree (the cross). In doing this he has paid the price for our sins and reconciled us to God. Jesus, on the cross, literally became the fruit of the Tree of Life for us. If we choose to eat of the Tree of Life then we will never die (be separated from God).

The Tree of Life we see in the New Jerusalem will be a constant reminder of Gods love, faithfulness and sacrifice for us. The Bible has come full circle. This will be how the story of Adam ends.

^{Rev 22:3}And there shall be no more curse: but the throne of God and of the Lamb shall be in it; and his servants shall serve him:

⁴And they shall see his face; and his name *shall be* in their foreheads.

⁵And there shall be no night there; and they need no candle, neither light of the sun; for the Lord God giveth them light: and they shall reign for ever and ever.

⁶And he said unto me, These sayings *are* faithful and true: and the Lord God of the holy prophets sent his angel to shew unto his servants the things which must shortly be done.

⁷Behold, I come quickly: blessed is he that keepeth the sayings of the prophecy of this book.

⁸And I John saw these things, and heard *them*. And when I had heard and seen, I fell down to worship before the feet of the angel which shewed me these things.

⁹Then saith he unto me, See *thou do it* not: for I am thy fellowservant, and of thy brethren the prophets, and of them which keep the sayings of this book: worship God.

¹⁰And he saith unto me, Seal not the sayings of the prophecy of this book: for the time is at hand.

¹¹He that is unjust, let him be unjust still: and he which is filthy, let him be filthy still: and he that is righteous, let him be righteous still: and he that is holy, let him be holy still.

¹²And, behold, I come quickly; and my reward *is* with me, to give every man according as his work shall be.

¹³I am Alpha and Omega, the beginning and the end, the first and the last.

¹⁴Blessed *are* they that do his commandments, that they may have right to the tree of life, and may enter in through the gates into the city.

¹⁵For without *are* dogs, and sorcerers, and whoremongers, and murderers, and idolaters, and whosoever loveth and maketh a lie.

¹⁶I Jesus have sent mine angel to testify unto you these things in the churches. I am the root and the offspring of David, *and* the bright and morning star.

[17]And the Spirit and the bride say, Come. And let him that heareth say, Come. And let him that is athirst come. And whosoever will, let him take the water of life freely.

[18]For I testify unto every man that heareth the words of the prophecy of this book, If any man shall add unto these things, God shall add unto him the plagues that are written in this book:

[19]And if any man shall take away from the words of the book of this prophecy, God shall take away his part out of the book of life, and out of the holy city, and *from* the things which are written in this book.

[20]He which testifieth these things saith, Surely I come quickly. Amen. Even so, come, Lord Jesus.

[21]The grace of our Lord Jesus Christ *be* with you all. Amen.

This chapter attempted to show the chronological nature of the Book of Revelation. To do this it was necessary to leave out the parenthetical passages. These passages are full of symbolism and provide valuable insight. The next chapter will examine these parenthetical passages.

Chapter Sixteen

Prophecy:

The Parenthetical Passages of Revelation

The last chapter was intended to show the sequential nature of the Book of Revelation. Seven seal judgments will be followed by seven trumpet judgments, the rapture occurs at the seventh trumpet judgment, and then the seven vial judgments are poured out. The sequence of judgments was interrupted at several points by what I call parenthetical passages. These passages constitute a pause or parenthesis in the timeline. There are many things going on during this time period. Many things are happening at the same time. The description of these concurrent events makes it difficult to see the sequential nature of the prophecy. For example, there are three chapters separating the sounding of the last (7th) trumpet in Rev 11:15 and the rapture of the saints in Rev 14:16. According to 1Corinthians 15:52, the rapture and the blowing of the last trumpet happen at virtually the same instant. Why would these events be separated by three chapters?

> 1Cor 15:52In a moment, in the twinkling of an eye, at the last trump: for the trumpet shall sound, and the dead shall be raised incorruptible, and we shall be changed.

The sounding of the last (7th) trumpet is one of the most significant events in the Book of Revelation. It is an important pivotal point in the prophetic timeline. John chooses to insert parenthetical passages before and after the sounding of the last trump. These passages are used to give additional insight into what has been going on to get us to that point. After these parenthetical passages are complete John picks up where he left off in the timeline.

In this chapter, we will examine the parenthetical passages and see why they are so significant.

Parenthetical Passage # 1

The Angel, The Seven Thunders and The Little Book.

^{Rev 10:1}And I saw another mighty angel come down from heaven, clothed with a cloud: and a rainbow *was* upon his head, and his face *was* as it were the sun, and his feet as pillars of fire:

²And he had in his hand a little book open: and he set his right foot upon the sea, and *his* left *foot* on the earth,

³And cried with a loud voice, as *when* a lion roareth: and when he had cried, seven thunders uttered their voices.

⁴And when the seven thunders had uttered their voices, I was about to write: and I heard a voice from heaven saying unto me, Seal up those things which the seven thunders uttered, and write them not.

The angel, the seven thunders and the little book are all mysteries. The Bible doesn't give much information regarding them, but we can examine their symbolism.

The Angel:

The identity of the angel is not given but he shares some attributes typically associated with the Lord.

He was clothed with a cloud.

Clouds are associated with the glory of Lord.

> ^{Ex 40:34}Then a cloud covered the tent of the congregation, and the glory of the LORD filled the tabernacle. ³⁵And Moses was not able to enter into the

tent of the congregation, because the cloud abode thereon, and the glory of the LORD filled the tabernacle.

His face was like the Sun.

> Mat 17:1 And after six days Jesus taketh Peter, James, and John his brother, and bringeth them up into an high mountain apart, 2And was transfigured before them: and his face did shine as the sun, and his raiment was white as the light.

A rainbow was upon his head.

A rainbow, in the Book of Genesis, is associated with God's covenant to never destroy the world again with water. Everywhere else in the Bible the rainbow is associated with the throne of God.

His feet were as pillars of fire.

Notice the similarities between the following passages and the description of the Angel.

> Rev 4:2 And immediately I was in the spirit: and, behold, a throne was set in heaven, and *one* sat on the throne. 3And he that sat was to look upon like a jasper and a sardine stone: and *there was* **a rainbow round about the throne**, in sight like unto an emerald. 4And round about the throne *were* four and twenty seats: and upon the seats I saw four and twenty elders sitting, clothed in white raiment; and they had on their heads crowns of gold. **5And out of the throne proceeded lightnings and thunderings and voices**

> Ezek 1:26 And above the firmament that *was* over their heads *was* the likeness of a throne, as the appearance of a sapphire stone: and upon the likeness of the throne *was* the likeness as the appearance of a man above upon it. **27And I saw as the colour of amber, as the appearance of fire round about within it, from the appearance of his loins even upward, and from the appearance of his loins even downward, I saw as it were the**

appearance of fire, and it had brightness round about. [28]**As the appearance of the bow that is in the cloud in the day of rain**, so *was* the appearance of the brightness round about. This *was* the appearance of the likeness of the glory of the LORD. And when I saw *it,* I fell upon my face, and I heard a voice of one that spake.

The Seven Thunders:

We can only speculate as to what the Seven Thunders said. Why even mention the Seven Thunders if we are not supposed to know what they said? It was important enough for God to tell us the thunderings would occur and yet he refuses to tell us what they will say. It is as if God is trying to tell his people he has a plan of action, while at the same time he tries to prevent the enemy from learning the details of his plan. Hopefully, we will understand what is going on when the Seven Thunders utter their voices.

There are instances in the Old Testament where the Lord's thundering can be seen and these verses seem to be prophetic in nature.

1 Sam 2:10The adversaries of the LORD shall be broken to pieces; **out of heaven shall he thunder upon them**: the LORD shall judge the ends of the earth; and he shall give strength unto his king, and exalt the horn of his anointed.

Ps 18:13**The LORD also thundered in the heavens,** and the Highest gave his voice; hail *stones* and coals of fire. [14]Yea, he sent out his arrows, and scattered them; and he shot out lightnings, and discomfited them. [15]Then the channels of waters were seen, and the foundations of the world were discovered at thy rebuke, O LORD, at the blast of the breath of thy nostrils. [16]He sent from above, he took me, he drew me out of many waters. [17]He delivered me from my strong enemy, and from them which hated me: for they were too strong for me

Psalm 18 mentions 7 things that happen when the Lord thunders.

1)   He sends hail stones.
2)   He sends coals of fire
3)   He sends out his arrows, and scatters them.
4)   He shoots out lightnings, and discomfits them.
5)   The channels of waters are seen.
6)   The foundations of the world are discovered
7)   He sends from above, he takes me, he draws me out of many waters

Could Psalm 18 give us a general idea of what will happen when the Seven Thunders sound?

If so, then what does item 7 mean?

"He sent from above, he took me, he drew me out of many waters"

This sounds like a description of the rapture. To be drawn from many waters would symbolically mean his people would be taken out of many population groups.

Considering the rapture will occur at the last (7ᵗʰ) trumpet does this make sense?

Yes it does. To see why let's continue reading this parenthetical passage.

> Rev 10:5 And the angel which I saw stand upon the sea and upon the earth lifted up his hand to heaven,
>
> 6And sware by him that liveth for ever and ever, who created heaven, and the things that therein are, and the earth, and the things that therein are, and the sea, and the things which are therein, that there should be time no longer:
>
> 7But in the days of the voice of the seventh angel, when he shall begin to sound, the mystery of God should be finished, as he hath declared to his servants the prophets.

In verses 6 and 7, the angel swears there will no further delay. When the 7ᵗʰ (last) Angel sounds, the "Mystery of God" will be finished.

What is the mystery of God?

> [1 Corr 15:51] **Behold, I shew you a mystery**; We shall not all sleep, but we shall all be changed, [52]In a moment, in the twinkling of an eye, **at the last trump**: for the trumpet shall sound, and **the dead shall be raised incorruptible, and we shall be changed.** [53]For this corruptible must put on incorruption, and this mortal *must* put on immortality. [54]So when this corruptible shall have put on incorruption, and this mortal shall have put on immortality, then shall be brought to pass the saying that is written, Death is swallowed up in victory. [55]O death, where *is* thy sting? O grave, where *is* thy victory?

The mystery is when and how the Lord will return for his bride. He will return "AT THE LAST TRUMP!" not at the beginning of the tribulation period as many have been falsely taught.

This parenthetical passage is appropriately located between the 6th and the 7th trumpet judgment. It is as if the stage is being set for the 7th trumpet to be blown.

> [Rev 10:8]And the voice which I heard from heaven spake unto me again, and said, Go *and* take the little book which is open in the hand of the angel which standeth upon the sea and upon the earth.
>
> [9]And I went unto the angel, and said unto him, Give me the little book. And he said unto me, Take *it,* and eat it up; and it shall make thy belly bitter, but it shall be in thy mouth sweet as honey.
>
> [10]And I took the little book out of the angel's hand, and ate it up; and it was in my mouth sweet as honey: and as soon as I had eaten it, my belly was bitter.
>
> [11]And he said unto me, Thou must prophesy again before many peoples, and nations, and tongues, and kings.

The Little Book:

Here again, there isn't a lot of detail given about the little book. We know there was a duality about it. It tasted sweet but it made the stomach bitter. The symbolism of this suggests the book contains wonderfully good news as well as terribly bad news. John was told to eat the little book. By doing this, the book literally becomes a part of him. Then he was told he would prophesy to many peoples, nations, tongues and kings.

The little book John ate was most likely the book of Revelation. It was given to him to write. He would understand better than anyone its ultimate joyful climax as well as its sorrowful trials and tribulations. To him it would be both sweet and bitter.

Parenthetical Passage # 2

The Two Witnesses.

Rev 11:1And there was given me a reed like unto a rod: and the angel stood, saying, Rise, and measure the temple of God, and the altar, and them that worship therein.

2But the court which is without the temple leave out, and measure it not; for it is given unto the Gentiles: and the holy city shall they tread under foot forty and two months.

John was instructed to measure the temple but not the court that was outside of the temple because it is given to the Gentiles. This tells us two things. The temple will be rebuilt and the holy city will have to accommodate the Gentiles for 42 months. This may give us a clue about the circumstances surrounding the rebuilding of the temple. It sounds as if the temple mount will be shared. I suspect a compromise, like land for peace, will allow the rebuilding of the temple.

Dan 9:27And he shall confirm the covenant with many for one week: and in the midst of the week he shall cause the sacrifice and the oblation to cease, and for the overspreading of abominations he shall make it desolate, even until the consummation, and that determined shall be poured upon the desolate.

Rev 11: 3And I will give *power* unto my two witnesses, and they shall prophesy a thousand two hundred *and* threescore days, clothed in sackcloth.

The two witnesses prophesy 1260 days. This is exactly 42 months which is the same amount of time the Gentiles will be occupying the holy city.

Rev 11:4These are the two olive trees, and the two candlesticks standing before the God of the earth.

5And if any man will hurt them, fire proceedeth out of their mouth, and devoureth their enemies: and if any man will hurt them, he must in this manner be killed.

6These have power to shut heaven, that it rain not in the days of their prophecy: and have power over waters to turn them to blood, and to smite the earth with all plagues, as often as they will.

Who are these two witnesses? Most scholars agree they will be either Moses and Elijah or Enoch and Elijah. Moses and Elijah were the two saints Jesus met with on the Mount of Transfiguration. While Enoch and Elijah were the only two men who never physically died. I think Enoch and Elijah are the most likely candidates but I could be wrong.

Rev 11:7And when they shall have finished their testimony, the beast that ascendeth out of the bottomless pit shall make war against them, and shall overcome them, and kill them.

8And their dead bodies *shall lie* in the street of the great city, which spiritually is called Sodom and Egypt, where also our Lord was crucified.

9And they of the people and kindreds and tongues and nations shall see their dead bodies three days and an half, and shall not suffer their dead bodies to be put in graves.

[10]And they that dwell upon the earth shall rejoice over them, and make merry, and shall send gifts one to another; because these two prophets tormented them that dwelt on the earth.

[11]And after three days and an half the Spirit of life from God entered into them, and they stood upon their feet; and great fear fell upon them which saw them.

[12]And they heard a great voice from heaven saying unto them, Come up hither. And they ascended up to heaven in a cloud; and their enemies beheld them.

[13]And the same hour was there a great earthquake, and the tenth part of the city fell, and in the earthquake were slain of men seven thousand: and the remnant were affrighted, and gave glory to the God of heaven.

[14]The second woe is past; *and,* behold, the third woe cometh quickly

The seventh angel sounds his trumpet at this point.

Rev 11:15And the seventh angel sounded; and there were great voices in heaven, saying, The kingdoms of this world are become *the kingdoms* of our Lord, and of his Christ; and he shall reign for ever and ever. [16]And the four and twenty elders, which sat before God on their seats, fell upon their faces, and worshipped God, [17]Saying, We give thee thanks, O Lord God Almighty, which art, and wast, and art to come; because thou hast taken to thee thy great power, and hast reigned. [18]And the nations were angry, and thy wrath is come, and the time of the dead, that they should be judged, and that thou shouldest give reward unto thy servants the prophets, and to the saints, and them that fear thy name, small and great; and shouldest destroy them which destroy the earth. [19]And the temple of God was opened in heaven, and there was seen in his temple the ark of his testament: and there were lightnings, and voices, and thunderings, and an earthquake, and great hail.

Four parenthetical passages are inserted between where the Seventh Trumpet is sounded and when the rapture is described. These parenthetical passages are important but they tend to hide the fact the Seventh Trumpet and the rapture occur at virtually the same time. The key to understanding the placement of these passages is to realize these parenthetical passages are describing concurrent events but they will all culminate with the rapture of the saints (at the last trump). Let's look at these parenthetical passages.

Parenthetical Passage # 3

The nature of the struggle between God, Israel and the Devil

Rev 12:1And there appeared a great wonder in heaven; a woman clothed with the sun, and the moon under her feet, and upon her head a crown of twelve stars:

2And she being with child cried, travailing in birth, and pained to be delivered.

3And there appeared another wonder in heaven; and behold a great red dragon, having seven heads and ten horns, and seven crowns upon his heads.

4And his tail drew the third part of the stars of heaven, and did cast them to the earth: and the dragon stood before the woman which was ready to be delivered, for to devour her child as soon as it was born.

Rev 12:5 And she brought forth a man child, who was to rule all nations with a rod of iron: and her child was caught up unto God, and *to* his throne.

6And the woman fled into the wilderness, where she hath a place prepared of God, that they should feed her there a thousand two hundred *and* threescore days.

The symbolism associated with the woman is unmistakable. We see the same imagery in Joseph's dream in the book of Genesis.

> ^{Gen 37:9}And he (Joseph) dreamed yet another dream, and told it his brethren, and said, Behold, I have dreamed a dream more; and, behold, **the sun and the moon and the eleven stars made obeisance to me**. ¹⁰And he told *it* to his father, and to his brethren: and his father rebuked him, and said unto him, What *is* this dream that thou hast dreamed? **Shall I and thy mother and thy brethren indeed come to bow down ourselves to thee to the earth?** ¹¹And his brethren envied him; but his father observed the saying.

In Joseph's dream the Sun, Moon and Stars were symbolic of Joseph's family. The Sun was Jacob, the Moon was Rachael and the stars were the brothers of Joseph. In the Book of Revelation, the woman is described as being clothed with the sun. She has the moon under her feet, and twelve stars are in her crown. The woman gives birth to a man child who would rule all nations with a rod of iron.

The man child is obviously Jesus. The woman that births him is the nation of Israel and the individual stars in her crown are representative of the 12 tribes of Israel. The symbolism of the Sun and Moon is not as readily obvious. She is clothed with the Sun. It is her covering. The Sun in Joseph's dream was Jacob. God made a covenant with him. This covenant is her covering. She is the beneficiary of Gods covenant to Abraham, Isaac, and Jacob. Through their seed all nations of the Earth will be blessed. In this vision, the Moon is under the woman's feet. The moon in Joseph's dream was his mother. Having the Moon under her feet does not denigrate the mothers in Israel but rather it suggests they have formed the solid ground necessary for the woman to stand on. Sarah, Rebecca and Rachael were all very special women.

> ^{Rev 12:7}And there was war in heaven: Michael and his angels fought against the dragon; and the dragon fought and his angels,
>
> ⁸And prevailed not; neither was their place found any more in heaven.

⁹And the great dragon was cast out, that old serpent, called the Devil, and Satan, which deceiveth the whole world: he was cast out into the earth, and his angels were cast out with him.

¹⁰And I heard a loud voice saying in heaven, Now is come salvation, and strength, and the kingdom of our God, and the power of his Christ: for the accuser of our brethren is cast down, which accused them before our God day and night.

¹¹And they overcame him by the blood of the Lamb, and by the word of their testimony; and they loved not their lives unto the death.

¹²Therefore rejoice, *ye* heavens, and ye that dwell in them. Woe to the inhabiters of the earth and of the sea! for the devil is come down unto you, having great wrath, because he knoweth that he hath but a short time.

The reference to Michael and his angels fighting against the dragon is reminiscent of a similar verse in the book of Daniel. Michael is mentioned by name. He stands as a defender of the people of Israel. This is supposed to be the greatest time of trouble in the history of the nation.

Dan 12:1And at that time shall Michael stand up, the great prince which standeth for the children of thy people: and there shall be a time of trouble, such as never was since there was a nation *even* to that same time: and at that time thy people shall be delivered, every one that shall be found written in the book.

Rev 12:13And when the dragon saw that he was cast unto the earth, he persecuted the woman which brought forth the man *child*.

¹⁴And to the woman were given two wings of a great eagle, that she might fly into the wilderness, into her place, where she is nourished for a time, and times, and half a time, from the face of the serpent.

¹⁵And the serpent cast out of his mouth water as a flood after the woman, that he might cause her to be carried away of the flood.

¹⁶And the earth helped the woman, and the earth opened her mouth, and swallowed up the flood which the dragon cast out of his mouth.

¹⁷And the dragon was wroth with the woman, and went to make war with the remnant of her seed, which keep the commandments of God, and have the testimony of Jesus Christ.

The dragon making war with the "remnant of her seed" is curious. This remnant is described as having the testimony of Jesus Christ. This does not describe what we currently think of as Jewish Israel. The nation of Israel does not accept Jesus as their Messiah. This is why the temple will be rebuilt to reinstitute Old Testament temple worship. The Jewish desire for a temple will be the tool the beast will use to manipulate the nations. What kind of compromises will the nation of Israel be willing to make to achieve peace and to regain the temple? What kind of promises will the beast have to make to the Islamic enemies of Israel to get them to relinquish their control over the temple mount?

Parenthetical Passage # 4

The Nature of the Government in the Last Days And the Mark of the Beast.

^{Rev 13:1}And I stood upon the sand of the sea, and saw a beast rise up out of the sea, having seven heads and ten horns, and upon his horns ten crowns, and upon his heads the name of blasphemy.

²And the beast which I saw was like unto a leopard, and his feet were as *the feet* of a bear, and his mouth as the mouth of a lion: and the dragon gave him his power, and his seat, and great authority.

It is interesting to note the beast has 7 heads and 10 horns just like the dragon. The dragon is cast down from the heavens and the beast rises up out of the sea. The spiritual power behind the beast is the dragon (Satan).

The sea the beast rose out of is the wicked sea of humanity.

Is 57:20But the wicked *are* like the troubled sea, when it cannot rest, whose waters cast up mire and dirt.

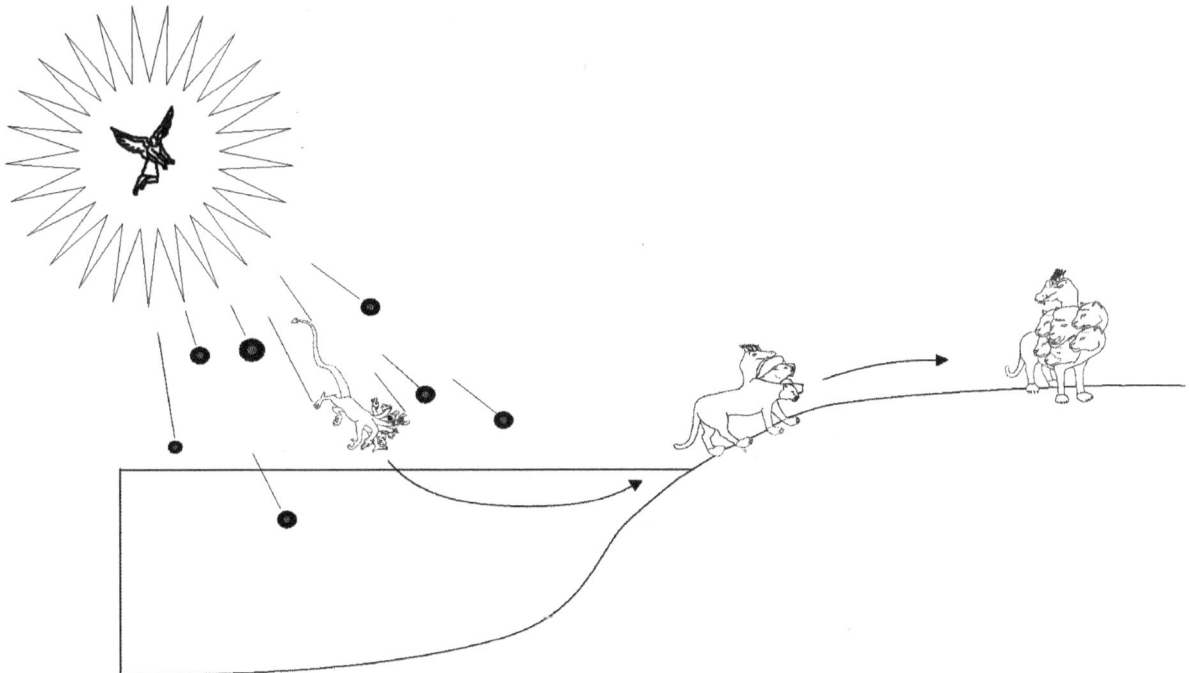

As we previously compared Daniel's prophetic images to the description of the beast in revelation we see the individual governments, which have had dominance over Israel, come together in the latter days. In Daniel's vision each government was described as a type of animal. In Revelation the beast is described as a composite of the animals described by Daniel.

Rev 13:3And I saw one of his heads as it were wounded to death; and his deadly wound was healed: and all the world wondered after the beast.

⁴And they worshipped the dragon which gave power unto the beast: and they worshipped the beast, saying, Who *is* like unto the beast? who is able to make war with him?

One of the countries (or its leader) in the beast alliance will be destroyed or seriously wounded but the wound will be healed. Healing most likely means the country or its leader will recover from its deadly wound. The recovery will be so astounding that the world will be astonished.

Rev 13:5And there was given unto him a mouth speaking great things and blasphemies; and power was given unto him to continue forty *and* two months.

⁶And he opened his mouth in blasphemy against God, to blaspheme his name, and his tabernacle, and them that dwell in heaven.

⁷And it was given unto him to make war with the saints, and to overcome them: and power was given him over all kindreds, and tongues, and nations.

⁸And all that dwell upon the earth shall worship him, whose names are not written in the book of life of the Lamb slain from the foundation of the world.

⁹If any man have an ear, let him hear.

¹⁰He that leadeth into captivity shall go into captivity: he that killeth with the sword must be killed with the sword. Here is the patience and the faith of the saints.

The beast exists during the tribulation period but it (he) is not given power over all kindreds and tongues and nations until after the wounded head is healed. This is the point when he is allowed to make war with the saints and overcome them. He is allowed to continue 42 months after the wound is healed.

These verses (Rev 13:5-7) give us a reference point whereby we can establish a relative timeframe for some of the prophetic events.

The beast is given power to continue 42 months. As we shall see later, the beast will be thrown into the bottomless pit at the end of the tribulation period when Jesus returns with his armies. This would mean the 42 months the beast is allowed to continue are the last 42 months (3.5 years) of the tribulation period.

The last half of the 7 year tribulation period is when the beast and the false prophet take control.

Rev 13:7 says the beast will make war with the saints at this point; therefore the saints must endure the tribulation period beyond its 3.5 year midpoint. This also suggests the worst persecution for the saints will begin at the 3.5 year midpoint. The prophet Daniel says those who make it to the 1335th day will be blessed. This would be 75 days after the midpoint of the tribulation period. Will the blessing be the rapture of the saints?

> Dan 12:12Blessed *is* he that waiteth, and cometh to the thousand three hundred and five and thirty days.

The next beast coming up out of the earth is the false prophet.

> Rev 13:11And I beheld another beast coming up out of the earth; and he had two horns like a lamb, and he spake as a dragon.

> 12And he exerciseth all the power of the first beast before him, and causeth the earth and them which dwell therein to worship the first beast, whose deadly wound was healed.

> 13And he doeth great wonders, so that he maketh fire come down from heaven on the earth in the sight of men,

> 14And deceiveth them that dwell on the earth by *the means of* those miracles which he had power to do in the sight of the beast; saying to them that dwell on the earth, that they should make an image to the beast, which had the wound by a sword, and did live.

> 15And he had power to give life unto the image of the beast, that the image of the beast should both speak, and cause that as many as would not worship the image of the beast should be killed.

¹⁶And he causeth all, both small and great, rich and poor, free and bond, to receive a mark in their right hand, or in their foreheads:

¹⁷And that no man might buy or sell, save he that had the mark, or the name of the beast, or the number of his name.

¹⁸Here is wisdom. Let him that hath understanding count the number of the beast: for it is the number of a man; and his number *is* Six hundred threescore *and* six.

Verse 18 suggests the beast is more than a confederation of nations. The beast is a man. He will be the leader and figurehead of the new world order. The false prophet will be another demonically controlled individual. He will glorify the beast through his "miracles" and will portray the beast as God. He will also institute an economic tracking system (the mark) whereby all monetary transactions can be monitored and controlled.

On the surface, a biologically affixed monetary tracking system makes sense. It would mean every transaction would be electronically tracked but credit or debit cards would not be needed. It could also be used for identification and to help prevent identity theft. If all transactions were tracked it would reduce crime immediately. You couldn't be robbed for the money in your wallet. Nothing could be done in secret on a cash basis. You couldn't make any money "on the side" without the government knowing. It would virtually eliminate tax cheating. In many ways a cashless society seems like a good idea and it is the direction the world is going.

If the mark of the beast is a method of tracking transactions and the Bible warns us against taking the mark, then is it o.k. to use things like credit or debit cards? What is the difference?

First of all, the Bible says that we should not put marks in our flesh.

> ^{Lev 19:28}Ye shall not make any cuttings in your flesh for the dead, nor print any marks upon you: I *am* the LORD.

Is there any wonder tattoos and body piercing have become so popular in the last few years? Satan is preparing the people to receive his mark. Compared to the tattoos and piercings, his mark will seem insignificant.

Secondly, credit or debit cards are different from a mark because they are something you can use or not use. You can put them down or cut them up with a pair of scissors. The mark of the beast, on the other hand, actually becomes part of the person. The most important aspect of the mark is its symbolic meaning. It has to do with ownership. When you own something, how do you show it is yours? You put your name on it. You mark it. This is what the mark of the beast is. When you allow the beast to put his mark on you… you become his.

This is where the idea of a pre-tribulation rapture is going to cause many unsuspecting Christians to lose their soul. The pre-trib rapture believers have not prepared themselves in any way to endure the trials of the tribulation period. They will be totally confused by the things going on around them. They will be easily manipulated by those who would take advantage of their confusion.

> Mat 24:24For there shall arise false Christs, and false prophets, and shall shew great signs and wonders; insomuch that, if *it were* possible, they shall deceive the very elect.

God also puts a mark on his servants. He identifies the ones who are his with a seal.

> Rev 7:2And I saw another angel ascending from the east, having the seal of the living God: and he cried with a loud voice to the four angels, to whom it was given to hurt the earth and the sea,
>
> **3Saying, Hurt not the earth, neither the sea, nor the trees, till we have sealed the servants of our God in their foreheads.**
>
> 4And I heard the number of them which were sealed: *and there were* sealed an hundred *and* forty *and* four thousand of all the tribes of the children of Israel.

The next verses will give us further insight into the nature of the woman with the 12 stars in her crown.

Parenthetical Passage # 5

The Lords Presence is With His People

^{Rev 14:1}And I looked, and, lo, a Lamb stood on the mount Sion, and with him an hundred forty *and* four thousand, having his Father's name written in their foreheads.

²And I heard a voice from heaven, as the voice of many waters, and as the voice of a great thunder: and I heard the voice of harpers harping with their harps:

³And they sung as it were a new song before the throne, and before the four beasts, and the elders: and no man could learn that song but the hundred *and* forty *and* four thousand, which were redeemed from the earth.

⁴These are they which were not defiled with women; for they are virgins. **These are they which follow the Lamb whithersoever he goeth**. These were redeemed from among men, *being* the firstfruits unto God and to the Lamb.

⁵And in their mouth was found no guile: for they are without fault before the throne of God.

In Rev 7:4 we read that 144,000 of Gods servants were sealed (Twelve thousand from each tribe). These twelve tribes correspond to the twelve stars in the woman's crown.

This brings up an interesting question. Is this woman the same as modern Israel? It would seem unlikely. During the reign of King Rehoboam Israel was divided into two nations. The 10 northern tribes were known as the kingdom of Israel and the remaining two tribes were known as kingdom of Judah.

The 10 northern tribes were eventually conquered by the Assyrians and were dispersed. They have come to be known as the 10 lost tribes.

The southern kingdom of Judah consisted of the tribe of Judah, Benjamin and some, if not all, of Levi (Levi was not counted as one of the twelve tribes because they were the priests). Judah continued to exist as a nation until the time of the Romans but even after they were dispersed they kept their identities as Jews. In 1948 Israel was reborn and the Jews returned to their homeland.

As you can see, the 144,000 servants of God from the 12 tribes cannot all come from the modern nation of Israel because 10 of the tribes of Israel are unaccounted for. The modern Jewish nation of Israel will not likely be the source of any of the 144,000. The only descendants of Judah who will be part of the 144,000 will be those who follow Jesus. Only Messianic Jews or Christians of Jewish descent can be counted as part of the 12,000 of Judah.

> Rev 14:4These are they which were not defiled with women; for they are virgins. **These are they which follow the Lamb whithersoever he goeth**. These were redeemed from among men, *being* the firstfruits unto God and to the Lamb

As for the other lost tribes, God knows who is who. He will gather the faithful descendants of Jacob as his first fruits. All of them will have been followers of Jesus. In Rev 13:7, the beast is given power to make war with the saints and to overcome them. By chapter 14 the 144,000 are redeemed from the Earth and are in Heaven. They are with the lamb on mount Zion. The 144,000 were most likely martyred for their unwillingness to submit to the beast.

Parenthetical Passage # 6

The warning goes out against taking the mark of the beast.

> Rev 14:6And I saw another angel fly in the midst of heaven, having the everlasting gospel to preach unto them that dwell on the earth, and to every nation, and kindred, and tongue, and people,

⁷Saying with a loud voice, Fear God, and give glory to him; for the hour of his judgment is come: and worship him that made heaven, and earth, and the sea, and the fountains of waters.

⁸And there followed another angel, saying, Babylon is fallen, is fallen, that great city, because she made all nations drink of the wine of the wrath of her fornication.

⁹And the third angel followed them, saying with a loud voice, If any man worship the beast and his image, and receive *his* mark in his forehead, or in his hand,

¹⁰The same shall drink of the wine of the wrath of God, which is poured out without mixture into the cup of his indignation; and he shall be tormented with fire and brimstone in the presence of the holy angels, and in the presence of the Lamb:

¹¹And the smoke of their torment ascendeth up for ever and ever: and they have no rest day nor night, who worship the beast and his image, and whosoever receiveth the mark of his name.

¹²Here is the patience of the saints: here *are* they that keep the commandments of God, and the faith of Jesus.

¹³And I heard a voice from heaven saying unto me, Write, Blessed *are* the dead which die in the Lord from henceforth: Yea, saith the Spirit, that they may rest from their labours; and their works do follow them.

In the previous verses, an angel is proclaiming the everlasting gospel and warning the people against taking the mark. It is uncertain if this is an angelic being or some other sort of messenger like a satellite broadcast. Angel means messenger. If it is a literal angelic being flying through the sky preaching then the mere spectacle of it should have a tremendous impact on those hearing the message.

The voice from heaven says, "Blessed *are* the dead which die in the Lord from henceforth..." Why is there a special blessing for those who die in the Lord after this point?

These are not the descendants of Jacob like the 144,000 were. These are most likely gentiles who followed Jesus. Death will be a release to them. They will rest from their labors and they will be rewarded according to their works.

Revelation 14:8 says Babylon is fallen. Who is Babylon? Is it the same Babylon that was symbolized as the golden head in Nebuchadnezzar's vision of the multi-metallic statue? I don't think so. I think the imagery goes further back. I think the imagery goes back to the tower of Babel which is the root word in the name Babylon.

The tower of Babel was where the descendants of Noah came together in one accord to build a tower unto heaven (presumably for the purposes of astrology). This displeased God so he confused their language and caused the people to scatter.

During the tribulation period, the scattered people of the world will reunite behind a common leader. The composite beast shows us how the various governments will merge into an evil world order. Babylon will most likely be the religious system that will support the formation of this new world order.

More information on the mystery of Babylon will be provided later when we consider Revelation chapter 17 and 18.

Parenthetical Passages Occurring After the Rapture.

Parenthetical Passage # 7

The Godly are in Heaven now!

The Rapture has occurred but those who were raptured could not enter directly into the temple of God. They had to wait for the 7 angels to pour out their vials filled with God's wrath on those who remain on the earth.

Rev 15:1 And I saw another sign in heaven, great and marvellous, seven angels having the seven last plagues; for in them is filled up the wrath of God.

²And I saw as it were a sea of glass mingled with fire: and them that had gotten the victory over the beast, and over his image, and over his mark, *and* over the number of his name, stand on the sea of glass, having the harps of God.

This Sea of Glass corresponds to the Brazen Laver which was positioned at the entrance of the Tabernacle of Moses. Everything in the Tabernacle of Moses was representative of what was contained in God's heavenly Tabernacle. As the people stand on the Sea of Glass waiting to enter the heavenly Tabernacle they start to sing the song of Moses and the song of the Lamb.

Rev 15:3 And they sing the song of Moses the servant of God, and the song of the Lamb, saying, Great and marvellous *are* thy works, Lord God Almighty; just and true *are* thy ways, thou King of saints.

⁴Who shall not fear thee, O Lord, and glorify thy name? for *thou* only *art* holy: for all nations shall come and worship before thee; for thy judgments are made manifest.

⁵And after that I looked, and, behold, the temple of the tabernacle of the testimony in heaven was opened:

⁶And the seven angels came out of the temple, having the seven plagues, clothed in pure and white linen, and having their breasts girded with golden girdles.

⁷And one of the four beasts gave unto the seven angels seven golden vials full of the wrath of God, who liveth for ever and ever.

⁸And the temple was filled with smoke from the glory of God, and from his power; and no man was able to enter into the temple, till the seven plagues of the seven angels were fulfilled.

Verse 8 answers one of the primary objections the pre-tribulation rapture believers have with the rapture being at the 7th (last) trumpet. They say, God has not appointed us to wrath; therefore we must be raptured out at the beginning of the rapture. They point to the following verse.

^{1Thes 5:9}For God hath not appointed us to wrath, but to obtain salvation by our Lord Jesus Christ.

As the previous verses show, God's wrath is not poured out until <u>AFTER</u> the 7th Trumpet is sounded. This timing is consistent with 1Thes 5:9. A 7th trumpet rapture is consistent with this because God's people are removed before his wrath is poured out.

Parenthetical Passage # 8

Mystery Babylon

The final parenthetical passage in the Book of Revelation concerns Mystery Babylon.

^{Rev 17:1}And there came one of the seven angels which had the seven vials, and talked with me, saying unto me, Come hither; I will shew unto thee the judgment of the great whore that sitteth upon many waters:

²With whom the kings of the earth have committed fornication, and the inhabitants of the earth have been made drunk with the wine of her fornication.

We are immediately told two things about the Mystery of Babylon. First, Babylon is a whore and secondly, she sits upon many waters.

Once again, understanding Biblical symbolism will help us here.

The term whore is used to describe a relationship. The whore takes money to provide fleshly pleasures. There is no commitment, love or loyalty. It's all about money. This should be contrasted to the relationship between a husband and wife. The husband and wife are bound to one another in the eyes of God. They become each others help meet. They provide for each other and hopefully bring forth children.

The unfaithful wife can become a whore just like Israel and Judah did.

> [Jer 3:6]The LORD said also unto me in the days of Josiah the king, Hast thou seen *that* which backsliding Israel hath done? she is gone up upon every high mountain and under every green tree, and there hath played the harlot.

> [7]And I said after she had done all these *things,* Turn thou unto me. But she returned not. And her treacherous sister Judah saw *it.*

> [8]And I saw, when for all the causes whereby backsliding Israel committed adultery I had put her away, and given her a bill of divorce; yet her treacherous sister Judah feared not, but went and played the harlot also.

> [9]And it came to pass through the lightness of her whoredom, that she defiled the land, and committed adultery with stones and with stocks

God uses Israel and Judah to symbolically show the relationship between himself and his people as being like the relationship between a husband and a wife. Israel and Judah were not faithful to God and worshiped idols made of stones and stocks (wood).

God offered forgiveness:

> [Jer 3:12]Go and proclaim these words toward the north, and say, Return, thou backsliding Israel, saith the LORD; *and* I will not cause mine anger to fall upon you: for I *am* merciful, saith the LORD, *and* I will not keep *anger* for ever.

> [13]Only acknowledge thine iniquity, that thou hast transgressed against the LORD thy God, and hast scattered thy ways to the strangers under every green tree, and ye have not obeyed my voice, saith the LORD.

> [14]Turn, O backsliding children, saith the LORD; for I am married unto you: and I will take you one of a city, and two of a family, and I will bring you to Zion:

God considers worshiping false gods as being spiritual adultery. The Whore of Revelation was a spiritual prostitute and she sits on many waters. As we have seen, waters are symbolic of people groups.

The whore is a religious institution which is not faithful to the Lord and has great influence over many population groups. She does what she does for money.

> ^{Rev 17:3}So he carried me away in the spirit into the wilderness: and I saw a woman sit upon a scarlet coloured beast, full of names of blasphemy, having seven heads and ten horns.

> ⁴And the woman was arrayed in purple and scarlet colour, and decked with gold and precious stones and pearls, having a golden cup in her hand full of abominations and filthiness of her fornication:

> ⁵And upon her forehead *was* a name written, MYSTERY, BABYLON THE GREAT, THE MOTHER OF HARLOTS AND ABOMINATIONS OF THE EARTH.

> ⁶And I saw the woman drunken with the blood of the saints, and with the blood of the martyrs of Jesus: and when I saw her, I wondered with great admiration.

The woman is called "The Mother of Harlots".

She gave birth to other harlots which would be offshoots or denominations which would also go after false gods for the love of money.

She is drunk with the blood of the saints and with the blood of the martyrs which were the true worshipers of God.

The only institution that is perfectly described by all of this is the Catholic Church.

She was the mother of the modern Christian denominations. She embraced pagan religions and practices but redefined them as if they were Christian. (The Catholic exaltation of the Virgin Mary is not biblical. It is a repackaging of Isis worship.) The pantheon of pagan gods were renamed and called patron saints. What good catholic doesn't have a saint Mary charm or a

Saint Christopher medallion? These are graven images which are meant to bring supernatural protection to the wearer.

The Catholic Church changed the 10 commandments to accommodate her worship of the pagan gods. (She removed the 2nd commandment which prohibits the making of any graven images and, to avoid having only 9 commandments, she split the 10th commandment into two separate commandments. Thou shall not covet thy neighbor's wife and thou shall not covet thy neighbor's goods. The 10th commandment list 6 specific things not to covet. Why split it up into only two commandments if not to fill in the gap left by removing the 2nd commandment?)

> Ex 20:17Thou shalt not covet thy neighbour's house, thou shalt not covet thy neighbour's wife, nor his manservant, nor his maidservant, nor his ox, nor his ass, nor any thing that *is* thy neighbour's.

She sold indulgences to make the people think they could buy their way into Heaven. She will be used by the seven headed, ten horned beast government

The daughters of the harlot are the protestant denominations. They are not innocent either. They have also refused to turn from their pagan roots. Their adoption of the Easter (fertility) and Christmas (winter solstice) celebrations is totally pagan. These holidays have been assigned superficial Christian meanings to justify continuing these pagan rituals. I don't think God would approve of being linked with the Easter bunny or Santa Clause. The Bible doesn't say Jesus was born on December 25th and it doesn't even tell us to celebrate his birth. The Holy Days God wants us to observe have been declared to us by him. To add pagan holidays to his Holy Days shows that we have not totally given up our other gods. It is spiritual adultery. An increasing number of the protestant denominations are also embracing homosexuality and ordaining homosexual ministers. This is an abomination of the highest order. Any denomination who embraces such behavior has sold out to the popular culture and has become a spiritual harlot.

> Rev 17: 7And the angel said unto me, Wherefore didst thou marvel? I will tell thee the mystery of the woman, and of the beast that carrieth her, which hath the seven heads and ten horns.
>
> 8The beast that thou sawest was, and is not; and shall ascend out of the bottomless pit, and go into perdition: and they that dwell on the earth shall wonder, whose

names were not written in the book of life from the foundation of the world, when they behold the beast that was, and is not, and yet is.

⁹And here *is* the mind which hath wisdom. The seven heads are seven mountains, on which the woman sitteth.

Rome is the seat of the Catholic Church. It is also known as the city of seven hills. This seems to fit Rev 17:9 very nicely. The earlier imagery we saw also identified the heads as kingdoms which would merge during the tribulation period.

The preceding verses are very confusing, but if we consider the next few verses and put them into the context of when this vision was given to John, we will start to gain some understanding.

> ᴿᵉᵛ ¹⁷:¹⁰And there are seven kings: five are fallen, and one is, *and* the other is not yet come; and when he cometh, he must continue a short space.

At the time of John there had been five kingdoms which had subjugated Israel. These 5 are Egypt, Assyria, Babylon, Medo-Persia and Greece. These 5 constitute the 5 fallen kings.

Israel was currently being subjugated by Rome which was "the king that is".

There is also one which hadn't yet come. This indicates there will be another subjugation of Israel. This will be the revived Roman Empire.

> ᴿᵉᵛ ¹⁷:¹¹And the beast that was, and is not, even he is the eighth, and is of the seven, and goeth into perdition.

The beast will be more than a king. He will be an Emperor. The kingdoms symbolized by the seven heads and ten horns will be brought together under his authority. As for his lineage, he will be descended from one of the seven kingdoms symbolized by the heads of the beast.

> ᴿᵉᵛ ¹⁷:¹²And the ten horns which thou sawest are ten kings, which have received no kingdom as yet; but receive power as kings one hour with the beast.

¹³These have one mind, and shall give their power and strength unto the beast.

These 10 horns (kings) seem to rotate their power suspiciously like the Council of the European Union which allows each of its member states to preside over the council for a period of 6 months. Admittedly, there are currently more than 10 member states but this could easily change. If there were 10 member states which presided for 6 months each then it would take 5 years to rotate through them all. But something is going to happen to 3 of the 10 horns.

Consider what Daniel had to say about the 10 horns.

> ᴰᵃⁿ ⁷:⁸I considered the horns, and, behold, there came up among them another little horn, before whom there were three of the first horns plucked up by the roots: and, behold, in this horn *were* eyes like the eyes of man, and a mouth speaking great things.

According to Daniel, three of the horns are going to be plucked up by the little horn (the Anti-Christ). This would leave only 7 horns to rotate through which would require only 3.5 years to complete the cycle. This fits very well because the beast is given power to continue for 42 months (3.5 years)

> ᴿᵉᵛ ¹³:⁴And they worshipped the dragon which gave power unto the beast: and they worshipped the beast, saying, Who *is* like unto the beast? who is able to make war with him?
>
> ⁵And there was given unto him a mouth speaking great things and blasphemies; and power was given unto him to continue forty *and* two months.

> ᴿᵉᵛ ¹⁷: ¹⁴These shall make war with the Lamb, and the Lamb shall overcome them: for he is Lord of lords, and King of kings: and they that are with him *are* called, and chosen, and faithful.

¹⁵And he saith unto me, The waters which thou sawest, where the whore sitteth, are peoples, and multitudes, and nations, and tongues.

¹⁶And the ten horns which thou sawest upon the beast, these shall hate the whore, and shall make her desolate and naked, and shall eat her flesh, and burn her with fire.

¹⁷For God hath put in their hearts to fulfil his will, and to agree, and give their kingdom unto the beast, until the words of God shall be fulfilled.

¹⁸And the woman which thou sawest is that great city, which reigneth over the kings of the earth.

Verse 18 says the woman was a great city that rules over the kings of the Earth. Vatican City is a unique city state. It is the seat of Catholic power. In many ways the Pope is more powerful than any head of state and when heads of state visit him they must bow to him and kiss his ring.

Parenthetical Passage # 9

Babylon is Judged.

^{Rev 18:1}And after these things I saw another angel come down from heaven, having great power; and the earth was lightened with his glory.

²And he cried mightily with a strong voice, saying, Babylon the great is fallen, is fallen, and is become the habitation of devils, and the hold of every foul spirit, and a cage of every unclean and hateful bird.

³For all nations have drunk of the wine of the wrath of her fornication, and the kings of the earth have committed fornication with her, and the merchants of the earth are waxed rich through the abundance of her delicacies.

All nations have drunk of the wine of the wrath of her fornication and committed fornication with her. What does this mean? Babylon is called a whore because she has not been faithful to her husband. God had similar words for Judah and Israel when they went after other gods. Catholicism is supposed to be Christian but she has embraced other religions. She has adapted to the worship of other gods in order to absorb as many "converts" as possible. This is spiritual fornication.

Rev 18:4And I heard another voice from heaven, saying, Come out of her, my people, that ye be not partakers of her sins, and that ye receive not of her plagues.

5For her sins have reached unto heaven, and God hath remembered her iniquities.

6Reward her even as she rewarded you, and double unto her double according to her works: in the cup which she hath filled fill to her double.

7How much she hath glorified herself, and lived deliciously, so much torment and sorrow give her: for she saith in her heart, I sit a queen, and am no widow, and shall see no sorrow.

8Therefore shall her plagues come in one day, death, and mourning, and famine; and she shall be utterly burned with fire: for strong *is* the Lord God who judgeth her.

9And the kings of the earth, who have committed fornication and lived deliciously with her, shall bewail her, and lament for her, when they shall see the smoke of her burning,

10Standing afar off for the fear of her torment, saying, Alas, alas, that great city Babylon, that mighty city! for in one hour is thy judgment come.

11And the merchants of the earth shall weep and mourn over her; for no man buyeth their merchandise any more:

12The merchandise of gold, and silver, and precious stones, and of pearls, and fine linen, and purple, and silk, and scarlet, and all thyine wood, and all manner vessels of ivory, and all manner vessels of most precious wood, and of brass, and iron, and marble,

¹³And cinnamon, and odours, and ointments, and frankincense, and wine, and oil, and fine flour, and wheat, and beasts, and sheep, and horses, and chariots, and slaves, and souls of men.

¹⁴And the fruits that thy soul lusted after are departed from thee, and all things which were dainty and goodly are departed from thee, and thou shalt find them no more at all.

I think Vatican City is the only candidate that fits as Babylon because it is a religious institution as well as a city. Its status is unique in the world and it is wealthy beyond belief.

^{Rev 18:15}The merchants of these things, which were made rich by her, shall stand afar off for the fear of her torment, weeping and wailing,

¹⁶And saying, Alas, alas, that great city, that was clothed in fine linen, and purple, and scarlet, and decked with gold, and precious stones, and pearls!

¹⁷For in one hour so great riches is come to nought. And every shipmaster, and all the company in ships, and sailors, and as many as trade by sea, stood afar off,

¹⁸And cried when they saw the smoke of her burning, saying, What *city is* like unto this great city!

¹⁹And they cast dust on their heads, and cried, weeping and wailing, saying, Alas, alas, that great city, wherein were made rich all that had ships in the sea by reason of her costliness! for in one hour is she made desolate.

Verse 19 shows the destruction of Babylon will be quick and complete. Rev 17: 16 shows us she will be attacked by the nations she has been in alliance with.

^{Rev 17:16}And the ten horns which thou sawest upon the beast, these shall hate the whore, and shall make her desolate and naked, and shall eat her flesh, and burn her with fire.

Rev 18:20Rejoice over her, *thou* heaven, and *ye* holy apostles and prophets; for God hath avenged you on her.

21And a mighty angel took up a stone like a great millstone, and cast *it* into the sea, saying, Thus with violence shall that great city Babylon be thrown down, and shall be found no more at all.

22And the voice of harpers, and musicians, and of pipers, and trumpeters, shall be heard no more at all in thee; and no craftsman, of whatsoever craft *he be,* shall be found any more in thee; and the sound of a millstone shall be heard no more at all in thee;

23And the light of a candle shall shine no more at all in thee; and the voice of the bridegroom and of the bride shall be heard no more at all in thee: for thy merchants were the great men of the earth; for by thy sorceries were all nations deceived.

24And in her was found the blood of prophets, and of saints, and of all that were slain upon the earth.

Verse 24 shows us that Babylon was complicit in the deaths of the prophets and saints during the tribulation period. She was dunk with their blood.

> Rev 17:6And I saw the woman drunken with the blood of the saints, and with the blood of the martyrs of Jesus: and when I saw her, I wondered with great admiration.

The woman (Babylon) will be a total abomination. Any Catholic who truly desires to serve Jesus needs to come out of her. Seek Jesus directly while there is still time. Salvation is through him ONLY! Not the church. Not Mary and Not the Pope.

> Rev 18:4And I heard another voice from heaven, saying, Come out of her, my people, that ye be not partakers of her sins, and that ye receive not of her plagues.

Did you notice that God tells **his people** to come out of her? There are those who God considers to be his within her but if they do not come out of her they will suffer her fate.

This is the end of the parenthetical passages in the Book of Revelation. The chronology picks back up with chapter 19. The insertion of these parenthetical passages has complicated the study of Revelation. The parenthetical passages are filled with details which will be helpful to those who will enter into the tribulation period. These passages will give people an understanding of the true nature of what is happening around them. Some will be martyred while others will endure until the Lord returns at the last trump. Either way, we must be steadfast and determined to stand in the face of evil and never give in. Our souls are on the line. Do not be afraid to choose poverty, hunger or death over taking the mark of the beast. God has repeatedly shown his ability to feed and provide for his people when they are not able to provide for themselves. He did it with the Israelites in the wilderness and he fed the multitude with only a few loaves and fishes.

Faith is a combination of belief, trust and action. We must believe and trust God. He has the ability to prepare a place for us in the midst of our enemies. I would not be surprised if God uses the manna to once again feed his people in the wilderness. The manna could have been a foreshadowing of the miracle he will perform for his people during the tribulation period. Remember Rev 12:6.

> Rev 12:6And the woman fled into the wilderness, where she hath a place prepared of God, that they should feed her there a thousand two hundred *and* threescore days.

The woman is Israel but Christian believers have been grafted into the same vine as Israel, so why wouldn't God provide for us as well?

On the next page is a diagram which will attempt to put the timelines of Daniel and Revelation into their proper sequence. The one thing that needs further clarification is the placement on the timeline of the woman who fled into the wilderness for 1260 days. This woman has been shown to be Christian Israel. She flees into the wilderness during the first 3 ½ years of the tribulation while the non-Christian portion of Israel returns to Old Testament style temple worship. She will only be fed for 3 ½ years until the beast is allowed to make war with her. He will overcome the saints and make martyrs of them.

> ^{Rev 13:5}And there was given unto him a mouth speaking great things and blasphemies; and power was given unto him to continue forty *and* two months.

> ^{Rev 13:7}And it was given unto him to make war with the saints, and to overcome them: and power was given him over all kindreds, and tongues, and nations.

> ^{Rev 14:1}And I looked, and, lo, a Lamb stood on the mount Sion, and with him an hundred forty *and* four thousand, having his Father's name written in their foreheads.

The Number of Days

(Fitting it all together)

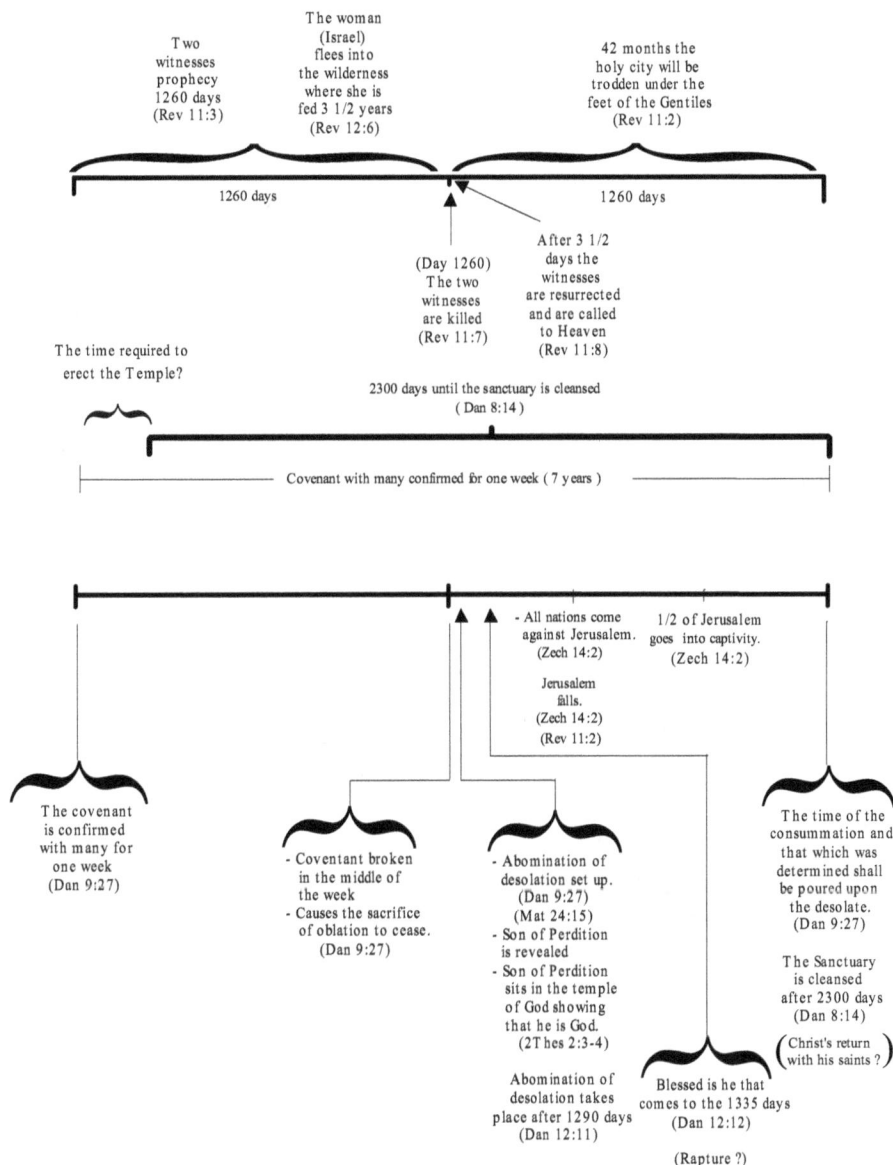

Two witnesses prophecy 1260 days (Rev 11:3)

The woman (Israel) flees into the wilderness where she is fed 3 1/2 years (Rev 12:6)

42 months the holy city will be trodden under the feet of the Gentiles (Rev 11:2)

1260 days

1260 days

(Day 1260) The two witnesses are killed (Rev 11:7)

After 3 1/2 days the witnesses are resurrected and are called to Heaven (Rev 11:8)

The time required to erect the Temple?

2300 days until the sanctuary is cleansed (Dan 8:14)

Covenant with many confirmed for one week (7 years)

- All nations come against Jerusalem. (Zech 14:2)

1/2 of Jerusalem goes into captivity. (Zech 14:2)

Jerusalem falls. (Zech 14:2) (Rev 11:2)

The covenant is confirmed with many for one week (Dan 9:27)

- Covenant broken in the middle of the week
- Causes the sacrifice of oblation to cease. (Dan 9:27)

- Abomination of desolation set up. (Dan 9:27) (Mat 24:15)
- Son of Perdition is revealed
- Son of Perdition sits in the temple of God showing that he is God. (2Thes 2:3-4)

Abomination of desolation takes place after 1290 days (Dan 12:11)

Blessed is he that comes to the 1335 days (Dan 12:12)

(Rapture ?)

The time of the consummation and that which was determined shall be poured upon the desolate. (Dan 9:27)

The Sanctuary is cleansed after 2300 days (Dan 8:14)

(Christ's return with his saints ?)

In the next chapter we will consider the prophecies Jesus gave concerning the last days. We will once again see the astounding interconnectedness of the scriptures.

Chapter Seventeen

Prophecy:

The Olivet Discourse

So far, in our search to understand prophecy, we have examined the Book of Daniel and the Book of Revelation. We've seen how these two books compliment each other. They fit together perfectly like the gears in a machine. Other prophets throughout the Bible provide important parts which are required to construct the machine. The prophecies were given to special men who obediently recorded what they saw without necessarily understanding their prophecies. In this chapter we will study the prophecies that were given to us by the Lord himself on the Mount of Olives. We will put what he said into the context of what we were told by Daniel and John. What Jesus said will become the third major gear in the machine. When we finish, the purpose of the machine will become obvious. We will see the machine is a clock. It allows us to see what time it is.

> Mat 16: 2He (Jesus) answered and said unto them, When it is evening, ye say, *It will be* fair weather: for the sky is red.
>
> 3And in the morning, *It will be* foul weather to day: for the sky is red and lowring. O *ye* hypocrites, ye can discern the face of the sky; but can ye not *discern* the signs of the times?

There are three different accounts of what is known as the "Olivet Discourse". These accounts are found in Mathew, Mark, and Luke. They are all very similar but Luke gives additional information that Mathew and Mark do not.

Just prior to the Olivet Discourse, Jesus and his disciples were leaving the temple and one of his disciples commented about the stones and the buildings of the temple. Jesus responded by telling them these buildings would be destroyed.

> Mat 24: 2And Jesus said unto them, See ye not all these things? verily I say unto you, There shall not be left here one stone upon another, that shall not be thrown down.

The thought of the temple being destroyed disturbed the disciples. Later when Jesus was sitting on the Mount of Olives Peter, James, John and Andrew came to him and asked him the following questions…

> Mat 24: 3And as he sat upon the mount of Olives, the disciples came unto him privately, saying, Tell us, when shall these things be? and what *shall be* the sign of thy coming, and of the end of the world?

> Mar 13: 4Tell us, when shall these things be? and what *shall be* the sign when all these things shall be fulfilled?

> Luk 21: 7And they asked him, saying, Master, but when shall these things be? and what sign *will there be* when these things shall come to pass?

It's curious the three gospels which recorded the Olivet Discourse were not written by the people who came to Jesus privately and asked him the questions concerning the destruction of the temple. From this we can conclude either the accounts of the Olivet Discourse where recorded as a second hand account of what Jesus said or Jesus was asked privately but he answered so all of his disciples could hear.

The disciples asked Jesus 3 separate questions.

1) When will these things be?
2) What shall be the sign of thy coming?
3) and of the end of the world?

It seems as if the disciples thought they were asking 2 questions but they were really asking 3. They assumed that the coming of Jesus would be at the end of the world. Jesus didn't specifically tell them his second coming would precede the "end of the world" by more than a thousand years but he did answer all three of their questions.

When shall these things be?

False Christs

Mat 24: 4And Jesus answered and said unto them, Take heed that no man deceive you. 5For many shall come in my name, saying, I am Christ; and shall deceive many.

Mar 13: 5And Jesus answering them began to say, Take heed lest any *man* deceive you: 6For many shall come in my name, saying, I am *Christ;* and shall deceive many.

Luke 21: 8And he said, Take heed that ye be not deceived: for many shall come in my name, saying, I am *Christ;* and the time draweth near: go ye not therefore after them.

The first thing Jesus was concerned about was the deception that would take place prior to his return. Jesus says many would come in his name saying "I am Christ" and they will deceive many.

The wording of this has two possible meanings. It could mean there would be imposters who would pose as Jesus in order to deceive many. It could also mean there would be those who would come in the name of Jesus and say Jesus was the anointed one (Christ) and by doing this they could deceive many.

I believe both readings are correct.

Mat 24: 11And many false prophets shall rise, and shall deceive many.

Mat 24: ²³Then if any man shall say unto you, Lo, here *is* Christ, or there; believe *it* not.

²⁴For there shall arise false Christs, and false prophets, and shall shew great signs and wonders; insomuch that, if *it were* possible, they shall deceive the very elect.

Lies are often hidden inside a truth. If the very elect can be deceived then the false Christs and false prophets will have to be very convincing. Jesus is the anointed son of God. He is the Christ and the Christians are looking for his return. Satan knows this and he intends to use this against the followers of God.

There will be much confusion during this time. Most modern day (Laodicean) Christians are not strong in the word and have been taught the comforting pre-tribulation rapture doctrine. These Christians will not believe their own eyes when the tribulation period starts and they will continue to expect the rapture to come at any minute. They will be very vulnerable to the false prophets who proclaim the coming of their false Christ, and the supernatural signs they are able to perform will give the false prophets all the credibility they need. The confused Christians, as well as the rest of the people, will be totally vulnerable to the deceit of the false prophet.

Rev 13: ¹³And he doeth great wonders, so that he maketh fire come down from heaven on the earth in the sight of men,

¹⁴And deceiveth them that dwell on the earth by *the means of* those miracles which he had power to do in the sight of the beast; saying to them that dwell on the earth, that they should make an image to the beast, which had the wound by a sword, and did live.

¹⁵And he had power to give life unto the image of the beast, that the image of the beast should both speak, and cause that as many as would not worship the image of the beast should be killed.

¹⁶And he causeth all, both small and great, rich and poor, free and bond, to receive a mark in their right hand, or in their foreheads:

¹⁷And that no man might buy or sell, save he that had the mark, or the name of the beast, or the number of his name.

¹⁸Here is wisdom. Let him that hath understanding count the number of the beast: for it is the number of a man; and his number *is* Six hundred threescore *and* six.

How could the pre-tribulation rapture believers be convinced to take the mark of the beast? Wouldn't they wake up?

Maybe some will wake up but I think the mark of the beast will be marketed as something other than swearing your allegiance to the devil. Satan is very cunning. The mark of the beast will seem to make sense. It will be linked with money. No man will be able to buy or sell without it. The pre-tribulation believing Christians will not recognize it for what it is because they think the mark of the beast will not come until after they are raptured into Heaven.

I can even see the false prophet twisting the scripture to give the impression that the mark of the beast is really the Seal of God.

> ^{Rev 7: 2}And I saw another angel ascending from the east, having the seal of the living God: and he cried with a loud voice to the four angels, to whom it was given to hurt the earth and the sea,
>
> ³Saying, Hurt not the earth, neither the sea, nor the trees, till we have sealed the servants of our God in their foreheads.
>
> ⁴And I heard the number of them which were sealed: *and there were* sealed an hundred *and* forty *and* four thousand of all the tribes of the children of Israel.

The preceding verses could be twisted by the false prophet to make them seem to describe his mark of the beast. The scripturally unprepared Christians would gladly receive the mark if they could be convinced it were the Seal of God described in Rev 7:3.

The Beginning of Sorrows

The next thing Jesus told us to look for was wars, famines and earthquakes.

Mat 24: [6]And ye shall hear of wars and rumours of wars: see that ye be not troubled: for all *these things* must come to pass, but the end is not yet.

[7]For nation shall rise against nation, and kingdom against kingdom: and there shall be famines, and pestilences, and earthquakes, in divers places.

[8]All these *are* the beginning of sorrows.

Wars, famines and earthquakes are nothing new to this planet but for Jesus to call them the "beginning of sorrows" indicates their intensity will dramatically increase prior to his return.

Persecution

Mat 24: [9]Then shall they deliver you up to be afflicted, and shall kill you: and ye shall be hated of all nations for my name's sake.

[10]And then shall many be offended, and shall betray one another, and shall hate one another.

[11]And many false prophets shall rise, and shall deceive many.

[12]And because iniquity shall abound, the love of many shall wax cold.

[13]But he that shall endure unto the end, the same shall be saved.

Mat 24:9-12 shows the turmoil and persecution the followers of Jesus will have to endure. Notice the false prophets are mentioned again. They will be instrumental in turning the Christians against each other through their deception.

Luke gives the Christians during this timeframe additional instruction.

> Luke 21: 10Then said he unto them, Nation shall rise against nation, and kingdom against kingdom:
>
> 11And great earthquakes shall be in divers places, and famines, and pestilences; and fearful sights and great signs shall there be from heaven.
>
> 12But before all these, they shall lay their hands on you, and persecute *you,* delivering *you* up to the synagogues, and into prisons, being brought before kings and rulers for my name's sake.
>
> 13And it shall turn to you for a testimony.
>
> 14Settle *it* therefore in your hearts, not to meditate before what ye shall answer:
>
> 15For I will give you a mouth and wisdom, which all your adversaries shall not be able to gainsay nor resist.

True Christians will be persecuted early on by the government (rulers and kings) and by the religious establishment (synagogues). We are told not to think about what we will say at that time but rather we should let Jesus give us the words to speak when that time comes. He will speak through us and they will not be able to deny the truth of what is said.

> Luke 21: 16And ye shall be betrayed both by parents, and brethren, and kinsfolks, and friends; and *some* of you shall they cause to be put to death.
>
> 17And ye shall be hated of all *men* for my name's sake.
>
> 18But there shall not an hair of your head perish.
>
> 19In your patience possess ye your souls.

The deception of the times will cause even the people who you would normally be able to trust to become your enemy. Family and friends will betray you. You will be hated by everybody. We can only imagine what kind of lying treachery will be used to turn people violently against real Christians. I expect this will be the result of our refusal to take the mark of the beast. All of us will become instant criminals. We will lose all of our possessions and we will have to scavenge for our survival.

Verse 16 says some of you will be put to death but verse 18 says not a hair of your head will perish. How can this be?

I think the key is the difference between the words death and perish. Death is referring to the physical loss of life. Perishing is referring to spiritual perishing. The passage is saying, no matter what they do to you physically, they cannot get to you spiritually if you do not give up. If they pluck out your eyes, don't worry. They will not perish. They will be restored to you at the resurrection. God will preserve even something as inconsequential as your hair if it is lost because of your obedience to him.

We Must Endure

Mat 24: 11And many false prophets shall rise, and shall deceive many. 12And because iniquity shall abound, the love of many shall wax cold. 13But he that shall endure unto the end, the same shall be saved

Mark 13:13And ye shall be hated of all *men* for my name's sake: but he that shall endure unto the end, the same shall be saved.

Luke 21: 19In your patience possess ye your souls.

All three versions of the Olivet discourse stress that endurance to the end is required to be saved. A good try is not good enough. Giving up is not an option. Iniquity will abound, people will be deceived and true Christians will be persecuted.

What shall be the sign of thy coming?

The Gospel Preached

^{Mat 24:} ¹⁴And this gospel of the kingdom shall be preached in all the world for a witness unto all nations; and then shall the end come.

^{Mark 13:10}And the gospel must first be published among all nations.

^{Rev 14:} ⁶And I saw another angel fly in the midst of heaven, having the everlasting gospel to preach unto them that dwell on the earth, and to every nation, and kindred, and tongue, and people,

⁷Saying with a loud voice, Fear God, and give glory to him; for the hour of his judgment is come: and worship him that made heaven, and earth, and the sea, and the fountains of waters.

⁸And there followed another angel, saying, Babylon is fallen, is fallen, that great city, because she made all nations drink of the wine of the wrath of her fornication.

⁹And the third angel followed them, saying with a loud voice, If any man worship the beast and his image, and receive *his* mark in his forehead, or in his hand,

¹⁰The same shall drink of the wine of the wrath of God, which is poured out without mixture into the cup of his indignation; and he shall be tormented with fire and brimstone in the presence of the holy angels, and in the presence of the Lamb:

Matthew and Mark tell us the Gospel must be published among all nations. The Book of Revelation tells us about an "angel" who flies through the heaven preaching the Gospel to all nations and it warns against taking the mark. I don't know if this is a literal angel or a Christian broadcast from satellite. Either way, the people will not be able to claim ignorance as an excuse.

The Abomination of Desolation and Great Tribulation

After Jesus tells his disciples about the coming persecution and the need to endure to the end he mentions what he calls the "abomination of desolation".

Mat 24: [15]When ye therefore shall see the abomination of desolation, spoken of by Daniel the prophet, stand in the holy place, (whoso readeth, let him understand:)

[16]Then let them which be in Judaea flee into the mountains:

[17]Let him which is on the housetop not come down to take any thing out of his house:

[18]Neither let him which is in the field return back to take his clothes.

[19]And woe unto them that are with child, and to them that give suck in those days!

[20]But pray ye that your flight be not in the winter, neither on the sabbath day:

[21]For then shall be great tribulation, such as was not since the beginning of the world to this time, no, nor ever shall be.

[22]And except those days should be shortened, there should no flesh be saved: but for the elect's sake those days shall be shortened.

Matthew doesn't tell us what the abomination of desolation is. He says it was spoken of by Daniel the prophet.

Mark gives us a very similar version of the abomination of desolation.

> ^{Mark 13:} ¹⁴But when ye shall see the abomination of desolation, spoken of by Daniel the prophet, standing where it ought not, (let him that readeth understand,) then let them that be in Judaea flee to the mountains:

> ¹⁵And let him that is on the housetop not go down into the house, neither enter *therein,* to take any thing out of his house:

> ¹⁶And let him that is in the field not turn back again for to take up his garment.

> ¹⁷But woe to them that are with child, and to them that give suck in those days!

> ¹⁸And pray ye that your flight be not in the winter.

> ¹⁹For *in* those days shall be affliction, such as was not from the beginning of the creation which God created unto this time, neither shall be.

> ²⁰And except that the Lord had shortened those days, no flesh should be saved: but for the elect's sake, whom he hath chosen, he hath shortened the days.

Mark gives us an additional piece of information about the abomination of desolation. He says it stands where it ought not. It sounds as if an object standing where it shouldn't is part of the abomination.

Let's see what Daniel had to say about the abomination of desolation.

> ^{Dan 9:27}And he shall confirm the covenant with many for one week: and in the midst of the week he shall cause the sacrifice and the oblation to cease, and for the overspreading of abominations he shall make *it* desolate, even until the consummation, and that determined shall be poured upon the desolate.

If we look at the Book of Revelation we can get additional information about this time period.

> Rev 13: 14And deceiveth them that dwell on the earth by *the means of* those miracles which he had power to do in the sight of the beast; saying to them that dwell on the earth, that they should make an image to the beast, which had the wound by a sword, and did live.
>
> 15And he had power to give life unto the image of the beast, that the image of the beast should both speak, and cause that as many as would not worship the image of the beast should be killed.

The Temple will be taken over during this time.

> Dan 12: 11And from the time *that* the daily *sacrifice* shall be taken away, and the abomination that maketh desolate set up, *there shall be* a thousand two hundred and ninety days.

The antichrist will set himself up in the Temple.

> 2 Thes 2: 3Let no man deceive you by any means: for *that day shall not come*, except there come a falling away first, and that man of sin be revealed, the son of perdition;
>
> 4Who opposeth and exalteth himself above all that is called God, or that is worshipped; so that he as God sitteth in the temple of God, shewing himself that he is God.

There is something else you should notice when reading the passages in Matthew and Mark. You should notice how they identify this period as being the greatest period of tribulation that will ever exist (see Mat 24:21 and Mark 13:19). They also say the Lord will shorten the days (for the elect's sake) otherwise no flesh would be saved.

I don't know what Matthew and Mark mean by "shortening the days", but God does it for the elect's sake. Which means God's elect will be here during the worst part of the tribulation period (No pre-tribulation rapture). We can also conclude the worst part of the tribulation will occur while the church is still here. We can conclude this because the rapture doesn't occur until Mat 24: 30-31, Mark 13: 26-27 and Luke 21: 27.

Luke doesn't mention the abomination of desolation specifically but he does mention the desolation of Jerusalem. He says when Jerusalem is compassed with armies, the desolation is near. By comparing Luke's account with that of Matthew and Mark we can see the abomination of desolation and the desolation of Jerusalem happen at virtually the same time.

> Luke 21: 20And when ye shall see Jerusalem compassed with armies, then know that the desolation thereof is nigh.
>
> 21Then let them which are in Judaea flee to the mountains; and let them which are in the midst of it depart out; and let not them that are in the countries enter thereinto.
>
> 22For these be the days of vengeance, that all things which are written may be fulfilled.
>
> 23But woe unto them that are with child, and to them that give suck, in those days! for there shall be great distress in the land, and wrath upon this people.
>
> 24And they shall fall by the edge of the sword, and shall be led away captive into all nations: and Jerusalem shall be trodden down of the Gentiles, until the times of the Gentiles be fulfilled.

Verses 20-24 are unique to the book of Luke. These verses place the focus on Jerusalem. We are told what to look for (Jerusalem being surrounded with armies). At that point the desolation of Jerusalem will be near. Verse 24 says they (those who inhabit Jerusalem) will be lead away captive into all nations until the times of the gentiles be fulfilled. This sounds similar to what happened when Nebuchadnezzar defeated Judah and took its people for slaves. Jesus was obviously describing a future event which brings us back to the concept of dual fulfillment in scripture. Is this another example of type and shadow?

It has been thought the destruction of the Jewish Temple in 70 AD was the fulfillment of these verses. There may be some merit to this interpretation but Matthew and Mark's assertion this will be the time of the greatest tribulation the world would ever know would argue against the fulfillment in 70 AD hypothesis. Luke 21:22 says these will be the days of vengeance when all things which are written will be fulfilled. The 70 AD fulfillment hypothesis would mean the last 2000 years have been God's days of vengeance. This seems unlikely. It is more likely God's days of vengeance will be seen during the tribulation period. Considering all three accounts, we can expect to see Jerusalem compassed with armies in the future. Then the wise inhabitants of Jerusalem will flee into the mountains and the remaining inhabitants will be lead away captive into other nations.

If you look at most current maps of modern Israel (see the map on the following page) you will find Jerusalem approximately in the center of Israel but you will see it is surrounded on 3 sides by a contested area known as the West Bank. This is an area Israel obtained as a result of the 1967 Six Days War. Their "right" to this land has been questioned by many of the surrounding nations and has been used as a justification for all sorts of hostile and terrorist attacks against Israel. I believe resolving the West Bank issue will be the key to the rebuilding of the Jewish Temple. President Obama, as well as previous administrations, have been pushing to make the West Bank an independent state for the Palestinians. They have been doing everything within their power to limit and reduce Israeli settlements there and to push forward their "Two State" solution.

Modern Map of Israel

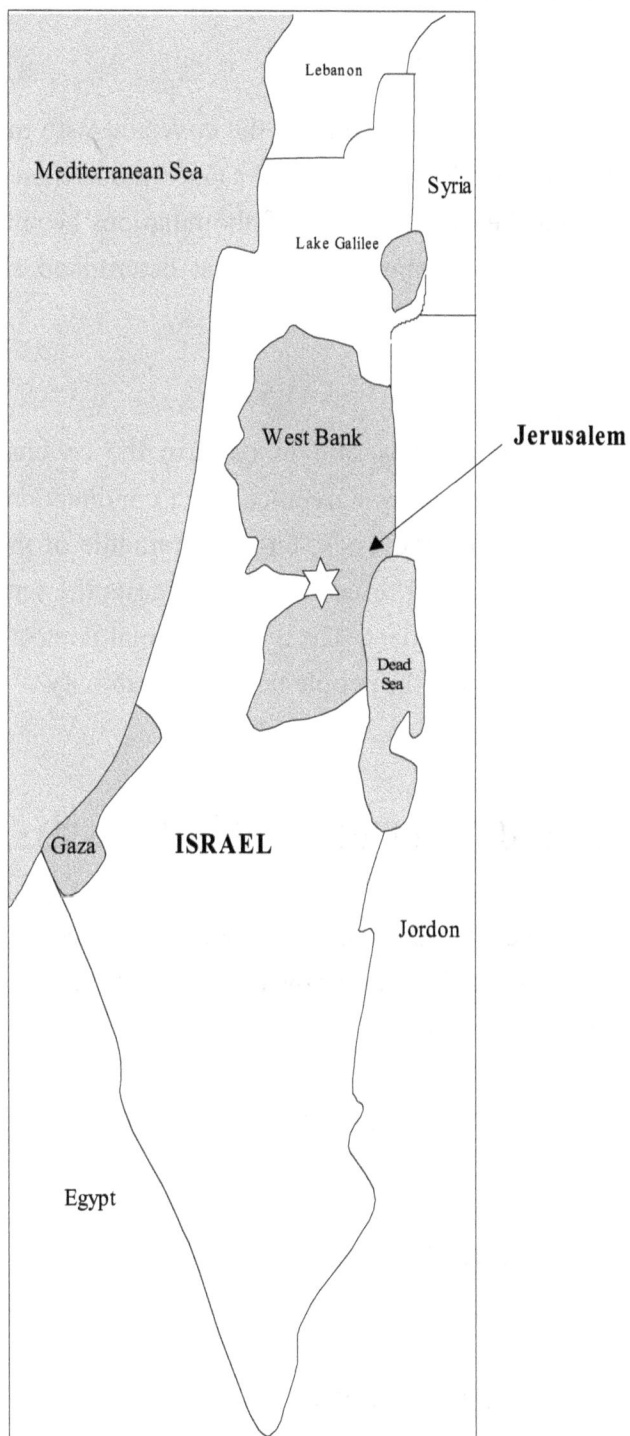

Mediterranean Sea

Lebanon

Syria

Lake Galilee

West Bank

Jerusalem

Dead Sea

Gaza

ISRAEL

Jordon

Egypt

I believe Israel will finally give up the West Bank with the understanding Jerusalem will be shared and the Temple will be allowed to be rebuilt. This will be part of a seven year plan. The plan will probably be something like a New Oslo Accord or a Renewal of the Oslo accord. It may not be based on Oslo at all but it will be a 7 year plan and it will probably be a renewal of a previous agreement.

> Dan 9: 27 And he shall confirm the covenant with many for one week: and in the midst of the week he shall cause the sacrifice and the oblation to cease, and for the overspreading of abominations he shall make *it* desolate, even until the consummation, and that determined shall be poured upon the desolate.

He (presumably the antichrist) is said to confirm the covenant for one week (seven years). This implies there was a previous agreement or a continuation of a current agreement. This agreement will be renewed for one week, but in the middle of the week he will cause the sacrifice and oblation (temple worship) to cease. This suggests the temple will exist during the first 3 ½ years of the seven year agreement. The 3 ½ year point is most likely when you will see Jerusalem compassed with armies and the people taken into captivity.

Another Warning Against Deceivers

Matthew and Mark give an additional warning against deceivers just prior to describing the manner of Jesus coming and the Rapture of his people. This reinforces the idea that deception will be rampant just prior to Jesus' return.

> Mat 24: 23 Then if any man shall say unto you, Lo, here *is* Christ, or there; believe *it* not.
>
> 24 For there shall arise false Christs, and false prophets, and shall shew great signs and wonders; insomuch that, if *it were* possible, they shall deceive the very elect.
>
> 25 Behold, I have told you before.
>
> 26 Wherefore if they shall say unto you, Behold, *he is* in the desert; go not forth: behold, he is in the secret chambers; believe *it* not.

There will be mass confusion among the people because of the disasters going on all around them. The people will be searching for answers and will be easily deceived by imposters who can seemingly perform great signs and wonders. Verse 24 says if it were possible, they would even deceive the very elect. The believers in a pre-trib rapture will be easily deceived at this time. At some point, the failure of the rapture to occur prior to the start of the tribulation period will become undeniable. Those who have invested all their faith in that doctrine will become perplexed. They will not know what the truth is. The false Christs will be very convincing. What they say will seem to make sense. The disillusioned pre-trib believers will be easy prey for the antichrist and his prophets. This is the reason I believe the pre-trib rapture doctrine is one of the most dangerous false doctrines ever. The pre-trib believers could conceivably be convinced to take the mark of the beast because they didn't expect the mark of the beast to implement prior to their rapture.

Mark says virtually the same thing.

Mark 13: 21And then if any man shall say to you, Lo, here *is* Christ; or, lo, *he is* there; believe *him* not:

22For false Christs and false prophets shall rise, and shall shew signs and wonders, to seduce, if *it were* possible, even the elect.

23But take ye heed: behold, I have foretold you all things.

It is so important not to be deceived that Jesus warned against it twice during the Olivet Discourse. The elect will be here and the deception will be so great even they will be susceptible to it. Only Christians who know what to expect will see through the lies of the false Christs and the false prophets. Those Christians who got their doctrine from sources like the "Left Behind" series or their favorite televangelist will not have enough understanding to resist the deceptions in front of their face. They will be lost. This is why I keep hammering against the pre-tribulation rapture.

__The Manner of His Coming__

Mat 24: 27For as the lightning cometh out of the east, and shineth even unto the west; so shall also the coming of the Son of man be.

28For wheresoever the carcase is, there will the eagles be gathered together.

Matthew tells us the coming of Jesus will be unmistakable. It will be like a lightening strike. He will cover the Earth in an instant. He will not come secretly or be hidden in some secret chamber. Only the counterfeit Christs will be there.

I think verse 28 is telling us the eagles (some think this would be better translated vultures) seek out carcasses like the false Christs will seek out the spiritually dead to consume them.

__The Powers of the Heavens are Shaken__

The three Gospels agree there will be a great shaking just prior to Jesus return.

Mat 24:29Immediately after the tribulation of those days shall the sun be darkened, and the moon shall not give her light, and the stars shall fall from heaven, and the powers of the heavens shall be shaken:

Mark 13: 24But in those days, after that tribulation, the sun shall be darkened, and the moon shall not give her light,

25And the stars of heaven shall fall, and the powers that are in heaven shall be shaken.

Luke 21: 26Men's hearts failing them for fear, and for looking after those things which are coming on the earth: for the powers of heaven shall be shaken.

There are some Christians who believe in post-tribulation rapture. They reference the previous verses in Matthew and Mark as a two of their main "proof texts". They think these verses say Jesus will return immediately after the tribulation period. A closer reading of these verses will show Jesus returning immediately after the tribulation of THOSE days or after THAT tribulation. This refers to the tribulations that were described previously in the chapter. It does not say the tribulations are over. Only the first part is over.

As we learned in our study of the book of Revelation, Jesus will return at the last (7ᵗʰ) trumpet. When the last trump sounds, the rapture will occur but there will still be 7 vial judgments to be poured out on the Earth.

Even though the post-trib rapturists are wrong in their beliefs concerning the timing of the rapture, I don't have the same concerns about them as I do about the pre-trib rapturists. The post-trib rapturists expect to be here during the tribulation period. They fully expect to suffer for their faith and they understand the need to endure. I am sure they will not regret being raptured earlier than they expected.

The Rapture

The Rapture is the fulfillment of the mystery described in 1 Corrinthians.

> 1 Cor 15: ⁵¹Behold, I shew you a mystery; We shall not all sleep, but we shall all be changed, ⁵²In a moment, in the twinkling of an eye, at the last trump: for the trumpet shall sound, and the dead shall be raised incorruptible, and we shall be changed.

Notice the reference in Matthew to the sounding of the trumpet just before the gathering of the elect. The consistency between these three gospels, the book of Revelation and the other books in the Bible is more than coincidence.

> Mat 24: [30]And then shall appear the sign of the Son of man in heaven: and then shall all the tribes of the earth mourn, and they shall see the Son of man **coming in the clouds** of heaven with power and great glory.

> [31]And he shall send his angels with a great **sound of a trumpet**, and they shall gather together his elect from the four winds, from one end of heaven to the other.

> Mar 13: [26]And then shall they see the Son of man **coming in the clouds** with great power and glory.

> [27]And then shall he send his angels, and shall gather together his elect from the four winds, from the uttermost part of the earth to the uttermost part of heaven.

> Luke 21: [27]And then shall they see the Son of man **coming in a cloud** with power and great glory.

> [28]And when these things begin to come to pass, then look up, and lift up your heads; for your redemption draweth nigh.

You also should notice all three gospels made reference to Jesus coming in the clouds. This is consistent with what we read in Thessalonians and in the book of Revelation.

> 1 Thes 4: [16]For the Lord himself shall descend from heaven with a shout, with the voice of the archangel, and with the trump of God: and the dead in Christ shall rise first: [17]Then we which are alive *and* remain shall be caught up together with them **in the clouds**, to meet the Lord in the air: and so shall we ever be with the Lord.

Rev 14: 14And I looked, and **behold a white cloud**, and **upon the cloud** *one* sat like unto the Son of man, having on his head a golden crown, and in his hand a sharp sickle. 15And another angel came out of the temple, crying with a loud voice to him that sat **on the cloud**, Thrust in thy sickle, and reap: for the time is come for thee to reap; for the harvest of the earth is ripe. 16And he that sat on the cloud thrust in his sickle on the earth; and the earth was reaped.

There can be no doubt; all of these scriptures are describing the same event. The rapture is when Jesus comes for his bride the church. The last trumpet is the midnight cry Jesus referred to in his parable about the ten virgins.

Mat 25:1Then shall the kingdom of heaven be likened unto ten virgins, which took their lamps, and went forth to meet the bridegroom. 2And five of them were wise, and five *were* foolish. 3They that *were* foolish took their lamps, and took no oil with them: 4But the wise took oil in their vessels with their lamps. 5While the bridegroom tarried, they all slumbered and slept. 6And at midnight there was a cry made, Behold, the bridegroom cometh; go ye out to meet him. 7Then all those virgins arose, and trimmed their lamps. 8And the foolish said unto the wise, Give us of your oil; for our lamps are gone out. 9But the wise answered, saying, *Not so;* lest there be not enough for us and you: but go ye rather to them that sell, and buy for yourselves. 10And while they went to buy, the bridegroom came; and they that were ready went in with him to the marriage: and the door was shut. 11Afterward came also the other virgins, saying, Lord, Lord, open to us. 12But he answered and said, Verily I say unto you, I know you not. 13Watch therefore, for ye know neither the day nor the hour wherein the Son of man cometh.

In the parable of the ten virgins, the wise virgins took oil for their lamps but the foolish virgins didn't take any oil. All ten were virgins (believers) but only five prepared themselves for the coming darkness (tribulation). The foolish virgins thought the bridegroom (Jesus) would come for them before the darkness came. They were unprepared to endure the darkness so they went back into the market to buy what they needed to endure the night. They missed the coming of the bridegroom and were later rejected by him.

Why would the bridegroom reject them for going back into the market to buy what they needed? Maybe the following verses from the book of Revelation will answer the question.

> Rev 13: 16And he causeth all, both small and great, rich and poor, free and bond, to receive a mark in their right hand, or in their foreheads: 17And that **no man might buy or sell, save he that had the mark**, or the name of the beast, or the number of his name. 18Here is wisdom. Let him that hath understanding count the number of the beast: for it is the number of a man; and his number *is* Six hundred threescore *and* six.

In my opinion, the pre-trib rapturists are setting themselves up to be like the foolish virgins. Their unpreparedness and lack of understanding will make them vulnerable to the deceptions of the antichrist. They will probably take the mark through fear or ignorance.

Watch For the Signs

After the rapture is described, the Lord tells us to watch for the signs of his coming.

> MAT 24: 32Now learn a parable of the fig tree; When his branch is yet tender, and putteth forth leaves, ye know that summer is nigh:

> 33So likewise ye, when ye shall see all these things, know that it is near, *even* at the doors.

> 34Verily I say unto you, This generation shall not pass, till all these things be fulfilled.

> 35Heaven and earth shall pass away, but my words shall not pass away.

> 36But of that day and hour knoweth no *man,* no, not the angels of heaven, but my Father only.

The fig tree is commonly thought to be symbolic of Israel. This is a reasonable assumption. It is thought the return of Israel as a nation was the start of the prophetic time clock and the prophetic time clock does seem to be ticking. We don't know exactly how long it will tick but we are told it will not tick for more than a generation. Matthew wrote **"**when ye shall see **all these things**, know that it is near, *even* at the doors. " The Gospels of Mark and Luke also agree.

> Mark 13: 29So ye in like manner, when ye shall see these things come to pass, know that it is nigh, *even* at the doors.

> Luke21: 31So likewise ye, when ye see these things come to pass, know ye that the kingdom of God is nigh at hand.

Israel becoming a nation was a wakeup call. We may not know the tribulation period has started until we are well into it. Even so, it will eventually become obvious the tribulation period is upon us. When that happens, these passages in Matthew, Mark and Luke will comfort us. They will assure us everything will be resolved within our generation.

Luke says something at this point which needs to be addressed.

> Luke 21: 36Watch ye therefore, and pray always, that ye may be accounted worthy to escape all these things that shall come to pass, and to stand before the Son of man.

This verse indicates it is possible to be counted worthy and escape all of these things. How could this possibly be? Could this verse be the definitive proof text for the pre-tribulation rapture believers? Could they be right?

Nope!

While a pre-tribulation rapture would not contradict Luke 21:36 it would not satisfy the requirements of the rest of the Bible. A pre-trib rapture would obviously not occur at the "last trump" as required.

The Bible has to be understood as a whole. All of the scriptures are true. Any theory we have concerning the scriptures must be consistent with the whole of the Bible.

Let's reconsider Luke 21: 36. Is there anywhere else in the Bible that could explain a way to escape all of these judgments based on your worthiness? The answer would have to be consistent with the rest of the Bible and be taken in the correct context.

The Book of Revelation has the answer to Luke 21:36

> Rev 2: 7And to the angel of the church in Philadelphia write; These things saith he that is holy, he that is true, he that hath the key of David, he that openeth, and no man shutteth; and shutteth, and no man openeth; 8I know thy works: behold, I have set before thee an open door, and no man can shut it: for thou hast a little strength, and hast kept my word, and hast not denied my name. 9Behold, I will make them of the synagogue of Satan, which say they are Jews, and are not, but do lie; behold, I will make them to come and worship before thy feet, and to know that I have loved thee. **10Because thou hast kept the word of my patience, I also will keep thee from the hour of temptation, which shall come upon all the world, to try them that dwell upon the earth.** 11Behold, I come quickly: hold that fast which thou hast, that no man take thy crown. 12Him that overcometh will I make a pillar in the temple of my God, and he shall go no more out: and I will write upon him the name of my God, and the name of the city of my God, *which is* new Jerusalem, which cometh down out of heaven from my God: and *I will write upon him* my new name. 13He that hath an ear, let him hear what the Spirit saith unto the churches.

The Lord's messages to the different churches were symbolic of the church ages throughout history. The Church of Philadelphia was the second to the last church. The Laodicean church will be the last. The answer to Luke 21:36 is simple. Those Christians who were counted among the Philadelphia church age will be allowed to die out before the tribulation period starts. The Laodicean church will be left to endure the tribulation until the rapture occurs.

Jesus tells us the Earth will be full of sin before he returns.

> Mat 24: 37But as the days of Noe *were,* so shall also the coming of the Son of man be. 38For as in the days that were before the flood they were eating and drinking, marrying and giving in marriage, until the day that Noe entered into the ark,

39And knew not until the flood came, and took them all away; so shall also the coming of the Son of man be. 40Then shall two be in the field; the one shall be taken, and the other left. 41Two *women shall be* grinding at the mill; the one shall be taken, and the other left. 42Watch therefore: for ye know not what hour your Lord doth come. 43But know this, that if the goodman of the house had known in what watch the thief would come, he would have watched, and would not have suffered his house to be broken up. 44Therefore be ye also ready: for in such an hour as ye think not the Son of man cometh. 45Who then is a faithful and wise servant, whom his lord hath made ruler over his household, to give them meat in due season? 46Blessed *is* that servant, whom his lord when he cometh shall find so doing. 47Verily I say unto you, That he shall make him ruler over all his goods. 48But and if that evil servant shall say in his heart, My lord delayeth his coming; 49And shall begin to smite *his* fellowservants, and to eat and drink with the drunken; 50The lord of that servant shall come in a day when he looketh not for *him,* and in an hour that he is not aware of, 51And shall cut him asunder, and appoint *him* his portion with the hypocrites: there shall be weeping and gnashing of teeth.

Mat 24:40-44 has been used by those who hold to the pre-tribulation rapture theory to support their views. On the surface it sounds like it might be describing a pre-tribulation rapture because people are working in the fields and in the mills.

Although not in the Olivet discourse, Luke 17 has a similar passage that seems to refer to the same events.

Luke 17: 30Even thus shall it be in the day when the Son of man is revealed. 31In that day, he which shall be upon the housetop, and his stuff in the house, let him not come down to take it away: and he that is in the field, let him likewise not return back. 32Remember Lot's wife. 33Whosoever shall seek to save his life shall lose it; and whosoever shall lose his life shall preserve it. 34I tell you, in that night there shall be two *men* in one bed; the one shall be taken, and the other shall be left. 35Two *women* shall be grinding together; the one shall be taken, and the other left. 36Two *men* shall be in the field; the one shall be taken, and the other left.

Do these passages really support the pre-tribulation rapture? It can be "spun" in such a way as to make it seem the people are living their lives normally (before the tribulation starts) and then "poof" they are gone.

To put these passages in their true context will require two things. The use of logic and adherence to the principle that all of the Bible's prophecies are true therefore they must all fit together. Any seeming contradictions between Bible prophecies are the result of a misunderstanding or misapplication of those prophecies. When properly understood, all of the prophecies will (and must) fit together perfectly.

Once again, we must consider 1Cor 15:52 which tell us the Lord returns at the "last trump". From the book of Revelation we know the seven seal judgments and six trumpet judgments will occur prior to the last (seventh) trump. We can also see how many trials will be endured prior to Jesus return in Mat 24:31. These verses and many others are consistent with a mid-tribulation rapture but not a pre-tribulation rapture. So, using the principle of Biblical consistency how can we reasonably reconcile the above passages? To do this we must use simple common sense and logic.

It will obviously take a while for the seal judgments and trumpet judgments to be executed. This will most likely take us well into the seven year tribulation (Daniel's 70th week). Daniel even gives us a general timeframe.

> Dan 12: [8]And I heard, but I understood not: then said I, O my Lord, what *shall be* the end of these *things?* [9]And he said, Go thy way, Daniel: for the words *are* closed up and sealed till the time of the end. [10]Many shall be purified, and made white, and tried; but the wicked shall do wickedly: and none of the wicked shall understand; but the wise shall understand. [11]And from the time *that* the daily *sacrifice* shall be taken away, and the abomination that maketh desolate set up, *there shall be* a thousand two hundred and ninety days. [12]**Blessed *is* he that waiteth, and cometh to the thousand three hundred and five and thirty days**.

Why is it blessed to come to the 1335th day? This works out to 3 years, 8 months and 15 days. Is this when the rapture will occur? I don't know but something will occur then that will be a real blessing to those who serve the Lord. Regardless, Christians will be here at least until that point.

If the rapture does occur at that point, the people will have to survive until then. They will have to work in the fields and in the mills in order to keep from starving. People cannot survive three plus years without food. People must eat and drink and they have always come together in marriage no matter how hard times get. People will be doing these things all the way until the Lord returns.

The Bible also tells us some people groups will not be under the control of the anti-christ.

> Dan 11: 41He shall enter also into the glorious land, and many *countries* shall be overthrown: but these shall escape out of his hand, *even* Edom, and Moab, and the chief of the children of Ammon.

So far we have focused on the first two parts of the question the disciples asked Jesus on the Mount of Olives.

> Mat 24: 3And as he sat upon the mount of Olives, the disciples came unto him privately, saying, Tell us, when shall these things be? and what *shall be* the sign of thy coming, and of the end of the world?

The final part of their question was about the end of the world. To answer the third part of the question Jesus used what has come to be known as the Parable of the Talents.

In the parable of the talents Jesus describes a man who gives his servants talents (money) to invest for him while he was gone. Two of the servants were faithful and caused their lord's money to increase. They were rewarded with greater responsibilities and they were able to enter into the joys of their lord.

The third servant was wicked and slothful. Rather than taking any efforts to increase his master's money, he just hid the talent in the ground until his lord returned. The lord was not pleased with him and threw him into the outer darkness where there was weeping and gnashing of teeth.

The very next thing Jesus describes is the judgment.

> Mat 25:31When the Son of man shall come in his glory, and all the holy angels with him, then shall he sit upon the throne of his glory: 32And before him shall be gathered all nations: and he shall separate them one from another, as a shepherd divideth *his* sheep from the goats: 33And he shall set the sheep on his right hand, but the goats on the left. 34Then shall the King say unto them on his right hand, Come, ye blessed of my Father, inherit the kingdom prepared for you from the foundation of the world... 41Then shall he say also unto them on the left hand, Depart from me, ye cursed, into everlasting fire, prepared for the devil and his angels... 46And these shall go away into everlasting punishment: but the righteous into life eternal.

The rebellious goats were obviously not destroyed at the beginning of the millennium because the book of Revelation tells us there will be a rebellion at the end of the millennium. This separation of the sheep from the goats must take place at the end of the thousand years when the nations rebel and come against the camp of the saints.

> Rev 20: 7And when the thousand years are expired, Satan shall be loosed out of his prison, 8And shall go out to deceive the nations which are in the four quarters of the earth, Gog and Magog, to gather them together to battle: the number of whom *is* as the sand of the sea. 9And they went up on the breadth of the earth, and compassed the camp of the saints about, and the beloved city: and fire came down from God out of heaven, and devoured them. 10And the devil that deceived them was cast into the lake of fire and brimstone, where the beast and the false prophet *are,* and shall be tormented day and night for ever and ever. 11And I saw a great white throne, and him that sat on it, from whose face the earth and the heaven fled away; and there was found no place for them.

> Rev 20:11And I saw a great white throne, and him that sat on it, from whose face the earth and the heaven fled away; and there was found no place for them. 12And I saw the dead, small and great, stand before God; and the books were opened: and another book was opened, which is *the book* of

life: and the dead were judged out of those things which were written in the books, according to their works.

In the parable of the talents, the profitable servants who served the lord faithfully were given greater responsibilities and were allowed to enter into the joys of their lord. This most likely means they were able to enter in to the Lord's millennial kingdom.

The unprofitable servant was sent to outer darkness to await his judgment on the last day. This judgment occurs at the end of the world.

When the judgments are completed, the sheep are separated from the goats, and God will create a new Heaven and a New Earth.

> Rev 21:1 And I saw a new heaven and a new earth: for the first heaven and the first earth were passed away; and there was no more sea.
>
> 2 And I John saw the holy city, new Jerusalem, coming down from God out of heaven, prepared as a bride adorned for her husband.
>
> 3 And I heard a great voice out of heaven saying, Behold, the tabernacle of God *is* with men, and he will dwell with them, and they shall be his people, and God himself shall be with them, *and be* their God.

All three versions of the Olivet discourse are consistent with one another and with the rest of the Bible.

In this chapter we talked extensively about the erroneous pre-tribulation rapture doctrine but there is another erroneous doctrine that will prove to be equally destructive to Christians during the tribulation period. This is the doctrine of "eternal security" or "once-saved-always-saved". The idea of eternal security for the believer takes the pressure off. If you can't be "unsaved" then you can do whatever it takes to get by until the rapture occurs.

How easy will it be for someone who believes he can't be "unsaved" to compromise and take the mark rather than loose everything he has, starve and face the real possibility of torture and death? What will the Christian who believes in unconditional security do to prevent his wife or daughters from being abused? Will he feel justified in taking the mark in order to save them? Surely, God would understand such a "selfless" act. After all, a Christian cannot be unsaved, right?

??? Right ???

<u>WRONG!!!</u>

God has gone to extreme lengths to warn believers about the coming deception. His instructions were given to believers. The Bible says…

> Rev 14:9And the third angel followed them, saying with a loud voice, **If any man** worship the beast and his image, and receive *his* mark in his forehead, or in his hand, [10]The same shall drink of the wine of the wrath of God, which is poured out without mixture into the cup of his indignation; and he shall be tormented with fire and brimstone in the presence of the holy angels, and in the presence of the Lamb: [11]And the smoke of their torment ascendeth up for ever and ever: and they have no rest day nor night, who worship the beast and his image, and **whosoever receiveth the mark** of his name.

Did God make any allowances for Christians taking the mark in the previous passage? No he didn't! If taking the mark were allowable for Christians in some circumstances then why wouldn't God have said so?

The Christian who believes in eternal security will read these verses and say it takes three things for Gods wrath to be poured out in this instance. A person must worship the beast AND his image AND take the mark. Also, since God has not appointed us (his people) to wrath, then it's O.K. to take the mark as long as you don't worship the beast and his image.

This type of reasoning is nothing more than a word play which will allow the believer in eternal security to do what he wants (avoid persecution by taking the mark.)

This type of logic fails because taking the mark is the form of worship the beast and his image will require. By taking the mark you are submitting to the beast system and symbolically becoming the property of the beast. Any clever word plays will not prevent a person from being thrown into the lake of fire when the time for judgment comes. You have been warned!

In my opinion, the doctrine of once-saved-always-saved is the second most dangerous false doctrine in the church today (second only to the doctrine of the pre-tribulation rapture). The pre-tribulation rapture doctrine doesn't prepare its adherents for the coming persecution and the once-saved-always-saved doctrine will convince many Christians to take the easy way out rather than suffer and die for their faith. It will be the ultimate one-two punch for Satan against the majority of Laodicean believers.

> 2Thes 2:3Let no man deceive you by any means: for *that day shall not come,* except there come a falling away first, and that man of sin be revealed, the son of perdition;

Who will be falling away in the preceding verse? What will they be falling away from? They will be Christians and they will be falling away from God.

> Mat 24:24For there shall arise false Christs, and false prophets, and shall shew great signs and wonders; insomuch that, if *it were* possible, they shall deceive the very elect.

Will it be possible to deceive the very elect? The answer is obviously, YES. If it were not possible then why would Jesus even mention it? The "false Christs" will be able to deceive some of the very elect. Jesus is giving YOU a warning so that it will not be possible to deceive YOU. **PAY ATTENTION!!!**

In the next chapter we will compare these versions of the Olivet discourse with the seal and trumpet judgments in the book of Revelation. The similarities are beyond coincidence.

Chapter Eighteen

Prophecy:

The Seals and the Olivet Discourse

In the last chapter we considered what Jesus said concerning the tribulation period in the various versions of his Olivet Discourse. We saw how they were consistent with the Book of Revelation. This chapter will take that consistency one step further and show how all three versions of the Olivet Discourse have a one-to-one correspondence with the Seal judgments in the Book of Revelation.

The Last three pages in this chapter summarize this correspondence and should be referred to during the explanations that follow. I apologize for the small typeset, but I felt it was necessary to fit the summaries onto singular pages. This makes comparisons between the different versions easier to see.

All three versions of the Olivet Discourse have a similar sequence of events, as would be expected, but the interesting part is what these events are and how they relate to the events described in the Book of Revelation. The events, in a broad general way, describe the events associated with the seal and trumpet judgments in Book of Revelation but they don't describe the vial judgments at all. I suspect the reason Jesus didn't describe the vial judgments is because the church would be removed prior to the vial judgments.

I will focus on Mathew's version of the Olivet Discourse but I will reference the others as necessary to explain any differences.

False Christs

The first thing Jesus describes is the false Christs.

> Mat 24: 4And Jesus answered and said unto them, Take heed that no man deceive you.

⁵For many shall come in my name, saying, I am Christ; and shall deceive many.

Seal #1 (False Christ)

Rev 6:1And I saw when the Lamb opened one of the seals, and I heard, as it were the noise of thunder, one of the four beasts saying, Come and see.

²And I saw, and behold a white horse: and he that sat on him had a bow; and a crown was given unto him: and he went forth conquering, and to conquer.

The first seal is all about the man who rides the white horse and has a crown. A white horse has come to symbolize what is good. (The good guy rides the white horse.) The crown symbolizes a king. Could this good king who goes forth to conquer be a counterfeit Jesus? Notice how Jesus is described when he returns.

Rev 19:11And I saw heaven opened, and **behold a white horse**; and he that sat upon him *was* called Faithful and True, and in righteousness he doth judge and make war.

¹²His eyes *were* as a flame of fire, and **on his head** *were* **many crowns**; and he had a name written, that no man knew, but he himself.

The pre-tribulation rapture believers are expecting Jesus to return just before the tribulation period. It's curious the first horseman sounds similar to what they are expecting.

<u>The Beginning of Sorrows</u>

Mat 24: 6And ye shall hear of wars and rumours of wars: see that ye be not troubled: for all *these things* must come to pass, but the end is not yet.

Seal # 2 (War)

Rev 6: [3]And when he had opened the second seal, I heard the second beast say, Come and see.

[4]And there went out another horse *that was* red: and *power* was given to him that sat thereon to take peace from the earth, and that they should kill one another: and there was given unto him a great sword.

The second seal is the logical progression of the first. The conquering king brings war.

Mat 24: [7]For nation shall rise against nation, and kingdom against kingdom: and there shall be **famines**, and **pestilences**, and earthquakes, in divers places.

Seal # 3 (Famine)

Rev 6: [5]And when he had opened the third seal, I heard the third beast say, Come and see. And I beheld, and lo a black horse; and he that sat on him had a pair of balances in his hand.

[6]And I heard a voice in the midst of the four beasts say, A measure of wheat for a penny, and three measures of barley for a penny; and *see* thou hurt not the oil and the wine.

Seal # 4 (Pestilence / Death)

Rev 6: [7]And when he had opened the fourth seal, I heard the voice of the fourth beast say, Come and see.

[8]And I looked, and behold a pale horse: and his name that sat on him was Death, and Hell followed with him. And power was given unto them over the fourth part of the earth, to kill with sword, and with hunger, and with death, and with the beasts of the earth.

Mat 24:7 describes seals 3 and 4. Famine, pestilence and death are a natural consequence of war. Seal number 4 says the pale horse kills with the sword, hunger, death, and the beasts of the Earth. To kill with death in verse 8 could be better translated disease or pestilence.

Persecution

Mat 24: [9]Then shall they deliver you up to be afflicted, and shall kill you: and ye shall be hated of all nations for my name's sake.

[10]And then shall many be offended, and shall betray one another, and shall hate one another.

Seal # 5 (Martyrs)

Rev 6: [9]And when he had opened the fifth seal, I saw under the altar the souls of them that were slain for the word of God, and for the testimony which they held:

[10]And they cried with a loud voice, saying, How long, O Lord, holy and true, dost thou not judge and avenge our blood on them that dwell on the earth?

[11]And white robes were given unto every one of them; and it was said unto them, that they should rest yet for a little season, until their fellowservants also and their brethren, that should be killed as they *were,* should be fulfilled.

Rev 6:11 refers to the same ongoing persecution as Mat 24:9.

The Powers of Heaven are Shaken

Mat 24: 29Immediately after the tribulation of those days shall the sun be darkened, and the moon shall not give her light, and the stars shall fall from heaven, and the powers of the heavens shall be shaken:

Seal # 6

Rev 6: 12And I beheld when he had opened the sixth seal, and, lo, there was a great earthquake; and the **sun became black** as sackcloth of hair, and the moon became as blood;

13And the **stars of heaven fell** unto the earth, even as a fig tree casteth her untimely figs, when she is shaken of a mighty wind.

14And the heaven departed as a scroll when it is rolled together; and **every mountain and island were moved out of their places**.

15And the kings of the earth, and the great men, and the rich men, and the chief captains, and the mighty men, and every bondman, and every free man, hid themselves in the dens and in the rocks of the mountains;

16And said to the mountains and rocks, Fall on us, and hide us from the face of him that sitteth on the throne, and from the wrath of the Lamb:

17For the great day of his wrath is come; and who shall be able to stand?

It is easy to see the correlation between Mat 24:29 and Seal number 6. Jesus summed it all up in one verse, whereas Revelation gave more detailed information.

The Rapture

Mat 24: 30And then shall appear the sign of the Son of man in heaven: and then shall all the tribes of the earth mourn, and they shall see the Son of man coming in the clouds of heaven with power and great glory.

31And he shall send his angels with a great sound of a trumpet, and they shall gather together his elect from the four winds, from one end of heaven to the other.

Seal # 7 (The Rapture)

Rev 8: 1And when he had opened the seventh seal, there was silence in heaven about the space of half an hour.

2And I saw the seven angels which stood before God; and to them were given seven trumpets.

Rev 11: 15And the seventh angel sounded; and there were great voices in heaven, saying, The kingdoms of this world are become *the kingdoms* of our Lord, and of his Christ; and he shall reign for ever and ever.

Rev 14: 14And I looked, and behold a white cloud, and upon the cloud *one* sat like unto the Son of man, having on his head a golden crown, and in his hand a sharp sickle.

15And another angel came out of the temple, crying with a loud voice to him that sat on the cloud, Thrust in thy sickle, and reap: for the time is come for thee to reap; for the harvest of the earth is ripe.

16And he that sat on the cloud thrust in his sickle on the earth; and the earth was reaped.

Just as Jesus broadly described the events associated with the sixth seal with one verse, he described the events of the seventh seal with just two verses. The seventh seal had the most things associated with it. It initiated the seven trumpet judgments which culminated with the rapture of the church as described in Mat 24:30-31. The seven trumpet judgments are contained within the seventh seal judgment. To say it another way, the seven trumpet judgments are a subset of the seventh seal judgment.

The Olivet Discourse can be seen as a condensed version of the Book of Revelation. We are told what to expect. We are given clues about the coming abomination and we are warmed against being deceived. We know Jerusalem will fall and the abomination will stand where it ought not. We will be betrayed and persecuted but if we endure to the end we will be saved.

The Olivet Discourse came straight from the lips of Jesus. It is totally consistent with the Book of Daniel, Revelation and all of the other Books in the Bible. The consistency between all of these books is a testimony to the truth of these books. The way they fit together (as seen in chapter 11 with the Tabernacle) is beyond coincidence. The divine hand of God has ensured the preservation of these particular books which form the Bible.

The Olivet Discourse, the book of Daniel, and Revelation give us the most organized and complete vision of the tribulation period but there are many other scriptures throughout the Bible which seem to be referring to the same events. In the next chapter we will examine one of these lesser known prophecies.

Matthew 24:1-51 And Jesus went out, and departed from the temple: and his disciples came to him for to shew him the buildings of the temple.

2And Jesus said unto them, See ye not all these things? verily I say unto you, There shall not be left there one stone upon another, that shall not be thrown down.

3And as he sat upon the mount of Olives, the disciples came unto him privately, saying, Tell us, when shall these things be? and what shall be the sign of thy coming, and of the end of the world?

Seal #1 Riding a white horse.
Crown given to him.
went forth conquering
and to conquer.

False Christs

4And Jesus answered and said unto them, Take heed that no man deceive you.

5For many shall come in my name, saying, I am Christ; and shall deceive many.

Seal #2 Riding a red horse.
Takes peace from the Earth.
Men kill one another.
A great sword is given to him.

Beginning of Sorrows

6And ye shall hear of wars and rumours of wars: see that ye be not troubled: for all these things must come to pass, but the end is not yet.

7For nation shall rise against nation, and kingdom against kingdom: and there shall be famines, and pestilences, and earthquakes, in divers places.

8All these are the beginning of sorrows.

Seal #3 Riding a black horse.
Had a pair of balances
in his hand.
Food is rationed.

Seal #4 Riding a pale horse.
Death sat on the horse and
hell followed with him.
Power given him to kill
with sword.
with hunger.
with death.
with beasts.

Persecution

9Then shall they deliver you up to be afflicted, and shall kill you: and ye shall be hated of all nations for my name's sake.

10And then shall many be offended, and shall betray one another, and shall hate one another.

We must endure

11And many false prophets shall rise, and shall deceive many.

12And because iniquity shall abound, the love of many shall wax cold.

13But he that shall endure unto the end, the same shall be saved.

Seal #5 martyrs cry for justice.
They are told to wait until
the rest of the martyrs
could be slain.
White robes given to the martyrs.

Gospel Preached

14And this gospel of the kingdom shall be preached in all the world for a witness unto all nations; and then shall the end come.

Abomination of desolation and Great Tribulation

15When ye therefore shall see the abomination of desolation, spoken of by Daniel the prophet, stand in the holy place, (whoso readeth, let him understand:)

16Then let them which be in Judaea flee into the mountains:

17Let him which is on the housetop not come down to take any thing out of his house:

18Neither let him which is in the field return back to take his clothes.

19And woe unto them that are with child, and to them that give suck in those days!

20But pray ye that your flight be not in the winter, neither on the sabbath day:

This verse confirms that Daniel's prophecy concerning the "Abomination of Desolation" was meant for the end of this age!

21For then shall be **great tribulation** such as was not since the beginning of the world to this time, no, nor ever shall be.

22And except those days should be shortened, there should no flesh be saved: but for the elect's sake those days shall be shortened.

Seal #6 The wrath of the lamb.
Sun darkened.
Moon becomes blood.
Stars of heaven fall.
Heavens depart as a scroll
when it is rolled together.
Every mountain and island
is moved out of its place.
Rich and mighty men seek
shelter in the dens and in the
rocks of the mountains.
Winds halted.
144,000 of the tribes of Israel
sealed in their foreheads.
12,000 from each tribe.
White robed martyrs hold palms
and give glory to the lamb.

Another warning against the deceivers

23Then if any man shall say unto you, Lo, here is Christ, or there; believe it not.

24For there shall arise false Christs, and false prophets, and shall shew great signs and wonders; insomuch that, if it were possible, they shall deceive the very elect.

25Behold, I have told you before.

26Wherefore if they shall say unto you, Behold, he is in the desert; go not forth: behold, he is in the secret chambers; believe it not.

The manner of his coming

27For as the lightning cometh out of the east, and shineth even unto the west; so shall also the coming of the Son of man be.

The powers of the heavens shaken

28For wheresoever the carcase is, there will the eagles be gathered together.

29**Immediately after the tribulation of those days** shall the sun be darkened, and the moon shall not give her light, and the stars shall fall from heaven, and the powers of the heavens shall be shaken:

Seal #7 Silence about the space of 1/2 hour.
7 angels given trumpets.
Angel casts censer to Earth causing
voices, thunderings, lightnings,
and an earthquake.
The seven angels begin to sound.

Rapture

30And **then shall appear the sign of the Son of man in heaven** and then shall all the tribes of the earth mourn, and **they shall see the Son of man coming in the clouds of heaven** with power and great glory.

31And **he shall send his angels with a great sound of a trumpet, and they shall gather together his elect from the four winds, from one end of heaven to the other.**

Watch for the signs

32Now learn a parable of the fig tree; When his branch is yet tender, and putteth forth leaves, ye know that summer is nigh:

33So likewise ye, when ye shall see all these things, know that it is near, even at the doors.

34Verily I say unto you, This generation shall not pass, till all these things be fulfilled.

35Heaven and earth shall pass away, but my words shall not pass away.

36But of that day and hour knoweth no man, no, not the angels of heaven, but my Father only.

Mark 13:1-37 And as he went out of the temple, one of his disciples saith unto him, Master, see what manner of stones and what buildings are here!

2And Jesus answering said unto him, Seest thou these great buildings? there shall not be left one stone upon another, that shall not be thrown down.

3And as he sat upon the mount of Olives over against the temple, Peter and James and John and Andrew asked him privately,

Seal #1 Riding a white horse.
Crown given to him.
went forth conquering
and to conquer.

4Tell us, when shall these things be? and what shall be the sign when all these things shall be fulfilled?

False Christs

5And Jesus answering them began to say, Take heed lest any man deceive you:

6For many shall come in my name, saying, I am Christ; and shall deceive many.

Seal #2 Riding a red horse.
Takes peace from the Earth.
Men kill one another.
A great sword is given to him.

Beginning of Sorrows

7And when ye shall hear of wars and rumours of wars, be ye not troubled: for such things must needs be; but the end shall not be yet.

8For nation shall rise against nation, and kingdom against kingdom: and there shall be earthquakes in divers places, and there shall be famines and troubles: these are the beginnings of sorrows.

Seal #3 Riding a black horse.
Had a pair of balances
in his hand.
Food is rationed.

Gospel Preached

9But take heed to yourselves: for they shall deliver you up to councils; and in the synagogues ye shall be beaten: and ye shall be brought before rulers and kings for my sake, for a testimony against them.

10And the gospel must first be published among all nations.

Seal #4 Riding a pale horse.
Death sat on the horse and
hell followed with him.
Power given him to kill
with sword.
with hunger.
with death.
with beasts.

Persecution

11But when they shall lead you, and deliver you up, take no thought beforehand what ye shall speak, neither do ye premeditate: but whatsoever shall be given you in that hour, that speak ye: for it is not ye that speak, but the Holy Ghost.

12Now the brother shall betray the brother to death, and the father the son; and children shall rise up against their parents, and shall cause them to be put to death.

Seal #5 martyrs cry for justice.
They are told to wait until
the rest of the martyrs
could be slain.
White robes given to the martyrs.

13And ye shall be hated of all men for my name's sake: but he that shall endure unto the end, the same shall be saved.

14But when ye shall see the abomination of desolation, spoken of by Daniel the prophet, standing where it ought not, (let him that readeth understand,) then let them that be in Judaea flee to the mountains:

15And let him that is on the housetop not go down into the house, neither enter therein, to take any thing out of his house:

This verse confirms that Daniel's prophecy concerning the "Abomination of Desolation" was meant for the end of this age!

Abomination of desolation and Great Tribulation

16And let him that is in the field not turn back again for to take up his garment.

17But woe to them that are with child, and to them that give suck in those days!

18And pray ye that your flight be not in the winter.

19For in those days shall be affliction, such as was not from the beginning of the creation which God created unto this time, neither shall be.

20And except that the Lord had shortened those days, no flesh should be saved: but for the elect's sake, whom he hath chosen, he hath shortened the days.

Another warning against the deceivers

21And then if any man shall say to you, Lo, here is Christ; or, lo, he is there; believe him not:

22For false Christs and false prophets shall rise, and shall shew signs and wonders, to seduce, if it were possible, even the elect.

23But take ye heed: behold, I have foretold you all things.

Seal #6 The wrath of the lamb.
Sun darkened.
Moon becomes blood.
Stars of heaven fall.
Heavens depart as a scroll
when it is rolled together.
Every mountain and island
is moved out of its place.
Rich and mighty men seek
shelter in the dens and in the
rocks of the mountains.
Winds halted.
144,000 of the tribes of Israel
sealed in their foreheads.
12,000 from each tribe.
White robed martyrs hold palms
and give glory to the lamb.

The powers of the heavens shaken

24But in those days, **after that tribulation**, the sun shall be darkened, and the moon shall not give her light,

25And the stars of heaven shall fall, and the powers that are in heaven shall be shaken.

Rapture

26And then shall they see the Son of man coming in the clouds with great power and glory.

27And then shall he send his angels, and shall gather together his elect from the four winds, from the uttermost part of the earth to the uttermost part of heaven.

28Now learn a parable of the fig tree; When her branch is yet tender, and putteth forth leaves, ye know that summer is near:

Seal #7 Silence about the space of 1/2 hour.
7 angels given trumpets.
Angel casts censer to Earth causing
voices, thunderings, lightnings,
and an earthquake.
The seven angels begin to sound.

29So ye in like manner, when ye shall see these things come to pass, know that it is nigh, even at the doors.

30Verily I say unto you, that this generation shall not pass, till all these things be done.

31Heaven and earth shall pass away: but my words shall not pass away.

32But of that day and that hour knoweth no man, no, not the angels which are in heaven, neither the Son, but the Father.

Watch for the signs

33Take ye heed, watch and pray: for ye know not when the time is.

34For the Son of man is as a man taking a far journey, who left his house, and gave authority to his servants, and to every man his work, and commanded the porter to watch.

35Watch ye therefore: for ye know not when the master of the house cometh, at even, or at midnight, or at the cockcrowing, or in the morning:

36Lest coming suddenly he find you sleeping.

37And what I say unto you I say unto all, Watch.

Luke 21:1-36 And he looked up, and saw the rich men casting their gifts into the treasury.

2And he saw also a certain poor widow casting in thither two mites.

3And he said, Of a truth I say unto you, that this poor widow hath cast in more than they all:

4For all these have of their abundance cast in unto the offerings of God: but she of her penury hath cast in all the living that she had.

5And as some spake of the temple, how it was adorned with goodly stones and gifts, he said,

6As for these things which ye behold, the days will come, in the which there shall not be left one stone upon another, that shall not be thrown down.

7And they asked him, saying, Master, but when shall these things be? and what sign will there be when these things shall come to pass?

False Christs { 8And he said, Take heed that ye be not deceived: for many shall come in my name, saying, I am Christ; and the time draweth near: go ye not therefore after them.

Beginning of Sorrows { 9But when ye shall hear of wars and commotions, be not terrified: for these things must first come to pass; but the end is not by and by.

10Then said he unto them, Nation shall rise against nation, and kingdom against kingdom:

11And great earthquakes shall be in divers places, and famines, and pestilences; and fearful sights and great signs shall there be from heaven.

Persecution { 12But before all these, they shall lay their hands on you, and persecute you, delivering you up to the synagogues, and into prisons, being brought before kings and rulers for my name's sake.

13And it shall turn to you for a testimony.

14Settle it therefore in your hearts, not to meditate before what ye shall answer:

15For I will give you a mouth and wisdom, which all your adversaries shall not be able to gainsay nor resist.

16And ye shall be betrayed both by parents, and brethren, and kinsfolks, and friends; and some of you shall they cause to be put to death.

17And ye shall be hated of all men for my name's sake.

We must Endure { 18But there shall not an hair of your head perish.

19In your patience possess ye your souls.

Abomination of desolation and Great Tribulation { 20And when ye shall see Jerusalem compassed with armies, then know that the desolation thereof is nigh.

21Then let them which are in Judaea flee to the mountains; and let them which are in the midst of it depart out; and let not them that are in the countries enter thereinto.

22For these be the days of vengeance, that all things which are written may be fulfilled.

23But woe unto them that are with child, and to them that give suck, in those days! for there shall be great distress in the land, and wrath upon this people.

24And they shall fall by the edge of the sword, and shall be led away captive into all nations: and Jerusalem shall be trodden down of the Gentiles, until the times of the Gentiles be fulfilled.

25And there shall be signs in the sun, and in the moon, and in the stars; and upon the earth distress of nations, with perplexity; the sea and the waves roaring;

The powers of the heavens shaken { 26Men's hearts failing them for fear, and for looking after those things which are coming on the earth: for the powers of heaven shall be shaken.

Rapture { **27And then shall they see the Son of man coming in a cloud with power and great glory.**

28And when these things begin to come to pass, then look up, and lift up your heads; for your redemption draweth nigh.

29And he spake to them a parable; Behold the fig tree, and all the trees;

30When they now shoot forth, ye see and know of your own selves that summer is now nigh at hand.

31So likewise ye, when ye see these things come to pass, know ye that the kingdom of God is nigh at hand.

Watch for the signs { 32Verily I say unto you, This generation shall not pass away, till all be fulfilled.

33Heaven and earth shall pass away: but my words shall not pass away.

34And take heed to yourselves, lest at any time your hearts be overcharged with surfeiting, and drunkenness, and cares of this life, and so that day come upon you unawares.

35For as a snare shall it come on all them that dwell on the face of the whole earth.

36Watch ye therefore, and pray always, that ye may be accounted worthy to escape all these things that shall come to pass, and to stand before the Son of man.

Seal #1 Riding a white horse.
Crown given to him.
went forth conquering
and to conquer.

Seal #2 Riding a red horse.
Takes peace from the Earth.
Men kill one another.
A great sword is given to him.

Seal #3 Riding a black horse.
Had a pair of balances
in his hand.
Food is rationed.

Seal #4 Riding a pale horse.
Death sat on the horse and
hell followed with him.
Power given him to kill
with sword.
with hunger.
with death.
with beasts.

Seal #5 martyrs cry for justice.
They are told to wait until
the rest of the martyrs
could be slain.
White robes given to the martyrs.

Seal #6 The wrath of the lamb.
Sun darkened.
Moon becomes blood.
Stars of heaven fall.
Heavens depart as a scroll
when it is rolled together.
Every mountain and island
is moved out of its place.
Rich and mighty men seek
shelter in the dens and in the
rocks of the mountains.
Winds halted.
144,000 of the tribes of Israel
sealed in their foreheads.
12,000 from each tribe.
White robed martyrs hold palms
and give glory to the lamb.

Seal #7 Silence about the space of 1/2 hour.
7 angels given trumpets.
Angel casts censer to Earth causing
voices, thunderings, lightnings,
and an earthquake.
The seven angels begin to sound.

Chapter Nineteen

Prophecy:

Egypt in Prophecy

The Books of Daniel, Revelation and the Olivet Discourse were the most complete and well organized views of the future tribulation period. They give us an idea of what to expect and the general sequence of events. On the other hand, most of the Old Testament prophecies (with the exception of the Book of Daniel) seem rather jumbled. It is as if the prophets were seeing bits and pieces of future events without being able to put them into any type of chronological context. Prophecies concerning the coming of Jesus, the tribulation period or the millennium seem to be dispersed at random throughout the books of the Old Testament prophets like Isaiah. These prophecies were impossible to decipher until the New Testament scriptures were given. The following is a good example from the book of Isaiah.

> Is 61:1The Spirit of the Lord GOD *is* upon me; because the LORD hath anointed me to preach good tidings unto the meek; he hath sent me to bind up the brokenhearted, to proclaim liberty to the captives, and the opening of the prison to *them that are* bound;

> 2To proclaim the acceptable year of the LORD, and the day of vengeance of our God; to comfort all that mourn;

> Luke 4: 16And he came to Nazareth, where he had been brought up: and, as his custom was, he went into the synagogue on the sabbath day, and stood up for to read.

> 17And there was delivered unto him the book of the prophet Esaias. And when he had opened the book, he found the place where it was written,

¹⁸The Spirit of the Lord is upon me, because he hath anointed me to preach the gospel to the poor; he hath sent me to heal the brokenhearted, to preach deliverance to the captives, and recovering of sight to the blind, to set at liberty them that are bruised,

¹⁹To preach the acceptable year of the Lord.

²⁰And he closed the book, and he gave *it* again to the minister, and sat down. And the eyes of all them that were in the synagogue were fastened on him.

²¹And he began to say unto them, This day is this scripture fulfilled in your ears.

Notice how Jesus only read the first part of the prophecy from Isaiah. He left out the part about the day of vengeance of our God; to comfort all that mourn. Who would have thought the first part of the passage would be fulfilled 2000 years before the last part of the passage? We understand from the New Testament that Jesus initially came as a humble servant to teach, to heal and to give his life as a payment for our sins. We also know he will return as a vengeful judge to those who have rejected him and persecuted his people.

There is another prophecy in the Book of Isaiah which is very interesting when viewed with a New Testament understanding. It concerns Egypt. The prophecy is located at Isaiah 19:1-25 (see the diagram on the last page of this chapter).

This prophecy seems to start with the rapture.

^{Is 19:} ¹The burden of Egypt. Behold, the LORD rideth upon a swift cloud, and shall come into Egypt: and the idols of Egypt shall be moved at his presence, and the heart of Egypt shall melt in the midst of it.

As we learned earlier, the Lord rides on a cloud to gather his saints when the rapture occurs. This narrows down the timeframe for this prophecy.

> Is 19: 2 And I will set the Egyptians against the Egyptians: and they shall fight every one against his brother, and every one against his neighbour; city against city, *and* kingdom against kingdom.
>
> 3 And the spirit of Egypt shall fail in the midst thereof; and I will destroy the counsel thereof: and they shall seek to the idols, and to the charmers, and to them that have familiar spirits, and to the wizards.
>
> 4 And the Egyptians will I give over into the hand of a cruel lord; and a fierce king shall rule over them, saith the Lord, the LORD of hosts.

Egypt will be in total chaos. Civil unrest will be rampant and the people will pointlessly look to their false gods for understanding. Then they will be taken over by a cruel lord (Most likely, the antichrist).

> Is 19: 5 And the waters shall fail from the sea, and the river shall be wasted and dried up.
>
> 6 And they shall turn the rivers far away; *and* the brooks of defence shall be emptied and dried up: the reeds and flags shall wither.
>
> 7 The paper reeds by the brooks, by the mouth of the brooks, and every thing sown by the brooks, shall wither, be driven away, and be no *more.*
>
> 8 The fishers also shall mourn, and all they that cast angle into the brooks shall lament, and they that spread nets upon the waters shall languish.
>
> 9 Moreover they that work in fine flax, and they that weave networks, shall be confounded.
>
> 10 And they shall be broken in the purposes thereof, all that make sluices *and* ponds for fish.

The Egyptian economy will be in total ruins. The waters dry up. Fishing will not be possible.

Is 19: [11]Surely the princes of Zoan *are* fools, the counsel of the wise counsellors of Pharaoh is become brutish: how say ye unto Pharaoh, I *am* the son of the wise, the son of ancient kings?

[12]Where *are* they? where *are* thy wise *men?* and let them tell thee now, and let them know what the LORD of hosts hath purposed upon Egypt.

[13]The princes of Zoan are become fools, the princes of Noph are deceived; they have also seduced Egypt, *even they that are* the stay of the tribes thereof.

[14]The LORD hath mingled a perverse spirit in the midst thereof: and they have caused Egypt to err in every work thereof, as a drunken *man* staggereth in his vomit.

[15]Neither shall there be *any* work for Egypt, which the head or tail, branch or rush, may do.

[16]In that day shall Egypt be like unto women: and it shall be afraid and fear because of the shaking of the hand of the LORD of hosts, which he shaketh over it.

[17]And the land of Judah shall be a terror unto Egypt, every one that maketh mention thereof shall be afraid in himself, because of the counsel of the LORD of hosts, which he hath determined against it.

The Egyptian economy does not improve and the people realize their error. They have stood against Israel and the Lord. Their gods have proven to be false. Egypt finally recognizes the Jews (and Christians) were worshiping the one true God and they will cry out to the Lord for help.

> Is 19: ¹⁸In that day shall five cities in the land of Egypt speak the language of Canaan, and swear to the LORD of hosts; one shall be called, The city of destruction.

> ¹⁹In that day shall there be an altar to the LORD in the midst of the land of Egypt, and a pillar at the border thereof to the LORD.

> ²⁰And it shall be for a sign and for a witness unto the LORD of hosts in the land of Egypt: for they shall cry unto the LORD because of the oppressors, and he shall send them a saviour, and a great one, and he shall deliver them.

> ²¹And the LORD shall be known to Egypt, and the Egyptians shall know the LORD in that day, and shall do sacrifice and oblation; yea, they shall vow a vow unto the LORD, and perform *it.*

The Egyptian people do something astounding. They repent! They build an altar unto the Lord and put a pillar unto the Lord at their border. They make a vow to the Lord and they perform it. The Lord accepts them and sends them a savior. I believe this savior will be the Lord himself.

> Is 19: ²²And the LORD shall smite Egypt: he shall smite and heal *it:* and they shall return *even* to the LORD, and he shall be intreated of them, and shall heal them.

The Lord will smite Egypt to destroy their oppressors and he will heal the land and the Egyptian people.

> Is 19: ²³In that day shall there be a highway out of Egypt to Assyria, and the Assyrian shall come into Egypt, and the Egyptian into Assyria, and the Egyptians shall serve with the Assyrians.

[24]In that day shall Israel be the third with Egypt and with Assyria, *even* a blessing in the midst of the land:

[25]Whom the LORD of hosts shall bless, saying, Blessed *be* Egypt my people, and Assyria the work of my hands, and Israel mine inheritance.

The Lord loves a repentant heart so much that he calls Egypt "my people". This is astounding. Egypt has persecuted Israel and served false gods since ancient times and yet when they repented and called upon the Lord, he heard them, delivered them and made them his people. This should be comforting to all of us. If we repent and do what we should before God, he will also make us his people.

There is so much more in the Bible concerning the coming of Jesus but I have focused on the most complete and sequential passages in an attempt to show the interconnectedness of scripture. Isaiah 19 fits perfectly with the other prophetic texts we have discussed. Thanks to Isaiah, we can rejoice for Egypt and Assyria. They will survive the coming tribulation and gain a special place with the Lord. If only America would repent and turn to God like Egypt, God would bless us too.

Egypt in Prophecy.

This will most likely occur at the Rapture because the Lord is described as riding upon a cloud. (see Rev 14:14)

Isaiah 19:1-25 The burden of Egypt. Behold, the Lord rideth upon a swift cloud, and shall come into Egypt: and the idols of Egypt shall be moved at his presence, and the heart of Egypt shall melt in the midst of it.

Civil Chaos.

2And I will set the Egyptians against the Egyptians: and they shall fight every one against his brother, and every one against his neighbour; city against city, and kingdom against kingdom.

Egyptians seek guidance from mystics.

3And the spirit of Egypt shall fail in the midst thereof; and I will destroy the counsel thereof: and they shall seek to the idols, and to the charmers, and to them that have familiar spirits, and to the wizards.

May be the antichrist or one of his generals.

4And the Egyptians will I give over into the hand of a cruel lord; and a fierce king shall rule over them, saith the Lord, the Lord of hosts.

5And the waters shall fail from the sea, and the river shall be wasted and dried up.

6And they shall turn the rivers far away; and the brooks of defence shall be emptied and dried up: the reeds and flags shall wither.

7The paper reeds by the brooks, by the mouth of the brooks, and every thing sown by the brooks, shall wither, be driven away, and be no more.

Egyptian economy in ruins.

8The fishers also shall mourn, and all they that cast angle into the brooks shall lament, and they that spread nets upon the waters shall languish.

9Moreover they that work in fine flax, and they that weave networks, shall be confounded.

10And they shall be broken in the purposes thereof, all that make sluices and ponds for fish.

11Surely the princes of Zoan are fools, the counsel of the wise counsellors of Pharaoh is become brutish: how say ye unto Pharaoh, I am the son of the wise, the son of ancient kings?

12Where are they? where are thy wise men? and let them tell thee now, and let them know what the Lord of hosts hath purposed upon Egypt.

13The princes of Zoan are become fools, the princes of Noph are deceived; they have also seduced Egypt, even they that are the stay of the tribes thereof.

The Egyptians begin to doubt their "wise" men and they begin to fear the Lord.

14The Lord hath mingled a perverse spirit in the midst thereof: and they have caused Egypt to err in every work thereof, as a drunken man staggereth in his vomit.

15Neither shall there be any work for Egypt, which the head or tail, branch or rush, may do.

16In that day shall Egypt be like unto women: and it shall be afraid and fear because of the shaking of the hand of the Lord of hosts, which he shaketh over it.

17And the land of Judah shall be a terror unto Egypt, every one that maketh mention thereof shall be afraid in himself, because of the counsel of the Lord of hosts, which he hath determined against it.

18In that day shall five cities in the land of Egypt speak the language of Canaan, and swear to the Lord of hosts; one shall be called, The city of destruction.

The Egyptians shall call on the Lord, and the Lord will send them a savior to deliver them.

19In that day shall there be an altar to the Lord in the midst of the land of Egypt, and a pillar at the border thereof to the Lord.

20And it shall be for a sign and for a witness unto the Lord of hosts in the land of Egypt: for they shall cry unto the Lord because of the oppressors, and he shall send them a saviour, and a great one, and he shall deliver them.

21And the Lord shall be known to Egypt, and the Egyptians shall know the Lord in that day, and shall do sacrifice and oblation; yea, they shall vow a vow unto the Lord, and perform it.

The Lord smites the evil rulers, and accepts the repentant Egyptian people.

22And the Lord shall smite Egypt: he shall smite and heal it: and they shall return even to the Lord, and he shall be intreated of them, and shall heal them.

23In that day shall there be a highway out of Egypt to Assyria, and the Assyrian shall come into Egypt, and the Egyptian into Assyria, and the Egyptians shall serve with the Assyrians.

At least, these three groups will survive the tribulation period.

24In that day shall Israel be the third with Egypt and with Assyria, even a blessing in the midst of the land:

25Whom the Lord of hosts shall bless, saying, Blessed be Egypt my people, and Assyria the work of my hands, and Israel mine inheritance.

Chapter Twenty

Prophecy:

What Is Next?

We have read through the books of Daniel, Revelation and the Olivet Discourse. We expect to see wars, famines, disease, natural disasters, oppressive government and demonic manifestations. These things will eventually happen... but when? Haven't people throughout history expected the return of the Lord during bad times? Hitler must have seemed like an antichrist and he was an antichrist. He did all he could to destroy the Jews but he was not THE antichrist.

People have been saying Jesus was coming for thousands of years. Whenever times get bad, people think the tribulation period is right around the corner ... right? What does the Bible say about it?

> 2Peter 3:3Knowing this first, that there shall come in the last days scoffers, walking after their own lusts,
>
> 4And saying, Where is the promise of his coming? for since the fathers fell asleep, all things continue as *they were* from the beginning of the creation.

Isn't this what the people say whenever you warn them about the coming tribulation?

Even many of the so called "Christians" have this attitude. They are too busy with their lives to be concerned about some "far off" tribulation period. They have mortgages and car payments to deal with. There are also sporting events and school activities to attend to. They don't have time to worry about a coming tribulation. Sure, they agree in theory it will eventually happen, but they don't think it will happen any time soon. Why should they "live in fear"? They are not like those "crazy people" who are stocking up on gold, guns and food.

What is different now? Why should we think these are the last days?

First of all, Israel is a nation again. This was not the case during the days of Hitler. On the contrary, it can be argued that World War II was the thing which allowed Israel to become a nation. Prophecy requires a temple to be rebuilt in Jerusalem. A temple (sanctuary) is required before the beast can place his abominable image in it.

> ^{Dan 11:31}And arms shall stand on his part, and they shall pollute the sanctuary of strength, and shall take away the daily *sacrifice,* and they shall place the abomination that maketh desolate.

Right now in America we have a president (Obama) who is hostile toward Israel and is pressuring them to give up their land (the West Bank) for peace. This president is not the first to try to broker a peace between the Jews and their Islamic neighbors. The difference is this president is hostile towards Israel and favors the Palestinians (and all other Islamic countries). When the real antichrist arrives, his efforts at "peace" will be successful and temple worship will be reinstated.

Israel is thought to be symbolized as a fig tree.

> ^{Hos 9:10}I found Israel like grapes in the wilderness; I saw your fathers as the firstripe in the fig tree at her first time: *but* they went to Baal-peor, and separated themselves unto *that* shame; and *their* abominations were according as they loved.

> ^{Mat 24:32}Now learn a parable of the fig tree; When his branch is yet tender, and putteth forth leaves, ye know that summer is nigh:

> ³³So likewise ye, when ye shall see all these things, know that it is near, *even* at the doors.

> ³⁴Verily I say unto you, This generation shall not pass, till all these things be fulfilled.

Israel was reborn and put forth her leaves in 1948. We are seeing prophecy being fulfilled. According to the previous verses, shouldn't we expect to see the things Jesus told us about come to pass in this generation?

The technology to track everybody's personal financial transactions did not exist until this generation. We still have the ability to use cash anonymously for transactions but how long will this be allowed?

> Rev 13:16And he causeth all, both small and great, rich and poor, free and bond, to receive a mark in their right hand, or in their foreheads:

> 17And that no man might buy or sell, save he that had the mark, or the name of the beast, or the number of his name.

Do we think it will be more than a generation from now before the government decides to track us and monitor all of our financial transactions?

We already have Lojack ™ in our cars and traffic light cameras looking at us. How long before we are required to have a physical mark on us (or in us) for positive identification? We're already putting ID chips in our pets which can be scanned to identify who the owner is if the pet gets lost. Do we really think it will be more than a generation before we are forced to take a similar type of ID chip?

Is President Obama the antichrist? I don't think so. But I do think he is setting the stage for him. Obama is taking control of the bank sector, the health care sector, the manufacturing sector, the energy sector, education and the food sector. He is running up a multi-multi-trillion dollar deficit. It is as if he were deliberately trying to force America into a financial crash. His handling of the Gulf oil spill and initially refusing any help from other countries with oil skimmers defies common sense and will end in economic disaster. The effects of Obama's policies are inflicting so much harm on America, it would be wise for the terrorists to just stand by and watch as the Omaba administration wages war on America. Obama is doing the dirty work. The terrorist can stand back and laugh as Obama's policies strangle our economy to death.

We are not the only economy on the verge of collapse. Greece is rioting at the prospect of not being able to fund pensions and other entitlements. The entire European Union is in desperate shape. China is also thought to be on the verge of financial collapse due to the world economic slowdown. The world is so financially interconnected an economic domino effect seems almost certain in the near future. It is hard to say what else will have transpired by the time this book is published. Eventually, there will be a global economic collapse. At this point, it is almost unavoidable.

The Four Horsemen of the Apocalypse seem to be getting closer. War is one method of stimulating the economy that our corrupt leaders may try again out of desperation. Famine is a likely consequence of war. Pestilence follows war. Then widespread death follows the pestilence, famine and the war. This is not mere speculation it is prophecy. We don't know exactly how it will start but it will happen.

After the collapse happens, when the dust settles, there will be a new form of government, a government which will demand total submission. Financial transactions will be electronic by way of the "mark". The expectation will be that everyone must take the mark. To refuse will put you outside the system and will not be allowed.

> Rev 13:13 And he doeth great wonders, so that he maketh fire come down from heaven on the earth in the sight of men,

> 14 And deceiveth them that dwell on the earth by *the means of* those miracles which he had power to do in the sight of the beast; saying to them that dwell on the earth, that they should make an image to the beast, which had the wound by a sword, and did live.

> 15 And he had power to give life unto the image of the beast, that the image of the beast should both speak, **and cause that as many as would not worship the image of the beast should be killed.**

> 16 And he causeth all, both small and great, rich and poor, free and bond, to receive a mark in their right hand, or in their foreheads:

> 17 And that no man might buy or sell, save he that had the mark, or the name of the beast, or the number of his name.

Worshiping the image of the beast will be required prior to taking the mark. This leader will try to pass himself off as a divine manifestation of God. It will be as if he came to save us from the brink of destruction. What does it mean to worship the beast? Could it mean swear allegiance to him? Just taking the mark will be an act of submission to him. It is curious the word Islam means submission. Whatever worshiping the beast means, if you refuse to do it you will be killed.

> ^{Dan 9:36}And the king shall do according to his will; and **he shall exalt himself, and magnify himself above every god**, and shall speak marvellous things against the God of gods, and shall prosper till the indignation be accomplished: for that that is determined shall be done.

This is when Christians must make their stand. DO NOT COMPROMISE! Do not worship the beast, the image of the beast or even acknowledge it as anything other than demonic.

If you are forced to become a martyr for Jesus, be brave. Do not anticipate the pain. The pain will be what it is. There is nothing you can do about it. If you are tortured, call on God to help you endure. He also feels your pain. He is with you and knows what you can endure. May he be merciful to you and block some of the pain. Do not let anything stop you from serving God, even if it means other members of your family will die. Satan will use anything he can against you. Do not give in.

When Jesus sent forth his disciples in Matthew chapter 10 he gave them words of encouragement and told them what to expect. His words seemed to have additional prophetic applications. Jesus' words in Matthew chapter 10 would seem to apply equally well to the tribulation saints.

We have seen many dual fulfillments throughout the Bible. When Jesus sent forth his disciples, there seemed to be more to it than just a "missions trip." Could it have been symbolic of the journey his people would take during the tribulation period?

> ^{Mat 10:7}And as ye go, preach, saying, The kingdom of heaven is at hand.

> ⁸Heal the sick, cleanse the lepers, raise the dead, cast out devils: freely ye have received, freely give.

⁹Provide neither gold, nor silver, nor brass in your purses,

Rev 13:17And that no man might buy or sell, save he that had the mark, or the name of the beast, or the number of his name.

Mat 10:10Nor scrip for *your* journey, neither two coats, neither shoes, nor yet staves: for the workman is worthy of his meat.

Mat 24:17Let him which is on the housetop not come down to take any thing out of his house: ¹⁸Neither let him which is in the field return back to take his clothes.

Mat 10:11And into whatsoever city or town ye shall enter, enquire who in it is worthy; and there abide till ye go thence.

¹²And when ye come into an house, salute it.

¹³And if the house be worthy, let your peace come upon it: but if it be not worthy, let your peace return to you.

¹⁴And whosoever shall not receive you, nor hear your words, when ye depart out of that house or city, shake off the dust of your feet.

¹⁵Verily I say unto you, It shall be more tolerable for the land of Sodom and Gomorrha in the day of judgment, than for that city.

¹⁶Behold, I send you forth as sheep in the midst of wolves: be ye therefore wise as serpents, and harmless as doves.

Dan 11:33And they that understand among the people shall instruct many: yet they shall fall by the sword, and by flame, by captivity, and by spoil, *many* days.

Mat 10:17But beware of men: for they will deliver you up to the councils, and they will scourge you in their synagogues;

18And ye shall be brought before governors and kings for my sake, for a testimony against them and the Gentiles.

> Luke 21:12But before all these, they shall lay their hands on you, and persecute *you,* delivering *you* up to the synagogues, and into prisons, being brought before kings and rulers for my name's sake.

Mat 10:19But when they deliver you up, take no thought how or what ye shall speak: for it shall be given you in that same hour what ye shall speak.

20For it is not ye that speak, but the Spirit of your Father which speaketh in you.

> Luke 21:13And it shall turn to you for a testimony. 14Settle *it* therefore in your hearts, not to meditate before what ye shall answer: 15For I will give you a mouth and wisdom, which all your adversaries shall not be able to gainsay nor resist.

Mat 10:21And the brother shall deliver up the brother to death, and the father the child: and the children shall rise up against *their* parents, and cause them to be put to death.

22And ye shall be hated of all *men* for my name's sake: but he that endureth to the end shall be saved.

> Luke 21:16And ye shall be betrayed both by parents, and brethren, and kinsfolks, and friends; and *some* of you shall they cause to be put to death. 17And ye shall be hated of all *men* for my name's sake.

Mat 10:23But when they persecute you in this city, flee ye into another: for verily I say unto you, Ye shall not have gone over the cities of Israel, till the Son of man be come.

> Luke 21:20And when ye shall see Jerusalem compassed with armies, then know that the desolation thereof is nigh. 21Then let them which are in Judaea flee to the mountains; and let them which are in the midst of it depart out; and let not them that are in the countries enter thereinto.

Mat 10:24The disciple is not above *his* master, nor the servant above his lord.

25It is enough for the disciple that he be as his master, and the servant as his lord. If they have called the master of the house Beelzebub, how much more *shall they call* them of his household?

26Fear them not therefore: for there is nothing covered, that shall not be revealed; and hid, that shall not be known.

27What I tell you in darkness, *that* speak ye in light: and what ye hear in the ear, *that* preach ye upon the housetops.

28And fear not them which kill the body, but are not able to kill the soul: but rather fear him which is able to destroy both soul and body in hell.

The words of encouragement and warning Jesus gave his disciples did not seem totally appropriate for the mission he was sending then on. It was as if Jesus was using the mission trip he was sending his disciples on as an object lesson for the tribulation saints to learn from.

Each one of us is very important to God.

Mat 10:29Are not two sparrows sold for a farthing? and one of them shall not fall on the ground without your Father. 30But the very hairs of your head are all numbered. 31Fear ye not therefore, ye are of more value than many sparrows.

We must confess Jesus before men no matter what.

> [Mat 10:32]Whosoever therefore shall confess me before men, him will I confess also before my Father which is in heaven. [33]But whosoever shall deny me before men, him will I also deny before my Father which is in heaven.

Confessing Jesus may cause you to be at odds with your family and they may even become your enemy.

> [Mat 10:34]Think not that I am come to send peace on earth: I came not to send peace, but a sword. [35]For I am come to set a man at variance against his father, and the daughter against her mother, and the daughter in law against her mother in law. [36]And a man's foes *shall be* they of his own household.

We cannot allow our love for our family or anyone else to prevent us from confessing and obeying Jesus. If we put the well being of our families above our commitment to the Lord then we are not worthy of him and we will be lost.

> [Mat 10:37]He that loveth father or mother more than me is not worthy of me: and he that loveth son or daughter more than me is not worthy of me.

We must expect to suffer and we will have to make the choice to follow Jesus or not. If we choose to save our life we will lose our soul. If we choose to die for Jesus we will live with him forever.

> [Mat 10:38]And he that taketh not his cross, and followeth after me, is not worthy of me. [39]He that findeth his life shall lose it: and he that loseth his life for my sake shall find it.

The following is a promise of a blessing for those who will help the Lord's people.

> [Mat 10:40]He that receiveth you receiveth me, and he that receiveth me receiveth him that sent me. [41]He that receiveth a prophet in the name of a prophet shall receive a

prophet's reward; and he that receiveth a righteous man in the name of a righteous man shall receive a righteous man's reward. ⁴²And whosoever shall give to drink unto one of these little ones a cup of cold *water* only in the name of a disciple, verily I say unto you, he shall in no wise lose his reward.

This will be the time in history when miracles will be seen and the people who know their God will do exploits.

> ^{Dan 9:32}And such as do wickedly against the covenant shall he corrupt by flatteries: **but the people that do know their God shall be strong, and do** *exploits*.

Be strong and do exploits. You will see miracles during this time. He will provide for us when we are faithful and can't provide for ourselves. The miracles of the loaves and fishes, the multiplication of the widow's flour to feed Elijah and the manna in the wilderness are all examples of God's miraculous provision. We will most likely see these types of miracles again.

> ^{Dan 9:33}And **they that understand among the people shall instruct many**: yet they shall fall by the sword, and by flame, by captivity, and by spoil, *many* days.
>
> ³⁴Now when they shall fall, they shall be holpen with a little help: but many shall cleave to them with flatteries.
>
> ³⁵And *some* of them of understanding shall fall, to try them, and to purge, and to make *them* white, *even* to the time of the end: because *it is* yet for a time appointed.

I still encourage Christians to prepare themselves for the coming tribulation. Prepare spiritually and financially. The times leading into the tribulation period are going to be very bad. In Genesis chapter 41 God gave Joseph the interpretation to Pharaoh's dream. He said there would be seven fat (prosperous) years followed by seven lean years of famine. Joseph told the Pharaoh to prepare. Joseph was put in charge of the preparation and, in the process; he saved his own family as well as Egypt and the surrounding areas.

God has given us a warning. The tribulation period is coming. We are supposed to be the people of understanding who will instruct many. I cannot tell you how to escape the coming trials but I can give you some good advice that will help you in the future.

The best advice I can give you is to be spiritually ready for the coming persecution. Also, get out of debt. This is not a time for accumulating wealth or pursuing things. If this means selling your new car, boat or house, fine. Get out of debt! Buy only what you can afford.

Get out of the cities. The cities are not going to be safe when the economy collapses. There is no way to survive inside of a city.

Buy or rent a house in the country. Gardening and raising small livestock like chickens could be the difference between life and death. Having a well for water is also a necessity. Even if the electricity goes off for good, a well can still provide you enough water to survive. You may have to remove the well pump and pull up small amounts of water using a rope and something to dip into the water.

Storing food now is a cheap insurance policy against future hunger. Unfortunately, you can only store a finite amount and when people become desperate they will do anything to get what you have.

The same holds true for buying gold. Gold may be a great insurance policy against the coming hyper-inflation, but when the economy dissolves into total chaos people will forcibly take whatever you have of value.

Guns and ammo seem to be the only way to protect what you have, but I don't see anything in the scriptures about taking a stand to protect what you have during the coming tribulation period.

The bottom line is this… It is wise to do what you can to prepare for the coming tribulation but, in the end, you cannot save yourself. Get out of debt. Get out of the cities. Store food and grow a garden. Buy gold and have some guns (for hunting) but do not expect any of these things to save you. Be a person of understanding. People will need you. You will do exploits. This will be one of the primary focal points of history and you will be part of it.

Hopefully this book will help you to be one of the people of understanding and you will be used to instruct many during the tribulation period. Many Christians with good hearts will be totally unhinged when the tribulation starts. Daniel 9:35 reminds us we may die as martyrs during this time, but this is ok because we will be given white robes by Jesus. We will stand before his throne to serve him and he will dwell among us. I think this will be the most desired place to be in Heaven.

Conclusion:

The Bible cannot be understood in part. It must be understood as a whole. Origins, Symbolism and Prophecy are intertwined. They themselves are a trinity. They are linked in the same way the past, the present, and the future are linked. When understood together they perfectly demonstrate the Unity of Scripture.

The future is going to be a difficult time of persecution. It will require faith, courage and a steadfast determination to follow God. Even through these trials, God can provide us with the peace we need. When we look at the 23rd Psalm and consider the coming persecution, it seems to be more relevant than ever.

Psalm 23:1 The LORD *is* my shepherd; I shall not want.

2 He maketh me to lie down in green pastures: he leadeth me beside the still waters.

3 He restoreth my soul: he leadeth me in the paths of righteousness for his name's sake.

4 Yea, though I walk through the valley of the shadow of death, I will fear no evil: for thou *art* with me; thy rod and thy staff they comfort me.

5 Thou preparest a table before me in the presence of mine enemies: thou anointest my head with oil; my cup runneth over.

6 Surely goodness and mercy shall follow me all the days of my life: and I will dwell in the house of the LORD for ever.

The Lord will provide for us and lead us into paths of righteousness. Even when we walk through the valley of the shadow of death, the Lord's rod (power) and his staff (leading) will comfort us. David said he would fear no evil because the Lord is with him. You do not have to fear. The Lord is with you. He will prepare a place for you in the presence of your enemies.

Be brave, be bold and do not give in. Satan is looking to separate you from the shepherd.

> Rom 8:38For I am persuaded, that neither death, nor life, nor angels, nor principalities, nor powers, nor things present, nor things to come, 39Nor height, nor depth, nor any other creature, shall be able to separate us from the love of God, which is in Christ Jesus our Lord.

Only you can separate yourself from God. You must hold on to your salvation with both hands. Guard it. Satan will hit you where you are most vulnerable. He does not play fair.

I hope this book has inspired you to study the Bible more closely. The Bible is a divinely inspired book. There are so many levels of truth and understanding within it, no man can hope to fully comprehend its entire meaning. Making the Bible more understandable has been the primary goal of this book. It is also my hope this book will result in the salvation of some who have been unwilling to accept the truth of the Bible because of their lack of understanding. Fortunately, God has made the salvation part simple.

> Rom 10: 9That if thou shalt confess with thy mouth the Lord Jesus, and shalt believe in thine heart that God hath raised him from the dead, thou shalt be saved.

> 10For with the heart man believeth unto righteousness; and with the mouth confession is made unto salvation.

> 11For the scripture saith, Whosoever believeth on him shall not be ashamed.

> 12For there is no difference between the Jew and the Greek: for the same Lord over all is rich unto all that call upon him.

> 13For whosoever shall call upon the name of the Lord shall be saved.

I encourage you, if you have not already done so, to accept the Lord Jesus as your savior. The above scripture shows you that becoming a Christian is not complicated. It can be hard though. First you have to believe, and then you must confess Jesus before men. It may be unpopular and, in the future, it may get you killed but you MUST be willing to confess your faith in Jesus to anyone. He died for you and you may have to die for him. Be ready. Be willing, and don't look back.

May your journey end/begin with the words…

Well done, thou good and faithful servant.

Appendix A

Why the Theory of Evolution is Wrong.

The genetic code is so complex even our best scientists with their state of the art technology cannot create even a single celled organism from scratch. The genetic code is like the most complicated computer program ever created, but a program is worthless without a computer to interpret and execute the program. Conversely, a computer is useless without a program to tell it what to do. In this analogy the genetic code is the software of life and the cells are the hardware of life. Neither of these could have developed without the other.

There are two theories to explain the origins of life. These are Evolution and Special Creation. Evolution seeks to explain life through purely natural processes. Special Creation explains the origin of life by way of an external creator who designed the life forms on this planet deliberately.

The mechanism that supposedly drives evolution forward is thought to be survival of the fittest. Evolution and Survival of the fittest are often thought of as being the same thing. They are not. Evolution is an increase in genetic complexity, such as a single celled organism changing (evolving) into a multi-cell organism or a fish changing (evolving) into an amphibian. Evolution has NEVER been observed or demonstrated in any way.

Survival of the fittest is easily observed in nature. It does not provide an increase in genetic complexity. It simply says the healthiest, best adapted individuals are the ones who are most likely to reproduce and pass on their genetic information to the next generation.

Evolutionists would suppose random errors (mutations) in the genetic code could sometimes be beneficial, which would make the life forms with the beneficial mutation more fit to survive. They would also suppose the first form of life to appear would have been the simplest type of single celled organism.

There are a couple things wrong with the suppositions made by the evolutionists.

The first single cell organism to ever come into existence would have to come about through a lucky combination of non-living chemicals. Not only would this first organism have to spontaneously come to life from a lifeless chemical soup it would also need a fully functioning reproductive system. If this first generation organism did not have a fully functioning reproductive system then it would die without being able to propagate itself (life would end there). This first generation organism would also need a fully functioning digestive system or some way of extracting sufficient energy from it's environment or it would not survive (life would end there). I repeat... these obstacles are so hard to overcome that even our best scientists can't produce life under ideal controlled conditions and we expect it to have happened randomly? Preposterous!

As for random mutations causing beneficial changes, it is astronomically unlikely. The more complicated the machine, the more things there are which can go wrong. Let's go back to the computer analogy. With all the computers that exist on this planet, how many have had software malfunctions that were beneficial? Let's assume there were some, and whenever it happens we will make sure every computer on the planet gets updated with the beneficial error.

How long do you expect it would take before our Windows 95 software would randomly become Windows 98 software? How long before Windows 2000? These beneficial errors would also require a simultaneous compatible evolution of the hardware used to interpret the newly evolved software.

If the previous example seems ridiculous, you should stop and consider that our genetic code is exponentially more complicated than our most advanced computer software. Evolution proposes that errors are responsible for the eventual transformation from amebas to men. Even if Survival of the fittest preserved every beneficial error (assuming there were any), it still doesn't make sense.

Survival of the fittest is a demonstrable fact. It is not a mechanism which increases the complexity within the genetic code. It rather preserves the genetic complexity and minimizes the amount of genetic error that gets passed on to the next generation. In the animal kingdom, the strongest (healthiest) males fight for the right to mate with the females. This ensures only the strongest, healthiest individuals get to pass on their genetic information to the next generation.

All living creatures have a genetic code that has a certain degree of diversity within it. If there wasn't a degree of diversity then all of us would be identical. This diversity explains the differences among similar animals. Dogs are the most popular example of genetic diversity.

There are dogs of all different sizes and shapes and yet a small dog is not more highly evolved than a large dog. They are just different.

An artificial form of Survival of the fittest is called Selective Breeding. It is used to develop animals with desirable characteristics. There is a common misconception that desirable characteristics can be bred into animals. In fact, it is just the opposite. Desirable characteristics are not bred into an animal but rather undesirable characteristics are bred out! To demonstrate this let's imagine we wanted to develop a new breed of dog. We would only allow the puppies with the characteristics we wanted to develop to survive and reproduce. With each generation we would select the same types of puppies to survive and reproduce. Within several generations, we would see the majority of puppies with the desired characteristics. What we have done is to remove the diversity from the puppy's genes and the result was the puppies became more and more similar. Their genetic code was not made more complex. It was made less complex because the diversity in their genes was removed.

To prove Survival of the fittest is a process of exclusion lets consider the possibility of breeding a dog with wings. Could we do it? No. The genetic code for wings does not exist within a dog's genetic makeup.

The same thing holds true for antibiotic resistant bacteria. The only reason bacteria can become antibiotic resistant is because there are a few bacteria within the bacteria population that have a natural resistance to the antibiotics. The natural resistance to the antibiotics is due to the diversity in the bacteria's genetic code. These resistant bacteria continue to multiply while the regular bacteria die out. Before long all of the bacteria are of the resistant type. This is survival of the fittest. Not evolution.

What about the Age of the Earth?

What about the Fossils?

The Old Earth theories are not as scientific as the public education system would have you believe. Fossils of extinct animals are seen as undeniable proof the Earth is ancient when, in reality, it is just proof that there were more types of animals in the past than there are today. It also shows the animals were killed and buried quickly before their bodies could be destroyed by scavengers or the elements. The flood of Noah is the best explanation for the worldwide mass extinction and quick burial of billions of animals in sedimentary rock layers.

Radiometric dating techniques are typically used to justify the extremely old ages associated with the fossils. All radiometric dating techniques rely on the decay of radioactive isotopes. These Radioactive Isotopes decay at predictable rates. The radioactive isotopes decay into what are known as daughter products. We can measure how much of the radioactive isotope is present and how much of the daughter product is present. By comparing the ratio of Radioactive Isotope to daughter product you should be able to figure out how long it would take for the Radioactive Isotope to decay to produce the amount of daughter product present.

The theories behind Radiometric dating techniques are reasonable, but there are problems associated with them which make them virtually useless.

In order to find the age of a fossil using Radiometric Dating techniques you have to make some assumptions.

You must assume the Radioactive Isotope was present in the bone of the animal when it died and there were none of the daughter products present in the bone when the animal died.

You must also assume that none of the Radioactive Isotope or the daughter product leeched into or out of the bone during the process of fossilization.

The very process of fossilization proves the bone was experiencing the continual inflow and outflow of mineral deposits. These fossilized bones are contaminated with external minerals, elements, and isotopes. Any conclusions drawn from isotopes in a fossil are by definition inaccurate.

Minerals from the surrounding area fill the holes
left by the disolved calcium. These minerals harden
over time causing fossilization.

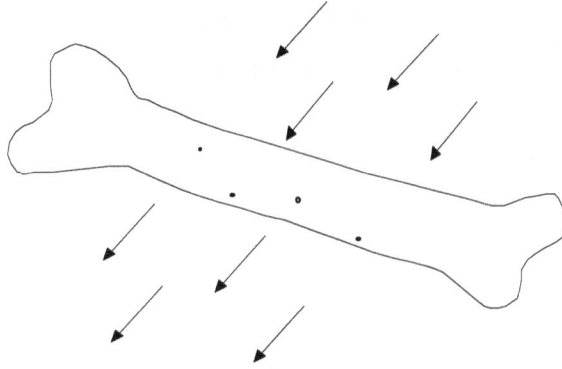

Calcium and other minerals disolve and are
carried away over time.

Radio Carbon dating (Carbon 14) is slightly different. It is used on supposedly "younger" specimens because Carbon 14 has a relatively short half life. Carbon 14 can be used on fossils or on regular flesh and bone.

The theory behind Carbon 14 testing is as follows. Carbon 14 is produced in the upper atmosphere when a cosmic ray (neutron) hits a regular Nitrogen 14 atom. This cosmic ray knocks off a proton and the cosmic ray (neutron) is absorbed thereby transforming the Nitrogen 14 atom into a radioactive Carbon 14 isotope. This carbon 14 isotope is has a half life of about 5730 years. This means that in 5730 years only half of the original Carbon 14 will remain in the specimen. 5730 years after that only one quarter of the original Carbon 14 will remain.

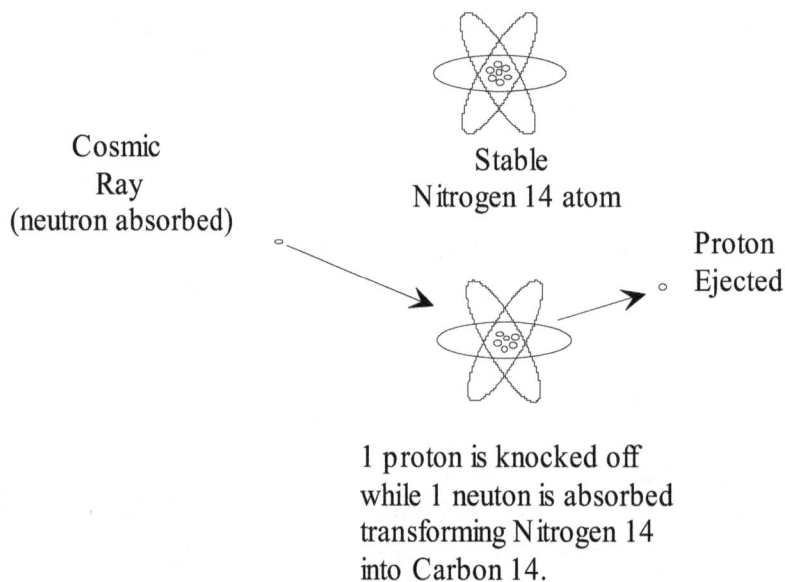

Cosmic
Ray
(neutron absorbed)

Stable
Nitrogen 14 atom

Proton
Ejected

1 proton is knocked off
while 1 neuton is absorbed
transforming Nitrogen 14
into Carbon 14.

The Carbon 14 isotopes will react chemically just like regular Carbon 12 atoms. Over many thousands of years, it is theorized, the Carbon 14 concentration in the atmosphere has reach stabilization where there are as many Carbon 14 atoms decaying as there are being made.

Scientists assume the Carbon 14 concentrations have been stabilized for millions of years. This would mean that the current ratio of Carbon 12 to Carbon 14 is a constant in our atmosphere.

Since plants get their carbon from the atmosphere and animals ultimately get their carbon from eating plants, the ratio of Carbon 12 to Carbon 14 within the animal's bodies should be the same as the atmospheric concentration.

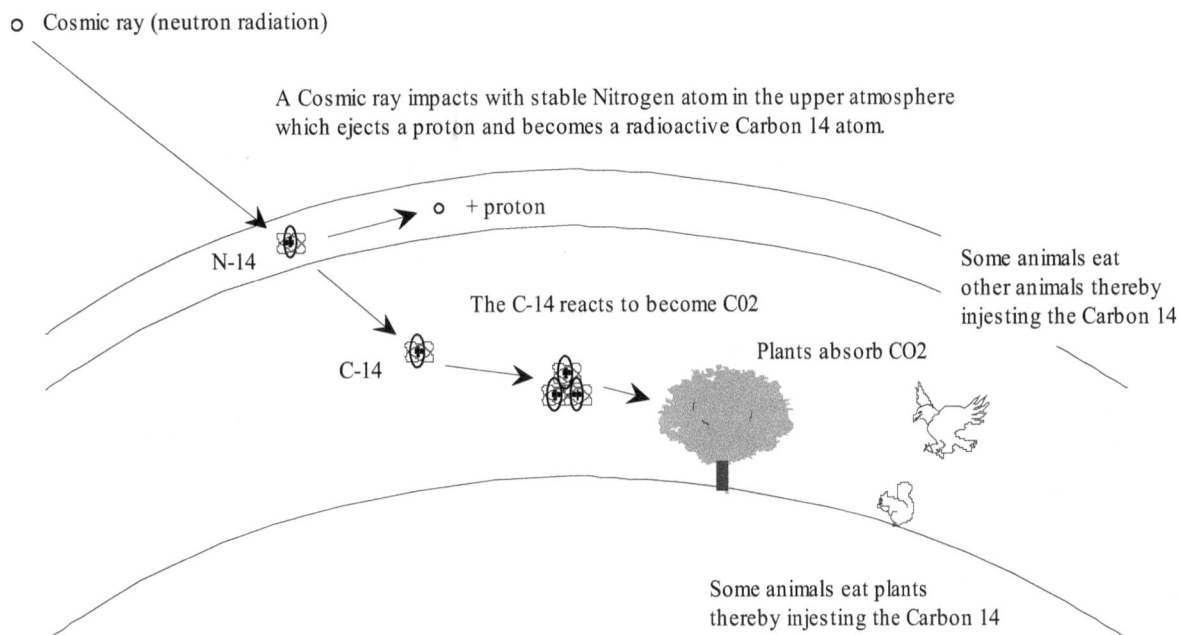

Cosmic ray (neutron radiation)

A Cosmic ray impacts with stable Nitrogen atom in the upper atmosphere which ejects a proton and becomes a radioactive Carbon 14 atom.

o + proton

N-14

The C-14 reacts to become CO2

Some animals eat other animals thereby injesting the Carbon 14

C-14

Plants absorb CO2

Some animals eat plants thereby injesting the Carbon 14

When the plant or animal dies, it no longer eats or intakes carbon. The Carbon 14 decays away over time leaving behind only the stable Carbon 12 atoms. By determining the ratio of the Carbon 12 to the remaining Carbon 14 atoms you should be able to determine how long the plant or animal has been dead.

The problem with this theory is the assumption the atmospheric concentration of Carbon 14 has been constant for millions of years. This is not necessarily so.

The Bible indicates the Earth is approximately 6000 years old. If God didn't initially make Carbon 14 when he created the Earth, then it would take many thousands of years to reach equilibrium.

372

The Bible also indicates God initially created a water vapor canopy in the upper atmosphere that could have acted as shielding to slow the production of Carbon 14. In the following verses the word Firmament means "sky", "atmosphere" or "heaven".

> Gen 1:6 And God said, Let there be a firmament in the midst of the waters, and let it divide the waters from the waters.

> 7 And God made the firmament, and divided the waters which *were* under the firmament from the waters which *were* above the firmament: and it was so.

> 8 And God called the firmament Heaven. And the evening and the morning were the second day.

The very small amounts of Carbon 14 in the early atmosphere would make fossils from that era appear much older than they actually were.

Volcanic eruptions would also throw off the ratios because volcanoes expel massive quantities of Carbon 12. This would change the Carbon concentration ratios and would make accurate Carbon dating impossible.

What about Dinosaurs?

Dinosaurs are extinct animals we are aware of because their bones have been preserved in sedimentary rocks. They were obviously buried very quickly so as to prevent scavengers and the elements from destroying them. These fossils are preserved in sedimentary deposits all over the world. The easiest and most obvious explanation for this would be the worldwide flood described in the Bible.

Noah was instructed to take two of every sort of animal into the Ark according to their kinds.

Noah was to take two of each type not two of every variety. Two wolves would suffice for the dog kind, two from the cat family, two from the lizards etc. I am sure God took part in the selection of which animals to pick. Dinosaurs could have been a specific variety of lizard that may not have been taken. A different type of lizard could have been chosen for the Ark.

It is possible Noah brought dinosaurs into the Ark. If he did, it would have been prudent to bring smaller adolescent specimens because they would take up less space and eat less.

If Noah did bring the dinosaurs with him, then what happened to them?

Answer: They died.

There are Biblical references to a dinosaur like creature described in the book of Job 40:15. It was called Behemoth. Animals such as this could be where the legends of dragon slayers came from.

It is not surprising many animals would become extinct after the flood. The animal populations would be so small that any disease, injury or attack by predators could be unrecoverable to that particular type of animal.

The post-flood environment could have also caused stress on many animals. It is theorized the atmospheric pressure after the flood was less than it was before the flood because the weight of the vapor canopy was no longer pressing down on the atmosphere. This reduction in atmospheric pressure would make it more difficult to breath, similar to the way it is harder for mountain climbers to breathe as they go higher in elevation.

This may also explain why the life spans of people after the flood dropped off dramatically. I expect many animals couldn't adequately adjust to the new environmental conditions.

We would expect to find evidence of many unexpected varieties of animals living before the flood and the fossil record supports this.

What about the Cave Men?

What about Cave Men Fossils?

Cave men are by definition men that lived in caves. Nothing special there, but the idea of cave men usually assumes an evolutionary past for humans where we evolved from ape-like ancestors.

The evidence for these "ape-men" is so flimsy as to be non existent.

Some of the recent candidates include:

Piltdown Man:	fraud: the skullcap of a human was paired with the lower jaw of an orangutan. The teeth were filed down and made to look human and made to match the teeth in the upper human jaw. The teeth were also dyed to make them appear to be very old.
Nebraska Man:	Mistake: An extinct pig's tooth was mistakenly thought to be that of an ancient human. An illustration of the ancient ape-man was made based on this tooth. It was later discovered that the type of pig that the tooth came from wasn't extinct either.
Australopithecus:	Lucy: 40% complete, No jawbone, Most of scull missing, No hands or feet. Other examples have now been found. It is now recognized to be a type of ape. Not man.
Homo habilis:	Mistakenly identified as human. It never existed as such. It was a combination of bones from different apes and humans.
Homo erectus:	This was a true human with a smaller than average brain cavity but was still within the range of modern human brain cavities.
Neandertal man:	The fossil discovered was a true human who suffered from a bone disease like rickets. Reconstructions of the diseased bones resulted in a stooped, ape-like posture. Had a slightly larger than average brain cavity.

Evolutionists are desperate to find a missing link but everyone they find is eventually proved to be in error. They desperately want to prove evolution because it is the only possible way to explain our existence without God. The idea that scientists will go anywhere the evidence takes them is not true. The theory of evolution is unreasonable, unproven and unsupported by the evidence but the "scientists" are determined to cling to it because the alternative (God) is unacceptable to them. So much for "Scientific Integrity".

Appendix B

Einstein and Genesis

The Bible was not meant to be a scientific document but what it describes is consistent with what true science has discovered about the nature of the universe.

This can be demonstrated by looking at the first 3 verses of the Bible (Gen 1:1-3). These verses describe the creation of time, space, matter, and energy in general terms.

Genesis 1

[1]In the beginning God created the heaven and the earth.

    In the beginning = Time

    Heaven = Space (units = distance)

    Earth = Matter (units = mass)

[2]And the earth was without form, and void; and darkness was upon the face of the deep. And the Spirit of God moved upon the face of the waters.

[3]And God said, Let there be light: and there was light.

    Light = Energy

Time, Space, Matter, and Energy are the most fundamental properties in the physical universe. This shows the great insight of the author of Genesis concerning the nature of the universe. Einstein would undoubtedly agree.

Consider Einstein's famous equation E=mc²

E = Energy

m = Mass

c = the speed of light (186,000 miles/second)

This equation basically states there is a demonstrable relationship between Energy and Matter. Matter can be converted into Energy and theoretically, Energy can be converted into matter.

The amount of energy contained in matter is equal to the amount of matter times the speed of light to the second power. Therefore, there is an incredible amount of potential energy contained in all matter.

Notice the speed of light constant is given in units of miles per second. The units for speed are actually Distance per unit Time.

So, Einstein's equation could be written as...

$E=m(d/t)^2$

E = Energy

m = Mass

d = Distance

t = time

These are exactly the same properties described in Gen 1:1-3. The Bible described the fundamental properties of the universe thousands of years before Einstein put them into specific mathematical terms.

The time component, found in the speed of light factor, is fundamental to the relationship between mass and energy. Time is the most basic quantity in the universe. I believe time is the one constant that holds this universe together. Everything in this universe is synchronized to the same time constant and yet time has not always existed. A simple thought experiment will demonstrate this. Let's define a day as the most basic unit of time. This day unit is based on 24 hourly periods and is independent of the Earth's rotation. Imagine if time had always existed, then it would have existed infinitely into the past. If time went an infinite number of days into the past, then an infinite number of days would have to pass before today could occur. Therefore today could never occur. This paradox demonstrates that time must have had a beginning for us to get to this point.

I also believe God is outside of time. God exists at all points of time simultaneously. I think God gave a hint of this when Moses asked God who he should say sent him and God told Moses to tell the Israelites that "I am" sent him. If God is outside of the bounds of time, then God lives in a nonlinear continuum of being. This is why God describes himself as "I am". This also explains why a day is as a thousand years and a thousand years is as a day with the Lord. Time to God is meaningless. His simultaneous existence at all points in time makes prophecy possible, because God knows the end from the beginning. It is also obvious the angels and demons do not exist in the same timeless state God does. If they did, then the demons would have known the consequences of their rebellion and would not have chosen to follow Lucifer.

The Bible says we were created a little lower than the angels. This could have a couple of meanings. I suspect that the demons (and the angels) exist in a realm with a time constant that is slightly out of phase with our own. The best way to explain this is to compare it to radio waves. There are many radio waves traveling thru the atmosphere. Many radio waves are occupying the same air space and yet an individual broadcast can be isolated using a receiver that is tuned into the proper frequency. I believe the time constant for our universe is the frequency everything is tuned to. We cannot perceive anything outside of our time constant.

Angels and demons can interact with us to some extent even though their time constants are different. How is this possible? Going back to the radio wave analogy will help explain this. If two broadcasts are relatively close in frequency and the band width of one of the frequencies is broad enough and powerful enough, then the broad bandwidth broadcast will bleed over onto nearby frequencies. I expect the time constant for our universe has a very tight bandwidth. The demons would have a higher time constant than we have with a bandwidth wide enough to allow them to perceive and interfere with our universe. The Angels would have a higher time constant than the demons and also a high enough bandwidth to reach our time constant. This would also allow the Angels to perceive and interact with our universe. Unfortunately, the Angels have to pass through the demon bandwidth to reach our time constant and the demons might be able to interfere with them as they try to pass through the demon bandwidth. In the Book of Daniel, he prayed and fasted for 21 days for the interpretation of a vision. When he was visited by "one like the similitude of the sons of men ", Daniel was told by the manlike being that he had tried to come immediately but the Prince of Persia (a demon) restrained him until the angel Michael came to help him. The manlike being had to pass through demon territory to reach Daniel. The manlike being came to make Daniel understand the vision. When the manlike being was finished he said, "and now will I return to fight with the prince of Persia: and when I am gone forth, lo, the prince of Grecia shall come."

The manlike being returns through the territory of the Prince of Persia and he fights with him. He obviously defeats the Prince of Persia because the Prince of Grecia comes to fill the void left by the absence of the Prince of Persia.

The point of this is to show there are beings (angels and demons) which exist in a different plane (Maybe with a different bandwidth and a different time constant.). Daniel existed in the physical plane. The Prince of Persia (a demon) had power and authority over the Babylonian kingdom. In order to reach Daniel in the physical realm, the manlike being had to fight his way past the demon (with the help of Michael). The manlike being would have to return through the demonic territory when he was ready to leave the physical realm.

The Identity of the manlike being was most likely the pre-incarnate Jesus. The description of the manlike being is very similar to the description of Jesus in the book of Revelation. Jesus is also referred to as the Son of Man.

This is explanation of how angels and demons can interact with the physical universe is highly speculative. It is not a matter of doctrine but it is something to consider. The bottom line is… Angels and demons do exist. We don't normally see them but the Bible tells us they can interact with us. My explanation is just a personal theory. You can take it for what it is worth.

Appendix C

What calendar does the Bible use?

Note: The following concerning the origins of our methods of time keeping and angular measure are purely speculative on my part.

The timeline of the great flood:

> Gen 7:11In the six hundredth year of Noah's life, in the second month, the seventeenth day of the month, the same day were all the fountains of the great deep broken up, and the windows of heaven were opened.

> Gen 8:3And the waters returned from off the earth continually: and after the end of the hundred and fifty days the waters were abated.

> Gen 8:4And the ark rested in the seventh month, on the seventeenth day of the month, upon the mountains of Ararat.

It was 150 days before the waters of the great flood abated enough for the ark to come to rest on the mountains of Ararat.

It was exactly 5 months before the ark came to rest.

Therefore each month was exactly 30 days long.

Projecting this 30 day month over an entire year would result in a 360 day year.

This may also explain why it has been customary for mathematicians and craftsmen to divide a circle into 360 equal divisions called degrees. This could be a carry over from ancient astronomy. Logically, dividing a circle into 360 degrees does not result in the most convenient units to use. It would be much more logical to divide a circle in half and divide those sections in half and divide those sections in half again and so on until the desired precision is achieved. Another common method of dividing a circle into sections is to compare a circles circumference to its radius. As it turns out, a circles circumference is always 2π larger than its radius. The symbol π is an irrational number roughly equal to 3.1415. This system is known as the Rad system. While the previous two methods are more logical and useful, the most commonly used system is the arbitrary 360 degree system. Comparing the 360 degree system to the ancient calendar is the only thing that seems to make sense.

To take it further we could consider why days are divided into hours and hours are divided into minutes and seconds.

The most ancient time measuring device was the sun dial. Time could only be measured during the daylight hours. So the ancient time keepers divided the daylight into 12 equal parts (hours) just as the year is divided into 12 equal parts (months). It should be noted that most dial clocks are 12 hour clocks. Eventually, it would be discovered how to tell time at night by plotting star movements or through some type of mechanical means like an hour glass. To be consistent, the night time hours were also divided into 12 equal parts just like the daytime hours. Presumably, this is how we end up with our current 24 hour day.

If we count the number of seconds per hour we will see there are 3600 seconds in an hour. The number of seconds in an hour is also evenly divisible by 360.

In summary, the number 360 seems to have particular significance.

There is the same number of daylight hours as there are months in the year.

Our methods of measuring angles and time support the idea that the ancient year was considered to be 360 days long.

Why would the number 360 be so important unless it was something that could be observed by the ancient astronomers?

The big question is... Was the year really 360 days long or were the ancient time keepers slightly off?

Both possibilities can be reasonably argued.

The ancient year could have been 360 days long before the great flood. It could be theorized God used a large meteor impact to initiate the great flood. This could have caused the fountains of the great deep to break open and the Earth's vapor canopy to collapse. Depending on the angle of the impact the asteroid could have caused the rotation of the Earth to speed up slightly. Since water has less mass per unit volume than dirt and stone the fountains of the deep breaking open would allow the less dense water to rise to the surface while the more dense dirt and rock would fall inward toward the center of the Earth. This would increase the Earths angular velocity. Much like when an ice skater spins around. When she brings her arms in closer to the center of her body she spins faster. Her angular velocity goes up. The water vapor canopy collapsing would have the same effect to increase the Earths angular velocity because water is more dense than the air, if a great deal of mass was transferred from the Earths upper atmosphere to the Earths surface the angular velocity of the Earth would increase.

More angular velocity means the Earth would spin faster as it goes around the Sun. The final result would be more days per year.

Additionally, it is unlikely the ancient time keepers could have been off by as much as 5 days per year. Since a year is roughly 365 days long, counting 360 days as a year would mean the seasons would arrive at different times each year. Within 6 years the calendar would be off by a month. The errors would add up quickly making planting and harvesting times harder to predict.

A more reasonable option would be to have the years be 360 days long and include an extra month (a leap month) every 6 years. This would mean most years would have 360 days but every sixth year there would be an added month making the leap year 390 days long. This would resynchronize the calendar before the seasons were off by too much.

There is still a slight inaccuracy with this method because a year is actually closer to 365 ¼ days long. This would mean that every 4th year the calendar would be off by a day. If this inaccuracy were allowed to continue, the seasons would become significantly out of sync in less than 100 yrs. The easiest way to compensate for the ¼ day inaccuracy would be to add 3 days to every other leap year. This would mean a normal year would be 360 days long. When the sixth year comes it would be a leap year of 390 days. Then 5 more 360 day years and a second leap year of 393 days would occur.

By alternating the leap years between 390 and 393 days long, the seasons would stay in sync for thousands of years.

It is my belief that before the flood of Noah, the year was exactly 360 days long. The flood resulted from a catastrophe caused by God. This catastrophe caused massive Earth changes that caused the rotational speed of the Earth to increase causing the 365 ¼ day years we have become accustomed to.

The 360 Day Prophetic Year
The Key to Understanding Bible Prophecy

The importance of the calendar used becomes obvious when trying to study Bible prophecy. Some prophecies are given in terms of days, some in Months and Some in years. It appears that these prophecies only make sense if we assume a 360 day year.

Prophecies Duration.	360 day year	365 ¼ day year
1260 days =	3 ½ yrs no leap Month	3.449 yrs
1290 days =	3 ½ yrs with a 30 day leap Month.	3.532 yrs
1335 days =	44.5 months	3.655 yrs Unable to determine because months have different durations
2300 days =	76 2/3 months	6.297 yrs Unable to determine because months have different durations
Middle of the Week	3.5 yrs	3.5 yrs

From the above comparison, It is obvious that the 360 day per year model fits better mathematically than the 365 ¼ day per year model.

The prophecies in the Bible fit together very nicely when a 360 day year is assumed.

A 365 ¼ day year makes the interrelation of the prophecies much more confusing.

The Number of Days

(Fitting it all together)

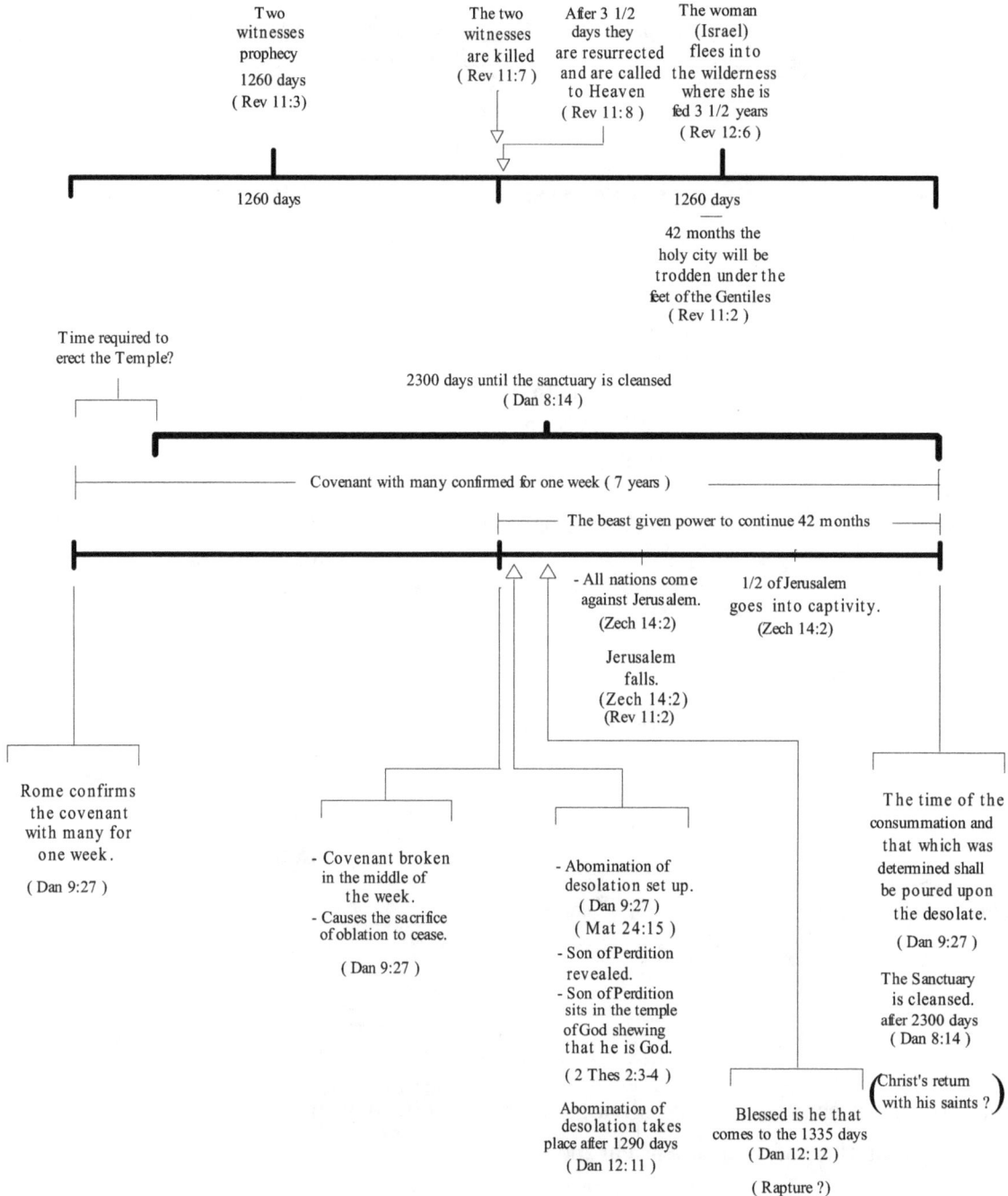

Two witnesses prophecy 1260 days (Rev 11:3)

The two witnesses are killed (Rev 11:7)

After 3 1/2 days they are resurrected and are called to Heaven (Rev 11:8)

The woman (Israel) flees into the wilderness where she is fed 3 1/2 years (Rev 12:6)

1260 days

1260 days

42 months the holy city will be trodden under the feet of the Gentiles (Rev 11:2)

Time required to erect the Temple?

2300 days until the sanctuary is cleansed (Dan 8:14)

Covenant with many confirmed for one week (7 years)

The beast given power to continue 42 months

- All nations come against Jerusalem. (Zech 14:2)

1/2 of Jerusalem goes into captivity. (Zech 14:2)

Jerusalem falls. (Zech 14:2) (Rev 11:2)

Rome confirms the covenant with many for one week. (Dan 9:27)

- Covenant broken in the middle of the week.
- Causes the sacrifice of oblation to cease.

(Dan 9:27)

- Abomination of desolation set up. (Dan 9:27) (Mat 24:15)
- Son of Perdition revealed.
- Son of Perdition sits in the temple of God shewing that he is God.

(2 Thes 2:3-4)

Abomination of desolation takes place after 1290 days (Dan 12:11)

The time of the consummation and that which was determined shall be poured upon the desolate. (Dan 9:27)

The Sanctuary is cleansed. after 2300 days (Dan 8:14)

Blessed is he that comes to the 1335 days (Dan 12:12)

(Rapture ?)

(Christ's return with his saints ?)

Appendix D

Was the Ark of the Covenant a Capacitor?

A theory has been proposed in recent years by supposed scholars who would attempt to explain the deadly nature of the Ark towards those who would touch it (other than the Levites who were assigned to carry it.) The theory has been promoted on several Bible mystery "documentaries". I remember one such "documentary" where a so-called expert on the subject was being interviewed and (to paraphrase his statement) he said, "The Ark of the Covenant was a very simple device. It was two conductors (gold) separated by an insulator (wood). The Ark of the Covenant was simply a capacitor." A couple of years later I saw a different "documentary" where a man had made a simplified replica of the Ark and hooked it up to a high voltage electrostatic generator. The man showed how a small electrical arc could be caused to jump from the Ark replica to a wire he was holding.

Let's consider the merits of both of these "documentaries". To do this we must consider how the Ark was constructed.

> Ex 25:10 And they shall make **an ark *of* shittim wood**: two cubits and a half *shall be* the length thereof, and a cubit and a half the breadth thereof, and a cubit and a half the height thereof. 11 And thou shalt **overlay it with pure gold, within and without** shalt thou overlay it, and shalt make upon it a crown of gold round about. 12 And thou shalt cast four rings of gold for it, and put *them* in the four corners thereof; and two rings *shall be* in the one side of it, and two rings in the other side of it. 13 And thou shalt make staves *of* shittim wood, and overlay them with gold. 14 And thou shalt put the staves into the rings by the sides of the ark, that the ark may be borne with them. 15 The staves shall be in the rings of the ark: they shall not be taken from it. 16 And thou shalt put into the ark the testimony which I shall give thee. 17 And thou shalt make a mercy seat *of* pure gold: two cubits and a half *shall be* the length thereof, and a cubit and a half the breadth thereof. 18 And thou shalt make two cherubims *of* gold, *of* beaten work shalt thou make them, in the two ends of the mercy seat. 19 And make one cherub on the one end, and the other cherub on the other end: *even* of the mercy seat shall ye make the cherubims on the two ends thereof. 20 And the cherubim shall stretch forth *their* wings on high,

covering the mercy seat with their wings, and their faces *shall look* one to another; toward the mercy seat shall the faces of the cherubims be. [21]And thou shalt put the mercy seat above upon the ark; and in the ark thou shalt put the testimony that I shall give thee.

The Construction of the Ark of the Covenant

The two Staves were constructed of shittim wood overlaid with pure gold

The two Cherubim were made of gold.

The Mercy Seat was made of pure gold.

Four Rings of pure gold were cast to hold the staves.

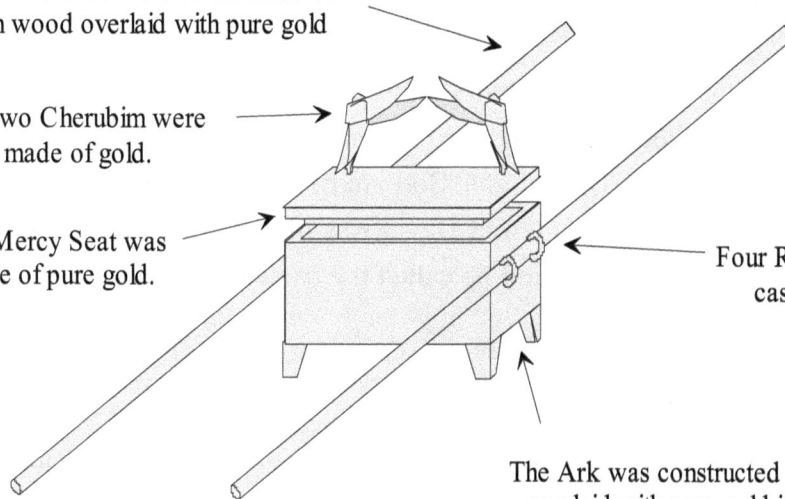

The Ark was constructed of shittim wood overlaid with pure gold inside and out.

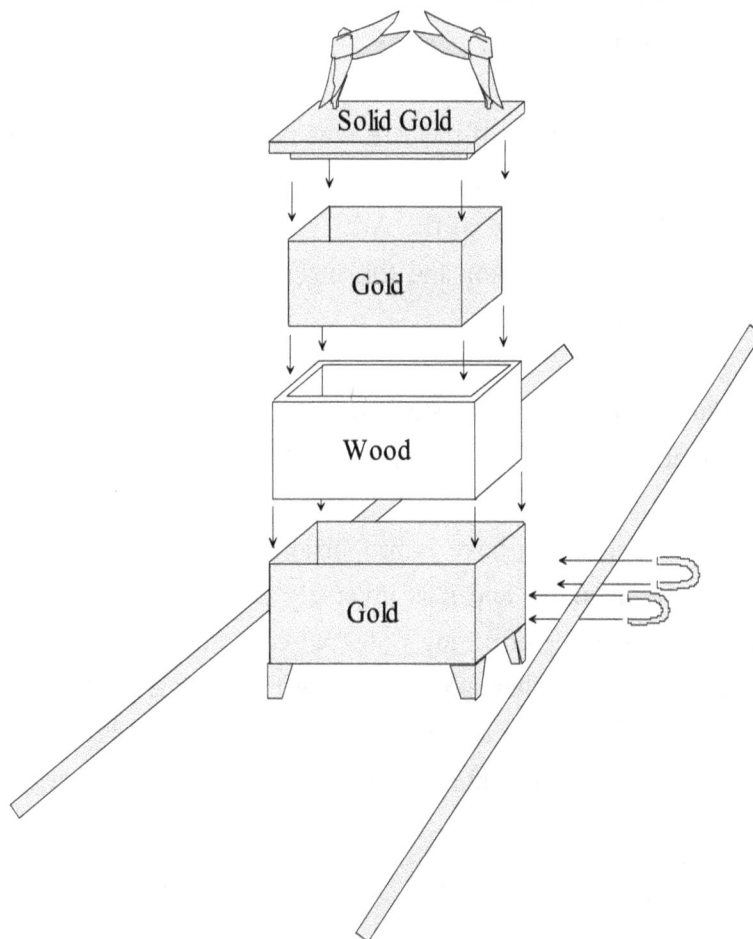

Solid Gold

Gold

Wood

Gold

The theory of the Ark being a capacitor may seem reasonable on a superficial level and the fact that a capacitor can retain an electrical charge would seem to explain why it could be deadly if touched. The Bible tells us one instance where the Ark killed a man who touched it.

> 2 Sam 6:6And when they came to Nachon's threshingfloor, Uzzah put forth *his hand* to the ark of God, and took hold of it; for the oxen shook *it*. 7And the anger of the LORD was kindled against Uzzah; and God smote him there for *his* error; and there he died by the ark of God. 8And David was displeased, because the LORD had made a breach upon Uzzah: and he called the name of the place Perez-uzzah to this day.

Did an electrical discharge from the Ark kill Uzzah? The Ark was constructed of an insulator (wood) and it did have a conductor (gold) on either side of the wood. Assuming the Ark was constructed in such a way as to take advantage of this capacitive effect then let's calculate how much capacitance it could have potentially had.

Assuming the gold overlay on the outside of the Ark was not allowed to touch the gold overlay on the inside of the Ark, we can use the dimensions given in the Bible to determine the approximate surface area of the inside and outside of the Ark. The surface area inside the Ark would effectively become one plate of the capacitor and the surface area of the outside of the Ark would become the other plate of the capacitor.

Capacitance can be calculated if you know the surface area of the conductor plates, how far they are separated from each other and what kind of insulator is between them.

The amount of capacitance an object can have is proportional to the surface area of the conductive plates on either side of the insulator and it is inversely proportional to the distance between the conductors. The third factor in determining potential capacitance is the insulator's dielectric constant (how well it insulates). In other words, the more surface area the conductive plates have, the greater the capacitive effect. The closer the plates are together, the greater the capacitive effect and the better the dielectric constant (permittivity), the better the charge will be retained.

We will have to make some assumptions about the dimensions of the Ark when trying to get a reasonable estimate of the Ark's performance as a capacitor.

*Note: all values will be converted to metric for the following calculations.

First we will assume the Ark was constructed using the 17.5 inch cubit (0.4445 meters). This being the case, the surface area of the inside and outside of the Ark would be...

$$\text{Sides and bottom} \quad = \quad 3 \cdot 2.5 \text{ cubits} \cdot 1.5 \text{ cubits} \cdot 0.1976 \frac{\text{meter}^2}{\text{cubit}^2} = 2.223 \text{ meters}^2$$

$$\text{Ends} \quad = \quad 2 \cdot 1.5 \text{ cubits} \cdot 1.5 \text{ cubits} \cdot 0.1976 \frac{\text{meter}^2}{\text{cubit}^2} = 0.889 \text{ meters}^2$$

$$\text{Total Surface Area} \ (A) = \quad 2.223 \text{ meter}^2 + 0.889 \text{ meter}^2 \quad = 3.112 \text{ meters}^2$$

Next we must guess at the thickness of the wooden walls of the Ark. To maximize the capacitive effect, I will assume a small wall thickness of ½ inch (0.0127 meters). I seriously doubt the walls of the Ark could have been much smaller than this and still be strong enough to support the weight of the Mercy Seat.

We will also maximize the capacitive effect by choosing the upper limit of permittivity for wood (6).

On the following page we will use the parallel plate formula to determine the capacitance of the Ark.

Capacitance can be determined using the following formula…

$$C = \frac{k \varepsilon_o \cdot A}{d}$$

C = Capacitance (farads)

k = relative permittivity of the dielectric material between the plates. (the relative permittivity of wood is 2-6) We will use a value of 6.

ε_o = Permittivity of empty space = 8.854×10^{-12} C ^{2}/Nm^2

A = Surface Area (square meters) = 3.112 square meters

d = Distance between the capacitor plates (meters) = 0.0127 meters

$$C = \frac{(8.854 \times 10^{-12})(6)(3.112)}{0.0127} = 1.302 \times 10^{-8} \text{ Farads} = 13.02 \text{ nF}$$

For those without an electronics background, let me assure you a capacitor with a value of 13 nano-Farads would be considered very-very small. A capacitor with a value 1000 times larger would still be considered a small capacitor. In most applications this amount of capacitance would be considered negligible. There is no way that this amount of capacitance could store enough of a charge to cause a life threatening jolt to anyone.

To put the final nails in the coffin of the capacitor theory, I suggest the way the Ark was constructed would have prevented even this small amount of capacitance from being created. If you look at exploded diagram of the Ark you will see the Mercy Seat acted as the lid of the Ark. It was made of pure gold and when it was placed on top of the Ark it would have touched both the inside gold overlay and the outside gold overlay thereby shorting the two together. The Ark wouldn't have ANY capacitive effect at all with the Mercy Seat in place. Similarly, the mounting rings for the staves were made of pure gold. They were mounted into the sides of the Ark. To have enough strength to lift such a heavy object, the rings would need to go entirely through the sides of the Ark. The wood was what gave the Ark its structural strength. The rings being inserted through the sides of the Ark with its gold-wood-gold construction would have also formed a short between the internal gold overlay and the external gold overlay. Once again, the capacitive effect would have been reduced to zero.

In conclusion, the construction of the Ark would suggest the internal golden overlay was not electrically isolated from the external golden overlay which is what would be required to achieve any sort of capacitive effect. Even if Moses took additional pains to ensure the inside overlay was electrically isolated from the outside overlay, which the Bible doesn't mention, the potential capacitance the Ark could have demonstrated would have been almost immeasurably small. The bottom line is …**The Ark of the Covenant was NOT a capacitor!**

As for the second "documentary" I mentioned earlier, there was a man who built a simplified model of the Ark using a wooden box covered with gold leaf. He hooked a high voltage generator up to it and a small electrical arc jumped between his Ark and one of the high voltage leads. AMAZING…. WOW…. STOP THE PRESSES!!!

I found this whole demonstration to be laughable. He hadn't demonstrated any unique electrical phenomenon by his sensationalistic experiment. What he demonstrated was the fact that gold is a conductor. The "documentary" didn't give the important details about how the high voltage Ark-circuit was set up but below is how I suspect they did it.

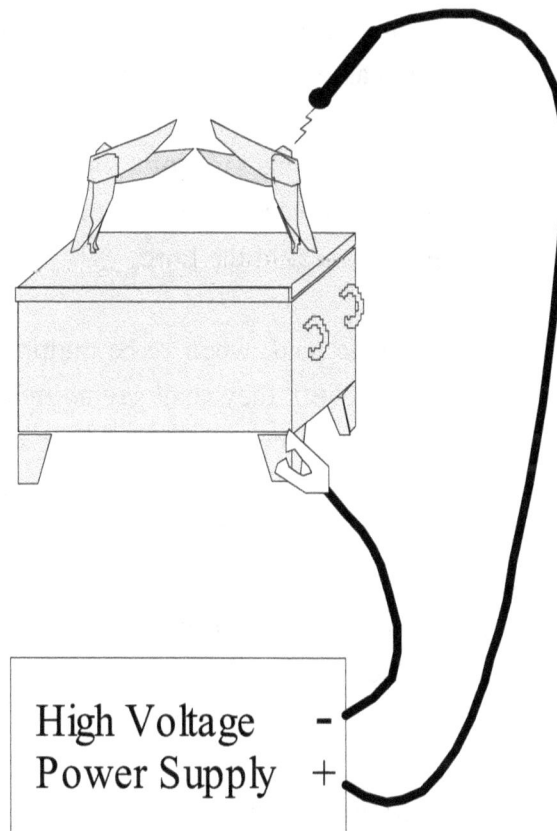

High Voltage
Power Supply
-
+

Sensationalism is rampant around things like the Ark of the Covenant. The theories these pseudo-science/educational channels push forward are so easily disproved with just a little effort it begs the question… Why do they promote such obvious nonsense? I believe there are two answers for this.

1) Sensationalism sells and most people aren't technically minded enough to question what they are being told.

2) If Biblical mysteries can be explained away using natural processes or science then there is no reason to believe the Bible. (God wasn't involved but rather it was Moses tricking the people with his knowledge of hidden Egyptian technology.)

Let me say this very clearly…

The Ark of the Covenant was not Technology… It was Symbology!

The Ark represented God's presence. It was symbolic of his throne. Physically, the Ark was just a box. Anything supernatural associated with it was the result of God's presence.

In the future, when Jesus has set up his kingdom, the Ark of the Covenant will not even be remembered. There will no longer be a need for a symbolic throne of God. The real one will be known as Jerusalem and it will be the seat of the Lord.

> Jer 3:16And it shall come to pass, when ye be multiplied and increased in the land, in those days, saith the LORD, they shall say no more, The ark of the covenant of the LORD: neither shall it come to mind: neither shall they remember it; neither shall they visit *it;* neither shall *that* be done any more.

> 17At that time they shall call Jerusalem the throne of the LORD; and all the nations shall be gathered unto it, to the name of the LORD, to Jerusalem: neither shall they walk any more after the imagination of their evil heart.

These pseudo-science/educational channels have an agenda. They try to explain away the power of God by discrediting the Ark of the Covenant. They also tell us Noah's flood was a local event, which made the building of his Ark seem pointless. God should have just told Noah and the animals to go to higher ground. Then they try to tell us that Jesus didn't die on the cross and resurrect on the third day, but rather, it was all an elaborate deception. They tell us Jesus and Mary Magdalene had a child through whom the royal families of Europe descended (how very convenient).

The Media attacks the Bible, Judaism and Christianity while all other religions are either embraced or ignored. Why is this? What do the Bible, Judaism and Christianity have in common?

The answer is...TRUTH!

The Bible is true and Judaism and Christianity are both based on this truth (to varying degrees).

It is a war of ideology... Truth vs. Lies.

The truth is unacceptable to many because of its consequences. For these people, discrediting the Bible is the only option. They do not want to answer to God for anything. They want to do whatever they desire. They justify themselves by discrediting the Bible. They are wise in their own eyes and want to be gods unto themselves. Regardless of what they want, the truth of the Bible stands on its own. Everyone will be judged by it. Rebelling against it is as pointless as rebelling against the law of gravity.

The truly wise person will love the truth and seek to understand it.

God rewards those who seek him and he gives them understanding.

> Ps 119:17Deal bountifully with thy servant, *that* I may live, and keep thy word. 18Open thou mine eyes, that I may behold wondrous things out of thy law. 19I *am* a stranger in the earth: hide not thy commandments from me. 20My soul breaketh for the longing *that it hath* unto thy judgments at all times. 21Thou hast rebuked the proud *that are* cursed, which do err from thy commandments. 22Remove from me reproach and contempt; for I have kept thy testimonies. 23Princes also did sit *and* speak against me: *but* thy servant did meditate in thy statutes.

Psalm 119 is probably the best expression of the truth of God's word. I suggest reading all of it.

Appendix E

Adam & Eve

130+800=930
Seth

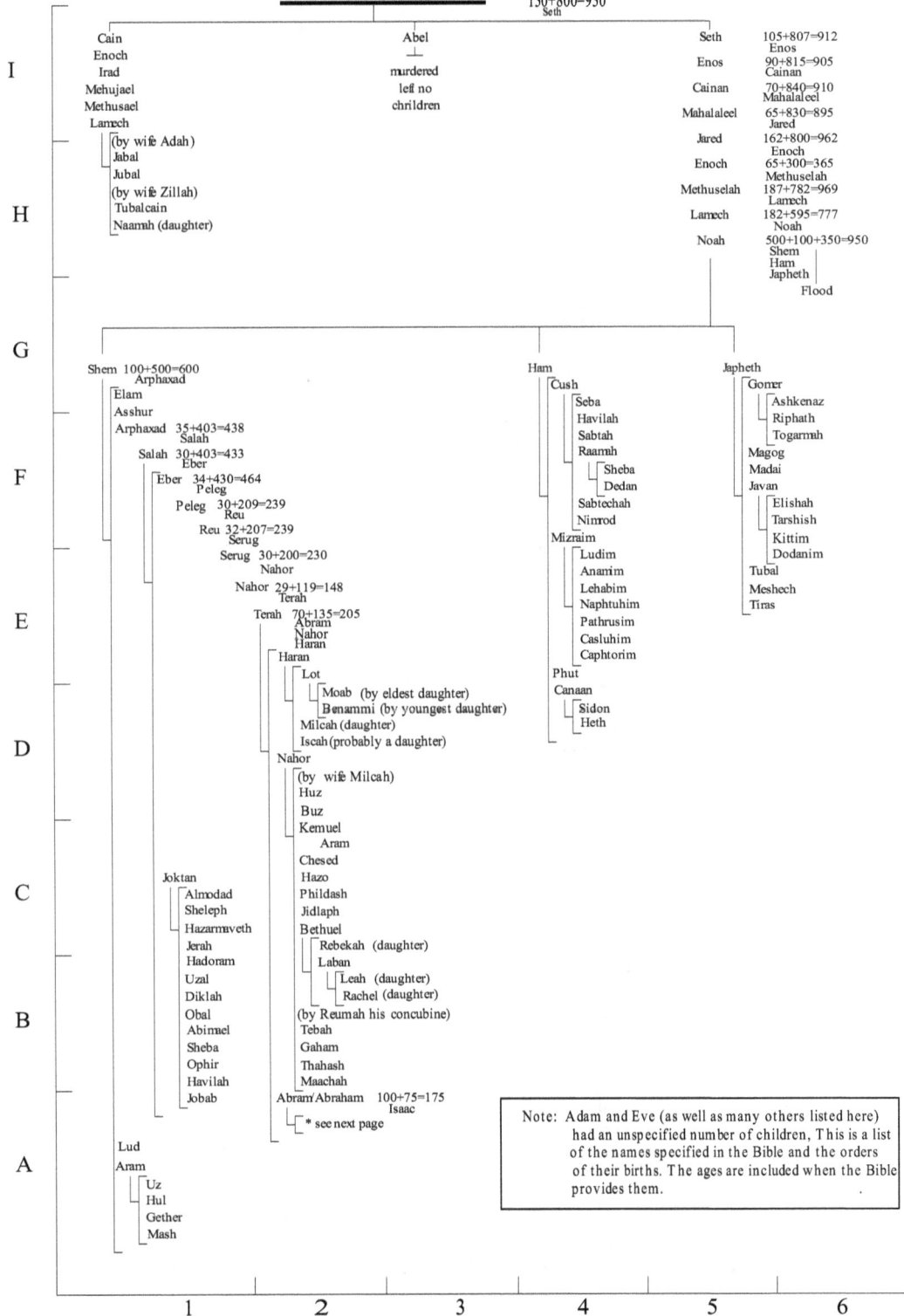

I	Cain — Enoch — Irad — Mehujael — Methusael — Lamech

Abel ⊥ murdered — left no children

Seth 105+807=912
Enos
Enos 90+815=905
Cainan
Cainan 70+840=910
Mahalaleel
Mahalaleel 65+830=895
Jared
Jared 162+800=962
Enoch
Enoch 65+300=365
Methuselah
Methuselah 187+782=969
Lamech
Lamech 182+595=777
Noah
Noah 500+100+350=950
Shem
Ham
Japheth
Flood

H
(by wife Adah)
Jabal
Jubal
(by wife Zillah)
Tubalcain
Naamah (daughter)

G

Shem 100+500=600
Arphaxad
Elam
Asshur
Arphaxad 35+403=438
Salah
Salah 30+403=433
Eber
Eber 34+430=464
Peleg
Peleg 30+209=239
Reu
Reu 32+207=239
Serug
Serug 30+200=230
Nahor
Nahor 29+119=148
Terah
Terah 70+135=205
Abram
Nahor
Haran

Ham
Cush
Seba
Havilah
Sabtah
Raamah
Sheba
Dedan
Sabtechah
Nimrod
Mizraim
Ludim
Anamim
Lehabim
Naphtuhim
Pathrusim
Casluhim
Caphtorim
Phut
Canaan
Sidon
Heth

Japheth
Gomer
Ashkenaz
Riphath
Togarmah
Magog
Madai
Javan
Elishah
Tarshish
Kittim
Dodanim
Tubal
Meshech
Tiras

F

E

Haran
Lot
Moab (by eldest daughter)
Benammi (by youngest daughter)
Milcah (daughter)
Iscah (probably a daughter)

D

Nahor
(by wife Milcah)
Huz
Buz
Kemuel
Aram
Chesed
Hazo
Pildash
Jidlaph
Bethuel
Rebekah (daughter)
Laban
Leah (daughter)
Rachel (daughter)
(by Reumah his concubine)
Tebah
Gaham
Thahash
Maachah

C

Joktan
Almodad
Sheleph
Hazarmaveth
Jerah
Hadoram
Uzal
Diklah
Obal
Abimael
Sheba
Ophir
Havilah
Jobab

B

Abram/Abraham 100+75=175
Isaac
* see next page

A

Lud
Aram
Uz
Hul
Gether
Mash

Note: Adam and Eve (as well as many others listed here)
had an unspecified number of children. This is a list
of the names specified in the Bible and the orders
of their births. The ages are included when the Bible
provides them.

1   2   3   4   5   6

Sons of Abram/Abraham

86 + 14 + 75 = 175
Ishmael
|
Isaac

I

Abram/Abraham

Ishmael (mother is Hagar, Sarai's Egyptian handmaid.
Ishmael lived 137yrs.)

Nebajoth
Bashemath (daughter, sister of Nebajoth)
Mahalath   (daughter, sister of Nebajoth)
Kedar
Adbeel
Mibsam
Mishma   Gen 25:12-17
Dumah
Massa
Hadar
Tema
Jetur
Naphish
Kedemah

H

G

Isaac (mother is Sarah, Abraham's wife.   Isaac 60+120 = 180
Isaac lived 180 yrs.)
Esau
Jacob

Esau/Edom

Eliphaz (mother is Adah, wife of Esau.)

Duke Teman
Duke Omar
Duke Zepho   } (mother is unknown.)
Duke Gatam
Duke Kenaz   }
Duke Amalek   (mother is Timna, Elephaz's concubine.)   Gen 35:27-36:19

Reuel (mother is Bashemath, wife of Esau.)

Duke Nahath
Duke Zerah
Duke Shammah
Duke Mizzah

F

E

Duke Jeush
Duke Jaalam   } (mother is Aholibamath, wife of Esau.)
Duke Korah   }

Jacob

Reuben
Simeon
Levi
Judah   (mother is Leah, Rachel's elder sister.)
Issachar
Zebulun
Dinah (daughter)   Gen 35:22-26
Dan
Naphtali } (mother is Bilhah, Rachel's handmaid.)
Gad
Asher   } (mother is Zilpah, Leah's handmaid.)
Joseph
Benjamin } (mother is Rachel.)

D

C

Zimran
Jokshan
Sheba
Dedan
Asshurim
Letushim
Leummim

Medan   (mother is Keturah, wife of Abraham
Midian   Gen 25:1-4)
Ephah
Epher
Hanoch
Abidah
Eldaah
Ishbak
Shuah

B

A

1   2   3   4   5   6

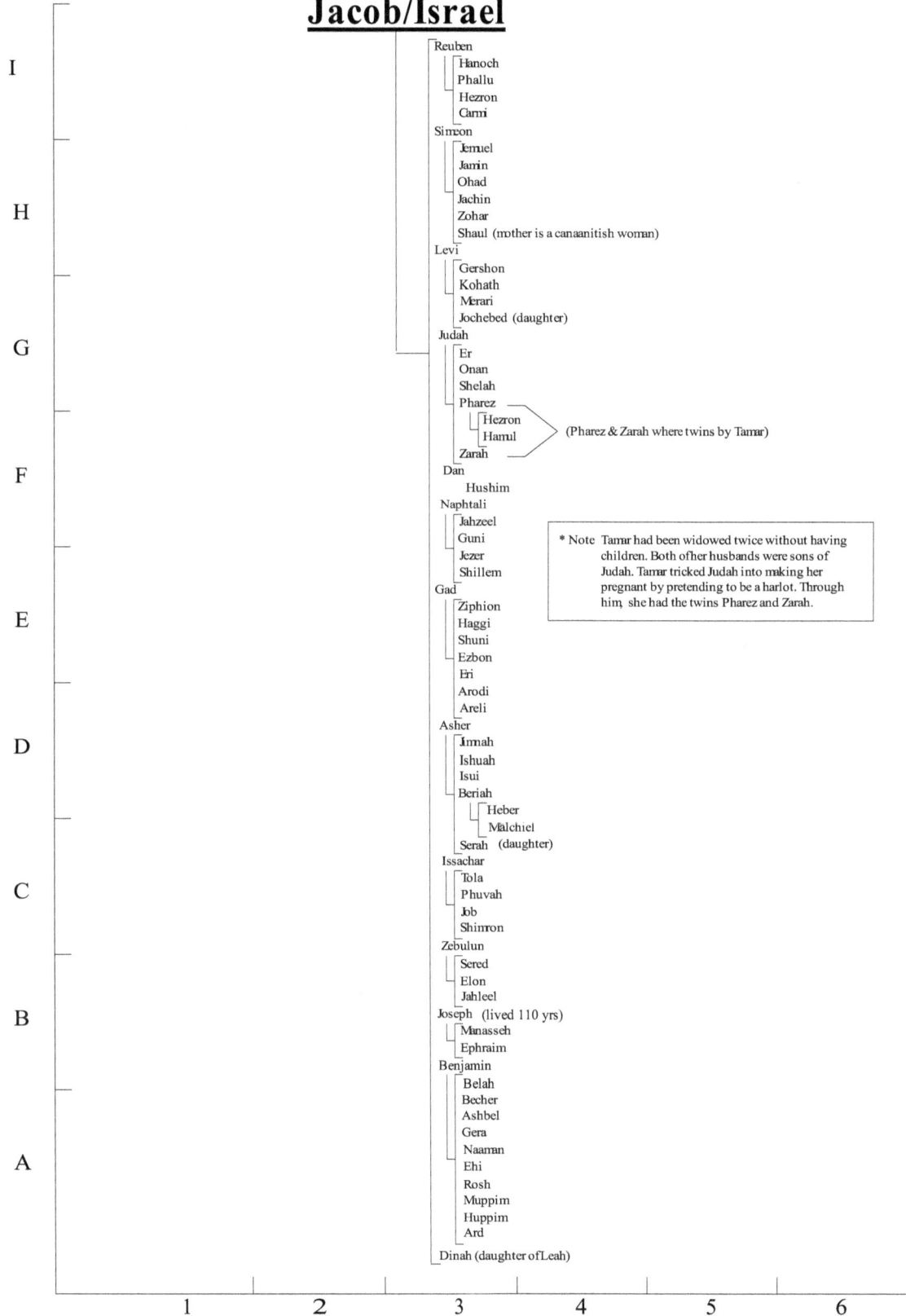

Gen 35:22-26

Jacob/Israel

```
┌ Reuben
│    ├ Hanoch
│    ├ Phallu
│    ├ Hezron
│    └ Carmi
├ Simeon
│    ├ Jemuel
│    ├ Jamin
│    ├ Ohad
│    ├ Jachin
│    ├ Zohar
│    └ Shaul (mother is a canaanitish woman)
├ Levi
│    ├ Gershon
│    ├ Kohath
│    ├ Merari
│    └ Jochebed (daughter)
├ Judah
│    ├ Er
│    ├ Onan
│    ├ Shelah
│    ├ Pharez
│    │    ├ Hezron
│    │    └ Hamul
│    └ Zarah
├ Dan
│    └ Hushim
├ Naphtali
│    ├ Jahzeel
│    ├ Guni
│    ├ Jezer
│    └ Shillem
├ Gad
│    ├ Ziphion
│    ├ Haggi
│    ├ Shuni
│    ├ Ezbon
│    ├ Eri
│    ├ Arodi
│    └ Areli
├ Asher
│    ├ Jimnah
│    ├ Ishuah
│    ├ Isui
│    ├ Beriah
│    │    ├ Heber
│    │    └ Malchiel
│    └ Serah (daughter)
├ Issachar
│    ├ Tola
│    ├ Phuvah
│    ├ Job
│    └ Shimron
├ Zebulun
│    ├ Sered
│    ├ Elon
│    └ Jahleel
├ Joseph (lived 110 yrs)
│    ├ Manasseh
│    └ Ephraim
├ Benjamin
│    ├ Belah
│    ├ Becher
│    ├ Ashbel
│    ├ Gera
│    ├ Naaman
│    ├ Ehi
│    ├ Rosh
│    ├ Muppim
│    ├ Huppim
│    └ Ard
└ Dinah (daughter of Leah)
```

(Pharez & Zarah where twins by Tamar)

* Note Tamar had been widowed twice without having children. Both of her husbands were sons of Judah. Tamar tricked Judah into making her pregnant by pretending to be a harlot. Through him, she had the twins Pharez and Zarah.

I   H   G   F   E   D   C   B   A

1   2   3   4   5   6

Contemporaries before the Flood

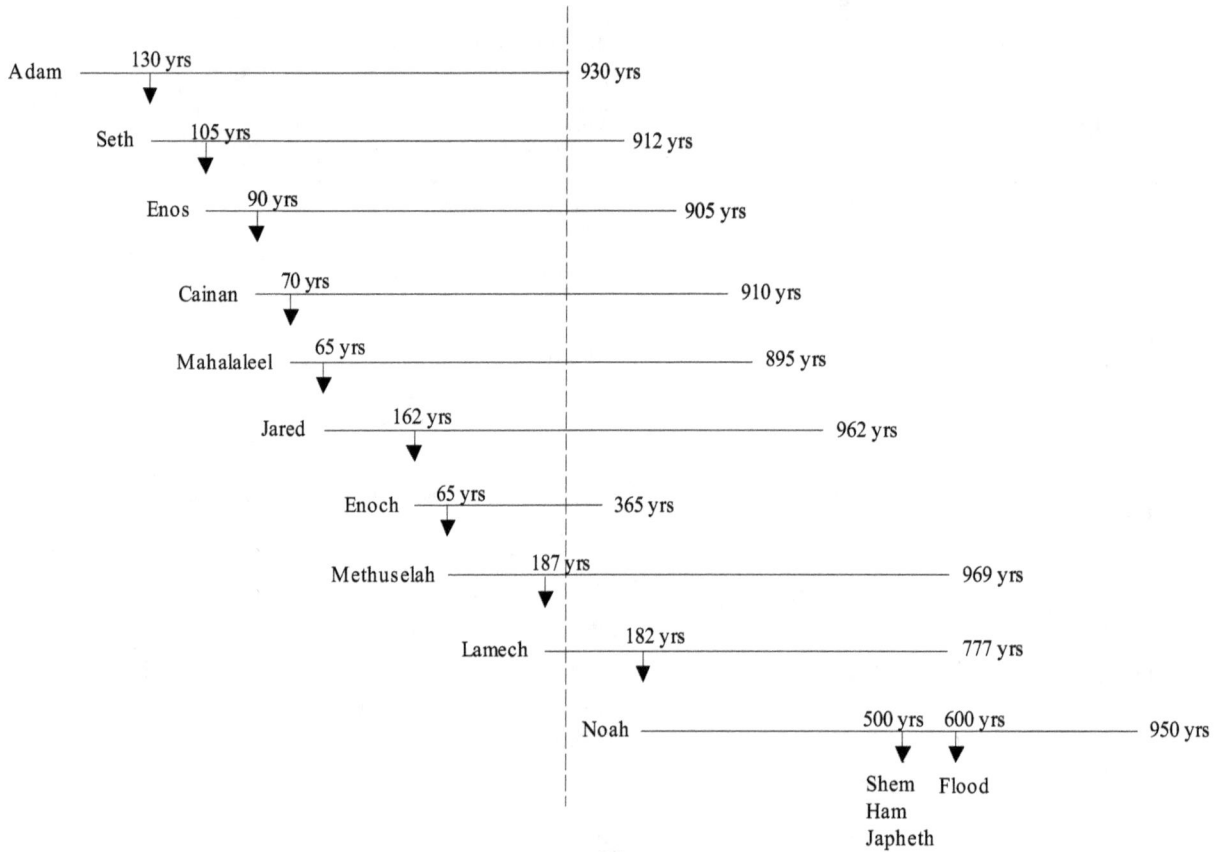

Adam	130 yrs	930 yrs
Seth	105 yrs	912 yrs
Enos	90 yrs	905 yrs
Cainan	70 yrs	910 yrs
Mahalaleel	65 yrs	895 yrs
Jared	162 yrs	962 yrs
Enoch	65 yrs	365 yrs
Methuselah	187 yrs	969 yrs
Lamech	182 yrs	777 yrs
Noah	500 yrs 600 yrs	950 yrs
	Shem Flood	
	Ham	
	Japheth	

It is curious to note that Noah was the first in his line who was not alive during the time of Adam.

God allowed everyone in Noah's lineage to die naturally (except Enoch) before sending the flood.

Contemporaries after the Flood

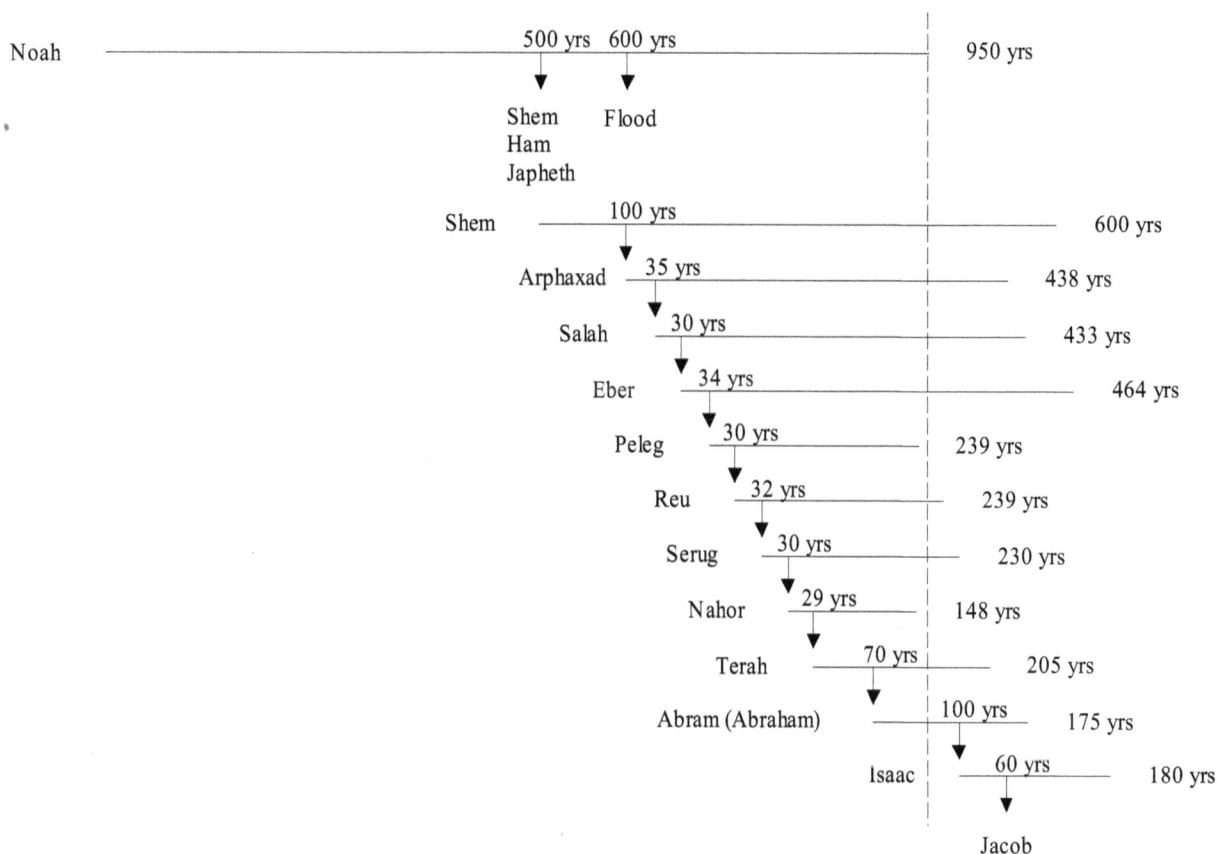

Noah	500 yrs	600 yrs		950 yrs
	▼	▼		
	Shem	Flood		
	Ham			
	Japheth			
Shem	100 yrs			600 yrs
	▼			
Arphaxad	35 yrs			438 yrs
	▼			
Salah	30 yrs			433 yrs
	▼			
Eber	34 yrs			464 yrs
	▼			
Peleg	30 yrs			239 yrs
	▼			
Reu	32 yrs			239 yrs
	▼			
Serug	30 yrs			230 yrs
	▼			
Nahor	29 yrs			148 yrs
	▼			
Terah	70 yrs			205 yrs
	▼			
Abram (Abraham)	100 yrs			175 yrs
	▼			
Isaac	60 yrs			180 yrs
	▼			
Jacob				

Everyone until the time of Abraham could have known all of their forefathers personally all the way back to Noah.

There is no Biblical record of Abraham meeting Noah or Shem but the possibility did exist considering the exceedingly long life spans of these men. If such a meeting ever took place it seems likely the Bible would have recorded it. Regardless, it makes for interesting speculation.

www.ingramcontent.com/pod-product-compliance
Lightning Source LLC
Chambersburg PA
CBHW080454110426

42742CB00017B/2883